Ghérasim Luca's *Francophonics*

Raphaël Sigal

CW01500355

Je suis l'Étranjuif.

G. L.

Dear reader, عزيزي القارئ

Ghérasim Luca's name doesn't resonate often in English-speaking mouths. He is nowhere to be found in the English-language anthologies of francophone literature. Nothing in the index of *French Global: A New Approach to Literary History*; he is buried below Lovejoy, Arthur (American); Lucian (ancient Greek); Lukacs (Hungarian). In the anthologies of French literature, he isn't anywhere either. Nothing in *A New History of French Literature*. In French, although he wrote in that language, his voice remains largely silent, despite his legacy. Thankfully, that silence is slowly dissipating. As I start writing this article, my friend Mathias sends me an email. It reads *"g l au cp!"* (decoded: *g*hérasim *l*uca au *c*entre *p*ompidou*!*). The official heart of French modern art is organizing a small exhibition of Ghérasim's books, art, and handwritten poems, on the occasion of the 2019 Franco-Romanian season. In French, we call that (political) *récuperation*. In English, it means (political) "appropriation," or "rip-off." Luca is neither French, nor Romanian: he spent his life rejecting any sense of belonging. He called it "Non-Œdipus" (a term that inspired Deleuze's and Guattari's "Anti-Œdipus")—a systematic logic grounded in the choice of the name he selected (he once wrote: elected).

"Né à Bucarest dans le quartier juif Dudesti-Vacaresti le 10 ou le 23 juillet 1913 (les documents officiels portent l'un ou l'autre date), il se prénomme soit 'Zola' soit 'Salman' selon que l'on se rapporte aux souvenirs de famille ou à l'acte de naissance" [Born in Bucharest in the Jewish neighborhood Dudesti-Vacaresti on July 10 or July 23, 1913 (official documents state both dates), his first name is 'Zola' or 'Salman,' depending on whether we refer to his birth certificate or his family's memories] (Luca 2001: i).[1] No fixed name, nor a fixed date of birth. "Le choix du nom d'écrivain, devenu en 1946 patronyme officiel, est en effet contemporain de l'adoption de la langue française comme langue d'écriture: Ghérasim Luca y ferait irruption en revendiquant son étrangeté" [The choice of the pen name, which became his official patronym in 1946, occurred at the same time as his adoption of French as his writing language: Ghérasim Luca bursts into that language by asserting his strangeness] (Carlat 1998: 20). His pen name is in fact a patronymic readymade, the name of an archimandrite found in the necrology of a daily newspaper. Ghérasim Luca—the poet—was born on the day of Ghérasim Luca's—the archimandrite's—death.

But there's more to the Centre Pompidou's exploitative irony, and it gets worse: one biographer even suggests that being forced to take French nationality by the French government in the 1990s was the event that, one thing leading to another, triggered his suicide (Velter 2001a). On the English version of the Centre Pompidou's website, he is described as follows, verbatim:

Nationality apatride (roumaine (avant 1948) à la naissance)

Born in 1913 in Bucarest (Royaume de Roumanie)

Died in 1994 in Paris (France). ("Ghérasim Luca": n. pag.)

The weird syntax, the (ab)use of parenthesis, the absence of punctuation between "nationality" and "apatride" (which means "stateless" but sounds a lot worse) are not there because of the strange mix of languages; that weirdness appears in the French version of the website as well. It is clear in Ghérasim's mind, however: "Fondamentalement et même légalement je suis nécessairement apatride. Ni ma langue passée ni ma langue présente ne justifient à mes yeux (après Auschwitz) l'appartenance à un patrimoine national" [Fundamentally and even legally, I am necessarily stateless. Neither my past tongue nor my present tongue justify in my eyes (after Auschwitz) the belonging to a national patrimony] (Carlat 1998: 251). No nationality, no patrimony, after Auschwitz. Only poetry. And when poetry

---

[1] All translations from French are mine, unless otherwise noted. One quote is intentionally left untranslated.

SOUNDS SENSES

FRANCOPHONE POSTCOLONIAL STUDIES

The annual publication of the Society for Francophone Postcolonial Studies
New Series, Vol. 12

Francophone Postcolonial Studies

The annual publication of the Society for Francophone Postcolonial Studies

The Society for Francophone Postcolonial Studies (SFPS) is an international association which exists in order to promote, facilitate and otherwise support the work of all scholars and researchers working on colonial/postcolonial studies in the French-speaking world. SFPS was created in 2002 with the aim of continuing and developing the pioneering work of its predecessor organization, the Association for the Study of Caribbean and African Literature in French (ASCALF). SFPS does not seek to impose a monolithic understanding of the 'postcolonial' and it consciously aims to appeal to as diverse a range of members as possible, in order to engage in wide-ranging debate on the nature and legacy of colonialism in and beyond the French-speaking world. SFPS encourages work of a transcultural, transhistorical, comparative and interdisciplinary nature. It implicitly seeks to decolonize the term Francophone, emphasizing that it should refer to all cultures where French is spoken (including, of course, France itself), and it encourages a critical reflection on the nature of the cognate disciplines of French Studies, on the one hand, and Anglophone Postcolonial Studies, on the other.

Our vision for this publication with Liverpool University Press is that each volume will constitute a sort of *état présent* on a significant topic embracing various expressions of Francophone Postcolonial Cultures (e.g. literature, film, music, history), in relation to pertinent geographical areas (e.g. France/Belgium, the Caribbean, Africa, the Indian Ocean, Asia, Polynesia) and different periods (slavery, colonialism, the post-colonial era, etc.): above all, we are looking to publish research that will help to set new research agendas across our field. The editorial board of *Francophone Postcolonial Studies* invites proposals for edited volumes touching on any of the areas listed above: proposals should be sent to Julia Waters (j.waters@ reading.ac.uk). For further details, visit: http://sfps.org.uk/.

General Editor: Julia Waters (University of Reading, UK)

SOUNDS SENSES

Edited by
yasser elhariry

Liverpool University Press

First published 2021 by
Liverpool University Press
4 Cambridge Street
Liverpool
L69 7ZU

British Library Cataloguing-in-Publication data
A British Library CIP record is available

ISBN 978-1-800-85688-2 cased

Typeset by Carnegie Book Production, Lancaster
Printed and bound by CPI Group (UK) Ltd, Croydon CR0 4YY

Contents

Cinema

Voices

Outro

Figures

Prelude

is cast out, life isn't possible anymore: by committing suicide, he writes to his wife, he leaves "ce monde où les poètes n'ont plus de place" [this world where poets haven't got a place anymore] (qtd. in Velter 1994). Displaced from birth to death.

This prelude thus begins with a perfect example of black humor—of the surrealistic kind—lodged in a perfect oxymoron—of the bureaucratic kind. Stateless *is*, in the administrative idiolect, Ghérasim's legal and desired nationality. Ghérasim is neither French nor Romanian. He is nothing, *apatride*, stateless. A Non-Œdipus walking on zero legs. He wrote in Romanian and in French but writing in this or that language never gave anyone a country, a patrimony, or a nationality. As such, there is no obvious postcolonial dimension to him. Or, at best, that dimension is oblique. The only comment in the literature that deals with the term uses Luca's poems to swiftly condemn the "domination" of "postcolonial periodization":

> Si la francophonie semble aujourd'hui être liée majoritairement à une périodisation postcoloniale dominante, il ne faut pas oublier que, pour de nombreux pays, l'histoire se scande autour du postcommunisme. C'est le cas du poète roumain Gherasim Luca qui, d'origine juive, va fuir son pays et venir en France où il commencera à traduire en français son œuvre écrite en roumain. (Gligore 2008: 127)

> If today *francophonie* seems to be mainly linked to a dominant postco-lonial periodization, let us not forget that, in many countries, history is articulated around postcommunism. This is the case of the Romanian poet of Jewish origin Gherasim Luca. He flees his country and comes to France, where he begins to translate his Romanian œuvre into French.

But that article ironically calls Luca, again, a "Romanian poet of Jewish origin" when he is at best a Stranjewish poet of Romanian origin. As Serge Martin notes, Luca's poems seem impermeable to political instrumentalization: "Non seulement il y aurait avec le poème un refus des instrumentalisations, politiques en l'occurrence, mais de plus il y aurait un travail de sape des assignations langagières [...] Ces réénonciations lancées par la force du poème constituent l'extension permanente du domaine des apatrides" [With his poems, there would be not only a refusal of instrumentalizations, in this case political, but also a sapping of linguistic assignations (...) The reenunciations emitted by the sheer force of the poems constitute the indefinite extension of the domain of statelessness] (Martin 2019).

As I start gleaning Ghérasim's quotes for my essay, I find a sentence he wrote in all caps in the preparatory notes for a book titled *Apostroph'Apocalypse* (qtd. in Carlat 1998: 253):

OUBLIE TA LANGUE MATERNELLE

SOIS ÉTRANGER À LA LANGUE D'ADOPTION ETRANGÈRE

SEULE

LA

NO MAN'S LANGUE

How should I translate it? Should I translate it? Do I have to translate, yasser? I don't remember what you told me when we talked about it. It doesn't sound very good in English: 'FORGET YOUR MOTHER TONGUE / BE FOREIGN TO THE ADOPTIVE FOREIGN TONGUE / ALONE (ONLY?) / THE / NO MAN'S TONGUE'—and of course, the pun is lost.

*

On September 3, 2018, you send me an email: "I am going to propose an edited volume called *Sounds Senses* for Liverpool University Press's annually published Francophone Postcolonial Studies series. The book would take a Sound Studies approach to francophone culture [...] I know you've been working on some new material which takes on Francophone texts and in the past I've read *brouillons* of yours on *the sound of literature*, so [...] do you think you might be able to contribute a creative/critical chapter (*au choix*) on any aspect of Francophone culture that adopts a sound-centric approach?" Sure, I tell you, "i'd love to contribute. would ghérasim luca count as *francophone*? in that case, i would do a piece about him." Yes, you answer me, "Luca is *absolutely francophone*." Cool, I tell myself, as I put together a proposal that I send you two days later. But:

...

BE FOREIGN TO THE ADOPTIVE FOREIGN TONGUE

...

Does he still count as francophone? Does that even sound francophone? Is there a francophone sound? Some sort of francophonics?

(Questions for this essay.)

*

I hear Ghérasim for the first time in 2005, in the library of the Musée d'Art et d'Histoire du Judaïsme, in Paris. He is standing there, straight, on the bookshelf facing the stairwell which I take to go up to get a book or go to the bathroom. Poetry is not really my thing at the time, nor is French. I am spending my days at the library in Walter Benjamin and Gershom Scholem's company, trying to make sense of their sefirotic trees, angels, and hunchbacks—the Jews' accursed share—and to incorporate them into my stammering scholarly lexicon. I am after some kind of secret narrative lodged between the lines of their super-convoluted texts.

That summer, I travel to Vilnius to swallow as much of the Yiddish grammar and dictionary as I can in three weeks. I plan to write a thesis about Lamed Shapiro's short stories of ultraviolence (*The Cross and Other Jewish Stories*, 2007). I need to be able to read them in the language of my grandfathers. There is something deeply unsettling about Yiddish. It is as familiar as it is impenetrable. I get it and I don't. I can't sense it. It is not dead, they tell us. But it is death, I realize, as I accumulate proofs:

One Sunday morning, we hop on a bus to go see a shtetl. The sky is gray, it takes us two hours, maybe three, to get there. Once there, no shtetl. In its place, a commemorative stone saying, in Yiddish, "Once there was a shtetl here." The guide, a Lithuanian Jew who decided to stay in Vilnius after the war to tell stories of extermination in the original language, repeats what the stone is already stating clearly: "Once there was a shtetl here."

On a Saturday, another visit is organized with our guide. She must be seventy-something. She survived the Shoah in Vilnius, a miracle. She rectifies history: don't believe what everybody says, she says. Look around, Hitler won the war. On another Saturday, she guides us through a thick bucolic forest right outside Vilnius: Ponar. Teenagers seem to come here to French kiss in the woods. Seventy thousand Jews were shot there, then incinerated in six enormous pits originally dug for oil storage. "She kept repeating the word *farbrent*" (Benjamin) my friend Jordan recalls. *Burnt*.

On the last night of our trip, in a hip club, Jordan and I meet a tall slender ghost with a violin and a ponytail. He hears us speak the extinct language and starts to cry. "I know your faces. I have missed th... I had friends wh... I am so drunk ... please forgive me right ... please ... tell me your names?" (Benjamin). He hears voices and insists on taking us to his home. He stutters, his voice is full of vodka, he squeaks like the strings of the violin he is too drunk to play. He knows our faces and we can't take it. End of our trip in the giant cemetery.

The sound of death infiltrates all the letters of my aleph-beys.

After the summer, I'm back in the museum's library. The dictionary is sticking in my throat, I slowly read Shapiro's short stories in Yiddish: murder, rape, cannibalism in the original language. I take breaks, I go upstairs, to the bathroom, to the literature section. I open a book again, I hear Ghérasim again, he is chanting a vivid Death Fugue.

> "La mort, la mort folle, la morphologie de la méta, de la métamort, de la métamorphose ou la vie, la vie vit, la vie-vice, la vivisection de la vie" étonne, étonne et et et est un nom, un nombre de chaises, un nombre de 16 aubes et jets, de 16 objets contre, contre la, contre la mort ou, pour mieux dire, pour la mort de la mort ou pour contre, contre, contrôlez-là, oui c'est mon avis, contre la, oui contre la vie sept, c'est à, c'est à dire pour, pour une vie dans le vidant, vidant, dans le vidant vide et vidé, la vie dans, dans, pour une vie dans la vie. (Luca 2001: 15)

That year, I put a final period on my master's thesis and abandon Yiddish's infinite sadness. I commit myself to French and elect Ghérasim as my personal angel, "for a life within life." I do not suspect, at that time, that he too, like his friend Paul Celan, will commit suicide, that he too, like Celan, will throw himself into the Seine. I find solace on Wikipedia, weirdly, when I read that although he kills himself on February 9, his body isn't found until one month later, on March 10. He floats for a whole month between earth and sky. I can't verify that information, it seems to be a perfect fabrication. Precisely the type of fabrication that Ghérasim digs.

*

I have an auditory hallucination: I hear Yiddish when I read Ghérasim. It is the essential metaphor, the means of transportation, the ghostly hand that guides me through his writings, the ghostly voice that punctuates his recordings.

*

Ghérasim writes on the occasion of a recital he gives in 1968:

Il m'est difficile de m'exprimer en langage visuel. Il pourrait y avoir dans l'idée même de création—créaction—quelque chose, quelque chose qui échappe à la description passive telle qu'elle découle nécessairement d'un langage conceptuel. Dans ce langage, qui sert à désigner des objets, le mot n'a qu'un sens, ou deux, et il garde la sonorité prisonnière. Qu'on brise la forme où il s'est englué et de nouvelles relations apparaissent: la sonorité s'exalte, des secrets endormis surgissent, celui qui écoute est introduit dans un monde de vibrations qui suppose une participation physique, simultanée, à l'adhésion mentale. Libérez le souffle et chaque mot devient un signal. Je me rattache vraisemblablement à une tradition poétique, tradition vague et de toute façon illégitime. Mais le terme même de poésie me semble faussé. Je préfère peut-être: « ontophonie ». (Luca 2001: xi–xii)

It is hard for me to express myself in visual language. There may be something in the idea of creation—creaction—something that evades a passive description as it is necessarily derived from a conceptual language. In that language, which is used to designate objects, the word has only one meaning, or two, and it keeps sonority imprisoned. As soon as we break the form in which it got stuck, new relationships appear: sonority is exalted, sleeping secrets arise, the listener is introduced to a world of vibrations that presupposes simultaneous physical participation and mental adhesion. Free the breath and each word becomes a signal. I am likely part of a poetic tradition, a tradition that is vague and illegitimate in any case. But the very term "poetry" seems distorted to me. I think I prefer: "ontophonics."

It is an important piece of text, often quoted, the closest thing we have to Luca's *ars poetica*. Like others before him, he insists on the necessity of breaking the mold of language: the mold of linguistic language after Saussure, the referential language of signs in which sound is subordinated to a drastically finite quantity of meaning. Our poor, unexpansive, translatable, vernacular languages are so crammed into the world of objects they designate that they are blind to their sounds. Blind to the fact that in French, morphology is a "mad death," that objects are phonically made of "dawns and spurts" and that vice binds together life and vivisection, if you hear what I mean. Sound is the great word-opener. It does not represent actual objects but points at potential ones. It rescues words from the passive world of signs and makes them flourish in an active world of "signals," Luca's secret territory where "the listener is introduced to a world of vibrations that presupposes a physical, simultaneous participation to mental adhesion."

To non-believers, Luca may appear esoteric here, but to the listeners of Rimbaud, Lautréamont, Tzara, Artaud, and other members of the "poetic tradition" he may allude to, what he says here is fairly profane: when freed from the signifying, stultifying relationship, language is active and effective— "it granulates, it crackles, it caresses, it grates, it cuts, it comes" (Barthes 1975: 67). It speaks to the body. Like Artaud, Luca stages "the acoustic deconstruction of the voice, the liberation of sound from the tyranny of speech" (Hollier 1997: 28). Hence that neologism, "ontophonics," between quotation marks: a call to free linguistic language from the bonds of the bronze dictionary and to unleash its profound nature. Language is the being's soundtrack. Not a thing to read passively, but an essence to listen to actively. After all, Luca's secrets are not destined for his reader, but for his listener, *celui qui écoute.*

An attack on linguistic language is always a charge against what we call "to read." I look for synonyms in the thesaurus and here is what I find under the tab "look at and understand the written word": gather, interpret, know, learn, refer to, scan, see, study, translate, view, apprehend, comprehend, construe, decipher, discover, glance, perceive, peruse, etc. None of the synonyms Ghérasim convokes: create, break the form, vibrate, exalt, participate, listen. Brought to *you* by "ontophonics." You: *the one who listens.*

I take a deep dive into the depths, I read this paragraph over and over to extract a password (a translation, see below) from it, the magic glasses that would allow me to read below the crust of his poems. I continue to hallucinate: Luca's French is a Silent, Buried, Dead Yiddish. The recording of its choking and silencing. The undoing of a language, the tearing of its grammar and disarticulation of its lexicon. What remains: "Sleeping secrets," "vibrations," "breath," "signal," "ontophonics"—a Francophonics of the abyss. The silent Sound of Being. You recognize this, don't you? Césaire is here, somewhere. Jabès, too. And Cixous, of course! Meddeb, Kilito, other silent ones, and the ones to be. In Dead Yiddish, in Dead Arabic, in Dead Créole—*langues mortes à venir.* How would you translate that? Dead languages to come?

Another translation question. After "ontophonics," I don't know how to translate further. I send the next paragraph to our friends Matt and Youna: "I need you guys for an experiment (for an article) in translation," I email them. "I need several versions of the text below (Ghérasim Luca) in English [...] If you have time over the break, would you please try your hand at it?" Here is the French:

> Celui qui ouvre le mot ouvre la matière et le mot n'est que le support matériel d'une quête qui a la transmutation du réel pour fin. Plus que de me situer par rapport à une tradition ou à une révolution, je m'applique à dévoiler une résonance d'être, inadmissible. La poésie est un « silensophone », le poème, un lieu d'opération, le mot y est soumis à une série de mutations sonores, chacune de ses facettes libère la multiplicité des sens dont elles sont chargées. Je parcours aujourd'hui une étendue où le vacarme et le silence s'entrechoquent—centre choc—où le poème prend la forme de l'onde qui l'a mis en marche. Mieux, le poème s'éclipse devant ses conséquences. En d'autres termes: je m'oralise. (Luca 2001: xii–xiii)

Matt answers first: "Hope you're having a nice break. This was quite challenging! Below is what I've got. Not quite happy with it, but not sure it's possible to be!":

> Whoever opens words opens matter and words are not merely a material medium for a quest that has as its goal the transmutation of reality. More than situating myself in regard to a tradition or a revolution, I seek to unveil a resonance of being, inadmissible. Poetry is a "silensophone," the poem a place of operation, in which words undergo a series of acoustic mutations: every one of their facets frees the multiplicity of meanings with which they are charged. Today I'm moving across a space where din and silence clash—crashing and clasping—where the poem takes the form of the wave that set it in motion. Better yet, the poem slips away in the face of its consequences. In other words, I oralize myself, I m'oralize.

Youna sends hers a few days later:

```
He who discloses the word discloses matter, and the word serves as
material support for the pursuit of the transmutation of the real.

Rather than situate myself in relation to: a tradition or to a
revolution, I devote myself to unveiling an inadmissible
resonance of being.

Poetry is a "silensophone," and the poem a site of activity, where
the word is subjected to a series of aural mutations, xxxhxxxxxxxf
xhxxxxxxxxxxxxxxf so that the multiplicity of meanings with
which every facet of the word are laden, are set free.

Lately I range over a great expanse where clamor and silence
collide -- co-lie -- and where the poem assumes the shape
of the wave that first set it in motion.

Better still: the poem is eclipsed by its effects.

In other words: I put myself into words.
```

I extract the keywords according to Ghérasim's formula:

"ontophonics" [...] "silensophone" [...] resonance of being [...]

    I m'oralize [...] I put myself into words

                Cf. *Sounds Senses.*

*

What is fueling my hallucination? What is that tinnitus ringing in my ear? Why do I hear Yiddish when I read Ghérasim? I am looking for ways to legitimize my phantasm, to give some ground to its floating evidence. Is there a piece of paper in an archive buried somewhere that would sanction its origin? I find a first clue in the preface to Ghérasim's most widely available collection of poems (*Héros-Limite*, published by Poésie/Gallimard in 2001). In it, André Velter notes:

> Parler roumain, français, allemand, yiddish était habituel dans la communauté juive ashkénaze, libérale, d'une ville-carrefour comme Bucarest. Ce jeu des langues, qui semblait tonique, légitime, fondateur et formateur n'avait pourtant rien d'innocent. Non seulement il récusait l'idée d'une hiérarchie entre les idiomes, mais il gardait vivant le yiddish, qu'un programme gouvernemental d'inspiration ultra-nationaliste et antisémite entreprenait d'éradiquer. (Velter 2001b: ii)

> Speaking Romanian, French, German, Yiddish was common in the Ashkenazi liberal community of a gateway city like Bucharest. This game of languages seemed tonic, legitimate, foundational and formative. There was however nothing innocent about it. Not only did it recuse the idea of a hierarchy between idioms, it also kept Yiddish alive, which an ultra-nationalist and anti-Semitic governmental program was in the process of eradicating.

Is that enough? Did Ghérasim keep Yiddish alive in his poems intentionally, after the eradication? Am I following some indications he planted here and there, or am I fantasizing in an ivory tower far away from his words?

I find another piece of evidence in Dominique Carlat's book:

> Le yiddish serait bientôt l'objet d'une destruction programmée. D'une génération et d'une sensibilité où l'attachement à tout patrimoine paraissait une impasse, Ghérasim Luca écrit cependant sur le fond de cet événement. La défaillance "voluptueuse" de la lettre, son battement sans cesse ausculté dans les textes, acquièrent une résonance particulière dès lors que s'entend ce silence mat. (1998: 20)

> Yiddish would be soon the object of a programmed destruction. Although he was part of a generation and a sensibility for whom the attachment to any given patrimony was a dead end, Ghérasim Luca writes in the context of that event. The "voluptuous" failure of the letter, its endlessly examined beat, acquire a peculiar resonance once this matte silence is heard.

This matte silence is heard. The silensophone of poetry reveals and conceals the destruction of Yiddish. Ontophonics: Yiddish-after-Auschwitz, distilled in the adoptive tongue. A dissolution of the being, silent echoes of its destruction. Margarete ... Shulamit ...

*

I'm sure you've had this experience. As you write every day about a text or a poet, everything else you read seems to point insistently to a center that conceals a revelation. Here is how it dawned on me. I was in Boston with Jordan—he, too, abandoned Yiddish—and he had Jabès's *The Book of Margins*, in English, on his bookshelves. I had never read Jabès in English. In the introduction of the book, the series editor, Mark Taylor, recalls some of the conversations he had with Jabès and quotes him saying, "Adorno once said that after Auschwitz we can no longer write poetry. I say that after Auschwitz we *must* write poetry but with wounded words" (Jabès 1993: ix–x).

Wounded words, *des mots blessés*, words echoing the silent wound of unimaginable death. With that sentence everything becomes clearer. Ghérasim makes that wound legible, visible, audible. Here is probably his most famous poem, typographically condensed (imagine more space between the lines and the words, and much more white on the page):

pas pas paspaspas pas
pasppas ppas pas paspas
le pas pas le faux pas le pas
paspaspas le pas le mau
le mauve le mauvais pas
paspas pas le pas le papa
le mauvais papa le mauve le pas
paspas passe paspaspasse
passe passe il passe il pas pas
il passe le pas du pas du pape
du pape sur le pape du pas du passe
passepasse passi le sur le
le pas le passi passi passi pissez sur
le pape sur papa sur le sur la sur
la pipe du papa du pape pissez en masse
passe passe passi passepassi la passe
la basse passi passepassi la
passio passiobasson le bas
le pas passion le basson et
et pas le basso do pas
paspas do passe passiopassion do
ne do ne domi ne passi ne dominez pas
ne dominez pas vos passions passives ne

ne domino vos passio vos vos
ssis vos passio ne dodo vos
vos dominos d'or
c'est domdommage do dodor
do pas pas ne domi
pas paspasse passio
vos pas ne do ne do ne dominez pas
vos passes passions vos pas vos
vos pas dévo dévorants ne do
ne dominez pas vos rats
pas vos rats
ne do dévorants ne do ne dominez pas
vos rats vos rations vos rats rations ne ne
ne dominez pas vos passions rations vos
ne dominez pas vos ne vos ne do do
minez minez vos nations ni mais do
minez ne do ne mi pas pas vos rats
vos passionnantes rations de rats de pas
pas passe passio minez pas
minez pas vos passions vos
vos rationnants ragoûts de rats dévo
dévorez-les dévo dédo do domi
dominez pas cet a cet avant-goût
de ragoût de pas de passe de
passi de pasigraphie gra phiphie
graphie phie de phie
phiphie phéna phénakiki
phénakisti coco
phénakisticope phiphie
phopho phiphie photo do do
dominez do photo mimez phiphie
photomicrographiez vos goûts
ces poux chorégraphiques phiphie
de vos dégoûts de vos dégâts pas
pas ça passio passion de ga
coco kistico ga les dégâts pas
le pas pas passiopas passion
passion passioné né né
il est né de la né
de la néga ga de la néga
de la négation passion gra cra

crachez cra crachez sur vos nations cra
de la neige il est il est né
passioné né il est né
à la nage à la rage il
est né à la né à la nécronage cra rage il
il est né de la né de la néga
néga ga cra crachez de la né
de la ga pas néga négation passion
passionné nez pasionném je
je t'ai je t'aime je
je je jet je t'ai jetez
je t'aime passionném t'aime
je t'aime je je jeu passion j'aime
passionné éé ém émer
émerger aimer je je j'aime
émer émerger é é pas
passi passi éééé ém
éme émersion passion
passionné é je
je t'ai je t'aime je t'aime
passe passio ô passio
passio ô ma gr
ma gra cra crachez sur les rations
ma grande ma gra ma té
ma té ma gra
ma grande ma té
ma terrible passion passionnée
je t'ai je terri terrible passio je
je je t'aime
je t'aime je t'ai je
t'aime aime aime je t'aime
passionné é aime je
t'aime passioném
je t'aime
passionnément aimante je
t'aime je t'aime passionnément
je t'ai je t'aime passionné né
je t'aime passionné
je t'aime passionnément je t'aime
je t'aime passio passionnément.

(Luca 2001: 169–176)

"The long citation (pp. 65–69) will need to be translated," one reviewer says. I try my hand at it: impossible, I think. I wonder why it isn't translated in English. I write to Mary Ann Caws, who published my favorite translations of Luca in English (Ghérasim Luca, *Self-Shadowing Prey*, Contra Mundum Press, 2012). "I'm currently revising an article about Luca that I wrote in English (a second language for me) in which [...] I quote his poem "Passionnément" in French in its totality (it has not been translated in English to my knowledge). [This] makes me curious about your own translations of Luca: I was wondering what decided you to opt for the poems you translated and not other ones?" "of course I wonder also," she replies the next day, "and can't find my Gherasim Luca book, sorry, but perhaps that wonderful poem was not in that book I had to translate! I would love to translate it, if I had it, but can't find it either, could I translate it for you if you send it? I would love to." My jaw drops. "What a truly wonderful gift it would be," I email her with the poem. And then again, one day later: "hi, Raphael, and here is an attempt at the impossible task of EVER translating a Gherasim Luca poem, and I am thinking of the repetitions and his five suicide notes I consulted in the library in Paris":

not not notnotnot not
notnnot nnot not notnot
the not not the faux pas the not
notnotnot the not the ba
the bade the bad not
notnot not the not the nonot
the bad nonot the bade the not
notnot note notnotnote
notes notes he notes he not not
the notes the not of the not of the nonote
of the nonote on the nonote of the not of the notes
notesnotes notesi the on the
the not the notesi notesi piss on
the nonote on nonot on the on tha on
the pipe of the nonot of the nonote piss in a mass
notes notes notesi notesnotsi the notes
the bass notesi notesnotesi the
notesio notesiobasson the bass
the not notesi the basson and
and not the basso off not
notnot off notes notesinotesi off
no off no offme no notesi no offmynose not
no offmynose not your notesis notifies no

no offmynos your notesi your your
snots your notesi no offoff your
your offmynoss of gold
it's offmoffmymag off offofgold
off not not no offme
not notnotes notesi
your not no off no off no offmynose not
your notes notesis your not your
your not offvo offvorants no off
no offmynose not your rats
not your rats
no off offvorants no off no offmynose not
your rats your rations your rats rations no no
no offmynose not your notesis rations your
no offmynose not your no your no off off
mynose mynose your nations nay but off
mynose no off no my not not your rats
your notesinantes rations of rats of not
not notes notesi minose not
minose not your notesis your
your rationnants ratastes of rats devo
devour-them devo deoff off offmy
offmynose not this to this before-taste
of rataste of not of notes of
notesi of notesigraphi gra phiphie
graphie phie of phie
phiphie phena phenakiki
phenakisti coco
phenakisticope phiphie
phopho phiphie photo off off
off mynose off photo mimez phiphie
photomicrographiez your tastes
these bugs choregraphiques phiphie
of your distastes of your wastes not
not that notesio notesion of ga
coco kistico ga the wastes not
the not not notesionot notesion
notesion notesionay nay nay
he is nay of the nay
from the nayga ga of the nayga
of the negation notesion gra spi

spit spi spit on your nations spi
of the snow he is he is nay
notesionay nay he is nay
to the swim to the rage he
is nay to the nay to the naycroswim spi rage he
he is nay from the nay of the nayga
nayga ga spi spit of the nay
of the ga not nayga naygation notesion
notesionay nose noteesionaym i
i have you i love you i
i i iyou i have you i you
i love you notesionnaym love you
i love you i i i notesion i love
notesionnay ay ay ayme aymayr
aymerge to love I I I love you
aymerge aymerge ay ay not
notssi notssi ayayayayay aym
aymay aymayrsion notesion
notesionay ay I
i have you i love you i love you
notes notesio o notesio
notesio o my gr
my gra spi spit on the rations
my grande my gra my tay
my tay my gra
my grande my tay
my terrible notesion notesionnay
I have you I terri terrible notesio I
I I love you
I love you I have you I
love you love love I love you
notesionmay ay love I
love you notesionm
I love you
notesionnayment lovingtay I
love you I love you notesionnayment
I have you I love you notesionnay nay
I love you notesionnay
I love you notesionnayment I love you
I love you notesio notesionnayment.

This is what a love poem looks like in wounded language. A single sentence, *Je t'aime passionnément*, contains the abyss of a thousand that are muted. One sentence that has to undergo all the nots, all the lacerations, the piss, the pain, the spit. *I love you notesionnayment*: a body with a thousand cuts.

*

Auschwitz: the name of the tinnitus ringing in my ear, when I hear Ghérasim Luca. The site of Yiddish's massacre. A whole fantasized topography of language—a vision. Poetry above the abyss. Ghérasim takes the words with both hands, stretches them past their point of breakage and observes all the klipot, all the shatters, left on his page: "Chaque mot est un trou, un abîme, un piège" [Every word is a hole, an abyss, a trap] (qtd. in Carlat 1998: 256). It sounds like Mallarmé: "Tout devient suspens, disposition fragmentaire avec alternance et vis-à-vis, concourant au rythme total, lequel serait le poëme tu, aux blancs" ["Everything is suspended, an arrangement of fragments with alternations and confrontations, adding up to a total rhythm, which would be the poem stilled, in the blanks"] (Mallarmé 2003: 211; 2007: 209). In French-after-Auschwitz, the "suspen[sion]" becomes a "hole," the "arrangement of fragments," an "abyss," the "blanks" a "trap." Franco(silenso)phonics: poetry in the key of death.

*

You asked me for a text about *francophonie*, and here I am again, following, despite myself, Jewy signs, traces, and tracks (but Jewishness in French is always *f*rancophone, as you know). It's been a year since I started this piece. It took a year to discover why I elected, thirteen years ago, Ghérasim as a personal angel (I have others): he (like the others) helps me name my ghosts. He helps me write in French. He helps me connect the depths of the unsaid to the surface of my pages. Here is the quote I saved for the end:

> Nous franchissons un corridor, traversons un pont, inventons une forêt: la langue étrangère qui s'égare dans ma bouche, alors que sous une averse de feuilles et de larmes nous courons enlacés à la rencontre du premier abîme venu, a le goût indéchiffrable de l'air que seul le vide des gouffres émane. (Luca 1998: 31)

I try my hand at it:

> We go through a corridor, cross a bridge, invent a forest: the foreign tongue that gets lost in my mouth, as under a downpour of leaves and tears we run

together to the first abyss, has the undecipherable taste of air emanated by the void of chasms.

Do you hear that, reader? Isn't it the forest where we meet, you and I?
Paris–Amherst(–Paris), October 2018–February 2020(–January 2021)

Works Cited

Barthes, Roland. *The Pleasure of the Text.* Translated by Richard Miller, Hill and Wang, 1975.

Benjamin, Jordan. "The Languages of Vilnius." *Zeek*, May 2007, zeek.net/705vilna/index.php?page=2.

Carlat, Dominique. *Ghérasim Luca l'intempestif.* José Corti, 1998.

"Ghérasim Luca." centrepompidou.fr/cpv/resource/cAbnqjE/rajaoqK.

Gligore, Daliana. "Francophonie, périphérie et auto-traduction: le cas de Gherasim Luca." *Intercâmbio*, no. 1, 2008, pp. 127–140.

Hollier, Denis. "The Death of Paper, Part Two: Artaud's Sound System." *October*, no. 80, 1997, pp. 27–37.

Jabès, Edmond. *The Book of Margins.* Translated by Rosemarie Waldrop, University of Chicago Press, 1993.

Luca, Ghérasim. *Un loup à travers une loupe.* José Corti, 1998.

——. *Héros-Limite suivi de Le Chant de la carpe et de Paralipomènes.* Gallimard, 2001.

Mallarmé, Stéphane. *Œuvres complètes, II.* Edited by Bertrand Marchal, Gallimard, 2003.

——. *Divagations: The Author's 1897 Arrangement Together with "Autobiography" and "Music and Letters."* Translated by Barbara Johnson, Harvard University Press, 2007.

Martin, Serge. "Avec Ghérasim Luca (1913–1994), extension du domaine des apatrides." *Modern Languages Open*, no. 1, 2019, doi.org/10.3828/mlo.v0i0.223

Velter, André. "Une disparition Ghérasim Luca l'éveilleur." *Le Monde*, March 12, 1994.

——. "passio passionnément." *Ghérasim Luca.* Jean-Michel Place, 2001a.

——. "Parler apatride." Preface. *Héros-Limite suivi de Le Chant de la carpe et de Paralipomènes*, by Ghérasim Luca. Gallimard, 2001b, pp. i–xvi.

Introduction

Unsound french[1]

yasser elhariry

Nuicts

Such is the onward march of things, that the history of french is a history of progressive standardization, normalization, and normativity. From the rules of orthography, grammar, syntax, and semantics to the gatekeeping of dictionaries and learned societies, on to the codifying poetics of linguistics, prosody, versification, gender inclusivity, and pronunciation, french amounts to no less than an apparatus of creative and critical blockage, poetical and political stoppage. No one, today, for instance, really, dreams of composing verses that look like this anymore.

> Ie ne chante (Magny) ie pleure mes ennuys:
> Ou, pour le dire mieulx, en pleurant ie les chante,
> Si bien qu'en les chantant, fouuent ie les enchante:
> Voila pourquoy (Magny) ie chante iours & nuicts. (Du Bellay 1558: 3)

> But I don't sing (Magny), except to complain.
> You might say I've turned sobbing into singing,
> an enchanting chanting I've learned in the hope of bringing
> some relief to these days and nights of pain. (2004: 39)

And it's not just the queasiness of Joachim's feelings or the indeterminacy of sixteenth-century orthographical conventions, which, like *nuicts*, spell

---

[1] On the poetics and politics of small-f french, see elhariry 2016.

23

double trouble for the lingual-sensorial divide between the ocular and aural. Yes, the lines strike the contemporary reader as outdated. For who in their right mind, given the state of the world, invokes muses, patrons, fellow poets, then cries them a river?

But what if the varieties of disturbance in Du Bellay's lines have nothing to do with how outdated but how radical they are? If anything, the Pléiade poets, and the Grands Rhétoriqueurs before them, were the first francophones. They deterritorialized vernacular languages and became "extraterritorial *avant la lettre*" (Kinoshita 2010: 6). Armed with these languages, they invaded the realms of poetics, politics, and artistic invention. With the founding of the Académie française, still unthought, a full century away, french was a far way from the fixities of standardization. Which made it transgression and invention's closest ally. Vernacular french strove toward nobility and literary cred (don't forget that Montaigne's mother tongue was Latin), and garnered traction as "the best developed and most prestigious of the European vernaculars in the medieval Mediterranean" (7). In this context, La Pléiade's explosive sonnetry in vernacular, trumpeted by Du Bellay's 1549 manual-manifesto, sought to expand the language's artistic capacities, and elevate it over the hegemony, sacredness, and nobility of Latin and Occitan. Coinciding with the emergence of the modern nation-state, the new french sonnet in the sixteenth century called for an imitation and improvement of models past. A reboot. An upgrade. In a language of one's own.

Fast-forward to the twentieth and twenty-first centuries, and everything neatly has its place. Now, what if a return to the plasticity of french—which would reactivate the sixteenth-century ocular/aural smudge—were not only possible, but were also to lead to a renewed understanding of the sounds of french and francophone postcolonial cultures and how they are heard? What if the noncoincidence between sign (sight) and sense (sound)—that retinally irksome *c* in Du Bellay's *nuicts*—were capable of opening up the worlds of french and francophone postcolonial cultures to different modes of understanding alterity and ipseity, impelling us to hear the unheard? Such an approach would revalorize longstanding traditions within the field, like the subversive potential and political value of decolonizing the mind, writing (sassing) back, pacifically invading french, whether through recourse to *créolité*, orality, hybridity, intertextuality, translation, translingualism, postlingualism (elhariry and Walkowitz 2021). It would imbue them with the insights of sound studies, and place sonic cultures at the heart of the francophone postcolonialist's critical arsenal.

The novelty of this endeavor comes at the price of a number of assumptions and critical breaks. *Sounds Senses* neither addresses postcolonialism nor makes postcolonial arguments in a direct way. The book swerves away from postcolonialism as a hegemonic disciplinary formation that, in its vision of the structures and histories of power relations in the francophone world, strains practices of creative criticism. A cursory glance at many of the essays collected here reveals no explicit postcolonial framework, which nevertheless lingers beneath each and every word. The essays take Mediterranean studies, minor transnationalisms, or transcolonial identifications as a set of givens circulating in the midst of others. They assume that francophone postcolonial cultures now include the Mediterranean, Francis Bacon, Palestine, Iran, China. Theirs is an "oblique" cut-and-graft of francophone postcolonialism (Khatibi 1974: 96, 228, 233; see elhariry 2020; Feriani et al. 2020; McNeece 2020). Some essays hew closer to postcolonial praxis, while others maintain outlier-outsider modes of critique, betraying an implicit though, perhaps, for some, startling revelation. *Francophone postcolonial cultures have become unrecognizable.* Certainly when you cut their optic nerve. We see, we gaze, we get, we dig, we know, we recognize. But we listen, stop seeing, and suddenly no longer recognize. As Edwige Tamalet Talbayev, quoting Pierre Schaeffer, writes in her essay, "'écouter' points to a listening protocol invested in 'viser, à travers le son instantané lui-même, une autre chose que lui' [aiming, through sound itself at the moment of its emission, for something beyond] (Schaeffer 1966: 107)." "Exhum[ing] the acoustic subtilities" of these newly unrecognizable francophone cultures constitutes this book's deep, if oblique, postcolonial cut.

To this project of critical rejuvenation, *Sounds Senses* introduces two primary theoretical thrusts—the *unheard* and the *unintegrated*—since a concise history of francophone postcolonial studies (otherwise boasting no shortage of theories on alterity, otherness, ipseity, and the formations of subjects, subjecthoods, and subjectivities) reveals a primary tendency to value what is seen over what is heard.[2] Beginning over a century ago with *Batouala*, René Maran's *véritable roman nègre* from 1921 and the field's foundational text in the twentieth century, a long tradition of attentiveness to the *shape* of language forms the backbone of francophone postcolonial studies. Modulating this observation in relation to Amadou Kouourma's *Les Soleils des indépendances* (1968), Christopher Miller announces that the francophone shape of language "Africanizes French" (2001: 1028). Africanization here

---

[2] Scholars in adjacent fields have already started to address this lapsus. Martin Munro writes in his essay in this volume that, "not surprisingly, of all the work done by Western historians of aurality, it is the research on the American South and the experience of American slavery that is potentially the most useful critical bridge in beginning to listen to Caribbean history." See for instance Bronfman and Wood 2012. For an example from Middle East studies, see Simon 2019.

designates a broad practice of translational transparency within francophone cultures that, in different cultural contexts, could alternatively be called Arabization, Creolization, or Vietnamization, wherein idioms from, say, the Manding languages are directly rendered into french, such as the titular *soleils des indépendances* that stands in for *ère des indépendances*.[3] As for Maran, though he sates *Batouala* with the onomatopoeia of local life in Ubangui-Chari, he watches, gazes, remains passively "à l'écoute" (Diouf 2016), listening and transcribing from a distance. A Martinican whose presence in West Africa was justified by his official capacity as french colonial administrator (Ikonné 1974; 1976), Maran was at an exclusionary remove from indigenous relationships to sound.

The historical and intellectual implications gleaned from Maran, Kourouma, and Miller are that the seeds of decolonization and the subsequent struggles for independence brought with them a political mobilization of local cultures as a form of resistance with and against (within and counter to) the colonizer's language, a tactic heralded by Maran, amplified by Négritude, then championed by Jean-Paul Sartre, Albert Memmi, and Frantz Fanon. Writers such as Assia Djebar and Abdellah Taïa go further by gendering ongoing postcolonial struggles for emancipation and equality—Djebar turns her attention to the religious and lingual effacements of women across historical translations of early Islamic chronicles, while Taïa queers french that has been pacifically invaded with Quranic scripture (elhariry 2021a; 2022). Contemporaneous with decolonization were North African journals such as *Souffles/Anfas*, which enlarged the geographical scope of the era's political struggles, and garnered a reputation for transnational postcolonial affinities by publishing "seminal works by tricontinental writers and political activists, such as the Haitian writer René Depestre, the Syrian poet Adonis, and Amilcar Cabral, the leader of the struggle for independence from Portugal in Guinea-Bissau, as well as key revolutionary and postcolonial texts, such as the ten-point program of the Black Panthers," and offering "continuing coverage of the Palestinian-Israeli conflict, liberation struggles in the Portuguese colonies of Africa, and the independence movement in the Western Sahara" (Harrison and Villa-Ignacio 2015: 1–2).

In this view of the field, and ever since Edward Said's *Orientalism* (1978), with its heavy dose of debt to Michel Foucault, politics and power dynamics have formed a red thread running throughout the formations of cultural, political, and gendered subjectivities in postcolonial critique. But from *The Empire Writes Back* (1989) to *The Location of Culture* (1994) and beyond,

---

[3] For contrast, see Albert Cossery's explanation of his process of translating Egyptian Arabic into french prose in Mitrani 1995: 90.

francophone postcolonial critique has rarely evoked sound. And when it was, it rapidly took a backseat to questions of political representation and visibility.

The lapsus is revelatory. In the middle of wondering how a community may "stabilize and unify its address as an agency of *representation*, as representative of a people," Homi K. Bhabha unexpectedly shifts rhetorical gears into an earnest mode of metaphorical questioning:

> How do we avoid the mixing or overlap of images, the split screen, the failure to synchronize sound and image? Perhaps we need to change the *ocular language* of the image in order to talk of the social and political identifications and representations of a people. (1994: 44; my emphasis)

Elsewhere in *The Location of Culture*, Bhabha describes how "the familiar space of the Other [...] develops a graphic historical and cultural specificity" (67). If anything, he seeks to rectify the historical invisibility of "the postcolonial or migrant subject" (67), which, mysteriously, it appears, has ceded to sound. "We witness the alienation of the eye," writes Bhabha, "through the sound of the signifier as the *scopic desire* (to look/to be looked at) emerges and is erased in the *feint of writing*" (67; my emphasis).

That graphemic, "ocular language" is sovereign in francophone postcolonial studies is no overstatement. In fact, so thoroughly is "scopic desire" entrenched in the philosophies and theories informing francophone postcolonial studies, that even discussions of rhythm and orature once used to always threaten folding and collapsing under their own weight—rhythm was always signaled by the image of the drum, orality by the figure of the *griot* ... As we shall see, recent groundbreaking scholarship has begun to rectify and nuance such lapses within the field's predominantly ocular language. For, as Jennifer Solheim suggests, a "call to listen," which "embeds sound technologies as part of the cultural phenomenon" across all mediums, now constitutes the major imperative of postcolonial critique's inquiries into "who speaks, who is silent; what is heard, what is silent; when and where things are heard, when and where there is silence; and why some things are heard, and others silenced" (2017: 2). Otherwise, in an extension of an insight gleaned over years of reading Frantz Fanon, Tahar Ben Jelloun, Assia Djebar, and Gayatri Spivak, "what is articulated" quite simply "goes *unheard*" (Solheim 2017: 8; see Chapter 7).

The sonic is the other of the ocular. Like a needle dropped in the widening groove of francophone postcolonial studies, this introduction furrows deep in the *unheard*, and its corollary, the *unintegrated*. By unheard, I designate what has been muffled, muted by a cultural, sensorial hardening or ossification, over the course of the past six centuries, as a result of the progressive philosophical, imperial, empirical, scientific, economic, and technological values placed on sight, from Gutenberg's press in the 1440s all the way to the first image of a black hole in 2019. Bathed in noise, the world nevertheless goes silent. Sound goes under, has been going under for a while, pulling with it modes of being, feeling, and thinking that are inextricably intertwined with the spectrum of the senses. For this reason, critical attention to the sonic cannot entirely separate itself from an aporetic coupling with the visual, the conventional domain of silence. The inseparability elicits a "narrative performance" out of the silent cultural object, wherein "how the listener reacts determines whether the sound source resonates through sound or silence" (Solheim 2017: 16). And yet, by turning their attention to cultural sources, at turns silent, at others sonorous, sometimes whispering, elsewhere screaming, the critics united by *Sounds Senses* collectively sift cultural artifacts for what has been left unintegrated. Unheard remains. Unheard remainders. Unheard reminders.

In what follows, then, I stake a claim for revalorizing the sonic over the progressive historical hegemony of the visual, illustrated with select examples from the history of french poetry. My theoretical discussions of the concepts of the "inouï, qui libère un sens nouveau" [unheard, which frees new meanings] (Kilito 1986: 64), and the unintegrated alternate between close readings of Michel Serres's *Genèse* (1982) and François Jullien's *L'Inouï* (2019). Serres and Jullien offer complementary philosophical assessments of the critical ramifications of refocusing our attention on sound, within an enlarged human sensorium that places a particular accent on the activities of listening, hearing, and understanding. The motivations behind my in-depth consideration of the unheard and the unintegrated are twofold. First, the unheard opens a semantic sonic realm in the francophone postcolonial context that stems from an ethical injunction centered around the imperative of hearing the Other. Second, the unintegrated, which denotes a tension between noise, on the one hand, and phenomenæ rising against a background of noise on the other, probes the central notion of voice, critiqued throughout this book for being a supposedly "transparent, self-present medium" that "attempt[s] to capture presence" (Steintrager and Chow 2019: 9, 3; see Chapter 2).

The overarching endeavor in *Sounds Senses* to better grasp the theory, history, and nature of sound and voice in francophone postcolonial cultures is steeped in the thought of Roland Barthes, Michel Chion, Jean-Luc Nancy, and Peter Szendy on the auditive. It draws on groundbreaking work by Rey Chow and James A. Steintrager, Sarah Kay and François Noudelmann, Eric Méchoulan and David F. Bell, David Toop, and Alexander G. Weheliye. And it would not have been possible without trailblazing interventions, in both francophone postcolonial studies and the overlapping field of critical race studies, by Fred Moten, Martin Munro, Edwin Hill, Vlad Dima, Carrie Noland, and Jennifer Solheim. In the most general terms, each of the three sections in *Sounds Senses* presents a cluster of essays that approaches the unheard and the unintegrated from the perspectives of poetry, cinema, and voices. Two additional essays—the first on Ghérsim Luca, the second on the *tchip*—bookend the collection. I gesture to individual essays organically throughout these pages. Essays within each cluster subsequently adopt theoretical modes from the wider field of sound studies, which expands the scope of my introduction through the implementation of harmonizing frameworks for making sense out of the sounds of francophone postcolonial cultures.

Nomqs

french poetry teems with examples of unsound french. They pinpoint discrete moments in the history of french that offer a counter-corrective to the teleological force behind the rise of the "Western retinal paradigm" (Barbanti 2018: 69). Alexander J. Weheliye recognizes in "the structuration of the scopic [...] the disembodied sense of reason par excellence since the Renaissance" (2005: 5). Drawing on R. Murray Schafer's influential notion of the soundscape (1977), Martin Munro similarly observes how "the ear was superseded by the eye as the primary bodily gatherer of information around the time of the Renaissance as the result of developments in the printing press and perspective painting" (2010: 191; see Bailey 2004; Woolf 2004; Weheliye 2005: 27–29).[4] And Edwin Hill, in a riff on Mary Louise Pratt's seminal *Imperial Eyes* (1992), situates the extension of this tradition squarely within the "imperial gaze" of "the seeing man," specifically in writings by "French ethnographers and colonial missionaries dating back to slavery and Enlightenment," such as Jean Baptiste Du Tertre, Jean-Baptiste Labat, Jean Baptiste Thibault de Chanvalon, Médéric Louis Élie Morea de Saint-Méry, and Lafcadio Hearn (2013: 2–3). "Because the indefinite and fluid nature of sonic phenomena in New World environment did not lend itself well to the Enlightenment's catalog of the visible," Hill contends, "travelers and travel writers often had to supplement scientific method with sentimental or openly subjective assessments and practices of sound description that alternately jeopardized and facilitated both the literal and mythological mapping" (4).

---

[4] Edwin Hill critiques Schafer's soundscape for its "claims of ownership and patriarchal social ordering," and how such a conceptual model, at turns "specific and arbitrary," "decide[s] which accounts count and which can be discounted" (Hill 2003: 12–15).

Sounds Senses aims to recuperate the soundtrack of french, its unintegrated sonic substratum, what has long been left unsounded, or unheard, and mix it with the ongoing project of postcolonial critique and criticism. Here, for instance, is how retroversion to Renaissance-era typographical conventions is reactivated in the extreme contemporary context, which mollifies metropolitan and institutional poetic, prosodic, and prosaic ossifications in language. To be sure, as novel and unheard as Du Bellay may have been, singing your poetic blues and overdoing alliteration and rich rhyme to the point of saccharine OD (enchanting chanting, anyone?) are anathema for a twenty-first-century writer of any stripe. Going in the opposite direction? Ya bish.

.Loirq. Lorsq(on désgi désignait u,ne chose ,
On la désiga, désignait par deux nomq s
Deux nomqs, deux nomq s.

(Bénazet 2018: 51)

.Whinq. Whenq(we desgi designated a,no thing ,
It's desiga, designated by two namq s
Two namqs, two namq s.[5]

The lines by contemporary transmedial poet Luc Bénazet mimic the kinds of irreversible typos or *coquilles* a writer may once have produced seated at a typewriter (no ⌘ + z). But they also mirror the misprints and idiosyncratic orthographies of french prior to standardization, lingual remainders still dangling from times past, like the *c* in *nuicts*, transmuted here into the *q* of *nomqs*, which Bénazet insists on leaving "uncorrected." Recursion to earlier moments in the history of french curtly undoes the hard visual order of contemporary language.[6] It passes over the progressive dominance and historical imperative of poetic writing—the takeover, the overshadowing alignment, of sound and sense, by sight and sign—and presents more than a signal flickering on the page, a loud scream, emanating from the page, raging against standardization, or, perhaps, just the grating click, of an oral klutz.

In this regard, the lines sound and look none the weirder, nor any more foreign, than poetry from 1558. Bénazet is hardly different from Du Bellay. Neither poet kowtows to much of anything. For Du Bellay, there was no precedent for lingual conformity. For Bénazet, a predetermination (condemnation, even) to the contrary. Some 500 years separate them and a fundamental investment in language's soft, sonic plasticity unites them. It's as if french can

---

[5] Unattributed translations are mine.

[6] On the place of soft vowels in relation to the consonantal hardness of language, see elhariry 2021b.

never really totally harden. Or be contained. Forever it overbrims. They seek its unsound side. They unsound it, sound its unsoundness, what had been (left) unsounded. Tongues—in their transplantations from one epoch to the next, from one land and mouth to the next (Saussure 2005: 40, 267; 2011: 20, 195), before, during, and after colonialism, in the still-unfolding reconfigurations of global colonialisms and postcolonialisms and neocolonialisms and decolonialisms—refuse affixations and assignations. They refute stillness and quietude. For what, orthographically speaking, is the deep difference between Du Bellay's *nuicts* and Bénazet's *nomqs*? And it's not just that it's impossible to tell what they sound or once sounded like. (How was sixteenth-century french pronounced? What did Du Bellay's voice sound like? What was the grain of his voice? When did the *c* go silent? When was it altogether erased?) It's impossible to know whether or not to even sound the *c* of *nuicts*, the *q* of *nomqs*. (Though Bénazet sounds all the klutziness of his graphemic typos during public readings).[7] I am nevertheless tempted to hit mute on Du Bellay's *c*'s and Bénazet's *q*'s. Why? Because they're incorrect? Who am I to know? What are the lingual differences, physiological, auditory, separating *nuit* from *nuict*? *Nom* from *nomq*? What did (does) the past sound like?

Never having heard

Something unsound. Something unheard. Francophone postcolonial cultural production inherits more than the Pléiade's sonic ambiguities and lingual fixations. A sinister history invades and colonizes our ears, ghastly earworm, clamorous "ver d'oreille" (Szendy 2008: 11–13; Weheliye 2005: 1). In the closing salvo to *Different Drummers* (2010), Martin Munro blasts a series of arresting questions:

> We may think we know—from old images, paintings, and even films—
> what slavery *looked* like, but how did it *sound*? We can perhaps conjure

---

[7] A reading by the poet of extracts from *Incidents* (2018) for the monthly Lyon-based radio program *La Fabrique de la nuit* is available on SoundCloud (soundcloud.com/lfdln/dosage-les-cils), as are readings from related works like *Unités* (2014), recorded at the Centre international de poésie Marseille (cip*M*) in November 2014 (soundcloud.com/cipmarseille/99-luc-be-nazet-unite-s-nov). See the France Culture website for a short feature on *Incidents* (franceculture.fr/emissions/jacques-bonnaffe-lit-la-poesie/ce-jour-recu-44-incident-benazet) and a dialogue between Bénazet and Jérôme Game (franceculture.fr/conferences/fondation-dentreprise-ricard/poesie-plate-forme-balbutier). For more on french sound poetry, see Fabre 2005; Noland 2005; Bobillot 2009; Wall-Romana 2009; Noland 2015: 253 n. 20; Royère and Théval 2018.

up images of the slave ship, the plantation, slave revolts, and slave dances, but can we put a soundtrack to those images, or do they run muted in our imaginations like silent movies? Were the sounds of slavery similar across the plantations of the New World, from Brazil to Virginia? Do these sounds die with the passage of time and the institution of plantation slavery, or do they survive, mutate, and evolve so that they may be heard even today in their commuted forms? If sounds do not die completely, what particular sounds have persisted through time and can still be heard today, and do these sounds constitute living ties with the past, parts of history that have outlived slavery and yet still bear witness to the lived experience of bondage? How can we listen to the past when sound is, by its nature, evanescent, when it fades as quickly as it comes, and when the ability to record sounds is historically a new development? (2010: 190–191)

The "ephemoromateriality of sound" (Weheliye 2005: 8), as raised by Munro, begins to suggest the nature of the challenges that surround listening for the contemporary critic, who will unwittingly evoke latent "memories of previous inscriptions of colonial siting, fact and fantasy, realities and fictions, authored by, yet signaled from beyond, the French imperial imagination" (Hill 2013: 2). For his essay in this book, Munro expands some of his key takeaways from *Different Drummers*, such as how the politics of sound over the course of history have served "as markers of [...] social inferiority and of the boundary between civility and barbarity" (Munro 2010: 192). His essay develops concepts first elaborated by Édouard Glissant, in particular the intertwined notions that "language, sounds, and silences defined and shaped slave experience," that "the alienated body of the slave was [...] deprived of speech," and that "self-expression was not only forbidden but 'impossible to envisage'" (196). Indeed,

> for the Caribbean person, Glissant says, the word is first and foremost not written but sound and noise. As Glissant argues, the pitch of sounds— screams, shouts, cries—conveyed meanings that escaped the comprehension of the master, and slaves in this way "camouflaged the world" in the varying intensity of their sounds. (196)

Turning his attention to a remarkable corpus of nineteenth-century Haitian poetry (Chapter 3), Munro carefully traces the development of sonic semantics as the poems' primary sense-making feature. The nineteenth-century primacy of sound is extended by francophone contemporary culture, permeated, as Edwin Hill shows (Outro), by diasporic practices. Hill focuses on the *tchip* as both a sound and word that marked the channels of french culture and daily life with extremely high frequency between 2014 and 2017, in french schools, in the news, in linguistics, at music festivals, in fashion, in hip-hop, in comedy sketches, in Christiane Taubira, in cinema. "While rooted deep in African diasporic experiences," he writes, the *tchip* "functions in a range of new ways as it navigates the urban topographies and soundscapes, the linguistic, cultural, and affective flows, operative in contemporary France." It "sounds the (potentially radical) blackening of the *métropole*, suggesting the ways in which African diasporic practices deeply inform French social and cultural life" by operating its own modes of sonic rebellion. The *tchip* amounts to a sonic gesture whose pushing and pulling forces are capable of breaking in on the official record, and seizing our bodies, with the vibrations of affective dissonance.

Deafness to the past (Munro) and sonic censorship in the present (Hill) both originate in a historical visual primacy, hegemony, and reign. In poetry, the five centuries of literary and artistic history between Bénazet and Du Bellay have introduced successions of complication upon complication. From the sonnet's fourteen lines to the diagonal stretch of Bénazet's sequenced placements of verse on the page, the poem's visual aspect is chief among these. If anything, a poem is still primarily received as a visual form.[8] A poem is a painting. You see it before you read it. It calls out to you from inside its frame on the white page. While ludic typography and visual play have formed integral components of french poetry at least since the Grands Rhétoriqueurs, and while the white space of the layout of the page has been continually revivified ever since *Gaspard de la nuit* (1842) and *Un coup de dés jamais n'abolira le hasard* (1897), sound has been more difficult to talk about, precisely because of the muteness of the past, which, subsequently, amplifies the problem of sound's randomness.

At stake here is a different kind of ephemoromateriality. Stéphane Mallarmé famously bemoaned the incongruity between pronunciation and meaning, more specifically between sonic timbre and semantic sense. Is it any coincidence, then, that, heartbroken, he, too, would halt upon *nui(c)t*? Mallarmé's voice comes across as scratched through with genuine pain. At utter odds, though, with just how bummed out Du Bellay was at never making it big in Rome, he rues lingual-sonic incommensurability and non-correspondence instead:

---

[8] This is changing. Though Bernstein 1998, and Perloff and Dworkin 2009, dominate the Anglo-Saxon field (Baetens 2020), Puff 2015, Broqua and Weissmann 2019, and Lang et al. 2020 outline broader methodological considerations, from translation to archiving, pertaining to the intersection of sound and sense in french.

Mon sens regrette que le discours défaille à exprimer les objets par des touches y répondant en coloris ou en allure [...] quelle déception, devant la perversité conférant à *jour* comme à *nuit*, contrairement, des timbres obscur ici, là clair. (Mallarmé 2003: 208)

My own sense regrets that discourse fails to express objects by touches corresponding to them in shading or bearing [...] what a disappointment, in front of the perversity that makes *jour* [day] and *nuit* [night], contradictorily, sound dark in the former and light in the latter. (2007: 205)

Mallarmé shies away from claiming outright that the *c* in *nuict* may, historically, pronounced, have darkened, radically blackened, *nuit*, introducing a sudden, trenchant, voiceless velar stop between the lightness of the semi-consonant and vowel [*ui*], and the silent consonant [*t*]. He seeks something chewy, tangible, material, beyond or above or beneath the fleeting ephemerality and arbitrariness of the sign, and, in the process, in an "irritation de l'épiderme français" [irritation of the french epidermis] (Baudelaire 1846: 85), brushes against, grates the skin of language, its visual grain. He scratches out the eye of language. Odysseus-like, he blinds it.

Lamentations over the hegemony of oculocentrism in literary theory, art criticism, and cinema studies are now commonplace enough that within sound studies alone, as James A. Steintrager and Rey Chow observe, "it remains almost de rigueur to remark and often to bemoan that the object of interest [sound] has been overlooked" (2019: 13), since "both historical and ongoing theoretical inquiry and media studies in anxious, celebratory, or critical mode has generally condensed around visuality, and much less studied has been the position and role of aurality" (3).[9] From its biblical origins in Genesis, sound was more than just "a creative force," and has constituted "an unseen source of dread" ever since (3). This "sound whose origin is not obvious," dubbed the *acousmêtre* by Michel Chion, constitutes a "disembodied voice" that "seems to come from everywhere" and possesses "four principal qualities: ubiquity, panopticism, omniscience, and omnipotence" (Dima 2017: 35; see Chapter 4). As Martin Munro puts it, power in such instances "derives from a certain omniscience" of the gaze, and "exerts [its] authority through staring" (Chapter 3). Sound's all-encompassing

---

[9] Eric Méchoulan and David F. Bell's take on this basic premise of sound studies leads them to wonder whether "one can attempt to imagine an ultimate resource of the sonic to *situate* the place of critique" and of the critic's voice (2020: 25). Their argument involves, in order of appearance, a discussion of Mike Batt, John Cage, Emmanuel Kant, Dziga Vertov, Alexandre Dumas, Adriana Cavarero, Jean-François Lyotard, and Paul Zumthor, among others.

invisibility (unlike light, sound travels in all directions) offers one possible explanation for the rise and privilege of the retinal. So powerful is the ocular regime that in his reading of African Third Cinema, Vlad Dima asserts that "the visual is the most developed human sense, and one tends to believe what one sees" (2017: 34), which modulates Michel Foucault's assertion that "not only must people know, they must see with their own eyes" (1995: 58, qtd. in Dima 2017: 37). Though Chow and Steintrager stop short of critiquing the Orientalism of oculocentric Enlightenment philosophy, axing it with the ethics, politics, and poetics of postcolonial critique remains the prerogative of critics like Tarek El-Ariss, who takes the Enlightenment West's oculocentricity to task (2013: 6), relishing instead such triggers as the stench of Europe (76, 82) and the generalized sensorial "aversion to civilization" that they provoke (53–87). In terms of the æsthetics of the black radical tradition, Alexander G. Weheliye pushes against "the general hegemony of vision that permeates Western modernity" (2005: 2), as did Fred Moten before him, for whom the "attention to language is always through an implicit and powerful *visualization* of the sign, a visualization never not connected to the hegemony or law of the signifier" (2003: 183) in the "ocularcentric West" (257). Where Jonathan Sterne describes a counter-Enlightenment "Ensoniment" (2003: 2, qtd. in Weheliye 2005: 10), Moten makes a case for the phonography of "silent arts" (Delacroix 2004: 276–277, qtd. in Toop 2010: xiv; see also Campt 2017; Chapters 2 and 5) like painting and poetry, as well as more transmedial mediums such as performance and, engaging Kaja Silverman (1988; 1996), cinema (Moten 2003: 220–221).[10]

Fred Moten even posits the radical claim that "sound gives us back the visuality that ocularcentrism has repressed," through a "phonic recovery of the artwork's visual materiality" (235; see Weheliye 2005: 10–11). This potential is on remarkable display in Jill Jarvis's analysis of filmic near-silence, where subsonic or "low-frequency sounds" betray "an extremely abundant acoustical environment" (Chapter 5), as well as in Olivia C. Harrison's attentive tracking of the progressive silencing of the Palestinian subject, whom she marks as the inscription site of both cinema and literature's preprogrammed mimetic failures as political or politicized or politicizable artistic mediums (Chapter 7). Vlad Dima, too, argues that cinematic sound, for auteurs Ousmane Sembène, Djibril Diop Mambety, and Jean-Pierre

---

[10] Dima 2017: 14–16 offers a helpful overview of feminist critique of cinema. He acknowledges how Oyèrónké Oyěwùmí's *The Invention of Women* (1997) in particular mounts an assault against the "visual logic of Western thought," which drowns out "the dominance of the auditory in Yorùbá-land" (Oyěwùmí 1997: 15, qtd. in Dima 2017: 15).

Bekolo, "often supplants the visual as the primary narrative tool, flipping over the usual conceptualization of the filmic narrative (that is, image plus, as in 'coming after,' sound)" (Chapter 4). At stake in the narrative roles of the aural are the material ramifications of biopolitical space, or how "sound reterritorializes the colonial space," and "essentially turns that space back into an African space again." Dima's essay develops a subjective corporeal poetics of space, which uncovers a tension "between the visual body and the aural body created by the voice," wherein "the hollowing out of African bodies might occur when diegetic and nondiegetic voices escape the bodies from whence they originate." Voice, for Dima, becomes "our most external limb."

Alongside the subjections of individual dominated bodies, Jill Jarvis (Chapter 5) and Maya Boutaghou (Chapter 6) show how hearing rather than seeing or watching films helps us understand the African city's "place in the world in ways that inherited political cartographies and disciplinary geographies obscure" (Jarvis). What Jarvis dubs "sonic mapping" and "aural cartography" in Abderrahmane Sissako's *Timbuktu* (2014) offers "an alternative form of place-making that surfaces recessed networks of interdependency and relation." With care and precision, she irreversibly draws our attention—and sensitizes us—to the speciated and gendered meanings of sounds otherwise "not obviously significant or even audible to untrained human ears." In her essay, sonic mapping and aural cartographies create "spatial awareness, almost like sonar echolocation" out of the "ambient rumblings and rustlings that surround a film's visual field." The film's sound ultimately subverts "a perceptual dynamic centuries in the making that has rendered Timbuktu an ambivalent symbol of alluring emptiness, existential danger, and environmental desolation." Boutaghou similarly analyzes cinematic urban soundscapes in three films set in Algiers. She draws on Michel Chion's *L'Audio-vision* (1990) and a complementary semiotic approach in order to show how a "film's ambient sounds [form] an integral part of diegesis." She "interprets the soundscape of Algiers and its narrative of captivity" in *Pépé le Moko* (1937), *Omar Gatlato* (1976), and *Viva Laldjérie* (2003) as the depiction of a city that "exists through its sounds" and "displays a certain narrative of violence." Evocative of Alex DeLarge's torture by the constant blare of Beethoven in Stanley Kubrick's 1972 adaptation of *A Clockwork Orange*, sound for Boutaghou, as a medium of subjugation and sensorial pain, spatializes a form of acoustic architecture (Constable 2019), which creates (perceptions of) aural prisons, or places to escape and evade. Boutaghou's attention to silenced urban narratives demonstrates how sounds translate "a form of imprisonment and a need to escape." By focusing on three sound sources—noise, music, and speech (specifically the loving, feminine voice)—Boutaghou maintains that "throughout the three movies, there exists an overlap and confusion between each of the three sources of sounds. *Speech* and *music* blend together to become one *noise*, losing meaning and increasing another dimension of the films: their underlying symbolic narrative about Algiers, the city to escape from."

The essays on cinema go against the visuality of the most visual of artforms. Or, further still, sound lets us see (cinema) anew. Michel Serres all out rejects the visual world, the primacy of the ocular hierarchization of the human sensorium, for its failure to bring forth its numerous objects around him. He insists that "je vis ces objets-là plus que je ne les vois. Je crois que j'en reçois les bruits plus que je ne les vois, ne les touche, ne les conçois" ["these are objects I seem to live through more than view. I think I pick up noises from them more than I see them, touch them, or conceive them"] (1982: 22; 1995: 7). As for Mallarmé, poetry, ever eager, readily serves up a cocktail

> niant, d'un trait souverain, le hasard demeuré aux termes malgré l'artifice de leur retrempe alternée en *le sens et la sonorité*, et vous cause cette surprise de *n'avoir ouï jamais* tel fragment ordinaire d'élocution, en même temps que la réminiscence de l'objet nommé baigne dans une neuve atmosphère. (2003: 213; my emphasis)

> negating, with a sovereign blow, despite their repeated reformulations between *sound and sense*, the arbitrariness that remains in the terms, and gives you the surprise of *never having heard* that fragment of ordinary eloquence before, while the object named is bathed in a brand new atmosphere. (2007: 211)

The sounds and senses explored in these pages "move in the traditions of these passages," as well as "out and outside of" them, producing "a generative break," "a fundamental reorientation that we might call novelty" (Moten 2003: 21, 24, 99) in our sensorial and critical receptions and perceptions of francophone postcolonial cultures.

Phono graph

Sounds Senses adopts an approach to francophone postcolonial studies that valorizes the unheard (*phono*) over the tendency to dwell on or remedy the endemic critical and lingual deafness to sound, long abandoned in favor of the ocular, retinal, and visual (*graph*). Each essay in this book turns its attention to listening and hearing in a unique francophone postcolonial corpus of cultural production, ranging from silent arts like poetry in the Prelude and chapters 1–3 (then again, when did poetry ever go silent, that is, "when (if ever) did silent reading take precedence over live performance?"

[Bernstein 1998: 4]) to aural hollowing and emptying, and the soundscapes, at turns boisterous, others silent, of cinema in North, West, and sub-Saharan Africa (chapters 4–6); from the derisive dismissal and political censorship of a lingual tic like the *tchip* (Outro) to the implicit soundtracks of comics, and the historical and political agencies that they activate (Chapter 9); from Orientalist constructions of the primacy of the ideographic over the sonic in Chinese (Chapter 8) to renewed readings of voice, presence, absence, and the politics of silence, subaltern speech, and æsthetic failure (Chapter 7).

The uncanny capacity of a language—even a standardized language—for such a generous, unquestioning, hospitable potentiality bespeaks the *deux nomqs* that give this book its title. The essays in *Sounds Senses* foreground the audibility of poetics and a poetics of audition (Prelude, chapters 1–3), pay attention to the acousmatic voice (Chion 1982; Chion 1999; Chapter 4), and privilege the soundscape (Schafer 1977; Munro 2010: 191; Kay and Noudelmann 2018: 4–6; chapters 5–6). They seek to make sense out of the sounds of poetry, music, cinema, novels, and comics. Frequently, in the process, they fray the limits of competing histories, languages, and semantics, extending them to, straining them at their limits. In this regard, *Sounds Senses* is less concerned with reading literature and viewing cinema than hearing their languages, hearing history, hearing the Other, listening to voice, and learning how to hear the world and listen to it. It sounds poetry, cinema, novels, and comics out loud. It seeks the deep senses—semantic, spiritual, temporal, affective, political, poetical, physiological—hidden in the sounds of all the languages of the francosphère, whether french, French, francophone, Francophone, hexaphone, or "exophone," as Shuangyi Li puts it with regard to Dai Sijie and François Cheng (Li 2019; Chapter 8).

For instance, Olivia C. Harrison (Chapter 7) bridges cinema and voice, nudges us ever closer to the "infrasonic," and probes sound's in/capacity to "[mark] the failure of representation" in both cinema (Ari Folman, and Jean-Luc Godard and Anne-Marie Miéville) and literature (Jean Genet). Her tripartite analysis, a downward gradient that goes from voice to volume to silence, "stage[s] a critique of representation in sound." As she straddles the lines between sound as a "sense of perception" and "medium of representation," Harrison critiques the dual pitfalls of "ethical paralysis" and "representation as substitution" (the Spivakian speaking-for), revealing in the process how sound altogether fails. Her sensitive attunement to sonic politics in Folman, Godard and Miéville, and Genet amounts less to a critique of medium and the use of sound in cinema and literature than a mediation which undermines sonic representation. The aporia of sonic absence in the textually silent medium allows her to salvage the sound repressed by the visuality of cinema, for literature "represents all the gradations of sound, including silence," with the becoming-Palestinian of Genet's voice in his late writings as a case in point. For his part, Shuangyi Li (Chapter 8) outlines a becoming-sinophone in the exophonic literature of Franco-Chinese writers, long captive to a "view and misconception of the Chinese language, which routinely downplays or suppresses the voicing of sinographs." Because of this, "much of Western philosophy and theory signals a general 'muting of the sinograph' and 'an erasure of its connection to speech.'" Li offsets the bias by guiding the reader through "performative utterances" in Dai Sijie "that illustrate how sounds and voices come to *mean*," and François Cheng's "invisible, immaterial, and spiritual qualities of sound and voice." At play in Li's argument is a narrative strategy that "musicates" (Rancière 2016a: 48; 2016b: 44) Dai and Cheng's novels, following the arcs of the dual cultural heritages of Daoism and the Orphic patterns of myth. Jennifer Solheim (Chapter 9) takes further aim at the geopolitics of *francophonie*, and singles out a musicated trend wherein "authors, filmmakers, and playwrights establish a temporal cadence through listening, both as performed within the work, and by the audience," and set "their own narrative tempo." Her focus on listening as a narrative strategy in Marjane Satrapi's *Persepolis* (2000–2003) mobilizes dual notions of synchresis (Chion) and inthymnacy (Szendy) in order to conceive of music as part of a "social ecosystem," which "establishes and punctuates narrative time," while "set[ting] a beat alongside the historical organization of French literature." She forcefully delineates how the francophone tradition of the performance of listening perforates the hegemonic historical time of postcolonialism. "There is sense in sound," she writes, even if the postcolonial subject-object, in slipping the knot of temporal ensnarement, "is not necessarily safe and sound."

As they elicit and birth sound out of silence and silent mediums and artforms, the essays in this book tirelessly *unsound* sound or standard or standardized french. If I thematize the long and still unsettled history of the language of french verse as a synecdoche for sound, it is because poetry not only plays a major role in *Sounds Senses* as the focus of the first section of the book, but also because it educes the specific means by which language opens up and onto the possible and the multiple, as enabled and activated by the sonic. The tension between phoneme and grapheme—"the novel cleft between sound and source" (Weheliye 2005: 7)—has satiated the thought of thinkers such as Hélène Cixous and Abdelkébir Khatibi since the 1960s. In Cixous's first novel *Dedans* (1969), sonic and typographical/punctuational breakdowns—"Alle-ma-gne, Au-tri, ch'en Amé-ri, qu'en Palestine" [Ger-ma-ny, Aus-tri, y'in Ame-ri, c'in Palestine] (40), "Rosevalemouillejouecachetoncou" [Rosiegowetitplayhideyourneck] (50–51), "Nos langues font éclater les syllabes et nos talons font vibrer les murs" [Our tongues shatter syllables and our heels shake walls] (51)—densely populate the work's rich aural textures, as do the many sound-based, trans- and postlingual passages revolving around Jewish liturgy (90). And ever since his first collection of essays *La Blessure du nom propre* (1974), Khatibi has dwelt upon "la fissure entre la phonie et la graphie" [the phonemic-graphemic fissure] (76), "ce mouvement vacillant entre phonie et graphie" [this vacillating movement between the phonemic and the graphemic] (177), "cette mystique du signe" [this mysticism of the sign] (181) that founds "le rapport immotivé entre phonie et graphie" [the baseless phonemic-graphemic relation] (182). In a shrewd observation, Carrie Noland notes how "the reading eye" in this way "connect[s] to a sonorous body," which "results in a heightened sensitivity to language *as object*, as aural, graphemic, and rhetorical phenomenon, rather than language as transparent vehicle" (2005: 5, 18). She insists that

> *it is entirely possible to have a visceral experience of the written word.* A second language—even if it is that of the colonizer—can be experienced with the senses of the body, experienced even as an erotic object, a point made overtly in the works of Khatibi (and celebrated by his critics) [...] Graphemic-phonemic relations constitute a field of acoustic exploration available to all poets invested in bringing the visceral experience of negative injunctions to the reader's eyes. (22, 126)[11]

Kindred spirits to Du Bellay, Mallarmé, and Bénazet, Cixous and Khatibi exacerbate the artifice of ruptures differentiating sign from sound from sense. They amplify "le multiple bruyant, anarchique, noiseux, nué, tigré, zébré, bigarré, mélangé, traversé de mille couleurs et de mille tons" ["the raucous, anarchic, noisy, variegated, tiger-striped, zebra-striped, jumbled-up, mixed-up multiple, criss-crossed by myriad colors and myriad shades"] (Serres 1982: 45; 1995: 22).

Sound, as a sense-making sign in the open field of multiplicity, should thus be situated at the heart of critical thought in francophone postcolonial studies. Sound points to the thresholds of an extreme phonemic-graphemic limit, which doubles as a reading of the limits of *francophonie* as concept.

---

[11] Noland presents a sensitive and sensitizing reading of Aimé Césaire's *Cahier d'un retour au pays natal* (1939) as a case in point that "encourages through lexical means the transformation of marks into vibration, into sound," and promulgates "that strange and magical act by which letters of the alphabet morph into sounds," wherein "marks on the page" act "as generators of sound," "sound patterns," "sound values," "sound effects," and "paronomastic soundplay," such that "verbal sounds [...] take on affective meanings in context," dispersing "rich chains of sound glitter in print" (2015: 42–53).

Raphaël Sigal, whose Prelude moonlights as an intimate account of this project's genesis, has, in opening, already taken us to the edge of the francophone by way of a ludic, creative decomposition of Ghérasim Luca's "francophonics." Luca broke the mold of "linguistic language after Saussure." In a hallucinatory exercise where Matthew Amos and Youna Kwak ghosted the poet's deathly "silent Sound of Being," Sigal "read below the crust of [Luca's] poems," placing him within a broader francophonic network of sonic de(con)structors. Aimé Césaire. Edmond Jabès. Hélène Cixous. Abdelwahab Meddeb. Abdelfattah Kilito. And "other silent ones, and the ones to be. In Dead Yiddish, in Dead Arabic, in Dead Créole." "Sound," Sigal recanted upon the thresholds of *Sounds Senses*, is "the great word-opener. It does not represent actual objects but points at potential ones."

As if he were directly responding to Luca-Sigal, Thomas C. Connolly (Chapter 2) evokes the "thunderous presence" of Mohammed Khaïr-Eddine's voice, his penchant to scream and shout rather than read and recite texts, his subversive recitations of "Mallarmé out loud, as if it were an Islamic text." His essay explores the "uneven rhythms" of the "acoustic cracks" in a recording of the poet's voice during a radio program on France Culture in 1975. Khaïr-Eddine's unsettling poetics—"rhythmic territorializations," a "secret music," "incrusted in the landscape of Azro Wado," "the place of his birth and early childhood"—are drawn out through a revelatory juxtaposition, via Gilles Deleuze and Félix Guattari, with the work of Francis Bacon and what the Irish-born English painter obsessively termed "a Sahara of the mouth." As he plots the remarkable transcultural and historical intertextual reach of Khaïr-Eddine's lyric, which "relates to musical instruments" and the "sound of the flute," Connolly composes a heterodox assemblage out of "the form of its stanzas, the presence of diastolic, systolic, and attendant rhythms, and the fragments of the myth of Marsyas."

As precursors to some of the most sensorially liminal francophonic experiments—a "complex interplay of body, voice, violence, rhythm, and art" (Connolly)—the sonic and rhythmic malleability and plasticity of Luca's and Khaïr-Eddine's transcultural phonemic-graphemic assemblages pave the way for understanding how those *nuicts* and *nomqs* of french old and new more than scratch your eye—Khatibi already noticed that "il y a dans ton regard une étrange griffure" ["in your gaze there's a strange scratch"] (2008: 16; 2017: 9)—with all those intrusive silent/unsilenced plosives, the out-of-place *c*'s and *q*'s. *Nuicts* and *nomqs* designate the flip sides of sound and the phonemic-graphemic object, they designate a thing by two names, they "désignai[en]t u,ne chose [...] par deux nomq s" [designated a,no thing [...] by two namq s] (Bénazet 2018: 51). They burn your eye, leaving an indelible acoustic image first, rupturing your ear drum next. Then they trounce the division between the sound and the sense in the sign. Hot on the heels of sound unsoundness, the essays collected in *Sounds Senses* track the varieties of unsound french, sounded equally across sense and non-sense.

Touch me

The essays in this book amplify the unheard. It seems fitting for the unprincipled unsoundness of such an undertaking to revolve around Mallarmé's "n'avoir ouï jamais" ["never having heard"] (Mallarmé 2003: 213; 2007: 211). But if we've never heard something before, do we even know how to listen to it? How to listen for it? Will we just know when it strikes us? What if it never reaches us? Will it? How can we know? How do we track it? Seek it out?

In *L'Inouï*, François Jullien posits that the world has been so muffled, "recouvert" [covered], "enfoui, enfui, sous les mots et sous les images" [buried, fleeing, beneath words and images], that we must "apprendre (comprendre) enfin, en retrait de tout ce qu'on en a pu jamais dire—« ouïr »—quel « in-ouï » elle est" [learn (understand), at last, at a remove from all that we could ever once say—"hear"—just how "un-heard" it is] (2019: 10–11). His observation evokes Ferdinand de Saussure,[12] Jean Starobinski's magisterial gloss of the Swiss linguist in *Les Mots sous les mots* (1971), and Michel Serres's treatise in *Genèse* on multiplicity, noise, and what he calls "une fontaine informe de formes" ["a formless fount of forms"], "le possible" ["the possible"], "l'ouverture" ["the opening"] (1982: 39, 45; 1995: 18, 22). Yet the key distinction that lies at the heart of Jullien's statement draws a distinction between listening and hearing. His attunement to a haptic tradition in the philosophy of sound reconstructs the visceral, synesthetic aurality described above by Carrie Noland, itself preoccupied with the physical touch, penetration, and impregnation of sound, a "frôlement" [grazing] (Jullien 2019: 85–86, 184, 199) or "effleurement" [light touch] (141–142) or brushing-against. Jean-Luc Nancy, in *À l'écoute* (2002), splits no hairs when it comes to the sense-making potential of *écouter* and *entendre*. He describes "l'ouïe, l'oreille, *auris*, mot qui donne la première partie du verbe *auscultare*, « prêter l'oreille », « écouter attentivement », d'où provient « écouter »" [hearing, the ear, *auris*, a word that gives the first part of the verb *auscultare*, "to lend an ear"], and contrasts it to how

---

[12] For a Marxist critique of Saussure's assertion that sound is ancillary to the value of meaning, and how the formalism of Saussurean linguistics sidesteps phonic materiality and plasticity, see Moten 2003: 13–14, 189–191. Szendy 2008: 20–21 makes analogous use of Marx on the sonic and commodity values of hit songs. On Saussurean synesthesia, see Yamaguchi 2019.

« entendre » veut dire [...] « comprendre », comme si « entendre » était avant tout « entendre dire » (plutôt qu'« entendre bruire »), ou mieux, comme si dans tout « entendre » il devait y avoir un « entendre dire », que le son perçu soit ou non de la parole. (17–19)

entendre, "to hear" [...] means *comprendre*, "to understand," as if "hearing" were above all "hearing say" (rather than "hearing sound [bristle]"), or rather, as if in all "hearing" there had to be a "hearing say," regardless of whether the sound perceived was a word or not. (2007: 5–6)[13]

Nancy reverses Roland Barthes's insistence in 1977 that *"entendre* est un phénomène physiologique; *écouter* est un acte psychologique"* ["hearing is a physiological phenomenon; listening is a psychological act"] (2002: 340; 1991: 245). Whatever the case, they both agree on one thing. To hear me is to touch me. To speak to you is to touch you. You listen to me. I feel you hearing me. Because "we experience sounds as waves of air molecules that strike against our eardrums, creating vibrations inside the body" that are "felt, with palpable physical effects" (Munro 2010: 11). Sound assumes "a corporeal quality," and "a materiality of sounds makes its presence felt," which "mainly comes from the way it is produced" (Dima 2017: 1, 13, 21). Sounds create a "sonic space" where they "are assembled by a set of relations," and "their presence, their interactions as mobile elements [...] create space" (27). Indeed, sound "generate[s] an imagined, sonic space" (28). "Sonic qualities" even "much more literally cause spectators to tremble" (Chapter 5). For "with every sensory experience comes an *empathic* response, an engagement not just as the reader or listener to a story, but as one human being imagining another human experience," which compels sensitivity to "social context, æsthetic (or other) content, cultural form, and the interplay of all three aspects" (Solheim 2017: 4). "These demands," writes Carrie Noland, "transform a personal voice into a hybrid entity, a set of marks on the page that can be phenomenalized, given sensual and cognitive form in the mouth and mind of a reader" (2015: 5).[14] Hearing, then, if we listen closely to Barthes and our critics, is touching me, which Nancy encapsulates in his observation that "écouter, c'est entrer dans cette spatialité par laquelle, *en même temps*, je suis pénétrée: car elle s'ouvre en moi autant qu'autour de moi, et de moi tout autant que vers moi: elle m'ouvre en moi autant qu'au dehors, et c'est par une telle double, quadruple ou sextuple ouverture qu'un « soi » peut avoir lieu" ["to listen is to

---

13 For complementary readings of *écouter* and *entendre*, see Kay and Noudelmann 2018: 1–2; Chapters 1 and 7 of this volume.

14 On the cognition of silent reading and "sounding," see Dehaene 2009; Roubaud 2009.

enter that spatiality by which, *at the same time*, I am penetrated, for it opens up in me as well as around me, and from me as well as toward me: it opens me inside me as well as outside, and it is through such a double, quadruple, or sextuple opening that a 'self' can take place"] (2002: 33; 2007: 14).

Power differentials play decisive roles in such aurally minded constructions of the self. As Laurent Aubert observes in relation to world music, "dans les civilisations appartenant au tiers-monde de l'économie planétaire, l'oreille prêtée par l'étranger—qui plus est, par l'étranger doté de pouvoir—a paradoxalement contribué à vivifier la pratique d'arts au passé millénaire" [in civilizations belonging to the Third World of the planetary economy, the ear lent by the stranger—a stranger furthermore endowed with power—has paradoxically contributed to a vivification of age-old arts] (2001: 13). A complex interplay is triggered by "les déferlements migratoires" [migratory surges], and "les autoroutes de la communication remettent-ils en cause les principes de l'identité [musicale]" [communication highways requestion the bases of (musical) identity] (7), which resemble "un vaste jeu de miroirs déformants, dans lequel l'autre nous renvoie indéfiniment l'image altérée de notre identité mouvante" [a vast game of deformative mirrors, where the other indefinitely sends the altered image of our shifting identity back to us] (100).

Sounds Senses pushes back against the kind of "hybridation érigée en dogme" [hybridization elevated to dogma] (104) frequently at stake in the task of listening to the other and the sounds of the other, as well as the risk of "undercomplicat[ing] the dynamics of identity formation" (Agawu 2003: xviii), forever and "irreducibly allusive" (147). In her essay on Moncef Ghachem's lyric, Edwige Tamalet Talbayev (Chapter 1) focuses on the generic transmedial transposition of poetry to music, and her fine-grained analyses lend credence to the synesthetic principle that "the sensory experience of rhythm is not quite hearing, not quite touching or feeling, but an amalgam of these (and possibly other) senses" (Munro 2010: 12).[15] Her essay takes the premise and aspirations of "the openness and fluidity of 'world music'" to develop a tension between the flux (or *flou*) of live performance, the (seeming) fixity of capture, and the "apprehension and parsing [of sound] with each playback." "Belying the exclusive dominance of any paradigm of loss,"

---

[15] For a discourse analysis of the intertwined trope of Africa and rhythm, see "The Invention of 'African Rhythm'" (Agawu 2003: 55–70). On "musics broadly referred to in France as *la world music, la musique mondiale,* or *les musiques du monde,*" see Solheim 2017: 134. On rhythm in Négritude as a form of "oversound," after Robert Frost's usage of the term in the poem "Never Again Would Birds' Song Be the Same," see Noland 2015: 131–142.

she writes, "sound reproduction creates unexpected, endlessly modifiable counterpoints to the aural original in which the restitution of a minimalist soundtrack of captured orality can lead to an infinity of transpositions across variable, transmedial collaborations." Evocative of Jahan Ramazani's *A Transnational Poetics* (2009), Talbayev constructs in the process an affective "sujet résonant" (Nancy 2002: 44; 2007: 21; Kane 2012), a subject resonant "with the vibrations of the sonorous object," bringing "further nuance to the study of the transcultural movement of lyric by unlocking the forms of sonic and cognitive transfers and negotiations that occur between languages in the process of poetic circulation and intertextuality."

The circulatory spatiality described by Talbayev hints at the unheard as formulated by Jullien, who senses an unending assault of standardization by language. Language tirelessly hides the unheard beneath itself—"le langage [...] le laisse [le « réel »] peut-être à jamais in-ouï *sous* tout ce qui en a été dit" [language (...) perhaps leaves it (the "real") forever un-heard *beneath* all that has been said about it] (Jullien 2019: 12; my emphasis)—such that our task and calling becomes a processual uncovering, a "dé-couvrement" [dis-covering] (13, 51, 63, 78, 130), an "exhumation de l'inouï de la sensation" [an exhumation of the unheard of sensation] (77), in order to "creuse[r] un abîme qui toujours est vertigineux" [hollow out an ever more vertiginous abyss] (125). The unheard is

> ce *restant*—ce qui reste « in-ouï »—parce que demeurant en deçà de notre appréhension qui toujours déjà le recouvre: ce qui échappe au cadrage et captage de la perception, toujours pré-déterminée; à l'enregistrement et au rangement de la pensée, toujours pré-constituée. (24)

> this *remainder*—what remains "un-heard"—because it dwells beneath our apprehension, which is always already recovering it: what evades the framing and capture of perception, always predetermined; what evades the recording and classification of thought, always pre-constituted.

One of the aporias of the scopic regime is that the unheard presents visually, in the guise of "l'inconnu de ce qu'on a sous les yeux, précisément parce qu'on l'a continûment sous les yeux" [the unknown within what lies before our eyes, precisely because we continually have it before our eyes] (41). Show, reveal, demonstrate ... in our writing, we are all guilty. The oxymoron is discernible in the most idiomatic of slippages, like "[sound] has been *overlooked*" (Steintrager and Chow 2019: 13; my emphasis). Or, when, above, supercilious, ridiculous, I announced that my revalorization of "the sonic over the progressive historical hegemony of the visual" shall be "*illustrated* with select examples from the history of french poetry." So used are we to reading, to seeing, so heavily reliant are we on the ocular, that we don't think twice about mixing metaphors, or the sounds of the words on the page anymore. We appear to have succumbed to a form of *atonal atony*. Not only do we no longer hear, but because we have been not hearing for so long, we dwell in a state of sonic slackness or debility. "L'inconnu," writes Michel Serres, "est [...] la multitude du confus" ["The unknown is (...) the multitude of confusion"] (1982: 55; 1995: 28). Then, one day, out of left field, you are assailed by *nuicts* and *nomqs*.

Hear me

The degrees of nuance between the visual and the sonic impose an ethical injunction, which lies at the core of *Sounds Senses* as an integral axis of francophone postcolonial studies. Difference impels us to unveil the alterity hidden beyond the skin-deep visual, and which the sonic may *dé-couvrir* or dis-cover. A reversal or conversion is at play here, "ce qui la rend [l'éthique] enfin « renversante » ou de conversion: non par conversion du mal au bien, mais du *lassant* qui, par son atonie, atrophie et replie la vie, à l'*inouï* qui remet celle-ci en tension en la confrontant à ce qui met en défaut son pouvoir d'assimilation" [which ultimately makes (ethics) "astounding" or conversional: not by the conversion of evil into good, but of the *tedious*—which atrophies and folds up life with its atony—into the *unheard*, which resets life by confronting it with whatever invalidates its assimilative powers] (Jullien 2019: 71; see also ibid., 134, 181).[16] Atony petrifies. It sets the world in stone. The infamous "rapport immotivé entre phonie et graphie" [baseless phonemic-graphemic relation] (Khatibi 1974: 182) takes root. In Serres's view, "le vieux rationalisme est le béton du monde, la philosophie du langage est le béton du sens, nos philosophies de la politique et de l'histoire sont le béton du temps" ["the old rationalism is the concrete of the world, the philosophy of language is the concrete of meaning, our philosophies of politics and history are the concrete of time"] (1982: 50; 1995: 25). Ethics entails a conversional calling that would allow us not just to see but to hear the Other, "or c'est précisément le pari du concept d'*inouï* que de donner à envisager l'inouï de l'Autre dans la suite de l'inouï de la mer ou de l'aube, du monde ou de la vie" [for the wager of the concept of the *unheard* very much rests upon how it yields to considering the unheard of the Other in the wake of the unheard of the sea or dawn, of the world or life] (Jullien 2019: 178). "Reconnaître l'Autre en tant qu'autre,"

---

[16] Jullien gleans the concept of the haunting, tedious *lassant* from Mallarmé's line, "*Je suis hanté. L'Azur! L'Azur! L'Azur! L'Azur!*" ["*For I am haunted. The Sky! The Sky! The Sky!*"] (1998: 15; 1994: 20, qtd. in Jullien 2019: 19).

concludes Jullien, "c'est reconnaître l'ipséité de l'autre en tant qu'elle me reste inouïe" [Recognizing the Other insomuch as other is to recognize the ipseity of the other insomuch as it remains unheard to me] (189).

Leave me

The sonic re-cognizance of otherness takes root within one's own sensorium in relation to word and world. Michel Serres laments how fixed and transfixed we are by unity, to the extent that "nous méprisons les sens parce que leur information nous parvient en rafales" ["we scorn the senses, because their information reaches us in bursts"] (1982: 15; 1995: 2). The sounds of the world are unintegrated at their genesis, and remain so until filtered, classified, categorized, organized, hardened by the senses and the intellect. The world, thus aggregated, solidifies, becomes integral, integrated, integrative. "Un concept, ainsi," Serres pursues, "est solide, et le solide est presque déjà un concept. Nous avions peur des gaz et des liquides [...] notre savoir n'était pas fait pour les grandes multiplicités" ["Thus, a concept is solid, and the solid is almost already a concept. We were afraid of gases and liquids (...) our knowledge was not made for the great multiplicities"], for "le solide est le multiple ramené à l'unité" ["the solid is the multiple reduced to the unitary"] (175–176; 108). Serres seeks to retune his ears, and then reorient his sensorium and all his thought toward "turbulence" (178; 110), toward noise, primordial waters, magma of the possible.

John Ashbery once attempted to capture the invention of language, cutting against all the primeval noise. "Gloss on the fine / Freckled skin," he wrote, "lips moistened as though about to part / Releasing speech" (2010: 486). Serres recasts the Foucauldian dimensions of Ashbery's lines—that "language arose when the noise produced by the mouth or the lips had become a *letter*" (Foucault 2002: 311, qtd. in Steintrager and Chow 2019: 9)—by insisting that

> le bruit ne peut être un phénomène, tout phénomène se détache de lui, figure sur fond, comme un feu sur la brume, comme tout message, tout cri, tout appel, tout signal, doivent se détacher du vacarme occupant le silence, pour être, pour être perçus, pour être connus, pour être échangés. Dès qu'un phénomène se manifeste, il quitte le bruit [...] il traverse [...] canaux construits ou langues. (Serres 1982: 33; see also Attali 1977 [1985]; Hegarty 2007; Weheliye 2005: 97, 107, 114–120)

> noise cannot be a phenomenon; every phenomenon is separated from it, like a silhouette on a backdrop, like a beacon against the fog, as every message, every cry, every call, every signal must be separated from the hubbub that occupies silence, in order to be, to be perceived, to be known,

to be exchanged. As soon as a phenomenon appears, it leaves the noise [...] it moves through [...] constructed channels or languages. (Serres 1995: 13)

Sounds Senses pursues the sonically unintegrated. It hears, then leaves. The interventions collected in this book, too, hear, then leave. They pursue a dual objective in relation to the unintegrated: (i) to isolate sonic phenomenæ, in the broadest possible sense of the term, in francophone postcolonial cultural production, though (ii) not at the expense of muffling the generative ambient noise—prosody, history, news cycles, technology—that bore them to existence in the first place. *Sounds Senses* seeks the noise inside and behind this noise. It stresses and maintains the kinds of unsoundness operative from Du Bellay to Mallarmé to Cixous to Khatibi to Bénazet. The world produces sound, but sound is like writing on water (Serres 1982: 48, 106, 111; 1995: 24, 61, 65). And so each essay in this book builds a memory or repository of the sonic, each essay seeks to "capture" (Chapter 1), through marks on the page, something of that noise, something leaving the noise, like a message to be deciphered, "comme clignote ce message avec le bruit de fond qui le porte et qui l'intercepte, qui l'amène à nous, qui l'empêche et qui l'interdit ... le monde est cette immersion même, la pensée, les messages sont ces immersions, distributions dans les systèmes, systèmes immergés dans les distributions" ["as this message winks with the background noise that carries it and that intercepts it, that brigs it to us, that hinders it and that prohibits it ... the world is this very immersion, thought, messages are these immersions, distributions in systems, systems immersed in distributions"] (Serres 1982: 185; 1995: 114–115).

Sound, in the francophone postcolonial context, as it emerges over the course of *Sounds Senses*, both makes no sense (it is ephemeral, it is nowhere), and produces a ton of it (it is everywhere, all the time). It is unintegrated and unintegrable. It remains unfixed, unfixable. It refuses affixations, assignations. For it has remained unheard for so long. The unheard is unheard because it is unintegrable, or, rather, so integrated is it into our life that it goes by unperceived. Which triggers sonically oriented cycles of awakening, capture, and dis-covering. Language "nous a déjà emmurés, elle qui ne sait toujours qu'*intégrer*; donc qui ne peut que laisser échapper l'inintégrable, autrement dit l'« inouï »" [has already inwalled us, it only knows how to constantly *integrate*; so it cannot help letting go of the unintegrable, in other words, the "unheard"] (Jullien 2019: 18; see also ibid., 35, 108). And since "l'ouïe intègre mieux qu'elle ne peut analyser, l'oreille sait perdre ses comptes" ["hearing is better at integrating than analyzing, the ear knows how to lose track"] (Serres 1982: 22; 1995: 7). Our search, therefore, is for a "multiplicité inintégrable" ["unintegrable multiplicity"] (187, 200, 219; 116, 124, 137).

Find ptyx

In the history of modern and contemporary french, pure lingual invention is a *rara avis*. Even Mallarmé appears to have only ever written just one made-up word.[17] Why?

> Sur les crédences, au salon vide: nul ptyx,
> Aboli bibelot d'inanité sonore. (Mallarmé 1998: 37)

> On the credenzas in the empty room: no ptyx,
> Abolished shell whose resonance remains. (1994: 69)

In a letter dated May 3, 1868, addressed to his friend, the Egyptologist Eugène Lefébure, Mallarmé briefly describes the structure of "Ses purs ongles très haut dédiant leur onyx" ["Her pure nails on high displaying their onyx"], a sonnet with just two alternating rhymes. Along the way, he offers a hint to the enigmatic *ptyx*.

> Comme il se pourrait parfois que [...] je fisse un sonnet, et que je n'ai que trois rimes en *ix*, concertez-vous pour m'envoyer le sens réel du mot *ptyx*, ou m'assurer qu'il n'existe dans aucune langue, ce que je préférerais de beaucoup afin de me donner le charme de le créer par la magie de la rime. (Mallarmé 1998: 728–729)

> As it happens that sometimes [...] I write a sonnet, and that I only have three rhymes in *ix*, pray tell me the real meaning of the word *ptyx*, or assure me that it exists in no language, which I would find infinitely preferable, so I may charm myself for having created it with the magic of rhyme.

Language, Mallarmé suggests, is an eternal emitter of sound signals. So artists, poets, and critics alike must act like sentinels, keeping out a constant ear for the unheard. Their task consists of being "au monde à l'état de veille, de se river à la chaîne des instants, de s'en saisir, de capturer ceux qui se cristallisent dans le ferment perpétuel de l'alchimie intérieure" [in the world in a state of constant alertness, riveted to the chain of instants, seizing them, capturing the ones that crystallize in the perpetual fomentation of interior alchemy] (Meddeb 2000: 16–17; reproduced in 2001: 87). As Barthes notes, listening is a three-part search for meaning: (i) an orientation to

---

[17] But was Mallarmé ever even french in the first place? As Albert Thibaudet wondered nearly a century ago, "il conviendra de chercher la mesure dans laquelle fut ou non française l'œuvre de Mallarmé" [it behooves us to figure out just how french—or unfrench—Mallarmé's work was] (1930: 20, qtd. in Combe 2020: 214).

certain *indices*, certain *alertes*, paying notice, which the human and the animal share: a rabbit in the field, an owl circling the dead blue of night; (ii) *déchiffrement*, intercepting or capturing (*capter*) certain signs (*signes*): the human is not logos, but the deciphering of logos; and (iii) an openness to the unheard, for listening

> ne vise pas—ou n'attend pas—des signes déterminés, classés: non pas ce qui est dit, ou émis, mais qui parle, qui émet: elle est censée se développer dans un espace intersubjectif, où « j'écoute » veut dire aussi « écoute-moi »; ce dont elle s'empare pour le transformer et le relancer infiniment dans le jeu du transfert, c'est une « signifiance » générale, qui n'est plus concevable sans la détermination de l'inconscient. (2002: 240)

> does not aim at—or await—certain determined, classified signs: not what is said or emitted, but who speaks, who emits: such listening is supposed to develop in an inter-subjective space where "I am listening" also means "listen to me"; what it seizes upon—in order to transform and restore the endless interplay of transference—is a general "signifying" no longer conceivable without the determination of the unconscious. (1991: 246)

Listening to the sounds of francophone postcolonial cultures resembles something akin to listening for an *indice*, an *alerte*, a *ptyx*, a phenomenon emerging out of the primordial waters or magma or ambient noise of the world. Capturing and deciphering its magic, its alchemy, its "iconic sound shape" (Bernstein 1998: 21)—hearing the unheard in/of the Other, in all its/ their un/integrality—is the small gesture offered by *Sounds Senses*. It sounds the unsound and makes the unsound sound sound.

Works Cited

Agawu, Kofi. *Representing African Music: Postcolonial Notes, Queries, Positions.* Routledge, 2003.

Ashbery, John. "Self-Portrait in a Convex Mirror." *Collected Poems 1956–1987,* edited by Mark Ford, Carcanet, 2010, pp. 474–487.

Attali, Jacques. *Bruits: essai sur l'économie politique de la musique.* Presses universitaires de France, 1977.

——. *Noise: The Political Economy of Music.* Translated by Brian Massumi, University of Minnesota Press, 1985.

Aubert, Laurent. *La Musique de l'autre: les nouveau défis de l'ethnomusicologie.* Georg, 2001.

Baetens, Jan. "Les Archives sonores de la poésie." *Leonardo Reviews Archive,* June 2020, leonardo.info/review/2020/06/les-archives-sonores-de-la-poesie.

Bailey, Peter. "Breaking the Sound Barrier." *Hearing History: A Reader*, edited by Mark M. Smith, University of Georgia Press, 2004, pp. 23–35.

Barbanti, Roberto. "Listening to the Landscape for an Ecosophic Aesthetic." *Soundings and Soundscapes*, edited by Sarah Kay and François Noudelmann, special issue of *Paragraph*, vol. 41, no. 1, 2018, pp. 62–78.

Barthes, Roland. "Listening." *The Responsibility of Forms: Critical Essays on Music, Art, and Representation*. Translated by Richard Howard, University of California Press, 1991, pp. 245–260.

——. "Écoute." *Œuvres complètes, V: livres, textes, entretiens, 1980–1977*, edited by Éric Marty, Seuil, 2002, pp. 340–352.

Baudelaire, Charles. *Salon de 1846*. Michel Lévy frères, 1846.

Bénazet, Luc. *Unités*. cip*M*, 2014.

——. *Incidents*. Nous, 2018.

Bernstein, Charles, ed. *Close Listening: Poetry and the Performed Word*. Oxford University Press, 1998.

Bhabha, Homi K. *The Location of Culture*. Routledge, 1994.

Bobillot, Jean-Pierre. *Poésie sonore, éléments de typologie historique*. Le Clou dans le fer, 2009.

Bronfman, Alejandra, and Andrew Grant Wood, eds. *Media, Sound, and Culture in Latina America and the Caribbean*. University of Pittsburgh Press, 2012.

Broqua, Vincent, and Dirk Weissmann, eds. *Sound/Writing: traduire–écrire entre le son et les sens. Homophonic Translation–Traducson–Oberflächenübersetzung*. Éditions des Archives Contemporaines, 2019.

Campt, Tina. *Listening to Images*. Duke University Press, 2017.

Chion, Michel. *La Voix au cinéma*. L'Étoile, 1982.

——. *L'Audio-vision: son et image au cinéma*. Nathan, 1990.

——. *The Voice in Cinema*. Translated by Claudia Gorbman, Columbia University Press, 1999.

Chow, Rey, and James A. Steintrager. "In Pursuit of the Object of Sound: An Introduction." *The Sense of Sound*, edited by Rey Chow and James A. Steintrager, special issue of *differences*, vol. 22, nos. 2–3, 2011, pp. 1–9.

Cixous, Hélène. *Dedans*. Des femmes, 1969.

Combe, Dominique. "Khatibi and Derrida: A 'Franco-Maghrebian' Dialogue." Translated by Jane Hiddleston. *Abdelkébir Khatibi: Postcolonialism, Transnationalism and Culture in the Maghreb and Beyond*, edited by Jane Hiddleston and Khalid Lyamlahy, Liverpool University Press, 2020, pp. 197–217.

Constable, Liz. "Hearing Cultures: Acoustic Architecture and Cinematic Soundscapes of Algiers in Merzak Allouache and Nadir Moknèche." *Contemporary French Civilization*, vol. 33, no. 1, 2009, pp. 179–208.

Dehaene, Stanislas. *Reading in the Brain: The Science and Evolution of a Human Invention*. Viking, 2009.

Delacroix, Eugène. *The Journal of Eugène Delacroix*. Translated by Lucy Norton, Phaidon, 2004.

Dima, Vlad. *Sonic Space in Djibril Diop Mambety's Films*. Indiana University Press, 2017.

Diouf, Ibrahima. "Un véritable roman barbare? La langue française à l'écoute de la barbarie dans *Batouala* (1921) de René Maran." *Francofonia*, no. 70, 2016, pp. 83–99.

Du Bellay, Joachim. *Les Regrets et autres oeuures poetiques*. Federic Morel, 1558.

——. *The Regrets: A Bilingual Edition*. Translated by David R. Slavitt, Northwestern University Press, 2004.

El-Ariss, Tarek. *Trials of Arab Modernity: Literary Affects and the New Political*. Fordham University Press, 2013.

elhariry, yasser. "*f.*" *Literature in the World*, edited by Simon Gikandi, special issue of *PMLA*, vol. 131, no. 5, 2016, pp. 1274–1283.

——. "Khatibi Misses the Mark." *North African Poetry in French*, edited by Thomas C. Connolly, special issue of *Yale French Studies*, nos. 137–138, 2020, pp. 125–146.

——. "Hyphens & Hymens: francoarab Literature of the Maghreb." *A Companion to African Literatures*, edited by Olakunle George, Wiley-Blackwell, 2021a, pp. 133–149.

——. "Tarkos Births a Vowel." *The Postlingual Turn*, edited by yasser elhariry and Rebecca L. Walkowitz, special issue of *SubStance*, vol. 50, no. 1, 2021b, pp. 54–75.

——. "Unbearable: Early Islam and Transnational Poetics in Assia Djebar and Abdelwahab Meddeb." *Transnational French Studies*, edited by Charles Forsdick and Claire Launchbury, Liverpool University Press, 2022, forthcoming.

elhariry, yasser, and Rebecca L. Walkowitz, eds. *The Postlingual Turn*, special issue of *SubStance*, vol. 50, no. 1, 2021.

Fabre, Guilhem. "Poésie sonore: expérimentation de la voix et expérience du corps." *Recherches et travaux*, no. 66, 2005, pp. 175–186.

Feriani, Rim, Jasmina Bolfek-Radovani, and Debra-Kelly. "Reading Signs and Symbols with Abdelkébir Khatibi: From the Body to the Text." *Abdelkébir Khatibi: Postcolonialism, Transnationalism, and Culture in the Maghreb and Beyond*, edited by Jane Hiddleston and Khalid Lyamlahy, Liverpool University Press, 2020, pp. 237–260.

Foucault, Michel. *Discipline and Punish: The Birth of the Prison*. Translated by Alan Sheridan, Vintage, 1995.

——. *The Order of Things: An Archeology of the Human Sciences*. Routledge, 2002.

Harrison, Olivia C., and Teresa Villa-Ignacio, eds. *Souffles-Anfas: A Critical Anthology from the Moroccan Journal of Culture and Politics*. Stanford University Press, 2015.

Hegarty, Paul. *Noise/Music: A History*. Continuum, 2007.

Hill, Edwin C., Jr. *Black Soundscapes White Stages: The Meaning of Francophone Sound in the Black Atlantic.* Johns Hopkins University Press, 2013.

Ikonné, Chidi. "René Maran, 1887–1960: A Black Francophone Writer Between Two Worlds." *Research in African Literatures*, vol. 5, no. 1, 1974, pp. 5–22.

——. "What Is *Batouala*?" *Journal of African Studies*, vol. 3, no. 3, 1976, pp. 373–391.

Jullien, François. *L'Inouï.* Grasset, 2019.

Kane, Brian. "Jean-Luc Nancy and the Listening Subject." *Contemporary Music Review*, vol. 35, no. 5–6, 2012, pp. 439–447.

Kay, Sarah, and François Noudelmann. "Introduction: Soundings and Soundscapes." *Soundings and Soundscapes*, edited by Sarah Kay and François Noudelmann, special issue of *Paragraph*, vol. 41, no. 1, 2018, pp. 1–9.

Khatibi, Abdelkébir. *La Blessure du nom propre.* Denoël, 1974.

——. *Le Lutteur de classe à la manière taoïste.* 1976. *Œuvres de Abdelkébir Khatibi II: poésie de l'aimance.* Preface by Marc Gontard, Différence, 2008, pp. 9–35.

——. *Class Warrior—Taoist Style.* Translated by Matt Reeck, Wesleyan University Press, 2017.

Kilito, Abdelfattah. "Meddeb et ses doubles." *Lamalif*, no. 182, 1986, p. 64.

Kinoshita, Sharon. "Worlding Medieval French." *French Global: A New Approach to Literary History*, edited by Christie McDonald and Susan Rubin Suleiman, Columbia University Press, 2010, pp. 3–41.

Lang, Abigail, Michel Murat, and Céline Pardo, eds. *Archives sonores de la poésie.* Les Presses du réel, 2020.

Li, Shuangyi. "Novel, Film and the Art of Translational Storytelling: Dai Sijie's *Balzac et la Petite Tailleuse chinoise*." *Forum for Modern Language Studies*, vol. 55, no. 4, 2019, pp. 359–379.

Mallarmé, Stéphane. *Collected Poems: A Bilingual Edition.* Translated by Henry Weinfield, University of California Press, 1994.

——. *Œuvres complètes, I.* Edited by Bertrand Marchal, Gallimard, 1998.

——. "Crise de vers." *Œuvres complètes, II*, edited by Bertrand Marchal, Gallimard, 2003, pp. 204–213.

——. "Crisis of Verse." *Divagations: The Author's 1897 Arrangement Together with "Autobiography" and "Music and Letters."* Translated by Barbara Johnson, Harvard University Press, 2007, pp. 201–211.

McNeece, Lucy Stone. "Abdelkébir Khatibi: The Other Side of the Mirror." *Abdelkébir Khatibi: Postcolonialism, Transnationalism, and Culture in the Maghreb and Beyond*, edited by Jane Hiddleston and Khalid Lyamlahy, Liverpool University Press, 2020, pp. 261–278.

Méchoulan, Eric, and David F. Bell. "Are Sounds Sound? For an Enthusiastic Study of Sound Studies." *Listening to Sounds Studies*, edited by Eric Méchoulan and David F. Bell, special issue of *SubStance*, vol. 49, no. 2, 2020, pp. 3–29.

Meddeb, Abdelwahab. "La matière du poème." *Dédale*, nos. 11–12, 2000, pp. 15–19.

——. *Matière des oiseaux*. Fata Morgana, 2001.

Miller, Christopher. "*Francophonie* and Independence." *A New History of French Literature*, edited by Denis Hollier, Harvard University Press, 2001.

Mitrani, Michel. *Conversation avec Albert Cossery*. Joëlle Losfeld, 1995.

Moten, Fred. *In the Break: The Aesthetics of the Black Radical Tradition*. University of Minnesota Press, 2003.

Munro, Martin. *Different Drummers: Rhythm & Race in the Americas*. University of California Press, 2010.

Nancy, Jean-Luc. *À l'écoute*. Galilée, 2002.

——. *Listening*. Translated by Charlotte Mandell, Fordham University Press, 2007.

Noland, Carrie. "Phonic Matters: French Sound Poetry, Julia Kristeva, and Bernard Heidsieck." *PMLA*, vol. 120, no. 1, 2005, pp. 108–127.

——. *Voices of Negritude in Modernist Print: Aesthetic Subjectivity, Diaspora & the Lyric Regime*. Columbia University Press, 2015.

Oyěwùmí, Oyèrónké. *The Invention of Women*. University of Minnesota Press, 1997.

Perloff, Marjorie, and Craig Dworkin, eds. *The Sound of Poetry/The Poetry of Sound*. Chicago University Press, 2009.

Pratt, Mary Louise. *Imperial Eyes: Travel Writing and Transculturation*. Routledge, 1992.

Puff, Jean-François, ed. *Dire la poésie?* Cécile Defaut, 2015.

Ramazani, Jahan. *A Transnational Poetics*. University of Chicago Press, 2009.

Rancière, Jacques. *Le Sillon du poème: en lisant Philippe Beck*. Nous, 2016a.

——. *The Groove of the Poem: Reading Philippe Beck*. Translated by Drew S. Burk, Univocal, 2016b.

Roubaud, Jacques. "Prelude: Poetry and Orality." Translated by Jean-Jacques Poucel. *The Sound of Poetry/The Poetry of Sound*, edited by Marjorie Perloff and Craig Dworkin, Chicago University Press, 2009, pp. 18–25.

Royère, Anne-Christine, and Gaëlle Théval. "Le texte, le son, l'action dans les 'litanies du banal' d'Anne-James Chaton." *Poetry's Forms and Transformations*, edited by Nina Parish and Emma Wagstaff, special issue of *L'Esprit Créateur*, vol. 58, no. 3, 2018, pp. 58–70.

Saussure, Ferdinand, de. *Cours de linguistique générale*. Payot, 2005.

——. *Course in General Linguistics*, edited by Perry Meisel and Haun Saussy, translated by Wade Baskin, Columbia University Press, 2011.

Schaeffer, Pierre. *Traité des objets musicaux*. Seuil, 1966.

Schafer, R. Murray. *The Tuning of the World*. Knopf, 1977.

Serres, Michel. *Genèse*. Grasset, 1982.

——. *Genesis*. Translated by Geneviève James and James Nielson, University of Michigan Press, 1995.

Silverman, Kaja. *The Acoustic Mirror: The Female Voice in Psychoanalysis and Cinema*. Indiana University Press, 1988.

——. *The Threshold of the Visible World*. Routledge, 1996.

Simon, Andrew. "Censuring Sounds: Tapes, Taste, and the Creation of Egyptian Culture." *International Journal of Middle East Studies*, vol. 51, no. 2, 2019, pp. 233–256.

Solheim, Jennifer. *The Performance of Listening in Postcolonial Francophone Culture*. Liverpool University Press, 2017.

Starobinski, Jean. *Les Mots sous les mots: les anagrammes de Ferdinand de Saussure*. Gallimard, 1971.

——. *Words Upon Words: The Anagrams of Ferdinand de Saussure*. Translated by Olivia Emmet, Yale University Press, 1979.

Steintrager, James A., and Rey Chow. "Sound Objects: An Introduction." *Sound Objects*, edited by James A. Steintrager and Rey Chow, Duke University Press, 2019, pp. 1–19.

Sterne, Jonathan. *The Audible Past: Cultural Origins of Sound Reproduction*. Duke University Press, 2003.

Szendy, Peter. *Tubes: la philosophie dans le juke-box*. Minuit, 2008.

Thibaudet, Albert. *La Poésie de Stéphane Mallarmé: étude littéraire*. Gallimard, 1926.

Toop, David. *Sinister Resonance*. Bloomsbury, 2010.

Wall-Romana, Christophe. "Dure poésie générale." *Esprit Créateur*, vol. 49, no. 2, 2009, pp. 1–8.

Weheliye, Alexander G. *Phonographies: Grooves in Sonic Afro-Modernity*. Duke University Press, 2005.

Woolf, D. R. "Hearing Renaissance England." *Hearing History: A Reader*, edited by Mark M. Smith, University of Georgia Press, 2004, pp. 44–51.

Yamaguchi, Liesl. "Sensuous Linguistics: On Saussure's Synesthesia." *New Literary History*, vol. 50, no. 1, 2019, pp. 23–42.

Poetry

CHAPTER ONE

Sound Capture and Transmedial Resonance: Moncef Ghachem's Lyric

Edwige Tamalet Talbayev

When sound ceases to follow sense, when, that is, it *makes* sense of sound, then we touch on the matter of language. This is the burden of poetry; this is why poetry matters. (Bernstein 1998: 21)

In their introduction to their 2011 special issue on *The Sense of Sound*, Rey Chow and James A. Steintrager capitalize on the Romantic characterization of sound as a fleeting object. Their theorization of sonic materialization is twofold, resting on both technical reconstruction (the attempt to solidify sound into a fixed, fully objectifiable form through technology and machines, a project in futility on account of sound's elusive nature) and human sensoriness (a phenomenological effort resulting in the imperfect processing of sound by auditory subjects, a process sensitive to sound's tenuousness, to its intangible echo). In the critics' own words, *"sonic capture is understood implicitly as the capture of that which is lost*. More succinctly put, *sound is always capture, and capture is always loss"* (Chow and Steintrager 2011: 4; my emphasis). Finding their theoretical mooring in the certainty that sound is always already evanescent, Chow and Steintrager emphasize the ineffectuality that imbues any attempt at recording it. What surfaces from this transaction is an enduring tension between a "capturable" sonic matter, the palpable substance of sound endowed with material properties that can be reproduced on a variety of media to relative technological perfection, and the inescapable deperdition of sound, its vanishing resonance lost to posterity. The critics thus point the way to the ghostly remainders of sound that persist, unaccounted for, beyond the rational processes aiming to turn sound into reproducible objects. Redrawing the boundaries of sonic phenomena as "points of diffusion" (2)—nodes where the auditor comes front and center, turning the aural process into an *interactive* process—they isolate aural perception as the coalescing principle behind sound's constitution into bounded, discrete units ("the *work* of gathering—an effort to unify and make cohere—implies that subjectivity is involved whenever we try to draw some boundary in the sonic domain" [2]). Subjective mediation gives way to a new form of "plenitude" belying sound's inexorable loss—not simply as a function of the "puri[fied]" state of studio-remastered sound, as Chow and Steintrager intimate (5), but rather, here, as a novel form of *interaction* borne of the intersubjective, aural/oral relation between auditor and voice. While less-than-pristine sound is perceived and imperfectly processed by the auditor, new sense is projected back onto the original performance, *restituted* into the implicit dialogue with the listener that the production of sound activates in the ever-elusive "elsewhere" of sonic diffusion ("sound is forever elsewhere" [5]). Any "gesture of restitution," Jacques Rancière tells us, "is always also a new gesture of capture" (2006: 116). In the context of sound objectification, restituting sound through playback redoubles the original seizure, in its entropic dimension ("loss") but also in the diffusive, swerving élan that each successive materialization unleashes.

In a subversion of Walter Benjamin's reflections on the interruption of the work of art's aura by the advent of mechanical reproducibility, capture comes to shed light on the endurance of sound once its inceptive utterance has vanished—on its multiple, multifarious afterlives after the finite lifespan of the original has faded into silence. In its endless posthumous circulation, captured sound therefore supersedes the exiguous time-space of its elocution. Breaking down the barriers of specificity, time-stamped sound lends itself to infinite reincarnations and endless resemanticizations.[1] Sound capture paves the way for a sequence of hearing episodes through which a sense of continuity and memory in hearing comes to be formed in defiance of the entropy inherent in live performance.[2] Through its enmeshment

---

[1] In this respect, the materialization of sound ushers in the suppressed dimension of time. It deploys the aural experience on an elastic temporal plane where the interval during which sound is produced, evolves, and comes to vanish is elongated.

[2] For Makis Solomos, "music is so much harder to remember or anticipate. Just as it is easy, with a melody, to remember the first note and anticipate those that

into other orders of meaning (transmedial, multimedial), sound objectification cultivates a sustained, longer-term listening practice whereby the lyric
qualities of a recited text can be perceived in complex resonance with the
convolutions of its musical transpositions. This tangled unspooling of the
lyrical line sets in motion new sense-making protocols that are gradually
constructed and in constant evolution, following the flow and counterflow of
amended perception. For if digitized sound does not alter with time—at least
not in a way sensible to the human ear—its apprehension and parsing does
with each playback. In the immanence of listening, the subject's sensorium
filters through the acoustic environment, recasting sound as a source of
relationality—between listener and sound object, but also among the overlaid
dimensions of captured sound that can only fully unfurl in time through the
auditory subject's mediation. Capture, then, functions as "an aperture for
interventional creativity" (Chow 2012: 54). Belying the exclusive dominance
of any paradigm of loss, sound reproduction creates unexpected, endlessly
modifiable counterpoints to the aural original in which the restitution of a
minimalist soundtrack of captured orality can lead to an infinity of transpositions across variable, transmedial collaborations.

With these reflections in mind, this essay ponders the kind of insights that
an analysis focused on sound as material object open to resemanticization
and imaginative investment can bring to the study of Francophone lyric in
a transmedial, translingual context. Building on Stephen G. Kellman and
Natasha Lvovich's definition of translingual texts as "texts by authors using
more than one language or a language other than their primary one" (2015: 3),
it aims to bring further nuance to the study of the transcultural movement
of lyric by unlocking the forms of sonic and cognitive transfers and negotiations that occur between languages in the process of poetic circulation
and intertextuality.[3] Moving forward the purview of both fields, this essay
aims to pinpoint the multiple translational, heteroglossic registers laboring
underneath the Francophone text—here, through a study of the collaboration
Dalle Sponde del Mare Bianco [*From the Shores of the White Sea*],[4] a musical
transposition of Tunisian poet Moncef Ghachem's francophone verse in the
distinctive, incantatory register of the Sicilian band Dounia.

---

follow, it is challenging to memorize sonic forms and anticipate their evolution
precisely because of their complexity" (Solomos 2018: 99).

[3] For additional insight into the mechanisms of translingual readings of
francophone literature, see Sellin 2013; Forsdick 2015; Dutton 2016; and elhariry
2017.

[4] "The White Sea," which appears in Ghachem's Arabic poetry recorded in the
Dalle Sponde volume, is the Arabic name for the Mediterranean.

Entanglements

fare libri è un esercizio di ospitalità

[making books is an exercise in hospitality]. ("Chi siamo")

Chow conceptualizes "entanglement" as the coming together of two disparate elements in inchoate conversations,

> a topological looping together [...] a tangle, of things held together or laid over one another in nearness and likeness [...] meetings that are not necessarily defined by proximity or affinity [...] conceivable through partition and particularity rather than conjunction and intersection, and through disparity rather than equivalence. (2012: 1–2)

Teetering between analogy and contrast, these enmeshments speak directly to the "ineluctable noncoincidence of emission and reception and the entanglement of subjectivity and objectivity" (Chow and Steintrager 2011: 12) intrinsic to any acousmatic experience marked by deferred—that is, deviated, embellished, improvised—restitution.

It is one such entanglement between captured poetic voice and musical counterpoint that this essay is interested in parsing through a sound-based reading of Moncef Ghachem's 2003 translingual poetry anthology *Dalle Sponde del Mare Bianco* in relation to its musical adaptation by the band Dounia. In 2000, Ghachem, a Tunisian fisherman-turned-poet noted for his marine lyric and strong Mediterranean inspiration, and Dounia, a Sicily-based world music group, took to the stage for what was meant to be a single collaborative poetry reading with musical accompaniment. The recitation of Ghachem's Francophone poetry to the hybrid sound of Dounia became the backbone of a series of concerts produced under the name *Dalle Sponde del Mare Bianco*, one of which was eventually recorded live at Acireale, Sicily in December 2002. In 2003, Casa Editrice Mesogea, a Messina-based Sicilian publishing house specializing in the publication of original and translated works of Mediterranean literature, developed a book-cum-CD centered on the collaboration. The eponymous volume is divided into two parts. The first section, entitled "il libro" [the book], comprises the first ever Italian translation of a selection of poems from Ghachem's collections *Car vivre est un pays* [For Living Is a Country] (1978), *Cap Africa* (1989), and *Orphie* [Garfish] (1996), as well as one of his short stories from *L'Épervier* [The Hawk] (1994) and an article published on April 25, 2002 in the Tunisian daily *Le Temps*. A prefatory critical essay by the then Mesogea Mediterranean literature editor Costanza Ferrini brings this inaugural part to a close. The second section, "il CD" [the CD], includes a recording of eight tracks adapted by Dounia from Ghachem's poetry. It breaks down as follows: seven songs from *Car vivre est un pays*, *Cap Africa*, and *Orphie*; one original creation by Ghachem penned in Tunisian Arabic, and one text composed by band singer Faisal Taher. In addition, "il CD" includes a transcription of the French texts recited during the "Dalle Sponde" concert, alternately accompanied or replaced by their Italian, and occasionally Arabic or Sicilian, translations.

The author of verse in Arabic and French, Moncef Ghachem has made a name for himself in Maghrebi Francophone literary circles as a fisherman-poet rooted in the mobile geography of the Mediterranean (he mentions "les racines de la mer" [the roots of the sea] [1997: 28]). This bond with the maritime is ontological, as central to Ghachem's poetic persona as it is to the sustenance of the fishing community into which he was born: "It is in the midst of my family of fishermen that I encountered poetry. And since I went out to sea by day and by night, it was the sea that had given me a little of its memory, of its mystery, a crumb of its song" ("Curriculum vitæ," Ghachem and Dounia 2003: 10).[5] Ghachem's characteristic lyric flows from the poet's physical connection to the Mediterranean Sea, which he envisions almost on the molecular level, as substance.[6] Through this immersion, an acrid, rugged poetics develops with roots in the immemorial times of Ifriqiya and medieval conquests. Knotted around the minutiae of a fisherman's life of hardship on the Mahdia peninsula, Ghachem's verse reflects a rumbling disquiet following the awareness of being crushed by the violence of history's damaging course: "le mort-né arabe" [the Arab stillborn] ("Le veilleur," 54) partakes of the widespread ruination afflicting life along the sea ("Nomades de la mer noire et âpre / Pêcheurs de l'orphie erratique" [Nomads of the black and harsh sea / Fishers of the erratic garfish] ["*Orphie* X," 116]). Out at sea, poetry, revelatory, fulgurates, rending the shroud of silence overlaying the churning brew of the tide. Stoking the tension between sound and silence, the *orphie*, a garfish, emerges as a flashpoint of lyric creativity. "Erratic" on account of its elusiveness, the darting garfish fractures the soundlessness entombing the poetic word: "La nuit suave où tangue notre patiente barque / entraîne, vers notre silence, les éclats d'orphie" [The sweet night where our patient boat rolls / drags towards our silence bright garfish] (114). In its luminescent wake ("le passage lumineux de l'orphie" [the luminous passage of

---

[5] Ghachem readily comments on the "Mediterraneanness" of his verse: see Villain 2014. Unless otherwise noted, all translations from the French, Arabic, Italian, and Sicilian are mine.

[6] For in-depth explorations of Ghachem's poetics, see, among others, Kassab-Charfi and Khedher 2019; Bekri 1992; and Cailler 2007.

the garfish] [114]), a summons chips away at the silence ("nous convoquons" [we convoke] [114]), opening up the space of the poetic text to other echoes, other translations.

Sound structures Ghachem's reflections on the difficulties inherent in poetic translation. When faced with the task of finding the right rendition of the Arabic *hajar* [stone], Ghachem insists on finding the equivalence of the quintessential quality of the stone ("la luminance, la chaleur, le mystère, le battement de cette pierre" [the luminescence, the warmth, the mystery, the pulse of this stone] ["Le traducteur," 21]) but also, and perhaps more essentially, a translation equally faithful to the sonic texture of the original: "Il y a l'R, bien sûr, dans le mot français 'pierre' et dans son équivalent arabe 'hajar'" [there is the R, of course, in the French word "pierre" and in its Arabic equivalent "hajar"] (21). Yet, beyond fortuitous alliteration, translation needs to attend to the delicate balance between sound and silence: "Il faut que je rende exactement le son de chute de cette pierre inaugurale" [I need to render exactly the sound of this inaugural stone falling] (21). A double challenge besets the poet, a double translation—that of the words themselves and, beyond, that of their rippling sound.

If sound slices through the silence insulating the poetic word, conversely, lyric highlights silence's lasting shroud. Speaking of the mandate to preserve the aural integrity of each linguistic code, Ghachem remarks that translation requires

> juxtaposer les deux écritures, les deux voix, l'ancienne et celle qui naît, la source et l'œil du sourcier, le silex, le grès ou le marbre, et la respiration de leur regardeur, clos dans son propre rêve ou extasié [...] Recréer le temps du silence, conserver la marge entre ce temps et le premier mot proféré, la pourfendre pour mieux la retrouver dans un autre espace du désert inné. Où trouver l'équivalent de cette parole autre, comment la ressusciter, de quel langage user? (21–22)

> juxtaposing both writings, both voices, the ancient and the one being born, the spring and the diviner's eye, the flint, the sandstone, or the marble, and the breath of their beholder, enclosed in his own dream or ecstatic [...] To recreate the time of silence, to preserve the margin between this time and the first uttered word, to slice it up to better discover it anew in another space of the innate desert. Where to find the equivalent of this other word, how to resurrect it, what language to use?

Undoubtedly, the mystical resonance of this passage ("extasié") would deserve more attention than I am able to devote in these pages. Suffice it for our purposes to point out the poet's extreme care to enshrine the discrepancy between *paroles* (tapping into the inner logic of "entanglement" as tension), and to give full shrift to the density of silence, which both preexists the spoken word and outlasts it. Silence is displaced unto the inner time of the beholder—the dowser watchful for the concealed spring of inspiration that alone can do justice to the semantic and phonic transfer between languages. The language to be crafted is one held in suspense, one lurking beneath the threshold between idioms, ensconced in silence. Tentative like the diviner wielding his rod, it is this incipient, ever-deferred heuristic quest that the translation of lyric articulates. In its interstices a new voice emerges, upholding the gaps and striations borne of the poetic convergence between languages. There, the breath of the poetic voice reigns supreme, imposing its intimate rhythm. It is probing, the incarnation of the translator's mediation. But it is also his limit, and, ultimately, his ineffectuality—any translating act is always already entropic, any attempt at capturing sound, loss.

To Paul Ricœur, this loss is one that "we must mourn until we reach an acceptance of the impassable difference of the peculiar and the foreign" (2006: 9). Far from being an invalidating proposition, the open-endedness of translation facilitates the mutual contamination of languages. It fosters a form of "linguistic hospitality" that resurrects the "memory of the foreign" (9), what Abdelkébir Khatibi, reflecting on Spain, dubbed a "réconcili[ation] avec [...] *notre cœur étranger de ce pays*" [a reconciliation with *our foreign heart in this country*] (1988: 128; emphasis original). The ghostly presence of variegated Mediterranean origins suffuses the liminal space of Mahdia's marine cemetery. The coastal city of Ghachem's birth doubles as a city of death for the many specters woven into the fabric of everyday life—be they the Greek fishermen of yore or the phantoms of the Fatimid kings who established the city as a capital.[7] Through blurred demarcation lines, past and present commingle, puncturing any sense of temporal continuum. The domain of porosity and belatedness, Ghachem's lyric takes on sepulchral hues: "Les tombes des îles sont les écailles de la mémoire. Dans leurs vasques taries, la mer reptile" [The islands' graves are the scales of memory. In their dried-up basins, the sea slithers] (1997: 60). Both scales and peeling off chips (*s'écailler*), *écailles* betokens protection and dispersal, integrity and progressive corruption. Beneath the *écaillure* of memory, breaches are formed, yielding passage to deep-reaching resurgences. The synecdochical sea-turned-reptile, in its neologistic use as a verb, surreptitiously overruns

---

7 The Fatimid empire (tenth–twelfth centuries) stretched across North Africa from the Atlantic to the Red Sea. Interestingly in our context, it also extended across the Strait of Messina in its earlier years to include modern-day Sicily.

the space of remembrance. Speaking of the linguistic traces left throughout history by those who came before him, Ghachem adumbrates a sonic

> l[egs] d'une forme de présence, une part de moi-même, un peu de feu pour ma voix nue? Je plante à ma manière les éclats de leurs langues, le brouhaha de leurs fêtes et les échos de leurs défaites dans les tissus viscéraux de qui je serai. C'est-à-dire un livre palpitant de visages et de pierres, d'arbres et de semences, d'exils et d'errances, de reflux, de villages [...] les irruptions de mes corps réunis, les terrestres et les célestes, les marins et ceux-là même qui m'ont perdu ... (1994: 160)

> legacy of a form of presence, a part of myself, a little fire for my naked voice? I plant in my own way the shards of their tongues, the hubbub of their celebrations, and the echoes of their defeats in the visceral tissues of who I will be. That is to say, a palpitating book of faces and stones, of trees and seeds, of exile and wanderings, of ebb and flow, of villages [...] the irruptions of all my bodies, be they earthly or celestial, those of sailors and those who have lost me ...

This irruptive inlaying of vocal "éclats," reminiscent of the "éclats d'orphie" that sparked off poetic expression, performs a prosopopoeic function. Through it, other voices of Mahdia come to resonate through history—the Greek sponge fishermen of yore, but also the illustrious lineage that has left its imprimatur on Mahdia. Numidians, Punics, Romans, Byzantines, Arab conquerors advancing the *geste* of Islam, Normans, Christian Crusaders, Spaniards, Turks, Imazighen (151), all endure through the vocal "ravaud[age]" [stitching up] of memory's fishing net ("*Orphie* X," Ghachem and Dounia 2003: 114).

If Ghachem's lyric is ontologically anchored in the ferment of the sea, the Sicily-based band Dounia instead opts to "not operate by mixing elements of different Mediterranean musical traditions," preferring instead to "contaminate without predetermination" (Plastino 2005: 180). Made up of three Sicilians (Vincenzo Gangi, guitar; Giovanni Arena, bass; Riccardo Gerbino, drums) and one Palestinian (Faisal Taher, voice), the band aspires to the openness and fluidity of "world music," only lending itself to an oblique connection to the Mediterranean. Ghachem characterized the collaboration as "élever le chant métissé d'une méditerranée à la fois, polyphonique et proche [...] c'est un compagnonnage et un échange poétiques et musicaux avec la Sicile, la belle île où ont vécu avant nous de grands poètes arabes, tels: Ibn Hamdis et El Khayat" [elevating the hybrid song of a Mediterranean both polyphonic and proximal [...] these are poetic and musical companionships and exchanges with Sicily, the beautiful island where great Arab poets lived before our time: for instance, Ibn Hamdis and El Khayat] (qtd. in Ben Zineb 2012). To Ghachem, the connection to the twin city of Mazara del Vallo, across the Strait of Sicily, encapsulates a resonant, if slightly essentialist, Mediterranean identification: "And the Sicily of Ibn-Hamdis keeps living in the band Dounia. It carries a wide-ranging music [*dall' ampio respiro*] which unites the song of the whole Mediterranean" (Zorat 2006).

In a prefatory essay to the part of the book dedicated to transcriptions, Catania-born poet Biagio Guerrera, who was invited by Mesogea's Costanza Ferrini to join the collaboration, vibrantly delineates the perfect symmetry between Ghachem's poetic lyric and Dounia's attention to the ecology of spoken sound: "From that first fortuitous encounter, an immediate communication was established between the poet and the musicians, which went beyond language, perhaps because it embraced so many of them [languages] at the same time. It was the sign of a creative communion" (Ghachem and Dounia 2003: 84). The im-mediacy of the artists' creative encounter stems from their common ability to transcend the singularity of idiom and emplacement, to reunite in a shared mental territory lying beyond the boundaries of any single linguistic system or cultural logic. Theirs is an encounter throbbing with the pulse of the Mediterranean hospitality mobilized by Ghachem, one in which languages and discrete forms of belonging come undone and commingle, ever beckoning to one another in the rich ferment of the sea. Among the sonic fioriture of Dounia's melodies, its distinctive, colorful timbre, made up of a "minimalismo caldo" [warm minimalism] for Guerrera, constitutes a particularly welcoming environment for the expression of poetic lyric. For as the Sicilian poet opines, "the poetic word, on the other hand, is already music in itself" (84).

In this entanglement between poetic word and musical sound, affinity and discrepancy are set in tension as the poetic lines rub against the musical weft, supported by its reiterative rhythms yet chafing against its grain. These intersecting sonic matrices function as coexisting sound boards, *tables de résonance* as they are known in French: reverberating surfaces where acoustic tremors undulate outward toward other sonic systems. Caught in the web of their lyrical enmeshment, long-forgotten, transcultural echoes make their way through the harmonies, weaving their wail into the melodic lines. In Dounia's own words, "the result exceeds any form of contamination creating Dounia's little world, where each sound is given importance, even a mere chord. Thus causing a surge of emotion for the listener, letting them feel free in this open and interactive listening space: imagination" ("Drum Book: Dounia Live"). In the distinctive tension between each chord, the remanence of sounds past can be perceived. In this polycentric, shifting sonic landscape, affect guides the listening ear from note to vivid note, from phoneme to euphonic or dissonant phoneme, following the unfolding of lyric cross-pollinations through Mediterranean history. Against conceptions of the Mediterranean in terms of space and mobility, the examination of plurilingualism in *Dalle Sponde* instigates a focus on time. It is across time that the deterritorialization of form and language occurs across the maritime expanse, across time that lexical forms carrying within them the imprimatur of other languages come to assimilate and complete their evolution, across time also that musical influences can blend into a distinctive microcosm— such is "Dounia's little world" that sheds light on the endurance of the Mediterranean lyric chronotope that Ghachem's overlaid poetry engages.

In his analysis of Dounia's idiosyncratic sounds, Goffredo Plastino argues that "repeated listening" opens up the realm of affect, impressions, sensations, and granularity (2005: 180). Through recurrent listening, the audience's engagement produces a personal connection to the musicality of the phrase— lyric becomes affective, the playground of imaginative investments of the musical phrase with personal perceptions, memories, and improvisations. This performative listening stands at the intersection of reception and production. Only the trained ear inured to the interweaving of the recital's disparate registers can begin to identify a converging lyric carried in turn by the spoken word, the sung text, and the music. The persistent listener thus enacts an internalization of Dounia's plural register, calling to mind through this restitution an omniscient narrator speaking in indirect speech, filtering utterances, analyzing them, fomenting connections between them in an attempt to palliate the ambiguity of lyric's intermedial mode of enunciation. Under Ghachem's capacious French, embedded in the heterophonic imprints brought about by the swell of the Mediterranean Sea, other sound systems undulate, registering repressed Italian, Sicilian, Tunisian Arabic, and even Palestinian Arabic echoes.

The *Dalle Sponde* project is translational at its core. Ghachem himself is no stranger to translation, having rendered into Arabic the Greek poetry of Yannis Ritsos (Kassab-Charfi and Khedher 2019: 133). And although translation as an intellectual practice may not be as habitual an activity for Biagio Guerrera, his commitment to non-dominant languages spurred him to translate Ghachem's original Tunisian Arabic poem included in *Dalle Sponde*, "Lambuca," into Sicilian. Evoking the translational process at work in his collaboration with Ghachem in a second project, Guerrera divulges:

I do not know Tunisian or Arabic, so Moncef and I sat close together, speaking in French or a little English. He translated the poem for me into French and explained the meaning to me [...] It is a translation, but it is a sort of re-creation of the poem in another language, too. It is a live dialogue between two poet friends and between two cultures; close and different at the same time. (Reale 2012)

It is this live dialogue, I argue, that the transmedial scrutiny of *Dalle Sponde* permits to bring to the surface the hidden ongoing negotiations encapsulated in the choice of each translational act and, conversely, the radiating resonance of other linguistic coordinates within the grain of the original language. The remainder of this essay will take a closer look at some examples of transmedial transpositions featured in *Dalle Sponde*.

"where one loses the voice because it no longer disappears ..."[8]

Pierre Schaeffer's distinction in *Traité des objets musicaux* (1966) between *écouter* and *entendre* provides a fruitful entry point into the specifics of the listener's position on the outer edge of performance. *Écouter* points to a listening protocol invested in "viser, à travers le son instantané lui-même, une autre chose que lui" [aiming, through sound itself at the moment of its emission, for something beyond] (Schaeffer 1966: 107). *Entendre*, by contrast, lies in the intentional suspension of judgment, the inescapable Husserlian *epoché* that alone can make room for *écoute réduite* [reduced listening], the ability to shift the emphasis away from the semantic import of sound to its sonic texture. What Schaeffer intimates, then, is the potential of "non-indexical and non-significational modes of listening" (Kane 2012: 442) that rethink the tension between the perceptible and the intelligible. Unquestionably, Dounia's collaborative performance of Moncef Ghachem's lyric works is a far cry from Schaeffer's *musique concrète* frame of reference. Yet Brian Kane's expatiations on the "ideal objectivity" of Schaeffer's sound object shed light on the role that the listening subject might take on in the interactive process at the core of the Mesogea project: "the sound object is an ideal objectivity, something that is intersubjectively accessible (thus, objective) while being irreducible to any of its particular sensory moments (thus, ideal)" (444). Taking his cue from Jean-Luc Nancy, Kane proposes that the auditor be considered in terms of a "resonant subject," that is, a subject that resonates with the vibrations of the sonorous object as "both share a similar 'form, structure, or movement'" (445). In Nancy's configuration, meaning "consists in a reference [*renvoi* ...] Sound is also made of referrals [...] it resounds, that is, it re-emits itself while still actually 'sounding,' which is already 're-sounding'" (2007: 7–8). The back-and-forth movement

---

8 Kahn 1999: 8.

of *renvoi* colors both meaning and sound, as both surge from the eternal return of referrals between subject and object. Kane concludes that sound "is 'intentioned' by the subject, rather it is contemporaneous with the subject because meaning, sound and self all share the same 'form, structure or movement,' namely *renvoi*, resonance" (446). The multifarious restitution of captured sound contributes to the exploration of the multiple forms of "resonance," or *renvois*, uniting the listening subject and the sound object in an interactive ecology of mediation.

One such *renvoi* can be assessed in *Dalle Sponde*'s centerpiece—"J'écris" [I write], a near-twelve-minute-long performance of the entirety of one of Ghachem's most iconic poems. Indicting the multiple forms of oppression and destitution plaguing the wretched of the earth and professing the poet's filial devotion to his Tunisian homeland, the poem undoubtedly counts as one of Ghachem's most socially committed pieces. The reiterative structure—the anaphora of the titular verb form, the refrain regularly interjected every six stanzas—lulls the listener into a state of heightened sensitivity to any slight variation, be it rhythmic, harmonic, or prosodic. The piece is introduced by a simple, haunting four-beat ritornello on the guitar. Syncopated, inquisitive, and quizzical, the harmonies and four-beat structure will recur in altered and developed form throughout the piece. Underneath the theme, supporting it, an elliptical harmonic line, remarkable for its truncated, pizzicato sounds, anchors the dissonant chords—seconds scraping against the full-bodied melodic line. The rubbing heightens a sense of mild discomfort, a defamiliarization, as the listener is caught in the seemingly never-ending, unresolved phrase. Introducing the titular seme around which the poem unfurls, the chanter's voice comes in offbeat, drowning the powerful resonance of the spoken words into the musical line:

> J'écris avec la tyrannie des misères
> j'écris avec mes processions de poète errant
> j'écris avec les jachères sèches de la terre
> j'écris et la colère gronde dans mon cœur transparent.
>
> (Ghachem and Dounia 2003: 96)

> I write with the tyranny of destitution
> I write with my wandering poet's processions
> I write with the dry, fallow land of the earth
> I write and anger roars in my transparent heart.

Inconspicuous at first, the recited verse swells to prominence at key moments of its utterance, when the voice slows down to the rhythm of the drums and lays emphasis on the repeated phonemes and lexemes that lend unity to the piece: "errant" at the end of line 2, to emphasize the fluidity of movement of the poetic voice; "colère" and "transparent" in the last line, relaying the rumbling of an incipient revolution. Cohering through the alliteration in /ʁ/, which highlights both the harshness of circumstances and the sharpness of resistance, the two terms partake of the construction of what could be termed *acoustic fields*, that is, sonic pendants to semantic fields that interlace phonetically cognate words throughout the entire piece—in the first stanza, alongside "colère" and "transparent," "jachère," "terre," "gronde"; further, entire lines, such as the "amer exode rural des frères errances amères" [bitter rural exodus of brothers bitter wanderings] (97). Here, sound and scansion alone provide structure and cohesion to the lexical sequence. Devoid of punctuation or grammatical ordering beyond the epanalepsis, the line only acquires meaning once delivered—once the voice's ritardando perfectly aligns with the musical accompaniment's slacking tempo. It is through its tonguing that the line yields its inner meaning as the listener traces the contours of each semantic unit, the inner rhythm of the phrase come to life. In writing, the line had remained unresolved, inscrutable; in performance, its meaning accrues from the coincidence of diction and rhythmical scansion and from their subtle, occasional disjointedness. Through its musical transposition, the orality of Ghachem's verse is exhumed, captured; what Rancière has called the "mute word" can be reactivated "in the form of rhythm" (qtd. in Noland 2015: 134). Rubbing against the elasticity of the unmetered verse, new scanning patterns emerge, untethered from the usual dominance of the syllable as metrical unit in French prosody. They are revealed through diction, through the presence of the chanter's voice distributing stress along the syncopated line, accelerating or withholding the pace of the phrasing to match the musical phrases. A counterpoetics of improvisation develops, aligning the chanter, the musicians, and the listener, amplifying the intrinsic orality of the text unveiled by Dounia's revelatory interpretation. The refrain will reoccur alongside different musical lines. Yet it will always conserve this initial stress pattern, establishing a distinctive style for the piece and lifting the veil on the centrality of sound as an ordering principle within the Francophone poetic text.

This sounding of the muted human voice underpinning the poem brings to mind what Roland Barthes has called "the grain of the voice," the corporeal resonance of dramatic voice expressivity wherein the "materiality of the body [is] speaking its mother tongue; perhaps the letter, almost certainly *signifiance*" (1977: 182). Drawing on Julia Kristeva's concept of the "pheno-song," Barthes points to a hermeneutics of voice that places significant emphasis on "the volume of the singing and speaking voice, the space where significations germinate 'from within language and its very materiality' [...]

where the melody really works at the language—not at what it says, but the voluptuousness of its sound-signifiers, of its letters" (182). The model of intellection favored here is perceptual, phenomenological. It thrives in the gaps and interstices between words, feeding from the wellspring of prosodic enunciation, the calibrated delivery of each breath. Subordinating the communicative value of language to its sonic significance, a focus on voice's granularity highlights the diffuseness of language, its blurred edges. The idiosyncrasy of the chanter's articulation reveals the tenuousness of verbal elocution, the hazy nature of language's sound economy. The wear and tear of subjectivized, appropriated language (Ghachem's accented French) evinces a distinctive ambiguity, an occasional resistance to strict vocalic differentiation (/ø/ versus /e/, for instance, or /y/ versus /u/). But it is the chanter's trilled /r/ that discloses most clearly the powerful undertow of Arabic underneath the weft of the French. Emphasizing materiality over abstraction (/r/ as vibration rather than meaning, as a sound signifier of *étrangeté* rather than a lexical phoneme), the form of hearing advocated by Barthes encourages an affective recoding whereby the auditory experience produces sensations rather than opinion, impacts the sensorial apparatus of the listeners rather than their cognitive power. In a further nod to the granular, Barthes concludes, "the 'grain' of the voice is not—or is not merely—its timbre; the *signifiance* it opens cannot better be defined, indeed, than by the very friction between the music and something else, which something else is the particular language (and nowise the message)" (185). Barthes will provide no definitive answer as to the exact nature of this "signifiance." Yet some elements of clarification may be culled from his proposition that "there is a progressive movement from the language to the poem, from the poem to the song and from the song to its performance," as "the *mélodie* has little to do with the history of music and much with the theory of the text" (186). For here, he tells us, "the signifier must be redistributed" (186), a redistribution that implies a reconsideration of the signifying process involved in sung poetry.

In this oratory mode, lyric surges from a musical transposition of the sound lying beneath the poem's graph. Here, sound means "opacity" rather than "immediacy"; in Carrie Noland's memorable pronouncement, it "bears an almost graphemic heft" (2015: 126). As the "resonant subject" pieces together acoustic fields materializing over time, *renvois* (between unfolding lines, and between the subject and the sound object) probe the density of the poetic word. The endless dynamic of referral sheds light on the palimpsestic layers of the sound object, placing the multiple languages, translanguages, and transcultures that compose it into resounding tension. In this layering, Giacinto Scelsi's third dimension of sound—depth, bringing the pitch/

duration diptych to completion (2006: 126)—comes into focus. Depth enfolds the listening subject, submerging him in a reciprocal movement of involution, in *"the inextricable links between the vibrating object, the milieu in which the vibration spreads and the subject who listens"* (Solomos 2018: 99; emphasis original). The subject's aural mediation, therefore, produces a mobile ontology of sound centered on perpetual reroutings and transpositions, one whose intermediality unearths the translingual makeup of the Francophone text.

"Firaq" [parting], Ghachem's Arabic "adaptation" of an excerpt of his poem "Ce qui nous a quittés" [What Has Left Us], lifts the veil on the consubstantial presence of Arabic and French within a shared lyric space. That Ghachem himself interpreted the "original" French in Arabic and recited the translation recorded on the CD gives the listener unmatched access to the translingual creative process at the core of his verse. In this piece, the muted, redundant musical accompaniment of the lines recedes in the distance. In contradistinction to "J'écris," where the accompaniment's rhythm and phrasing impart semantic weight, "Firaq/Hier" derives its sonic *signifiance* exclusively from poetic diction—the length of a diphthong, the grating of guttural Arabic velars, the liquidity of lateral consonants. The performance consists in an expressive reading of the French lines, followed by a reading of their Arabic transposition accompanied by a circular, minimalist guitar tune that progressively swells up to incorporate drums and bass as sustenance for a freer, full vocal rendition of the Arabic verse. The paratactic configuration of the performance provides an ideal structure to pore over the circulation of sounds and timbres from the French to the Arabic and back.[9] The sounding of poetry across languages and media emphasizes the complexity of the free-flowing movement of lyric across time and idioms: rather than mere fluidity, sonic performance instigates a *transformational* recoding of language that the practice of translation underscores.[10]

---

[9] For lack of space, I will refrain from applying the same translingual lens to the Sicilian/Tunisian Arabic pairing in "Lambuca," but examples abound in the poem where the mutual imbrication of Arabic and a second Romance language beyond French delineates novel forms of intimacy beneath the surface of the verse—in the case of "Lambuca," in the absence of French altogether. See, for instance, the aural *renvoi* between the soft fricatives /f/, /s/, and /ʃ/ and the trilled /r/ in the original Tunisian Arabic "wa ʿalih ṭurraḥa shalbiya," Biagio Guerrera's Sicilian translation, which, as we remember, rests on communication with Ghachem: "supra u sparveru pisca a sarpa," and even Guerrera's matching Italian translation: "sopra lo sparvieto pesca la sarpa" [above it the sparrowhawk fishes the sarpa] (Ghachem and Dounia 2003: 108–109).

[10] I borrow this idea of transformation from Boutaghou 2018.

Sound sets in relief slippages across languages. When phonetic value overshadows semantics, new modes of intellection can be crafted. Let us look at one essential line in the composition of the imaginative microcosm of the poem, this "yesterday" that the poetic voice holds dear in his memory as the antithesis of the disillusion that is soon to set in. This halcyon past revolves around the maritime element, and the poet's communion with it. At the crucial moment of initial contact between body and sea, through the consumption of freshly harvested seafood, the French reads: "Pourpre je plongeais dans les rochers" [Crimson I threw myself amid the rocks]. In turn, Ghachem's Arabic rephrasing distills a slightly different meaning: "ramaitu binafsi ʿurjuwanan / fi sukhur al bihar" [I myself threw (the color) purple among the rocks of the sea] (Ghachem and Dounia 2003: 92–93). The signifier ʿurjuwanan here acts as the catalyzer for the open-ended recoding afoot in the performance. Semantically, ʿurjuwanan unambiguously points to the color purple, a mix of blue and red. Yet its sonic resonance hews closer to the French *orange* pronounced in Ghachem's Tunisian lilt, a defamiliarization of the attempted metaphorical use of the Arabic purple, possibly to denote the same sunburns rendered by the French *pourpre*. By reversing the syntax of the French line into a cross-linguistic, deep-time chiasmus ("Pourpre je plongeais [...] ramaitu binafsi ʿurjuwanan"), Ghachem's translation brings the sea and the sun into fecund tension on the surface of the subject's body. The "I" becomes mediation. Sunburnt, crimson, possibly purple, not to mention tangentially orange by virtue of the translingual warping of Ghachem's displaced lyric, the subject is enclosed in a fully formed circle of bodily communion with his natural environment. In turn, the rocks evoked at the close of the French line are relegated to the next Arabic line in an enjambement. The aurality of the Arabic verse both displaces the semantic cohesion of the French (*pourpre* to purple to orange-tinged) and elucidates it. Via the detour through Arabic, the intrinsic translingualism of Francophone lyric is unmasked. Subjected to these acoustic tactics, French bursts at the seams to divulge its (deviated) Arabic substrate—or possibly *original*. In the next line, the extraneous adjective "al wasiʿatain" [wide], missing from the French text, is added to the Arabic poem in a sonic *reprise* of the noun "al ʿaini" [my eye], both lexemes emphatically tensed to their enunciative limits by the reciting voice. In a repudiation of transla-tional conventions such as verisimilitude, the translingual lyric born of the recitation offers up a swirling blend of long vowels and plosives (/a/, /i/, ʿain) that exposes the deep-reaching Arabic echo of the assonance in /a/ and /i/ also perceptible in "soleil" [sun] and "entrailles" [entrails]—or in this case, its conceivable Arabic origin. Whether "ʿaini al wasiʿatain" precedes "soleil" and "entrailles" in Ghachem's diglossic poetic lineage, insufflating Arabic sound into the French poem from its inception, is ultimately irrelevant. Toggling between French and Arabic in this circulatory, translational dynamic, Ghachem's lyric unfolds precisely against considerations of tightly ordered genealogies. Languages are seized, *captured* in their time-defying gravity, in their existential intermingling, both melancholic and future-oriented. Unsurprisingly, this glimmering vocalic arrangement accompanies the first direct evocation of the Mediterranean as an ontological substance defeating any sense of bounded self-sameness: "j'avais la Méditerranée / plein les entrailles / et des soleils / plein les yeux" [the Mediterranean was filling my entrails, suns, my eyes]. The ontological import (Scelsi's "depth") of this Mediterranean affiliation is further compounded by the extension of the assonantal pattern to the noun "ʾaḥshaʾi" [my entrails] and, belatedly, in one final translation of the text into Italian, by the echo of the sibilation saturating the Arabic "ʾaḥshaʾi" in the Italian "viscere."

This polymorphic circulation of sounds and semes across the performative exercise that is the plurilingual transposition of Ghachem's "Francophone" verse pinpoints the capaciousness of French-language lyric when filtered through sound. Through lateral forms of acoustic connectivity, a polyphony of voices emerges bringing to mind the tradition of the tragic chorus, one remnant of Fernand Braudel's "many voices of the Mediterranean." In the prescient judgment of Ferrini, when diffracted through orality, "il canto diviene coralità" [the chant becomes chorus] (Ghachem and Dounia 2003: 7). A focus on sound exhumes the acoustic subtilities of French-language lyric in its erratic, nonlinear, and inchoate dimensions. As "an aperture for interventional creativity" (Chow 2012: 54), sound capture distills the enduring resonance of lyric's orality, its far-reaching, entangled echo. By resurrecting fecund plurilingualism at the heart of poetic expression, sound takes to task the illusion of monolingualism, revealing instead the internal travails continuously warping the integrity of language in any of its realized forms. Chipping away at any solid demarcating line between linguistic systems, the polyvocality of Ghachem's transmedial lyric invites a scrupulous reading of the multiple affinities between languages, of their sonic intimacies. For it is in the hospitable interval between sonic emission and deferred, transposed reception that lyric—as an intermedial, translingual process—fully resonates.

Works Cited

Barthes, Roland. "The Grain of the Voice." *Image, Music, Text*. Translated by Stephen Heath, Hill and Wang, 1977, pp. 179–189.

Bekri, Tahar. "On French-Language Tunisian Literature." Translated by Richard E. Morris, *Research in African Literatures*, vol. 23, no. 2, 1992, pp. 177–182.

Ben Zineb, Saida. "Entretien: Moncef ghachem, poète." *Le Temps*, April 10, 2012, turess.com/fr/letemps/65105.

Bernstein, Charles, ed. *Close Listening: Poetry and the Performed Word*. Oxford University Press, 1998.

Boutaghou, Maya. "*What Books Do You Read?* Toru Dutt, *A Sheaf Gleaned in French Fields* (1876) or Imagining Francophone Intertextual Maps." *Contemporary French and Francophone Studies*, vol. 22, no. 2, 2018, pp. 198–207.

Cailler, Bernadette. *Carthage ou la flame du brasier: Mémoires et échos chez Virgile, Senghor, Mellah, Ghachem, Augustin, Ammi, Broch et Glissant*. Rodopi, 2007.

Chow, Rey. *Entanglements, or Intermedial Thinking about Capture*. Duke University Press, 2012.

Chow, Rey, and James A. Steintrager. "In Pursuit of the Object of Sound: An Introduction." *The Sense of Sound*, edited by Chow and Steintrager, special issue of *differences*, vol. 22, nos. 2–3, 2011, pp. 1–9.

Dounia. "Drum Book: Dounia Live," eventu.it/eventi/drum-book-dounia-live.

Dutton, Jacqueline. "World Literature in French, *littérature-monde*, and the Translingual Turn." *French Studies*, vol. 70, no. 3, 2016, pp. 404–418.

elhariry, yasser. *Pacifist Invasions: Arabic, Translation, and the Postfrancophone Lyric*. Liverpool University Press, 2017.

Forsdick, Charles. "French Literature as World Literature: Reading the Translingual Text." *The Cambridge Companion to French Literature*, edited by John D. Lyons, Cambridge University Press, 2015, pp. 204–221.

Ghachem, Moncef. *Car vivre est un pays*. Caractères, 1978.

——. *Cap Africa*. L'Harmattan, 1989.

——. *L'Épervier*. SPM-Lettrage, 1994.

——. *Orphie*. Maison des écrivains étrangers et des traducteurs, 1997.

——. "Le traducteur." *Matin près de Lorand Gaspar*, L'Or du Temps, 1998, pp. 21–24.

Ghachem, Moncef, and Dounia. *Dalle Sponde del Mare Bianco con CD musicale*. Mesogea, 2003.

Kahn, Douglas. *Noise, Water, Meat: A History of Sound in the Arts*. MIT Press, 1999.

Kane, Brian. "Jean-Luc Nancy and the Listening Subject." *Contemporary Music Review*, vol. 35, nos. 5–6, 2012, pp. 439–447.

Kassab-Charfi, Samia, and Adel Khedher. "Moncef Ghachem et la *rumeur marine du poème*." *Un Siècle de littérature en Tunisie (1900–2017)*, Honoré Champion, 2019, pp. 128–135.

Kellman, Stephen G., and Natasha Lvovich. "Literary Translingualism: Multilingual Identity and Creativity." *L2 Journal*, no. 7, 2015, pp. 3–5.

Khatibi, Abdelkébir. "Au-delà du trauma." *Par-dessus l'épaule.* Aubier, 1988, pp. 123–135.

Mesogea. "Chi siamo," mesogea.it/casa-editrice.

Nancy, Jean-Luc. *Listening.* Translated by Charlotte Mandell, Fordham University Press, 2007.

Noland, Carrie. *Voices of Negritude in Modernist Print: Aesthetic Subjectivity, Diaspora, and the Lyric Regime.* Columbia University Press, 2015.

Plastino, Goffredo. "Open Textures: On Mediterranean Music." *The Mediterranean in Music: Critical Perspectives, Common Concerns, Cultural Differences,* edited by David Cooper and Kevin Sawe, Scarecrow, 2005, pp. 179–194.

Rancière, Jacques. *Film Fables.* Translated by Emiliano Battista, Berg, 2006.

Reale, Michelle. "Quelli Che Bruciano la Frontiera (Those Who Burn the Border): An Interview with Pocket Poetry Orchestra's Biagio Guerrera." July 11, 2012, sempresicilia.wordpress.com.

Ricœur, Paul. *On Translation.* Translated by Eileen Brennan, Routledge, 2006.

Scelsi, Giacinto. *Les Anges sont ailleurs ...,* edited by Sharon Kanach, Actes Sud, 2006.

Schaeffer, Pierre. *Traité des objets musicaux.* Seuil, 1966.

Sellin, Eric. "Translingual and Transcultural Patterns in Francophone Literature of the Maghreb." *Transcultural Identities in Contemporary Literature,* edited by Hansen Nordin and Zamorano Llena, Rodopi, 2013, pp. 223–244.

Solomos, Makis. "From Sound to Sound Space, Sound Environment, Soundscape, Sound Milieu or Ambiance ...." *Paragraph,* vol. 41, no. 1, 2018, pp. 95–109.

Villain, Jean-Claude. "Jean-Claude Villain, Moncef Ghachem, correspondance poétique." *Babel: littératures plurielles,* no. 30, 2014, pp. 255–263.

Zorat, Ambra. "Moncef Ghachem. Dalle Sponde del Mare Bianco. La coscienza del popolo mediterráneo." *Fucinemute.* May 1, 2006, fucinemute.it/2006/05/dalle-sponde-del-mare-bianco.

CHAPTER TWO

Mohammed Khaïr-Eddine's Secret Music

Thomas C. Connolly

ma flûte s'implique et termine.

(Khaïr-Eddine 2009: 100)

Rhythm-Chaos

In an edition of the weekly radio program *Poésie ininterrompue* broadcast on France Culture on October 19, 1975, the Moroccan poet Mohammed Khaïr-Eddine (1941–1995) is invited to begin by reading from two of his texts.[1] The first fragment—from *Agadir*, his best-known work, then as now—is a monologue by the seer who claims to know "comment s'écrit l'avenir et comment / naît une rose [...] de sang" [how the future is written and how / a rose of blood (...) is born] (Khaïr-Eddine 1967: 83).[2] The second is an untitled passage in prose from his new collection *Ce Maroc!* (Khaïr-Eddine 1975: 76–77). The opening poem of this collection—which contains the

---

[1] *Poésie ininterrompue* was produced by Claude Royet-Journoud and broadcast on France Culture between April 7, 1975 and April 1, 1979. Abigail Lang identifies this program as having provided a unique platform where poets could read from their own works in progress, enabling "l'essor de la lecture publique en France" [the rise of public reading in France] (Lang 2018: 5). Michel Murat (2019) notes the 1970s as a pivotal moment in the performance of poetry in French.

[2] Unattributed translations are my own.

verse "ma voix fut roide comme le tonnerre" [my voice was stiff like thunder] (11)—goes some way to capturing the aural dynamics of this one-hundred-and-sixty-second segment, because the poet does not read, or recite, so much as shout out his texts. As Lucette Finas, the interviewer, notes—once Khaïr-Eddine's voice has returned to normal—"the listener is struck by the fact that your diction is a continuous shout [*un hurlement continu*], or more accurately, continuously a shouting [*continuellement un hurlement*]" ("Poésie ininterrompue" 1975: 6:18ff.).[3]

Few who knew Mohammed Khaïr-Eddine fail to recall the sound of his voice, or what Tahar Ben Jelloun called his "often thunderous presence" (Ben Jelloun 1995: ii). His close friend and colleague Jean-Paul Michel specifically remembers the poet reciting Stéphane Mallarmé out loud, as if it were an Islamic text, and "from which he drew an incredible comic effect, his long ululation mimicking the call to prayer" (2011: 123). Jean-Roger Bourrec recalls "a wide and deep voice, a persuasive, full-mouthed voice that said everything bluntly with a sandy roughness" (Michel 2011: 113). If much of the testimony around Khaïr-Eddine's life evokes his "wide and deep voice," much of the criticism around his proteiform literary œuvre focuses on his readiness to say "everything bluntly." There is an implied equation between the violence of his delivery and the violence of his text, as if one justifies and explains the other. For some, his violence is aimed at literary forms and "the constitution of a wild language whose incessant splitting gives rise to a truly plural discourse" (Gontard 1981: 54). For others, Khaïr-Eddine is the "écrivain du refus" whose "cry of revolt" attacks social and political injustices, particularly those perpetrated under the regime of Hassan II (Tenkoul 1985: 145). For many, his violence is carried out "against all established orders and conventions—language, society, religion, and morality" (Abdel-Jaouad 1992: 146). If Khaïr-Eddine is one of Maghrebi literature's most (in)famous iconoclasts, we shouldn't be too surprised to hear him shouting on the radio.

My aim here is to analyze and explore[4] the gap between the perceived violence of Khaïr-Eddine's verbal delivery and that of his poetry by reading a poem that has never before been subject to critical scrutiny.[5] I situate the

---

[3] Lucette Finas (b. 1921) was professor of literature at Paris VIII–Vincennes at the time.

[4] Note that to "explore," from the Latin verb *explōrāre* [to inspect, inquire], originally meant "to scout the hunting area for game by means of shouting" (de Vaan 2008: 473).

[5] Besides the first publication of the short works *Nausée noire* (1964) and *Faune détériorée* (1966), his collections of poems include *Soleil arachnide* (1969), *Ce Maroc!* (1975), *Résurrection des fleurs sauvages* (1981), and *Mémorial* (1991).

impetus for this investigation in an acoustic crack in Khaïr-Eddine's reading on France Culture, a clear dislocation between the rhythm of the shouting voice and that of the written text. In the first of his two readings, for example, the poet inserts an explosive stress every third, fourth, or fifth syllable: "Je 'lis sur mon 'os, je ne lis 'pas je 'vois plutôt / sur mon 'os" [I 'read from my 'bone, I do 'not read I 'see rather from my 'bone] ("Poésie" 1975: 2:58ff.). At other moments, the acoustic structure of individual verbal units is inverted, such that a word like "l'instiga'teur" becomes "l'in'stigateur," "impecc'able" becomes "im'peccable." Most strikingly, in "peuple" [/'pœpl/], which appears six times in quick succession, the poet stresses the first syllable with such force that the terminal "-le" is inverted to give /'pœpɛl/. There are suggestions here of what Mladen Dolar has called an "antinomy of meaning and the voice" (2006: 71). Or, as Finas puts it: "This screaming doesn't necessarily follow the lines of meaning of the text itself" ("Poésie" 1975: 6:28ff.).

When challenged over these rhythmic discrepancies, Khaïr-Eddine refers to the place of his birth and early childhood—Azro Wado, next to Tafraout in the Anti-Atlas Mountains[6]—and to his Berber, specifically Chleuch, ancestry: "I am only bringing to light what is already in me, this rhythm which is that of my ancestors and which was transmitted to me genetically. I call it my secret music" (Michel 2011: 45). The association of a shout's dislocated rhythm with the secret music of a poetics might be compared to the marriage of steps and song in the refrain as presented in Gilles Deleuze and Félix Guattari's *Mille Plateaux*. Here, the refrain is "territorial, a territorial assemblage" that "always carries earth with it" (Deleuze and Guattari 1980: 383–384). Khaïr-Eddine's shout relates to his native countryside in similar ways: "When you cross [...] these lunar landscapes," he explains to Finas, "you scream [*on hurle*], you want to scream [*on a envie de hurler*], because suddenly you find yourself alone, you shout out for a bit [*on gueule un bon coup*] and it reverberates throughout the entire mountain" ("Poésie" 1975: 14:12ff.). Once uttered, the scream does not just disappear, but fashions the landscape: "What can you see?" he asks, "You only see stones and a voice that multiplies to infinity. This incrustation of the landscape and the echo which breaks

---

6 This is the site of "la montagne sèche, rougeâtre, impossible à franchir, le vieux Sud ..." (Khaïr-Eddine 1975: 77) and "la montagne violette [...] avec des diffractions simultanément jaunes et mauves quand le soleil l'embrase par-derrière du côté du levant" (Khaïr-Eddine 1976: 159). See also the description of Azro Wado after the poet's return in 1979: "Située au creux d'un cirque rocheux sur lequel planent indéfiniment des escadrilles de corbeaux qui hantent les abattoirs et la cime des palmiers environnants, elle croupit au soleil, loin de tout, mais fascinante" (Khaïr-Eddine 1980: 41).

down and dies. But no sooner is it dead than you want to bring it back to life again" (14:28ff.). Mallarmé speaks of a similar dynamic, albeit silent, on the "lunar" landscape of the white page: "and, when aligned, in a break, the least, disseminated, chance conquered word by word, unfailingly the white returns, just now gratuitous, certain now" (1998–2003: 2.234). Where for Mallarmé silence returns "authenticated," for Khaïr-Eddine, the voice adds another imperceptible layer onto the surface of the earth, sealing—in its dying echo— the rhythms, the music, and the part of chaos that the cry contains.

Mouthings

Following Deleuze and Guattari, who stress that rhythm only comes about through the encounter of different milieus, I propose to unearth something of the structures of Khaïr-Eddine's secret music by juxtaposing his poetry with the work of the Irish-born English painter Francis Bacon (1909–1992).[7] The open, screaming mouth becomes central to Bacon's iconography from the mid-1930s with his first crucifixion paintings, and continues to grow in importance in the dozens of "copies" of the *Retrato de Inocencio X* (Galleria Doria Pamphilj, Rome, 1650) by Diego Velázquez. These include the iconic *Study after Velázquez's Portrait of Pope Innocent X* (Des Moines Art Center, 1953) in which a spectral figure screams, seated on his papal throne, streaked with black bars, and enclosed in a makeshift yellow fence, "thunderstruck," as Claude Imbert puts it, "by the invisible evidence of an unspeakable disaster" (Imbert 2003: 144). By the early 1950s, Michael Peppiatt writes, the scream becomes "obsessive, dominating all other concerns" (2006: 24). Bacon's scream is commonly linked to prominent antecedents, such as the still of the nurse shot in the eye on the great steps of Odessa in Sergei Eisenstein's *Battleship Potemkin* (1925), and to Nicolas Poussin's *Massacre of the Innocents* (Musée Condé, Chantilly, 1628), where the cry emanating from the mother's half-open mouth is echoed and amplified by the ellipse of limbs and weapons.[8]

In his two-volume *Francis Bacon: logique de la sensation* (1981), Deleuze interprets Bacon's scream as much more than a simple representation, even of an extreme psychological state. This stands in contrast to Dolar's reading of Edvard Munch's 1893 painting *Der Schrei der Natur* [*The Scream*] as a limit instance of the scream: "we see the void, the orifice, the abyss, but with no

---

[7] I do this despite David Sylvester's assertion that Bacon's work is not "companionable" (1998: 22).

[8] Louis Marin insists it "could without hesitation be taken, well in advance of Munch's celebrated work, as *one of the most extraordinary pictorial representations of a scream*" (2001: 346).

fetish to protect us or to hold on to" (2006: 69). Deleuze instead traces the scream to the logic of painting itself, specifically to the relation of field and Figure, and to the rhythm that is created between them. Bacon's paintings are characterized by large, shallow fields of color (red, black, orange, ocher) against which human figures, "ordinary bodies in ordinary situations of constraint and discomfort" (Deleuze 2005: x) are superimposed. Much of the drama of a given image centers around the ways in which the pictorial elements of field and Figure encounter each other, usually through some spasm: "loving, vomiting, excreting, the body always attempting to escape *through* one of its organs, in order to rejoin the field [*aplat*], the material structure" (Deleuze 1981: 1.17; 2005: 12). For Dolar, there is a direct relationship between the screamer and the landscape, such that the scream can be read as emanating outwards (Munch's own reading) or as eddying back into the mouth (Dolar's reading) (2006: 69). Deleuze identifies a much more violent operation in Bacon. The shadows cast by his figures are not to be understood as silhouettes— mimetic figures cut from the light—but as the body as it escapes from itself: "the scream [...] is the operation by which the entire body escapes through the mouth" (Deleuze 1981: 1.17; 2005: 12). Imbert notes how Bacon's "body seems to get longer, flatten down and stretch out, as if it were contracting itself to pass through a hole" (2003: 144). Even objects lend themselves to this great tumultuous spasm between Figure and field: sinks, umbrellas, chairs, puddles of water and paint are all equipped with "exaggerated points" (Deleuze 2005: xii) through which the body tries to flee.

Where previous models of reading Khaïr-Eddine have struggled to account for the detail, breadth, obscurity, and insistence of his poetic diction, particularly at those points—and there are many—where the reader is taken beyond transparent references to the real, Deleuze's reading of Bacon's painting provides a guide to the complex interplay of body, voice, violence, rhythm, and art that may allow us to draw out some of the hidden dynamics of Khaïr-Eddine's secret music.[9] More than that, Bacon provides the alternative milieu, the other code, the counter-rhythm against which a new rhythm—a new secret music—might come into audition. The following untitled poem was first published in *Soleil arachnide* (1969). It contains few if any identifiable references to a historical moment, or to an ideology, or even to a particular place. As in the case of other such poems by Khaïr-Eddine, critics have passed over it in silence. Here, I explore the poem for traces of Khaïr-Eddine's secret music in three brief parts, noting that these "do not

---

[9] The poet and the painter have only ever been compared in passing: "Like painter Francis Bacon, whom Michel Leiris describes as an 'outlaw,' Khaïr-Eddine 'grabs and in a way rapes that which he wants to represent'" (Tenkoul 2018: 234).

reveal three successive movements in an evolution" (Deleuze and Guattari
1980: 383), so much as three possible aspects of his poetics:

> et qui rampe à mon nombril de torrents ocres
> et décapite mes cols de tonnerres fascinés
> hache autrefois rire
> ce ciel sans ange a retrouvé toutes ses griffes
> mais ce ramassis de chanvre occulte
> tourne mal à la base même du mur d'affres
> qui rampent à mon nombril de terreurs ocres
>
> tranchez donc mes oiseaux seuls
> je parle d'un œil versé dans chaque gramme
> d'ambre amer
> fumé craché sur cette publicité d'astres où tombe
> pygmée ma voix noire de sangsue
> tranchez donc mes oiseaux seuls
>
> voici criée sans virgule la menace
> par je sais quels clous coupés en sacres
> le hasard veut qu'un chemin
> gîte ici
> et les cous d'enfants vantés par le sexe gros du seigle
> et du sommeil
> voici criée sans virgule la menace
>
> lorsque ses ongles s'incrustent dans la chair bleue du sabre
> toujours hurler quoi pleurer qui
> trompé de silences obtus ivre nuit sans matrice
> où vole l'insecte ma femme
> à moins d'une barque dont la mer se souvienne
> lorsque ses ongles s'incrustent dans la chair bleue du sabre
>
> dossiers de tous les météores du cuivre halluciné
> cette affaire punique me jonche vaste
> et dévaste mon ombre de vin rouge
> par le cri femelle de l'oiseleur
> mais comme le soleil est un fruit très gâté
> ombre notoire
> cette ombre et son fil s'insinuent dans ma peau
> dossiers de tous les météores du cuivre halluciné
>
> et je pars avec ce qui me reste de moi hurlé
> à ras du trottoir

et je trinque avec mon défi luisant sable
sous l'arbre dru où mes serpents tornades
brisent les flûtes
et je danse ma fascination
sur l'épine malhabile de tes prunelles
et je pars avec ce qui me reste de moi hurlé

j'écume de poèmes censurés et d'absinthes
ineffacées d'un vol de genoux dérapant
et j'insulte le mollusque de cette conque
blanche où l'habitude a fixé ses barreaux
qui me nomment lion giclant à vareuse inédite
d'audaces connues du marais haut placé
j'écume de poèmes censurés et d'absinthes

maintenant je vous lance mes poumons cerfs-volants
dans la rigueur où se mouille mon espace
et je dis
le printemps n'existe pas il s'est rompu l'échine
contre la rafale sourde (palmier-prison
qui t'écris toi-même et t'étonnes)
maintenant je vous lance mes poumons cerfs-volants.
                              (Khaïr-Eddine 2009: 54–56)

and who crawls into my navel of ocher torrents
and beheads my necks of mesmerized thunder
[axe] erstwhile laughing
this unangeled sky has found its claws again
but this heap of arcane hemp
loses its way at the base of this wall of cramps
who crawl into my navel of ocher [terrors]

butcher then my solitary birds
I mean the eye poured into every gram
of bitter amber
smoked and spit onto the advertisement of stars
from which falls my leech-black pygmy voice
go on then butcher my solitary birds

here without commas the threat is announced
by a couple nails I know cut into blessings
chance wants a path
to bivouac here

and the necks of children exalted by the fat sex of rye
and sleep
here without commas the threat is announced

once its fingernails are embedded in the saber's blue flesh
always yelling what weeping who
deceived by obtuse silences drunken moldless night
in which my wife the insect hovers
at least one boat the ocean remembers
once its fingernails are embedded in the saber's blue flesh

files for all the meteors of hallucinated copper
this punic affair strews my debris widely
and unwinds my red wine shadow
with the birdcatcher's female call
but as the sun is a highly spoiled fruit
incontrovertible shadow
this shadow and its wire thread themselves into my skin
files for all the meteors of hallucinated copper

and I am leaving with what remains of me screamed
down as low as the curb
I toast with my glittering defiance sand
beneath the hearty tree where my tornadic snakes
shatter flutes
and I dance my fascination
on the incompetent thorn of your pupils
and I am leaving with what remains of me screamed

I froth with censored poems and absinthe
unerased by a flight of skidding knees
and I insult the mollusk of this conch shell
white in which habit has screwed the bars
which call me surging lion of the unprecedented peacoat
with known audacities from a highly placed swamp
I froth with censored poems and absinthe

now I launch at you the kites of my lungs
in the rigor that wets my space
and I say
spring does not exist it has broken its back
on the wind's deaf edge (palm tree prison
writing to and astonishing yourself)
now I launch at you the kites of my lungs. (Khaïr-Eddine 2019: 35–36)

Excavation of a Scream

I trace a first element of Khaïr-Eddine's secret music to a simple formal device. With the exception of the first, each stanza begins and ends with an identical line.[10] These liminal lines serve not only to create a verbal frame, stalling any promise of continuity between stanzas, they also create an uneven rhythm, in which the first line of each stanza, enounced in isolation, recurs amid the noise of the intervening lines. Relatively simple (if unusual) acts, statements, imperatives, observations—"tranchez donc mes oiseaux seuls" and "dossiers de tous les météores du cuivre halluciné"—are complicated through the course of each stanza. The difference between the first and last line might be compared to the examination, through a microscope, of some cellular phenomenon in a weightless vacuum (first line), and of the same in the noise of gravity and atmospheric pressure (final line). Between the repetition of the same, each stanza reveals the difference that was always there, hidden, bubbling away, baroque. It is an example of how a simple rhythm—that of repetition—becomes expressive, how it harnesses the chaos it contains to become a territory.

Our understanding of the form and function of Khaïr-Eddine's rhythmic territorializations can be enhanced by considering two related scenarios. First, Deleuze perceives something like this excavation of the invisible in Bacon's painting. He tracks it back to the expressive geometry of Paul Cézanne, whose work demonstrates that "rocks only exist through the forces of folding that they harness, landscapes through magnetic and thermal forces, apples through forces of germination: all nonvisual forces that have been made visible" (Deleuze and Guattari 1980: 422). For Bacon, Cézanne opens up a route beyond the illustrative and the figurative, past the abstract, and onto the way of the Figure, a way sometimes called "sensation" (Deleuze 1981: 1.27; 2005: 25). For Khaïr-Eddine, Cézanne enables us to better see and unpick the cry incrusted in the landscape of Azro Wado, and to experience its uneven rhythms. With each successive line of verse, the reader descends deeper into the initial line of verse, like an archeologist of sensation, until he or she bumps up against the same verse with which they started, but which has—in the time of reading—become radically different.

Second, Khaïr-Eddine's stanzas recall a formulation deployed by Bacon in the first of a series of three interviews with Michel Couturier, broadcast on France Culture six months before Khaïr-Eddine's interview. There, Bacon speaks—in faltering French—about painting the mouth: "Even if you want to

---

[10] Other poems in *Soleil arachnide* adopt a similar structure, including "Mutinéries" and "Flibuste" (Khaïr-Eddine 2009: 57–58, 59–60).

make the mouth, you can make the mouth [...] or even, or even make a Sahara of the mouth [*faire un Sahara de la bouche*]. You know. You can go very far, almost around the head [...] If you are lucky, at the same time, it gives you, ah, the appearance, at the same time, of the subject" ("Entretiens" 1975: 15:30ff.).[11] To "make a Sahara of the mouth" is to extend the mouth as far around the head as it is possible to go, much as each of these stanzas is stretched to include the chaos of the intervening lines. Elsewhere, Bacon calls this stretching a "graph" or a "diagram." Deleuze extends these images further:

> it is as if a piece of rhinoceros skin, viewed under a microscope, were stretched over it; it is as if the two halves of the head were split open by an ocean; it is as if the unit of measure were changed, and micrometric, or cosmic, units were substituted for the figurative unit [...] It is as if, in the midst of the figurative and probabilistic givens, a *catastrophe* overcame the canvas. (1981: 1.65; 2005: 71)

Deleuze insists that painting is the art that "necessarily, hysterically, integrates its own catastrophe" (1981: 1.67; 2005: 72). But, here, in each of these stanzas, Khaïr-Eddine's writing also seems to "pass through the catastrophe," to "embrace the chaos" (1981: 1.67; 2005: 72), attempting to emerge from it, in the final stanza, on kites made not of stretched rhinoceros skin, nor of a head split by the ocean, but of exposed lungs: "maintenant je vous lance mes poumons cerfs-volants."[12]

Each of Khaïr-Eddine's stanzas might therefore be considered a "diagram," specifically a diagram of the open mouth, probably as it screams. The identical line that begins and ends each stanza represent the limits of the mouth, its lips, its edges, of that which in Arabic is شَفَة [*shafa*]. The Hebrew cognate, שפה [*safa*] is—not coincidentally—also the word for "language," which is always a matter of lips and edges, of ends and borders, of indiscretions and limits, stretchings, translations, and slippages. The intervening lines are a

---

[11] Bacon returns to this notion—making a Sahara of the mouth—on several occasions: see for instance Sylvester 1980: 56.

[12] Compare this line to the passage in Michel Tournier's 1967 novel *Vendredi ou les Limbes du Pacifique* where Robinson climbs a tree and is reflecting on its function as a vast lung, when he sees Friday fly a kite made from the skin of a dead goat: "*La feuille poumon de l'arbre, l'arbre poumon lui-même, et donc le vent sa respiration*, pensa Robinson. Il rêva de ses propres poumons, déployés au-dehors, buisson de chair purpurine, polypier de corail vivant, avec des membranes roses, des éponges muqueuses [...] Du côté du rivage, un grand oiseau de couleur vieil or, de forme losangée, se balançait fantasquement dans le ciel. Vendredi exécutant sa mystérieuse promesse faisait voler Andoar" (167).

Sahara, stretched rhino skin, lung-kites, the extent to which the mouth can be extended—distorted, defaced—and still remain a mouth. Like Bacon's diagram, each of these stanzas is "a catastrophe, a chaos," even as each contains "a spark [*un germe*] of order or rhythm" (1981: 1.67; 2005: 72). But beyond any comparison, each stanza also invites us to explore the extent to which a poem can wander, divagate, lose itself, while still remaining a poem.

Three Beats

A second element of Khaïr-Eddine's secret music may be related to the rhythms of its language. At work in Bacon's triptychs, but also across his paintings more generally, Deleuze identifies three basic rhythms: "one steady or 'attendant' rhythm, and two other rhythms, one of crescendo or simplification (climbing, expanding, diastolic, adding value), the other of diminuendo or elimination (descending, contracting, systolic, removing value)" (2005: xv). In any given figure, one rhythm might dominate, but not without the "attendant" presence of another. Even as Deleuze presents this typology of rhythms, he warns against any overly conscious application. They are part of "this irrational logic [...] this logic of sensation that constitutes painting" (1981: 1.55; 2005: 59).

In Bacon's triptych *Three Studies of the Human Head* (private collection, 1953; see Figure 2.1), the figure bearing a creepy grin in the leftmost panel might be said to represent a steady rhythm—a pacemaker, so to speak; the screaming mouth in the central panel may be considered a crescendo, an extreme of simplification; and in the panel on the right, where what remains of the mouth and eyes are smudged beyond recognition, a sudden diminuendo or contraction.[13] Even as basic rhythms are ascribed to each picture, they interfere with one another, denying the apparent isolation of each picture. There are hints of the scream in the smile, of the smile in the scream, and of both in the devastation of the face. This is what Deleuze calls (with echoes of Augustine) "the distributive unity of the three" (1981: 1.56; 2005: 60).

Evidence of these three rhythms can be found throughout Khaïr-Eddine's poem. Consider the first two lines of the opening stanza. It is hard to draw any clear idea of what (if anything) is being evoked, even as the syntactic parallels and semantic differences of the two lines create a mini crescendo, a sudden expansion, a manifestation of the diastolic. From one line to the next,

---

[13] Sylvester locates this painting at the end of one of Bacon's two peaks, running from 1945 to 1953. The second peak, 1970–1976, saw the creation of a dozen large triptychs, most of them studies of the male nude, "realized in a conscious wish to exorcise the pain of [lover George] Dyer's death" (Sylvester 1998: 29).

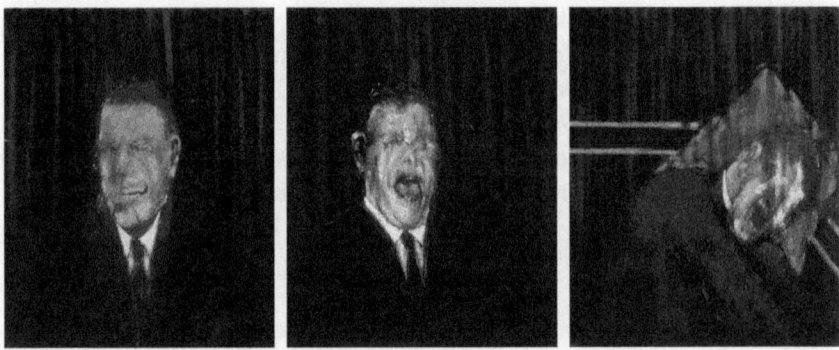

Figure 2.1. Francis Bacon, *Three Studies of the Human Head*, oil on canvas,
1953, triptych, each panel 61 x 51 cm (CR No. 53-23).
© The Estate of Francis Bacon. All rights reserved, DACS/ARS/Artimage 2021.
Photo: Prudence Cuming Associates Ltd.

the action of the singular verb shifts from "ramper" [climb] to "décapiter"
[behead]. The direct object moves from the body ["mon nombril"] to "mes
cols" which, although a part of the body in the singular (neck or cervix), can,
in plural form, no longer apply to any typical human. This in turn allows for
a geographical definition to emerge (as mountain passes, cols, or saddles),
unexpectedly translating the body to the landscape. In the acoustic shift
from "torrents" to "tonnerres," there is not only a metathesis of the internal
consonants (/n/ to /r/, and /r/ to /n/), but an acoustic and semantic escalation,
from gravity-bound flows of water to the unpredictable realm of electric skies.[14]

Although these lines precede the remainder of the text, there is no sense
that they begin the poem in any significant way. Rhythms do not need to
follow conventions of reading or of looking, but can begin anywhere, and
continue to be developed at any other point in the text. If we read the poem
with an ear for its most expressive rhythms, we might identify the opening
line of the third stanza as the fragment which most clearly dominates the
poem: "voici criée sans virgule la menace." As an invariable, impersonal,
unimodal, and unitemporal verb, "voici" stands apart from other verbal
units in the poem, drawing the sort of attention to the line that might more
usually be associated with the opening line of a poem. Here, the subject of

---

[14] More subtle traces of the diastolic are evident in the proliferation of the
conjunction *et* ("et qui rampe," "et décapite," "et les cous d'enfants," "et dévaste
mon ombre," "et je pars," "et je trinque," "et je danse," "et j'insulte," "et je dis,")
etc. pointing to a logic of accumulation and perhaps excess (Deleuze might say
of "hysteria"). See also "lion giclant," where *gicler* [to spurt] is related to the
Provençal *cisclar*, "to cry out loud; to whistle; to wind and rain."

this cry is "la menace" [the threat]. It stems from the Latin *minae* [threats] which is thought to have once designated the protruding parts of a wall.[15] The threat is "criée," which is to say it is an acoustic protrusion, an aural equivalent of all the spikes, sharpened objects, and tunneling body parts in Bacon's iconography. It is through these that the field flows into the Figure, and the Figure into the field, and that the body dispatches itself by pouring itself into its own shadow.

If the central panel of Bacon's triptych shows the threat as unpunctuated scream ("voici criée *sans* virgule la menace"), then the left-hand panel might display a punctuated scream, a potential scream, currently poised in the creepy grin ("voici criée *avec* virgule la menace"). The panel on the right realizes the full force of Khaïr-Eddine's verse, as the indistinct background with vertical lines of black paint becomes a wall with painted yellow tramlines, and a protrusion that causes some physical harm to the figure ("mur d'affres"). The tramlines turn at an obtuse angle right behind the figure's head (echoing the "silences obtus" in the fourth stanza), as if it is the angle of the yellow lines that becomes protrusive, knocking the figure down, exiling the figure from the realm of the figurative, and blocking the scream from the domain of sound. It may be that the hidden logic of the right-hand panel is primarily verbal, as "obtuse"—which geometrically defines the plane angle of two lines at greater than ninety but less than one hundred and eighty degrees—comes from the verb *obtundere*—to beat against, to blunt, to deaden, to deafen—all of which captures the ways the figure's torso is made to disintegrate before our eyes.

Flutes

A third element of Khaïr-Eddine's secret music relates to musical instruments. Throughout his poetry, the sound of the flute is subject to interruption. In *Ce Maroc!* it is obliterated by sand ("le son de flûte que le sable oblitère") and eaten by impatience ("un air de flûte rongé d'impatiences") (Khaïr-Eddine 1975: 42, 43). Its song is precarious in *Résurrection des fleurs sauvages* ("le sang siffle la précaire / flûte de ces bergers sicaires" [Khaïr-Eddine 1981: 10]). And here, in *Soleil arachnide*, flutes are destroyed: "sous l'arbre dru où mes serpents tornades / brisent les flûtes." Athena is often cited as the creator of the flute. In Ovid's *Fasti*, she carves one out of boxwood, but throws it away when she realizes how her "virgin cheeks" puff up in order to play it: "*ars mihi non tanti est; valeas, mea tibia*" ["I value not the art so high; farewell,

---

[15] Compare to *ēminēre*, to stick out, protrude; *ēminulus*, projecting; and *minēre*, to lean forward, project (de Vaan 2008: 380).

my flute"] (6.701; 1931: 372). Marsyas comes across the flute, teaches himself to play, and challenges Apollo—god of poetry and music—to a contest. In a curiously open (Baconian if not Khaïr-Eddinian) turn, they agree that the winner of the contest "should work his will on the vanquished" (Apollodorus 1.4.2; 1921: 1.31). Diodorus Siculus records that the judges were "amazed" by the "strange music" of the pipes that "in their opinion far excelled, by reason of [its] melody," that of Apollo's lyre (3.59; 1935: 2.273). There are differing accounts of what happens next. Apollodorus says that Apollo then impressed the judges by playing his lyre upside down, which Marsyas could not do with his flute. Diodorus says that Apollo went on to sing and play at the same time. Apollo then "attends" to Marsyas, hanging him from a tall pine, and flaying him until his skin comes away from his flesh.

Of the many versions of this myth, only Ovid pauses to—let's say—excavate the scream, to take a measure of its uneven rhythms. Only Ovid takes the time to inspect—like a haruspex—the satyr's innards. In a phrase that captures how Deleuze perceives Bacon's cry, Marsyas says: *"'quid me mihi detrahis?' inquit; / 'a! piget, a! non est' clamabat 'tibia tanti'"* ["'Why do you tear me from myself?' he cried. / 'Oh, I repent! Oh, a flute is not worth such price!'"] (Ovid 6.385–86; 1916: 1.314–315). The scream drags the body out of itself through the mouth. In light of Bacon, this question becomes an image of the body's emerging shadow. As Marsyas continues to scream, the skin is stripped from his limbs (*clamanti cutis est summos direpta per artus* [6.387]) until he is nothing but a wound (*nec quicquam nisi vulnus erat* [6.388]). Blood flows from all sides (*cruor undique manat* [6.388]), the sinews lie bare (*detectique patent nervi* [6.389]), his veins throb and quiver without any skin to cover them (*trepidaeque sine ulla / pelle micant venae* [6.389–390]) to the degree that one might count the fibers in his chest (*salientia viscera possis / et perlucentes numerare in pectore fibras* [6.390–391]). Even as the satyr screams through his mouth, the mouth extends to the entire body, revealing its ongoing, usually hidden functions, its own secret music. Ovid's depiction of Marsyas flayed is resumed in Deleuze's description of Bacon's *Fragment of a Crucifixion* (Stedelijk Van Abbemuseum, Eindhoven, 1950) as a painting "où toute la viande hurle" [where all the meat screams] (1981: 1.22; 2005: 19).

Both Ovid's and Deleuze's texts resonate with Khaïr-Eddine's poem. Here, there are not only screams—"voici criée sans virgule la menace,"[16] "toujours hurler quoi pleurer qui," "ce qui me reste de moi hurlé"—and expressions of pain associated with parts of the body: "mon nombril de torrents ocres." The stripping of skin from the body unveils new possible forms of action.

---

[16] Especially if we hear in *virgula* [little stick], the flute that Marsyas can no longer play.

The speaker adopts verbs normally associated with the elements: "j'écume de poèmes censurés." He projects his body out of itself: "je vous lance mes poumons cerfs-volants." Organs are no longer restricted in number or function, but spread and proliferate, or disappear altogether ("nuit sans matrice"). Much as Deleuze says that the eyes of Bacon's bodies become polyvalent and transitory organs—"Painting gives us eyes all over: in the ear, in the stomach, in the lungs" (1981: 1.37; 2005: 37)—the eyes of Khaïr-Eddine's body are also omnipresent: "un œil versé dans chaque gramme."

Further evidence of Apollo's torture and murder of Marsyas is present in references to decapitation ("et décapite mes cols"), in slicing ("tranchez donc"), in tearing ("ses ongles s'incrustent dans la chair bleue"), in bone-breaking ("il s'est rompu l'échine"), as well as in the axe that used to be a laugh—"hache autrefois rire"—a metamorphosis worthy of Bacon's dark imagination. In "cette ombre et son fil s'insinuent dans ma peau," we have not only the threads or strings of the god's lyre, but their insinuation into the speaker's skin.[17] We see Apollo's dull amorality, and more generally the immanence of the pagan, confirmed in "ce ciel sans anges a retrouvé toutes ses griffes" and "le hasard veut qu'un chemin / gîte ici." In "mur d'affres" there is the shallow field on which Bacon's detached figures wrestle. Where the acoustic remnants of Marsyas's name appear—appropriately defaced and disseminated in syntagms such as "mais ce ramassis," "la menace," "d'audaces [...] du marais" and "mouille mon espace," Apollo—often conflated with Helios, the sun—is more readily visible as both a notorious shadow ("ombre notoire") and a rotten fruit ("le soleil est un fruit très gâté").

When asked by Lucette Finas why he shouts out his poems, Khaïr-Eddine insists: "this theater could only be shouted [*hurlé*]. All the terms that make up this writing could only be said by being shouted" ("Poésie ininterrompue" 1975: 7:42ff.). But what this poem from 1969, and the recital of poems on the radio in 1975, establish is that Khaïr-Eddine's shout is only one rhythm in his poetics. The other is more musical, more lyrical even, although it is a music that is often dismissed as obscure. Marsyas provides a model for understanding the origin and interplay of these two unequal rhythms, both of which stem from a physical, acoustic understanding of language. More than

---

[17] Compare the sun's thread to the title of Celan's 1967 collection, *Fadensonnen* [Thread-Suns]. There appear to be several discreet references to Celan in Khaïr-Eddine. "Le roi" ends with the line: *"parmi les laits noirs de ma palmeraie"* [among the black milks of my palmery] (Khaïr-Eddine 2009: 73), which echoes the opening line of Celan's best known poem, "Todesfuge": "Schwarze Milch der Frühe wir trinken sie abends" [Black milk of dawn we drink it at evening] (2018: 46).

any stringed instrument, the flute imitates the human voice, but as it does so, it also prevents the voice from speaking or singing. Khaïr-Eddine's poem evokes the poet's own leech voice ("voix noire de sangsue"), speech that takes place so close to the instrument that it is often hard to make out the distance between the lip and the mouthpiece that would enable us to hear what the poet is saying. As Philippe Monbrun puts it, "the *aulos* tends to marginalize the *logos*" (2005: 273).

When Finas questions Khaïr-Eddine's shout, we see *in nuce* the same conflict between Apollonian propriety and Dionysian wildness dramatized in the myth of Marsyas. The fifth century BCE saw a debate not only on the value of music produced by the flute compared to the more established lyre, but also on whether melodies and rhythms should follow or distort the words they accompanied. Plato opined that "melody and rhythms must follow the words" (3.271; 2013: 1.271), and reserved the lyre and zither for the ideal city, leaving the pipes or *aulos* to the shepherds in the country. There is no reason to be surprised by the philosopher's conservatism. Apollo's citharody is the supreme manifestation of what Deleuze and Guattari call territorialization. It contains the roots of self and other, of dialogue, of the chorus, of democracy. Marsyas's new music is "incompatible with the citizen's moral education" (Monbrun 2005: 274), but has a much greater ability to move its listeners. The flute is the instrument of intense earthly sensations, pleasures as well as pains. It is verve, genius, hubris, the individual, the Romantic. Much like Bacon's painting, it seems not so much to "pass through the brain" as to "act immediately upon the nervous system" (Deleuze 1981: 1.27). In Khaïr-Eddine's poems we encounter, among other things, a relationship to sensation not all that far removed from Marsyas's flute and Bacon's canvas.

The expressiveness of this poem is by no means exhausted by the brief exploration of three aspects of Khaïr-Eddine's secret music undertaken here, namely the form of its stanzas; the presence of diastolic, systolic, and attendant rhythms; and the fragments of the myth of Marsyas. Any coherence is intended to be as fleeting as it is illuminating. By engaging with elements of Khaïr-Eddine's secret music, I hope not only to identify and maintain the dislocation between shout and poem audible in the recording of the poet's voice in 1975, but to articulate the nature of this gap, and to explore its depths. Despite claiming to be a proponent of "la voie de la guérilla linguistique!" [linguistic guerrilla warfare!] in *Moi, l'aigre* (Khaïr-Eddine 2011: 24), I maintain that Khaïr-Eddine is not primarily a poet of extremes, nor of violence, nor of iconoclasm, but rather of uneven rhythms. We find his music somewhere between that of Athena, who rejects the flute she has invented because it "disfigures her face" (Apollodorus 1.4.2; 1921: 1.29), and

Marsyas, who does not stop playing the flute in time to (literally) save his skin. Khaïr-Eddine's combat has much in common with Bacon's, for whom physical struggle, be it with man or bull or some other dark force, is always also an act of love. When, in April 1979, this "génial prospecteur et sacqueur" [genial prospector and harsh critic] (Sénac 1971: 38) returned to Morocco, after fourteen years of voluntary exile in France, he was briefly arrested. He explained then that his guerrilla warfare had never been meant politically, but was a matter of language, of "scriptural labor, of writing itself" (Abboubi 1998: 69). Without the uneven rhythm of Khaïr-Eddine's shout, there would be no secret music, but his shout may also have distracted us from much of what his poems still have to say.

Works Cited

Abboubi, Rachid, ed. *Mohammed Khaïr-Eddine, le temps des refus: entretiens 1966–1995*. L'Harmattan, 1998.

Abdel-Jaouad, Hédi. "Mohammed Khaïr-Eddine: The Poet as Iconoclast." *Research in African Literatures*, vol. 23, no. 2, 1992, pp. 145–150.

Apollodorus. *The Library*. 2 vols. Translated by James G. Frazer, Harvard University Press, 1921.

Ben Jelloun, Tahar. "Khaïr-Eddine ou la fureur de dire." *Le Monde*, December 1, 1995, p. ii.

Celan, Paul. *Die Gedichte. Neue kommentierte Gesamtausgabe in einem Band*, edited by Barbara Wiedemann, Suhrkamp, 2018.

Deleuze, Gilles. *Francis Bacon, logique de la sensation*. Différence, 1981.

——. *Francis Bacon: The Logic of Sensation*. Translated by Daniel W. Smith, Continuum, 2005.

Deleuze, Gilles, and Félix Guattari. *Capitalisme et schizophrénie 2: mille plateaux*. Minuit, 1980.

de Vaan, Michiel. *Etymological Dictionary of Latin and the other Italic Languages*. Brill, 2008.

Diodorus Siculus. *Library of History*. 12 vols. Harvard University Press, 1935.

Dolar, Mladen. *A Voice and Nothing More*. MIT Press, 2006.

"Entretiens avec Francis Bacon." France Culture, April 2, 3, and 4, 1975, franceculture.fr/emissions/les-nuits-de-france-culture/francis-bacon-parler-de-peinture-c-est-impossible.

Gontard, Marc. *La violence du texte: études sur la littérature marocaine de langue française*. L'Harmattan/Société marocaine des éditeurs réunis, 1981.

Imbert, Claude. "Empiricism Unhinged: From Logic of Sense to Logic of Sensation." *Introduction to the Philosophy of Gilles Deleuze*, edited by Jean Khalfa, Continuum, 2003, pp. 133–148.

Khaïr-Eddine, Mohammed. *Nausée noire: poème*. Siècle à mains, 1964.

——. *Faune détériorée*. Encres-vives, 1966.

——. *Agadir*. Seuil, 1967.

——. *Ce Maroc! Poèmes*. Seuil, 1975.

——. *Une odeur de mantèque: roman*. Seuil, 1976.

——. "Redécouverte du sud." *Lamalif*, no. 112, 1980, pp. 38–43.

——. *Résurrection des fleurs sauvages*. Stouky, 1981.

——. *Mémorial*. Preface by Jean Orizet. Le Cherche Midi, 1991.

——. *Soleil arachnide*. 1969. Gallimard, 2009.

——. *Moi l'aigre*. 1970. Tarik, 2011.

——. *Scorpionic Sun*. Translated by Conor Bracken, Cleveland State University Poetry Center, 2019.

Lang, Abigail. "Bien ou mal lire, telle n'est pas la question: *Poésie ininterrompue*, archives sonores de la poésie." *Poésie sur les ondes: la voix des poètes-producteurs à la radio*, edited by Pierre-Marie Héron, Marie Joqueviel-Bourjea and Céline Pardo, Presses universitaires de Rennes, 2018, pp. 1–12.

Mallarmé, Stéphane. *Œuvres complètes*. 2 vols, edited by Bertrand Marchal, Gallimard, 1998–2003.

Marin, Louis. *On Representation*. Translated by Catherine Porter, Stanford University Press, 2001.

Michel, Jean-Paul, et al., eds. *Hommage à Mohammed Khaïr-Eddine*. Préau des collines, 2011.

Monbrun, Philippe. "La notion de retournement et l'*agôn* musical entre Apollon et Marsyas chez le ps.-Apollodore. Interprétation d'un mythe." *Kernos*, no. 18, 2005, pp. 269–289.

Murat, Michel. "Lire ce qui est écrit comme ce qui est imprimé." *Fabula*, 2019, fabula.org/colloques/document6366.php.

Ovid. *Metamorphoses*. 2 vols. Translated by Frank Justus Miller, revised by G. P. Goold, Harvard University Press, 1916.

——. *Fasti*. Translated by James G. Frazer, revised by G. P. Goold, Harvard University Press, 1931.

Peppiatt, Michael. *Francis Bacon in the 1950s*. Sainsbury Centre for Visual Arts, 2006.

Plato. *Republic*. 2 vols, edited and translated by Christopher Emlyn-Jones and William Preddy, Harvard University Press, 2013.

"Poésie ininterrompue." France Culture, October 19, 1975, franceculture.fr/emissions/les-nuits-de-france-culture/poesie-ininterrompue-mohammed-khair-eddine-1ere-diffusion.

Sénac, Jean, ed. *Anthologie de la nouvelle poésie algérienne*. Librairie Saint-Germain-des-Prés, 1971.

Sylvester, David. *Interviews with Francis Bacon, 1962–1979.* Thames and Hudson, 1980.

——. *Francis Bacon: The Human Body.* Hayward Gallery/University of California Press, 1998.

Tenkoul, Abderrahman. *Littérature marocaine d'écriture française: essai d'analyse sémiotique.* Afrique Orient, 1985.

——. "Writing in Movement: A Poetics of Undecidability?" *The World in Movement: Performative Identities and Diasporas,* edited by Alfonso de Toro and Juliane Tauchnitz, Brill, 2018, pp. 229–237.

Tournier, Michel. *Vendredi ou les Limbes du Pacifique.* Seuil, 1967.

CHAPTER THREE

Listening to 19th-Century Haitian Poetry

Martin Munro

While the field of aural history, of listening and tuning in to the auditory elements of historical experience is expanding rapidly, much of the work done so far has focused on the United States and Europe and, as Mark M. Smith recognizes, the history of listening, sound, and noise in non-Western regions "begs for detailed attention and investigation" (2004a: x). Perhaps the most fundamental point made by auditory historians is that there is a close link between sound and subjectivity, that the "heard world" serves as "an index for identity" (Smith 2004b: 368). In a region shaped by the historical genocide (and thereby silencing) of one group of people, the brutal displacement and enslavement (and attempted silencing) of another, and the complete (and univocal) mastery of another, the control of sounds, voices, and languages has long been associated with defining and circumscribing identity. To adapt one critic's argument on the nature of noise (in Victorian England), in the Caribbean sounds have long been expressive and communicative resources that have registered, manipulated, distorted, and created collective and individual identities. In Caribbean history, noise (of carnivals, revolts, dancehalls, protests, wakes, religion) has been and remains a potent form of social energy with the capacity to "appropriate, reconfigure or transgress boundaries," and to convert space into territory (Bailey 2004: 34).

Not surprisingly, of all the work done by Western historians of aurality, it is the research on the American South and the experience of American slavery that is potentially the most useful critical bridge in beginning to listen to Caribbean history. In its music, its work sounds, its religious sounds, and its obstinate silences, the heard world of the American South echoes across the plantation world to the Caribbean, communicating with it in ways that require us to tune in to the sounds of the past, and to listen attentively for their reverberations in the present. While they are sensitive to the historical predominance of the visual in plantation societies and elsewhere, theorists of aurality also indicate ways in which sounds escape control, and how they can "disintegrate and reconfigure space" (Connor 2004: 56). Sounds can in this sense define, create, or even destroy spaces. On the plantations of the Caribbean, as in the American South, the sounds of machinery and work defined those spaces as sites of domination and subjugation, while the call-and-response singing of the enslaved to some extent reappropriated the plantation field as a space of cultural survival, of subjectivities repressed but not completely destroyed. Away from the fields, too, the sounds of slaves' laughter, dances, drumming, and quarreling marked out their own spaces as distinct from the places of work, and from the quietude of the planter's house. As Ralph Ellison argues, an enslaved person, and especially a musician, was one who expressed himself in music, "a man who realized himself in the world of sound" (1964: 60).

Frederick Douglass suggests a similar idea in a well-known passage from his *Narrative* (1845), in which he describes how enslaved people selected to go to the Great House Farm to collect the monthly allowance for themselves and their fellow enslaved would make the woods "reverberate with their wild songs," which revealed at once "the highest joy and the deepest sadness." These songs—like much subsequent black American music—had strong improvisational qualities: the enslaved would compose them as they went along. The aural elements of the songs were also not limited to the lexicon of the master's language, but were a mix of words and indeterminate sounds that expressed the "thought that came up." The words they did use were apparently unstructured, an "unmeaning jargon" to anyone else, but to the enslaved they were "full of meaning." The pitch and tone of the songs—"loud, long, and deep"—carried meanings beyond the jumble of words, and communicated to Douglass "the prayer and complaint of souls boiling over with the bitterest anguish." Every tone, he says, "was a testimony against slavery, and a prayer to God for deliverance from chains." The sounds of the songs, for Douglass, would do more to convince certain minds of the "horrible character" of slavery than reading entire volumes on the subject could ever do (259). Douglass in effect suggests that music and sound were the primary expressive outlets for slaves, that even at this stage, the experience of African-American life was explored and interpreted principally through sounds and music. This idea was taken up much later by LeRoi Jones, who similarly regards music as the most effective means of "getting into the history of the people." As Jones writes, black music has come to be understood as "the history of the Afro-American people as text, as tale, as story, as exposition, narrative" (2002: ix).

In the colonial Caribbean, the control of sounds and noises was a similarly important condition for the definition and demarcation of space, and thus of identity. The sounds of enslaved experience were primary elements in converting the alienating spaces of the Caribbean into new territories. Of primary importance in this regard are the sounds of language, particularly the various Creole tongues that evolved out of cross-cultural contact. For Édouard Glissant, as for Douglass above, language, sounds, and silences defined and shaped slave experience. The alienated body of the slave was, says Glissant, deprived of speech; self-expression was not only forbidden, but "impossible to envisage" (1989: 122). All pleasure for the slave was silenced, repressed, denied, and in such a situation expression is necessarily "cautious, reticent, whispered, spun thread by thread in the dark" (122–123). From the beginning of slave-master contact, when Creole language came into being, the spoken form imposed on the slave its "particular syntax" (123). For the Caribbean person, Glissant says, the word is first and foremost not written, but sound and noise. Glissant argues that the pitch of sounds—screams, shouts, cries—conveyed meanings that escaped the comprehension of the master, and enslaved people in this way "camouflaged the word" in the varying intensity of their sounds. This, Glissant says, is how the alienated slave organized his or her speech, by "weaving it into the apparently meaningless texture of extreme noise" (124). This historical speech tendency translates itself into Creole language in the speed of popular conversation, a seamless stream of language that makes speech into "one impenetrable block of sound" (124). The meaning of a sentence is again hidden in the sounds and pitch of the popular language, and in this sense, Creole was a "kind of conspiracy" that concealed meaning and thought (124). Crucially, Glissant sees (or hears) in these linguistic practices, and particularly in the speed of Creole speech, echoes of music—the "embryonic rhythm of the drum" (124). The rhythm of the speech, like the rhythm of the drum, carries meaning, and this meaning is occulted, available only to those attuned to the varying sounds, pitches, and rhythms of the language.

The corollary of Glissant's emphasis on sound, music, and language as vital and revealing markers of Caribbean being is his insistence on the power of the master's gaze. In his classic novel, *Le Quatrième siècle* (1964), the slave master La Roche, "an absolute and maniacal Patriarch," draws and exercises his power, through his "gaze that made them all, sons, employees, slaves and freedmen, shiver" (Glissant 1964: 128). Sitting high on his horse, his vision is uninterrupted, so that his power derives from a certain omniscience. Looking over those he seeks to control, "he would stare thoughtfully at those who had incurred his anger," so that the objects of his gaze become "more fearful than ever of his fixed stare" (128–129). Even in his exchanges with fellow planters, La Roche exerts his authority through staring: in one case he "looked [the planter] up and down without a word and the foolish man fell silent" (165). Significantly, in this example, the power of the gaze is enough to silence the one he seeks to control, even a white man. It is equally significant in the novel that the maroon figure of Longoué insists on the limitations of the master's gaze: "The master did not really exist except when he was looking at you [...] as if he could only rule by establishing a flow that dried up as soon as he turned away" (62). As the only character in the novel who dares return the master's gaze, he underscores Glissant's fundamental objection, which has less to do with being looked at than with not having the ability to return the gaze, either in the early colonial situations described in the novel or in Western ethnography. "We hate ethnography," Glissant writes, before adding: "The distrust that we feel is not caused by our displeasure at being looked at, but rather by our obscure resentment at not having our turn at seeing" (2010: 122).

Glissant is clearly aware that racism is a discourse of power "that thinks with its eyes," and that race itself is a product of history and not nature that sets human difference in visual terms (Bull and Back 2003: 14).[1] Implicitly, anti-racism involves not simply escaping the master's gaze, but returning it, an act that challenges and to some extent negates the racism of the master. In another context, the Haitian author Jean-Claude Charles is no less aware of the enduring power of the white gaze, for instance in a scene from his novel *Manhattan Blues* (1985), in which the black narrator and his white partner embrace in a New York museum. The white caretaker throws the couple a look full of hatred that leads the narrator to write of the "racism of the gaze":

> The racism of the gaze is the most treacherous there is, it does not speak, it does not strike, it does not emit audible insults, it is there, its recipient cannot be mistaken. It is a feeling that no non-discriminated person can know, because it is not part of their experience of the world. It is not planned in any analysis, it is not dissected, there is no law and it is desirable that there is no law against it. It's not paranoia. Usually I either don't pay attention or I don't care.
>
> I imagine women may have felt this unspeakable thing in certain circumstances. Or Arabs in France. Or Jews. Or anyone who could be

---

[1] As Bull and Back say, "It would be impossible to think about the history of racism without its scopic component" (2003: 14).

raped, lynched, beaten up, gassed. You can never say sir, madam, your gaze undermines. There is no agreed code for this. It's about the skin, if I dare say. A matter of the guts. The look of the gut feelings of a racist. (110–111)

It is no coincidence that in the case of Jean-Claude Charles, as for Douglass, Glissant, and many others, the recognition of the persistent and enduring power of the white gaze exists alongside a conviction that sound has long been a domain less easily controlled by white racism, and that if free expression of black subjectivity in the Americas has been achieved at all, it is chiefly in sound. Where Douglass hears the truth of the pain of the enslaved in the tones of their singing, and Glissant hears Creole language as a means of bypassing, or otherwise subverting the power of the master's gaze, Charles listens obsessively to black music, chiefly jazz and blues, as the sonic means of countering the racist gaze that he encounters still in 1980s New York.

*

This chapter extends and applies some of these ideas on the importance of sound to Caribbean (and broader black American) cultures and being onto early Haitian poetry, specifically the works anthologized in the 2015 collection edited by Doris Kadish and Deborah Jenson, *Poetry of Haitian Independence*, a bilingual volume that gathers together many forgotten and neglected poems written between 1804 and the late 1840s. In engaging directly with the poems, the chapter seeks to explore the ways in which sounds are used by the poets in various ways as the new nation sought to assert itself on its own terms and create a sense of unity and common purpose in a land torn apart by a long period of war, and by the legacies of colonialism and slavery. By reading and listening to the poems in this way, the reader gains a sense of the importance of sounds to the written form, and by extension to the broader culture, in ways that reflect Glissant's ideas on the ways in which sound was a vital element in forming early Caribbean subjectivities. More broadly, the chapter serves to underscore the argument that in contrast to the visually determined culture of colonialism and racism—critiqued by Glissant and Charles above—the cultures and subjectivities of slave-owning and post-slavery societies in the Caribbean were formed around strong vocal and aural elements. In short, sounds were of primary importance to the cultures of the enslaved, and have remained important in postcolonial societies. The chapter proposes that one of the future thrusts of Caribbean criticism should involve *listening* to the history and literature of the region, and that by paying close attention to the representations and uses of sounds of various kinds in written texts, sound is in a sense rescued from the historical oblivion more conventionally assigned to it—the idea that because sound is "intangible" and "transitory," it is necessarily "a haunting, a ghost" that "vanishes into air and past time" (Toop 2010: xv). The chapter instead argues that, because the written text in the Caribbean has never been a "silent medium" but has always had strong sonic elements, sound in literature has a presence and indeed permanence that requires the reader only to listen in to the sonorous qualities that echo across time and register ideas of culture and being that draw on the past but which are also future-oriented, vital means of sounding out times and situations to come.

In the case of the corpus of nineteenth-century Haitian poetry to be read and listened to here, the uses of sound may be broken down into the following categories: sound as voice and freedom; sound as veneration of male leaders (panegyric); sound as gender (the female voice); sound as nation-building; sound as a conventional trope of epic; and sound as a marker of slave time. In many cases, sound in the poems is closely associated with voice, with speakers vocalizing ideas of time, history, society, and culture in ways that insert sounds and voice into the discourse of history which, the poems suggest, would not be a simple matter of recording dates and events, but of registering and listening to voices and sounds as crucial parts of the construction of history.

*

Haiti's independence was announced in sound and words, in the 1804 Declaration of Independence that was, as Edwidge Danticat says, "itself a poetic text, filled with poignant and elaborate imagery and passionate language" (2015: xii). Early poetry in Haiti was similarly charged with declarative functions and forms; made to be heard, it was, as the historian Émile Nau put it, "the song of the multitude, a general outpouring, an epic" (qtd. in Kadish and Jenson 2015: xxi). To have an impact, to be heard, such a song for the people drew on the "oral, rhythmic traditions" of popular culture, the sounds that had survived slavery and served as markers of identity and solidarity during the long war of independence (Kadish and Jenson 2015: xxi). This was a time of transition and change, politically, but also culturally, and there is in the early post-independence poetry of Haiti a sense of a culture shifting "between the diverse arts and cultures brought from Africa and the poetry later in Haitian history that would represent the black republic in Creole" (xxiv). In the following analyses, I draw on this earliest Haitian poetry to show the ways in which sounds were important means of asserting the new nation's sense of itself, communicating its understanding of its place in the world, and imagining history and memory in a time marked by upheavals and uncertainty, and the persistent reminders of the legacies of the colonial past.

Sound as Voice and Freedom

Quite significantly, the earliest poems of Haitian independence invoke sounds as markers of freedom. Set to the tune of the "Marseillaise," the very title of the anonymously written poem "What? Native Race! Would You Remain Silent?" asserts in 1804 the importance of breaking the silence that was an inherent part of colonial experience: "What? Native race! Would you remain / Silent, unmoved when Hero's hand / Avenges you, breaks slavery's chain" (Kadish and Jenson 2015: 3). The hero in question is Dessalines, and in this charged, muscular poem, the speaker calls for the people to "sing with one manly voice" the praises of the leader, who "reigns wisely over us" (3). Quite interestingly, the call for the people to raise their voices is at once a call to sing their freedom, but also to express their deference to the new leader, the "Good father," in whom the poem urges the people to invest their faith and hope, and to some extent, hand over their freedom. When memory is evoked, it is also through sounds—the "anguished cries" of the "victims" of the crimes of slavery, who also "cry from the dark eternal night: / 'Good Father, he, who thus / Reigns wisely over us'" (5). The cries and songs of the dead further confirm the status of Dessalines as the rightful protector of the new nation, and in invoking the memory of the dead, the poem suggests that not to follow Dessalines would be to betray that memory. Singing as one creates a kind of unity, but also encourages an unquestioning spirit that serves to reinforce the power of the male leader. As the poem projects into the future, evoking the new-born citizens, who may all "Stammer his name in babblings dim," it is again through sounds and voice that Dessalines's name will be transmitted, and along with it, a certain vision of muscular government that would prove to have an enduring appeal (7).

Sound as Veneration of Male Leaders: Panegyric

Similar sentiments are expressed in C. César Télémaque's "Let Us Now Sing Our Glory!," which calls for the friends of Haiti to "sing our glory" and to be "eternally / Thankful" to the Emperor Dessalines (Kadish and Jenson 2015: 9). He is the father of the nation; the people are his "children" who, again, must sing his praises in order to create the post-revolution sense of nation and togetherness (9). One can perhaps sense some of the paradoxes and contradictions of independence in the poems' unquestioning veneration of a strongman leader, while they also call for freedom, as in the refrain of the piece "Nature, in Wisdom Infinite": "Sing we, sing we stoutheartedly: / Equality forevermore! / Banished, banished be cruel slavery: Equality forevermore!" (13). Thus, the poems vaunt the qualities of a self-appointed emperor, while singing for everlasting equality in ways that already pose the question of how any form of equality can exist while there exists a desire (and perhaps, to some extent, need) for an authoritarian form of leadership. These paradoxes are in fact part of the sound, the great cacophony that greets the early independence period, the "hurly-burly sound" as an 1805 poem by Justin Chanlatte puts it, and the noise of the crowd, "As the throngs the throne surround / In ecstasy" (Kadish and Jenson 2015: 19). Together, the crowd sing "with passion's voice, in manly wise: / We who accept the rule of Jacques Premier, / Fete our own feast on our king's holy day" (19). Dessalines's voice echoes through history, as in the later poem "There Did He Fall (The Pont-Rouge)" (1835), which remembers the leader through his words, and the cry, the "lion's cry," the "sublime cry" that turns slaves into warriors and which reinforces the connection between manly revolt and the cry, the scream of rebellion that characterizes the popular memory of Dessalines (180). Similarly, Ignace Nau's "Dessalines! ... At That Name, Doff Hats, My Friends!" (1839) remembers the leader "to the sound of the fanfare and the artillery," sounds of war that are intimately related to "the single cry," the noise that marked the people's unity, and a paradoxical sense of harmony and oneness that seems unattainable in the time of putative peace that has followed the revolution (184). Indeed, it is in this poem that we hear "the sound of battle" that precedes and announces a prophesied future of harmony, where "the bird will sing to us once more its songs of love / The voice of the forests will resonate again," sounds of peace that seem inseparable from those of war, and which suggest more broadly the difficulty in imagining peace without a preceding, clamorous war: conflict is a part of historical memory and is reassuring in the sense that history's most cherished moments are closely related to and indeed dependent on it. Already, in these works, Dessalines is an almost religious figure: a man, but also invested with superhuman qualities that implicitly call into question the particular notion of equality that is being promoted, its limits and contradictions.

The veneration of the male leader figure continues in the poems dedicated to Henri Christophe, notably the poem that was sung at his coronation in 1814, "What Sweet Chants, These, That Strike, Entrance My Ear" (Kadish and Jenson 2015: 23). The title is interesting in that it emphasizes the sounds, the sweetness of the chants and their entrancing effect, which could suggest that the songs have an almost mystifying effect, charming the listener into believing that the sweetness of the sounds is reflected in the spirit of the leader. Listening is the key to believing in the glory of the leader (and of the country): "Lo! Hear the blaring brasses joyously / Temper and blend their brash cacophony / With fanfares' trumpets, horns, resounding!" (23). The subtle sense of uncertainty and dreaminess is emphasized in the chorus, which asks, "Are we awake? Or are sleep's smiling, / Lying dreams, with fictions beguiling, / Lulling, plying our spirit and sense?" and which may be read as a statement of awareness that the sounds of the song may dull the senses, quite deliberately, and render "spirit and sense" suspect, and liable to being charmed or fooled (23). Sounds are also the means of recording history and transmitting memory, as the poem suggests: "Clio, fair Muse of History, / Shall sing his exploits, first to last, / And, hundred-voiced, cause them to shine, / In Glory's light forever cast, / Engraved in memory's hallowed shrine" (23). The leader's voice communicates his "brilliance" and has a dramatic effect: "Henry speaks. All at once, the waters / Bow to new masters" (27). The voice is thus the means through which power is manifested and deference and order maintained.

It seems every leader must have their poem, their song, and the work "Haitians All, Come and Rally Round" praises Alexandre Pétion: "'Long live PÉTION,' sings everyone! / Long live the FATHERLAND! All hail!" (Kadish and Jenson 2015: 43). The French version closely allies Pétion and the "patrie," so that between these poems one hears a growing number of voices clamoring to be heard, each one a father figure, the embodiment of the masculine nation. The poems stress harmony and unity, while in truth the nation was of course divided between the north, controlled by Henri Christophe, and the south, controlled by Pétion, a division that also had color and class connotations—Pétion was a French-educated mulatto, while Christophe was of so-called humble origins and darker skinned.

The call for unity is apparent in the anonymous poem "Join Now Our Voices," which asks to "Let the echoes ring / In accents of hearts' joy and love" (Kadish and Jenson 2015: 47), and which again equates Pétion with the fatherland. There is also an interesting historical debate hinted at in these early poems, and which will mark a lot of subsequent intellectual reflection on the revolution. Namely, the question of who were the real liberators of Haiti, the black or mulatto leaders. In this poem, it is the mulatto who saves the "weak, mortal men" from slavery, and who is presented as a wise hero figure and who is "Throughout the isle adored, revered" for delivering the slaves into their "blessed refuge" (47). The role, or duty, of the liberated is now to praise the glorious leader with their "flattering tongues," which through repetition reinforces the one-sided view of history. Even a poem such as Jules Solime Milscent's "To Smite the Tyrant's Shackle-Curse," which calls for a unified Haitian republic, does so by asking the south to cede to the north and to join together as "Liberty's children" (51).

Sound as Gender: The Female Voice

It is further striking that in a poem by Juste Chanlatte that marks the reunifi-
cation of Haiti following the suicide of Henri Christophe in October 1820, the
voice of reconciliation is that of a female "august patroness," who descends
from on high and bestows the boons of peace and justice (Kadish and Jenson
2015: 59). The figure brings new life to a "newborn" people (63), and offers
maternal support in a voice that contrasts with that of the male leaders:

> Her voice, imperious,
> Makes speak the gods; her shield,
> Hovering, covers us;
> Her glittering lance, revealed,
> Glimmers, dazzles our glance,
> As Nature, suddenly,
> In rich exuberance
> Unbound, luxuriantly
> Spreads around her greenery. (61)

The female voice is a form of intermediary, between the two factions and
between the time of war and the reinstatement of the male power, this time
in the form of Jean-Pierre Boyer, president of Haiti from 1820 to 1843. It is the
intervention of the female figure that brings new life and allows the people to
be "newborn," but following that her voice disappears and it is the male father
figure that dominates once more as the poem calls to Boyer: "Our judge and
our protector be! And yes, / Father, no less!" and to sow "fertility's / Seeds"
to ensure the continued vitality of the nation (63). Whereas some of the other
poems lay bare the race and class issues with which the new nation struggled,
in this poem the issue of gender is subtly but quite tellingly invoked in
ways that suggest the ambiguous situation of women, as peacemakers and
life-givers, intermediaries and conciliators, brought to the fore to resolve the
male-dominated conflict, but then silenced again as the primary role of the
male leader is reasserted and a national discourse of manliness and virility
gradually but quite decisively comes to prominence.

Independence is thus, as in an 1821 poem by Juste Chanlatte, "fair fruit of
manly pride," to be sung and praised in an act of memory, "recalling thus /
Our solemn righting of that wrong" (Kadish and Jenson 2015: 65). The same
poem features a succession of voices proclaiming the virtues of Boyer, and
virtually all of these voices are male: a trumpeter, a piper, lieutenants and
captains. The two female voices that are included serve to bolster the theme
of manly militarism. The first, that of a "Young Female Warrior," calls out to
"Haitian lads," to clean "our long-wrought wounds," for "Such is the surest

path to ply / If you would reach our hearts" (77). For their part, the young women will succumb to the virile male warrior: "Can a lover's zeal deny / When he avenges nature's woe?" (77). The second female voice is of a "Woman warrior pointing out to her child the column erected to Independence" (77), which is a metonym for the nation, clearly phallic in connotation, and designed to impress by its "soaring eminence," and also to strike fear into the child for, as the woman says, if the child should ever betray the nation, she will be eaten by a caiman (77). The message is then that the sexualized male metonym of the nation should be looked at in wonder, without questioning, and if such wonder and respect should fail, there will be violent consequences. Behind the chorus and praise, communicated at the end through sounds— "What sounds! What notes enchant the air!"—lies therefore a discernible note of menace, directed especially at women, and those who stray from their prescribed roles as willing lovers and virtuous mothers.

Sound as Nation-Building

It is important to realize in reading these poems that the idea of the new nation is being formed, and that works such as these form part of that effort. What was the significance of Haiti's independence? What kind of nation was it going to be? How would relations be between all of the nation's people? What could be done with the legacies of colonialism and slavery that were still so fresh in the memory? How could the complex events of the long war of independence be synthesized into a coherent national narrative? The very term "the Haitian Revolution" was coined a full twenty years after independence, possibly by Hérard Dumesle in his travel account, *Voyage dans le nord d'Haïti* (1824). It is also in this volume that appears the earliest known transcription of the "Oath of the Cayman Woods," which took place on August 14, 1791, at a Vodou ceremony that marked the beginning of the revolt. The oath appears in a poem composed by Dumesle, which frames the events with references to classical figures and symbols, such as Virgil, Aeolus, and Spartacus. The oath itself is important as it represents dramatically the power of the spoken word, and demonstrates how important the heard history of Haiti and the broader Caribbean is: with little or no popular written culture, the participants in the ceremony are electrified by the spoken word, which propels them into their long and deadly war of independence.

It is significant that as Dumesle sets the scene for the ceremony, the enslaved participants, the "poor oppressed," stand "in silence," voiceless against the "dread cacophony" of history, characterized in the image and sound of "gale winds howling" (Kadish and Jenson 2015: 93). The only sounds emitted by the people are "dour laments" that move "nature," a harmonizing force whose laws are held "in suspense" by the "foul crimes" of the colonists (93–94). The slaves' desire for vengeance is what motivates the uprising and animates the ceremony, which begins with an animal sacrifice (95). The animal is killed by "an orator" who, following the deed, pronounces his prophetic words: "Now you the noble purpose see / Whence heroes rise to immortality!" (97). The words are all the more potent and effective in that they are spoken in Creole, "that tongue that our forebears used, / So simple that it seemed to have suffused / Their very breath; tongue natural, naïve" (97). The language is closely related to their being; it is "the portrait of their soul" and it "electrified their hearts" (97). The speech itself talks of the "white man's sins against your land, your race," and draws a distinction between the whites' religion, which "leads to crime," and Vodou, which "leads to grace / And goodliness" (97). The oracle's words lead the fire to swirl "in an all-devouring hunger," a clear metaphor for the enflamed spirits of the participants (97). When the fire finally burns out, the slaves "consecrate this wood" with "prayer-chants and many a sacred vow," spoken acts that contrast with their initial silence, and which again show the importance of the oral elements, of finding a voice, and, in this case, of expressing themselves in their native tongue—all acts that mark their desire to take back the land and repossess their very selves (99).

Important occasions continued to be marked by songs and speeches, such as the poem "The World Has Hailed Your Sons" by Jean-Baptiste Romane that was sung at the festivities to mark France's recognition of Haitian independence in 1825. Romane's poem was sung to the dignitaries present, including a representative of France, and speaks of the celebration spreading across the land, in sounds and chants—the waters of the "Majestic Artibonite" river "murmur" and ring with the cry, "Vive Haïti! Vive la France!," while Boyer's pronouncement of the same phrase was "spoken to end our ills" (Kadish and Jenson 2015: 108–110). The song is finally addressed to God, who is called on to "accept our songs" and to bless Boyer and Charles X, and to hear them both call out to the glory of the two countries (111). In contrast to Dumesle's poem about Bois Cayman, this poem tends to look forward temporally, to a time that would never arrive, of Haiti's settled and peaceable external relations leading to national prosperity. Indeed, the poem is remarkable in that it does not mention Haiti's indemnity to France of 150 million gold francs, which was ten times the nation's annual revenues in 1825, and which threw it into a spiral of debt that it arguably has never recovered from. The chants celebrating the glory of the countries and the "clemency" of Charles in particular seem empty and to ignore the punitive aspects of the agreement, the effects of which would last far longer than the cries for peace and prosperity that ring throughout the poem, and which show the ways in which song and sound can capture a certain fleeting national feeling, which is subsequently forgotten and silenced as the realities of debt and economic hardship become clearer.

Sound as a Conventional Trope of Epic

Even as Haiti's economic independence and future prosperity were compromised by France's indemnity, the idea of a muscular, robust, male state persisted, and continued to be celebrated in poems such as *The Haïtiade*, which is, as Kadish and Jenson say, the "only formal epic of the Haitian revolution" (2015: xxviii). The first canto of the poem insists on the newness of what is to follow:

> O Muse, now to new songs I tune my lyre:
> Come, flame my heart with your mad passion-fire;
> Let my voice, proud, with manly accents, ring;
> Come, Muse, let us now Haiti's freedom sing. (121)

One senses still the freshness of the memory of the revolution, but also a concurrent feeling that the passage of time is eroding the memory, or at least that it needs to be set to words and music in order to preserve it. Again, manliness is seen as a virtue, and not a fundamental flaw in the political culture of the new nation. The song itself must by then have been somewhat familiar, and not altogether new; the tale of the slaves' overcoming and of how they transformed slavery into liberation and "beat to avenging blades their chains of old" (121). There is also a degree of revisionism in the way the poem states that there was an easy transition from slavery to nominally free field labor, that the hoe, previously "a burden so heavy when it fed / The cruel, slave-driving master" now "weighed ever so lightly in the withered hand / Of soldier citizen who saved his land" (123). In truth, attempts to force the freed people back onto the land were hugely unpopular and controversial.[2]

The glossing over of the issue of forced labor deliberately precedes the first mention of Toussaint Louverture, who is presented as a godly figure, "Heaven-endowed with power supreme" and one of those powers lies in his voice, as it was he "whose tongue decreed the Haitians' laws" (Kadish and Jenson 2015: 123). Having suffered "labors of the vilest king," he rose up, and

---

[2] See Laurent Dubois: "Louverture was the one who insisted on the maintenance of agricultural policies, set up by Sonthonax and Polverel, that forced ex-slaves to keep working as 'cultivators'; and his generals doubled as agricultural adminis- trators, using the armed forces to police the plantations and punish anyone who sought to run away from them" (2012: 31).

again this is presented in vocal terms: "his valor rang with cries of war" (125). Another noisy marker of revolt, the "conch shell's blaring sound," gathers the soldiers around Toussaint, though this sound is soon replaced by those that accompany the pious Toussaint's prayers: "Voices rise up, the Heavens' height inspires / Hymns intoned by celestial angel choirs" (127). Articulacy is a potent and necessary complement to the physical acts of revolt; much like Toussaint, the revolutionary general Télémaque is praised for "his eloquence," which "framed the laws / Adopted in the councils" (133); while Pétion's silence "binds all hearts," and his speech "conquers all" (139). Of all the heroes lauded in the poem, however, it is only Toussaint whose voice is communicated in direct speech, and who by implication becomes the voice of the revolution, which is ultimately a univocal phenomenon: the memory will be channeled through the voice of this single paternalistic figure, who "will govern like a father" (144). Similarly, Toussaint's singular voice is received by the crowd as it vows to "keep the law [...] all in one voice" (147). The memorial intentions of the speaker are subsequently reaffirmed in the call to "let our minds now stand free / Of deathly scorn's vile, hateful memory" (147), which suggests that Toussaint's voice can silence the memory of all that preceded him, and is also a kind of prophecy in that it projects forward into a future in which it is the manly, heroic voice that controls history, and leaves in silence aspects of that history that would call into question the value of promoting a univocal male version of history, and of maintaining a people in thrall to that voice.

Sound as a Marker of Slave Time

It is perhaps one of the signs of the early confusion over national identity—the unprecedented condition of being a "black nation" and modern at the same time—that there are very few mentions of popular culture in the poetry of the first three decades of independence. The derivative French style, language, and form in many of these works are reinforced by the classical themes and references. Even *The Haïtiade* is rather conventional in its attempt to present the events of the revolution in an epic form that seems to preclude any references to the culture of the newly freed people. This tension would endure for much of the rest of the century, and indeed into the indigenist period that began during the American occupation of 1915–1934. Coriolan Ardouin's 1835 poem "The Bechouans" prefigures the indigenists to some degree in its references to drums and dancing, even if the poem is largely situated in Africa, which is rather exoticized, not to say feminized and sexualized. The poem presents "Bechouan belles" who "dance through the night, casting the spells / That grace and fascinate the eye" (Kadish and Jenson 2015: 151). The ear is also attuned to the spectacle, and to the sounds of a drum that "echo deep into the forest" (150). The poet's awareness of Haitian popular culture is shown in the way the Bechouan maid dances rhythmically to the drum, "gliding above the *sotor's* sound," in the reference to the *assotor* drum, which is a Haitian instrument, used in Vodou ceremonies, and to send coded messages during the revolution (153). The sounds and sights are in harmony, in rhythm and time with each other, and with the natural environment, in that the "sweet music of the dance / carries through to the heart of the forest" (152). The dance is moreover "poetic," and the speaker encourages the young women to dance on, as they sing in one voice (152).

The subsequent scene of the maidens bathing peacefully in the river is interrupted by "a distant sound" that rises and dies so that they are not sure if it is real or "a dream" (Kadish and Jenson 2015: 156). The women flee as they realize the sound is that of the Bushmen, who are presented as barbaric hunters whose "terrible sounds" mix with the cries of a victim (157–158). The captured women are bound for the slave ship, and say farewell to the place and sounds of their homeland, notably the "sound of the drum," which echoes across the seas, in much the same way that the image of the idealized African woman is carried across the ocean, so that the exiled woman becomes an imagined figure, a fantasy, as the speaker puts it, "That angel who comes to us in our nightly dreams" (158, 160).

Ardouin's 1835 poem "Oh! I Recall That Day (Mila)" in a sense picks up where "The Bechouans" ends, in its romantic presentation of a beautiful "Daughter of Angola" and her doomed love affair with her "Creole beau," Osala. Mila marks out the plantation through sound, her songs that resonate across the "attentive valley," and the echoes of which betray her presence to the white master, Ebreuil (Kadish and Jenson 2015: 168). Her "simple song" charms him, though she sings of Osala, and this moves him to approach her, first in the "language [...] of a white," and then, "changing tone," he flatters her, saying "her voice is that of the dove" (170). When she rejects him, he walks away, falling into silence, and plotting to get rid of Osala (170).

Sounds mark out the slaves' time, and their relationship with space, as in a scene where "It is the silver bell / that sounds rest time," and during that time is heard the song of a nightingale (Kadish and Jenson 2015: 170–172). The speaker implores the slaves to come and hear the bird's song, as "this beloved cantor of the skies will be no less sweet / If it is a slave who hears her voice" (172). This is important, as it suggests something of the ways in which sounds escape the control of the planters, and remain accessible and enlivening to the enslaved people: the ear retains its freedom, and such sounds are there for all. It is also significant that the young Creole beau, Osala, appears whistling, a sound that connects him to the bird, and thus to nature; not only are sounds accessible to the enslaved, they are also able to make their own sounds that humanize them in a sense, and also are small acts of resistance that contrast with the gloomy silence of the master and the industrial clanging of the silver bell (172).

Osala's connection to natural things is reinforced in the presents he brings to Mila—fruits and flowers; and he says his "suffering" is over, "For I see you, and hear your voice," the two senses being markers of their intimacy and their freedom to communicate and be together (Kadish and Jenson 2015: 172). Her wish is that he "will sing / some of his airs on his mandolin" for her, while she will tell him a "story from the native land," which signals her love for Africa, and the ways in which songs and storytelling express that love and to some extent ease the suffering of their exile (174). Time is important in this, too, for the plans they make are for the night, when "They will be able to cradle each other in their sweet words" (174), and in the day, time is marked by the bell: when "Two o'clock tolls" she must run back to her work, and await the freedom that the night and its sounds bring. When their plans are foiled by the white planter, who sends Osala to work in chains "on another plain," his new exile is marked by sounds, or rather, their absence—the realization that "never will he hear / The gardens echo with the name of his Mila!" (178). Strikingly, too, Mila's pain is manifested in broken, interrupted sounds: she wanders "a dreamy and sad madwoman" who "Ceaselessly begins a Creole song / That she never completes!" and when she dies she is taken away "without a sound, without a flower" (178). The broken, unfinished song is also a sign of the ruptures of history and being that are the legacies of the colonial era, and which in this poem echo into the present via the contrasting sounds of the poem: the bird and human song, related to love and nature; the broody, ominous silence of the master; the sounds of work and time; and, finally, the broken songs and broken lives that emerge from it all.

It is interesting that it is in the poems that present "popular" or peasant characters that notions of memory and history are the most fragmented and troubling—although they are far from being realistic attempts to communicate trauma, there is a sense that the people's memory of the revolution is marked by ruptures and discontinuities, and that these broken memories are more important to them than the official, collective memory of glorious revolution, which is communicated, for example, at the end of the anonymous poem, "Father, Dear, How I Love to Cast My Glance Over These Hills and Fields" (1839). The sounds used here are quite different to the tears and broken songs of the popular poems. On the anniversary of independence, church bells ring out, priests chant their litanies of thanks, cannons "thunder long and loud," mixed with "the song of the horn," and the echoing sounds of the cannons, which carry the memory of war and victory: "So that your sounds, carried from mountain to mountain, / Remind today every last person /

That he had sworn to live independent!" (Kadish and Jenson 2015: 208). The sounds here are clamorous and loud, sounds of bells and cannons that may in other contexts be heard as contradictory—religious devotion mixed with a glorified memory of war—but which here indicate again the paradoxes of national memory: how memories of war announce feelings of peace; and how the booming sounds of war form the most coherent auditory memory of the revolution, where again notions of peace and togetherness are closely associated with conflict and suffering.

*

Slave revolts in the Caribbean often began with sounds—of shells, bells, drums, voices—and were spread in large part by the sounds of rumors, songs, half-truths, exaggerations, and language in general, so that sounds of Haitian revolts in particular were and are to a large extent the revolution, and the revolution was and is sound. This is one of the implications of Julius Scott's work which, in Marcus Rediker's words, shows how those who "inhaled the history of Toussaint and the revolution and who whispered it all out again as subversive stories [made it] circulate with velocity and force around the Atlantic" (2018: ix). That Rediker's commentary and the title of Scott's book refer to a poem—Wordsworth's famous 1802 sonnet to Toussaint Louverture—suggests that poetry was one of the most potent means of communicating meaning around the Atlantic, and indeed in the Caribbean itself. There was poetry in song, in the simple chants about Haiti sung across the Caribbean, in the expressive culture of the enslaved in general, in their knowing use of language and detour and mimicry, their proverbs taken from Africa and translated into Creole, and the slogans that echoed across the Atlantic and that resonate still today. Is there any more poetic statement of surrender than that attributed to Louverture in 1802: "By overthrowing me, they have only brought down the trunk of the tree of liberty in Saint-Domingue; it will grow back as its roots are deep and many"? Indeed, poetry played a part in the betrayal of Toussaint, as his son Isaac, duped by Napoleon into thinking the French would leave his father unharmed, "was so flattered that he composed a poem in the first consul's honor. It showcased a mastery of the French language that would have made his father proud, but a political naivete that would have horrified him. "'Young and valiant hero,' Isaac intoned in Napoleons' honor, 'your grandeur / Of the shining day, increase the splendor'" (Girard 2016: 232–233). When Haitian independence was declared in 1804, it was with great poetic flourishes: "I have avenged America," Dessalines announced. Great authors and thinkers, not just Wordsworth, but also Lamartine, Glissant, Walcott,

James, and countless others, have been drawn to the story of the revolution, its poetry. The revolution is sound; it is also poetry.

It is no coincidence that it is Louverture and Haiti that inspired Glissant to propose in his 1961 play *Monsieur Toussaint* a "prophetic vision of the past," and to insist that in the Caribbean the work of the historian must be complemented and indeed completed by the work of the poet, "in order to fill the considerable gaps specific to Caribbean history—the slave trade, Middle Passage, plantation slavery, anticolonial rebellion, and so on" (Douglas 2019: 23). Glissant's famous essay "The Quarrel with History" explains how the poetic and literary are integral parts of the work of understanding Caribbean history. Referring to a conference paper presented by Edward Baugh, Glissant questions initially the idea of a Caribbean non-history, before insisting on the disjuncture between a group's "relation with its surroundings (what we would call its nature)" and its "accumulation of experiences (what we would call its culture")" (1989: 61). In such a context, he says, history as a discipline that seeks to record the lived reality of a people "will suffer a serious epistemological deficiency: it will not know how to make the link." As such, a "creative approach" is required to understanding history in the Caribbean, which is the "site of a history characterized by ruptures and that began with a brutal dislocation, the slave trade" (61). Faced with the "erasure of the collective memory" (62), the Caribbean writer is charged with inscribing memory, and "history as a consciousness at work and history as lived experience are therefore not the business of historians exclusively" (65):

> A reality that was long concealed from itself and that took shape in some way along with the consciousness that the people had of it, has as much to do with the problematics of investigation as with a historical organization of things. It is this "literary" implication that orients the thrust of historical thought, from which none of us can claim to be exempt. (65)

Thus, the literary and the poetic are part of the process of understanding and knowing history: the form of the investigation is as important as the content. Poetics is, conversely, more than an issue of style and form, and poets are almost obliged to engage with history so that poetry becomes history to some extent and vice versa. It is not that poetry reveals history in any direct, visible way; rather, as Glissant says, "Little more than an indiscernible revelation, poetry is not formal knowledge" (2010: 54). The kind of knowledge he reaches for is not poetic thought, but what he calls a *"poetics of thought"* (57; emphasis original).

Described as a "Land of Poets," with more poets per square mile than anywhere else in the world, the recording of national history in Haiti begins in the poetry of the Declaration of Haitian independence, the grand rhetorical statements and lofty ideals that announced the arrival of the new nation (Hoffmann 1961: 62). And, as Hoffmann suggests, even if poetry is the "exclusive apanage of the elite," the Haitian oral traditions contain the three major literary forms: "The novel becomes the Creole folk tale, poetry is found in the lyrics of popular *méringues* and the embryo of a theater is found in pantomime and dance" (63). Haiti did not invent Caribbean poetry: it was already there, always, in the uses of language described by travelers, missionaries, and others, in the wordplay, the knowing uses of language, allegory, indirection, imagery, and of course, sound.

Accordingly, then, and as this chapter shows, the auditory aspects of these early written texts say much about the issues of independence, sovereignty, class, and color that were some of the young nation's main preoccupations. Sound was a contested domain during and after slavery, a means of control and potential, if incomplete and fleeting, liberation. History and memory were and are communicated through sounds, especially in a largely oral culture, the imprint of which is felt throughout the collection of early Haitian poetry. Poets wrote works that were to be spoken and heard, and knew that for their works to resonate they had to engage the listener's ear, and that the meaning of their works lay as much in how they sounded as in the words themselves. Through the poems, we can hear some of the clamor of history, the struggle for the new nation to assert itself internationally, and to come to terms with the legacies of its colonial history, notably the memories of war, the veneration of the "great men," the autocratic impulses of many of these male figures, and the class and color divisions that were expressed in part through sounds, through language, music, and noisy revolts. Official history tended to silence the contradictions of the new nations and to present a unified, masculine, univocal version of the past, while popular memories were more fragmented, multivocal, and often feminized, so that we gain a sense through the poems of the tensions, silences, and repressed sounds and voices of the people in this crucial time in the nation's history. Listening to these works, and to broader Caribbean history, allows us to tune into the past, to hear something of its chaos and clamor, and, importantly, to sound some of the forgotten parts, the silences that are no less important to understanding that history.

Works Cited

Bailey, Peter. "Breaking the Sound Barrier." *Hearing History: A Reader*, edited by Mark M. Smith, University of Georgia Press, 2004, pp. 23–35.

Bull, Michael, and Les Back. "Introduction: Into Sound." *The Auditory Culture Reader*, edited by Michael Bull and Les Back, Berg, 2003, pp. 1–18.

Charles, Jean-Claude. *Manhattan Blues*. Bernard Barrault, 1985.

Connor, Steven. "Sound and the Self." *Hearing History: A Reader*, edited by Mark M. Smith, University of Georgia Press, 2004, pp. 54–66.

Danticat, Edwidge. "Foreword." *Poetry of Haitian Independence*, edited by Doris Kadish and Deborah Jenson, translated by Norman R. Shapiro, Yale University Press, 2015, pp. xi–xvii.

Douglas, Rachel. *Making* The Black Jacobins: *C. L. R. James and the Drama of History*. Duke University Press, 2019.

Douglass, Frederick. *Narrative of the Life of Frederick Douglass, An American Slave*. Anti-Slavery Office, 1845.

Dubois, Laurent. *Haiti: The Aftershocks of History*. Metropolitan Books, 2012.

Ellison, Ralph. *Shadow and Act*. Vintage Books, 1964.

Girard, Philippe. *Toussaint Louverture: A Revolutionary Life*. Basic Books, 2016.

Glissant, Édouard. *Le quatrième siècle*. Seuil, 1964.

——. *Caribbean Discourse: Selected Essays*. Translated by J. Michael Dash, University of Virginia Press, 1989.

——. *Poetic Intention*. 1969. Translated by Nathanaël, Nightboat Books, 2010.

Hoffmann, Léon-François. "The Climate of Haitian Poetry." *Phylon*, vol. 22, no. 1, 1961, pp. 59–67.

Jones, LeRoi. *Blues People*. 1963. Harper and Collins, 2002.

Kadish, Doris, and Deborah Jenson. "Introduction." *Poetry of Haitian Independence*, edited by Doris Kadish and Deborah Jenson, translated by Norman R. Shapiro, Yale University Press, 2015, pp. xxi–xliii.

Rediker, Marcus. "Foreword." *The Common Wind: Afro-American Currents in the Age of the Haitian Revolution*, by Julius S. Scott. Verso, 2018, pp. ix–xiii.

Smith, Mark M. "Introduction: Onward to Audible Pasts." *Hearing History: A Reader*, edited by Mark M. Smith, University of Georgia Press, 2004a, pp. ix–xxii.

——. "Listening to the Heard Worlds of Antebellum America." *Hearing History: A Reader*, edited by Mark M. Smith, University of Georgia Press, 2004b, pp. 365–384.

Toop, David. *Sinister Resonance: The Mediumship of the Listener*. Continuum, 2010.

Cinema

CHAPTER FOUR

Hollowed Bodies: The Aural Skin of African Cinema

Vlad Dima

Djibril Diop Mambety's seminal *Touki Bouki* (1973) marks a turning point in our way of thinking about the narrative role that sound plays in African film.[1] This is not to say, of course, that sound had been completely missing from intellectual conversations about African films of the 1960s;[2] for example, Ousmane Sembène's *Black Girl* (1966) introduces a fascinating use of voice-over, which will be discussed shortly. However, it was Mambety, the quintessential sonic auteur, who first drew our attention to the malleability

---

[1] This chapter disregards worn-out conversations about authenticity and originality in African cinema. As Kenneth Harrow explains, "the attempt to validate African authenticity, or traditional identity, is a reaction to western domination and is betrayed by its dependence on western epistemological tools, western categories of knowledge" (2007: 27). That said, the early work of the pioneers of African film theory, Teshome Gabriel (1989: 45–52) and Manthia Diawara (1992: 141–164), represents an unavoidable springboard into any such discussion. For more on their categories of African film and on Third Cinema in general, see Dima 2017: 4–18.

[2] Roughly ten years separate Mambety's film from Sembène's *Borom Sarret* (1963), often considered to be the first African film. It is not the aim of this chapter to discuss the pros and cons in this debate, which often invokes Paulin Vieyra's *Afrique-sur-Seine* (1955) and Sembène's first two cinematics efforts, *Borom* and *Black Girl* (1966). Both Sembène films feature extensive use of voice-over.

of African cinematic sound, its narrative prowess, and the rich possibilities that stem from blurring the spatial lines usually delineated by the visual, the visualized source(s) of sound, and by sound itself. Following in Mambety's footsteps, several other African directors would continue to place a narrative emphasis on the role of sound, and perhaps none more consistently than the Cameroonian Jean-Pierre Bekolo, a veritable sonic heir to Mambety. If one follows the creative line between Mambety and Bekolo,[3] one may discover that cinematic sound in their films often supplants the visual as the primary narrative tool, flipping over the usual conceptualization of the filmic narrative (that is, image plus, as in "coming after," sound).[4] In other words, it is through sound that the stories are being narrated first, and the visual comes in only to complete or buttress that initial meaning. My first book, *Sonic Space* (2017), discusses sound at length, and posits that African cinematic sound reterritorializes the colonial space and that sound essentially turns that space back into an African space again. My second book, *The Beautiful Skin* (2020), gestures toward the materiality of African cinema, but only partially discusses the role that sound and voice have in creating an (aural) body, a body that reaches into the audience and touches the spectators. What I propose here is to revisit and expand some of those findings and hypotheses by focusing more intently on voice(s), agency, and the intentional blurring of spatial lines between the diegetic and the nondiegetic.[5]

---

[3] Bekolo reveres Mambety and he has made a very short documentary, *Grandmother's Grammar* (1996), documenting an intimate conversation about filmmaking with him.

[4] Sound theorist Michel Chion explains that because the "talkies" were born in the late 1920s, audiences had been trained to think through the image first. Therefore, it is simply by historical happenstance that sound was perceived as secondary to the image. Moreover, Rick Altman's important book, *Silent Film Sound*, establishes sound as "discontinuous" in its initial relationship with the image (Altman 2004: 92–93).

[5] Even though these terms are probably familiar, it may be worth explaining them in the context of sound studies. "Diegetic sound" occurs within the confines of what is seen on screen (or, what *logically* belongs to the world on screen, even if unseen), and thus has a clearly identifiable source; "nondiegetic sound" comes from off-screen and is seemingly not connected to the diegetic (at least not in a material way). Two other terms complete the possible types of sound: "extradiegetic sound" is sound connected to the diegetic but that has no place being heard on screen—an illogical sound within the diegesis (in narrative terms and in literary studies, the "extradiegetic" actually refers to the real world; both senses may be used in this chapter); finally, "intradiegetic sound" is sound

As a result, one of the tensions that this chapter aims to uncover is that between the visual body and the aural body created by the voice, as exemplified by selective parts from three films spanning from the beginnings of African cinema to the contemporary period. The hollowing out of African bodies might occur when diegetic and nondiegetic voices escape the bodies from whence they originate. These voices are paradoxical, though: on the one hand, they are needed in the process of post-independence affirmation, and on the other they have the potential to empty the visual bodies of these characters, to challenge that harmony of aural-visual unity, rendering them less "full," and thus posing a threat to their subjectivity. Emptiness, as it so happens, may already define the neocolonial African subject. At the beginning of his fundamental study, *Critique of Black Reason*, Achille Mbembe describes the "Black Man" as "powerfully possessed by emptiness" (2017: 11). Later in the book, Mbembe returns to the idea of emptiness, which he attaches to uttering the word "Africa" out loud. In his words, this pronunciation "identifies a certain litigious figure of the human as an emptiness of being, walled within absolute precariousness" (49). Voice certainly has the potential to help the African subject break out of these walls. Yet, to reiterate, it might also act as an emptying tool. Ultimately, the conflict between the fullness of one's voice, reigning on a narrative plane that is not immediately visualized, and the possible emptiness of the visual body, represents an apt metaphor for the condition of the neocolonial subject, a subject necessarily split.

In order to study this conflict, this chapter begins with the case of Diouana from Sembène's *Black Girl* (1966), whose visual body is flattened by the unforgiving machine of neocolonialism, but whose aural body (created by the voice-over) gives her both agency and volume. The chapter then moves to the nondiegetic voice of Josephine Baker in Mambety's *Touki Bouki* (1973), which, paradoxically, descends into the narrative and, I contend, actually becomes diegetic because of how the main characters, Mory and Anta, *react* to it. Baker's visual body remains unseen, yet we are all aware of the racial abuse it suffered in real life, in the extradiegetic. The power that comes with her acousmatic voice still transcends boundaries, though, and her aural body suffices to make her an actual, diegetic character in the film, searching for self-affirmation. Finally, this chapter engages with Jean-Pierre Bekolo's *The President* (2013), in which real-life rapper Valsero traverses all possible cinematic realms—diegetic, nondiegetic, and extradiegetic. Valsero controls all possible narrative spaces through his (singing) voice, which amounts in the end to a definitive filling out and fulfillment of the African subject. Taken

---

whose source is known (or becomes known), but whose source the audience cannot see at that particular moment.

together, these three films offer a fairly complete map of what voice means for African subjectivity and how the representations of voice have evolved.[6] To recapitulate, the first aim of this chapter is to show that sound as cinematic voice(s) indeed has a corporeal attribute—it creates an aural body; the second aim is to consider how this aural body affects neocolonial subjectivities, because it can both support and supplant the seen, visual body; the final aim is to consider the blurring of spatial lines as a necessary artistic strategy when facing the difficult, ongoing effects of neocolonialism.[7]

The Un/Corporeality of Sound

In one of his several books on sound, *Audio-Vision: Sound on Screen*, French theorist Michel Chion invokes "the physical nature of sound" in order to arrive at the following declaration:

> There is always something about sound that overwhelms and surprises us no matter what [...] The consequence for film is that sound, much more than the image, can become an insidious means of affective and semantic manipulation [...] sound works on us directly, physiologically (breathing noises in a film can directly affect our own respiration). (1994: 33–34)

If breathing noises on screen (which, like the voice, come out of one's mouth, of course) affect the physical bodies in the audience, it would not seem a stretch to imagine that a similar effect takes place whenever the audience hears any voice on or off screen, irrespective of that voice's pitch, tone, or possible accent. In other words, the voice does not need to be "special" in any way—no matter what, the voice on screen (diegetic) or off screen (nondiegetic) has a marked effect on the body of the spectator. Jean-François Lyotard is another French theorist who is aware of the physical quality of sound, and he

---

⁶ Widening the scope outside of Africa, it is certainly possible that these varied representations of voice force us to reconsider certain intellectual stances in sound studies, especially when it comes to acousmatics.

⁷ I prefer the term "neocolonial" to "postcolonial," because it offers more ambiguity and I believe the effects of colonialism are not completely erased in the global South. I am following here Ella Shohat's perspective: "The 'neocolonial,' like the 'postcolonial,' also suggests continuities and discontinuities, but its emphasis is on the new modes and forms of the old colonialist practices, not on a 'beyond'" (2006: 241). Perhaps a longer discussion is required about the appropriate terminology in 2021; are we really in a post-neocolonial moment? Mati Diop's successful film *Atlantics* (2019) centers on a return, the return of the dead to be exact—what is the metaphorical value of this return, if unconnected to the trauma of colonialism?

equates the term "matter" to sound (1988: 153, 155). In the United States, it is the work of Rick Altman that unveils the materiality of sound. According to Altman, the production of sound is a "material event, taking place in space and time, and involving the disruption of surrounding matter" (Altman 1992: 18). Furthermore, in a recent issue of the journal *Paragraph*, Sarah Kay and François Noudelmann endorse Altman's observation in the following way: "Sound is produced by the blow or shock of one solid body against another, or against air, and it is then perceived as an echoing blow when that moving air strikes against the ear" (2018: 7). In sum, a materiality of sound seems to exist, and, as a result, it might support the existence of a cinematic aural body that extends from the screen into the audience, perhaps making contact.

African filmmakers often construct the cinematic text in such a way that a confusion arises between the space(s) on the screen and the space(s) between screen and audience. Overlapping the diegetic with the nondiegetic usually leads to this confusion. The oscillation between the diegetic and the nondiegetic places the audience in a "transformative place of betweenness" (Deger 2006: 90). Sound studies theorist Robynn Stilwell theorizes this confusing split in similar terms: she calls the overlap the "fantastical gap," which is "a place of destabilization and ambiguity" (2007: 186) and also "a transformative space, a superimposition, a transition between stable states" (200). Film scholar Jennifer Barker supports both Deger's and Stilwell's ideas, when looking to explain the position of spectators: while "watching a film, we are certainly not *in* the film, but we are not entirely *outside* of it, either" (2009: 12). Our bodies may be going through a process of extension, then, and could find themselves in contact with the extended aural body coming out of the screen. Indeed, philosopher Jacques Derrida describes the body as an "*extension* [...] an incredible extension, that of the soul or thought" (2005: 24), which is a conclusion he draws from a very opaque segment in Jean-Luc Nancy's book *Corpus: "Feeling oneself touching you* (and not 'oneself')—or else, identically, *feeling oneself touching skin* (and not 'oneself'): the body is always forcing this thought farther forward, always too far" (2008: 39). Moreover, according to Nancy, the body, and specifically what he coins the being-exscribed (*l'être-excrit*), only makes sense at its limit, at the "external border, the fracture and intersection of anything foreign in a continuum of matter" (17). To me, there is nothing *more* exterior to our bodies than our voice.

As we turn toward the voice,[8] Mladen Dolar describes it as an excess that prolongs the body "like an excrescence" (2006: 73) and "embodies the

---

[8] Sound in cinema is already "vococentric." Chion explains that the voice is the main sound registered, above all other elements on the soundtrack (1994: 6; 2009: 73–75).

very coincidence of the quintessential corporeality and the soul" (71). The voice is paradoxical, because "not only does it detach itself from the body and leave it behind, it does not fit the body either, it cannot be situated in it [...] It floats [...] detache[s] itself from its source [...] yet remains corporeal" (73). So, the voice is capable of producing its own body of sorts. Moreover, Dolar's word choices—floats, detaches, corporeal—point to this body being different from the visual body. In the case of the voice-over specifically, it always "leaves a trace [that] marks the terrain" (Chion 2009: 79). The voice, then, could be understood as our most external limb, as it were, a part of us that comes out of a nebulous yet physical place, and extends our visual body to the surrounding areas. In other words, the voice carries the (Nancy) body out into this continuum of matter, making it mean well outside of itself.

The issue of overlap between the diegetic and the nondiegetic can perhaps be most clearly observed through the concept of the *acousmêtre*, another important contribution by Michel Chion to sound studies. The *acousmêtre* is, in short, a cinematic voice without a body, or without an obvious body, imbued with a number of powers. The *acousmêtre* seems to wander along the surface of the film, "*at once inside and outside*, seeking a place to settle [...] Neither inside nor outside: such is the acousmêtre's fate in the cinema" (Chion 1999: 23). Chion's description evokes Barker's placement of the spectator, not quite in nor quite outside of the film. This means that the *acousmêtre* has a body (an aural body to be exact) that cannot fit in a particular place.

If the acousmatic voice remains on the soundtrack and it is never given a visual body, then it is purely a nondiegetic voice, a traditional voice-over. However, if a diegetic body emerges and matches that voice, then the voice/sound becomes intradiegetic; this process is called de-acousmatization. One of the defining qualities of the acousmatic voice is that it "can be instantly dispossessed of its mysterious powers (seeing all, omniscience, omnipotence, ubiquity) when it is *de-acousmatized*, when the film reveals the face that is the source of the voice" (Chion 1994: 130). Chion considers de-acousmatization a type of "embodiment: a sort of enclosing of the voice in the circumscribed limits of the body—which tames the voice and drains it of its power" (131). Power is repossessed by the visible body, which can swallow back the voice. However, I contend that a voice may depart the body on several occasions and whether or not it comes back, fully or otherwise, does not diminish its (narrative) power. In other words, to me, the mysterious powers of the voice (and, more specifically, the voice-over) cannot disappear entirely. Once the voice extends the visual body in various directions, it cannot simply retract it entirely and limit it to the physical walls of that body.

Mladen Dolar makes a similar argument, but he comes at the problem from another angle. He focuses instead on the idea that the voice cannot make it back inside the body entirely, as opposed to weighing the possibility that it might maintain its acousmatic qualities. Dolar declares: "even when it finds its body, it turns out that this doesn't quite work, the voice doesn't stick to the body, it is an excrescence which doesn't match the body" (2006: 60–61). This impossible return is eerily similar to Frantz Fanon's musings on the returned *émigré* who does not quite fit back into his or her culture. Moreover, this *émigré* tries too hard to sound more French by exaggerating the proper French "r." In a fascinating footnote, Fanon muses on what these efforts mean: "the black man who returns home gives the impression of having completed a cycle, of having added something that was missing. He returns home literally full of himself" (2008: 3). Of course, this fullness is specious, because Fanon suggests quite the opposite here—the time away from home empties the subject. The neocolonial artistic space is replete with stories of return, with characters coming home empty-handed (for example, Moussa from Fatou Diome's novel *The Belly of the Atlantic* [2003], dejected by the realities of life in Europe). Even more auspicious returns, such as those of directors Mahamat Haroun Saleh (*Bye Bye Africa*, 1999) and Abderrahmane Sissako (*Life on Earth*, 1998), portray the main protagonists as fish out of water to an extent. Because the voice cannot be stuffed back in, as it were, Dolar posits that *"there is no such thing as disacousmatization"* (2006: 70; emphasis original). In other words, the voice always maintains a degree of *acousmatisme*. Dolar finds inspiration for this intriguing thesis in Slavoj Žižek's work. According the Žižek,

> an unbridgeable gap separates forever a human body from "its" voice. The voice displays a spectral autonomy, it never quite belongs to the body we see, so that when we see a living person talking, there is always a minimum of ventriloquism at work: it is as if the speaker's own voice *hollows* him out and in a sense speaks "by itself," through him. (1996: 92; my emphasis)

Žižek places the incongruity between voice and body in an everyday context, but this works similarly, of course, on the screen. Combined with the never-complete process of de-acousmatization, with the impossibility of a voice being fitted back into the originating body, the conclusion is that parts of that body are forever vacated and will likely remain hollowed.

African film is a propitious area in which to study the narrative roles of voice and the emerging aural body. The focus on and interest in voice in African film should come as no surprise given the wide array of theorists who establish a convincing link between African cinema and traditional orality (Ukadike 1994: 201–222; Diawara 1996: 209–218; Barlet 1996: 157–199, among others).[9] The following case studies—from *Black Girl* and Diouana's voice-over to Mambety's use of Josephine Baker, and finally to Bekolo's *The President*—are less interested in the question of orality, and more focused on what African film teaches us about the relationships between voice, agency, and the neocolonial body. The main issue to keep in mind is that once a voice garners agency, it may escape the body,[10] and in doing so empties it, leaving behind only a shell.

Black Girl

Ousmane Sembène's well-known film *Black Girl*, based on one of his short stories from the volume *Voltaïque* (1962), follows the story of Diouana, who moves to the south of France from Dakar to help her white employers raise their children. Once in France, she discovers that she is meant to do everything around the house and slowly becomes more and more alienated in her new condition (that is, the matron of the house, Madame, controls her physical body), to the point that she takes her own life. While Diouana shares her inner thoughts in voice-over throughout the film, one particular scene exaggerates the split between her body and voice, thus allowing the voice to create an aural body.[11] It should be noted that having full access to the character's thoughts through the voice-over is a tremendous advantage for the spectators, but the problem is that it does not bring any discernible advantage for Diouana, who still suffers and ends up dead. Unfortunately, her voice does not yield the power that one would normally ascribe to the voice-over—the all-knowing voice that controls the narrative space of the film.

The scene in question follows her around the living room as she cleans, while on the soundtrack she rhetorically wonders about her role in the family. At one point, back to the audience, she faces a mask on the wall—this was the gift she had brought the family from Dakar. Slightly decentered, hands

---

[9] I discuss orality myself in *Sonic Space* (Dima 2017: 25, 172–173).

[10] Sembène's *Guelwaar* (1992) extensively uses the main character's voice-over, which dominates the film, in spite of the fact that the main character, Guelwaar, is already dead. In essence, he speaks from the beyond, which lends his voice an unmatched magical aura. This is also a perfect example of an always-acousmatic voice.

[11] At least seemingly, because it must be specified that for the voice-over Sembène chose the voice of another actress, and therefore the actual distance between the two women enhances the perceived cinematic distance between body and voice.

on the wall, Diouana projects a well-defined shadow to her right. Visually, her physical body splits in three: her back toward the audience (she is faceless, and thus somewhat universalized), mask on the wall (a metonymy for her identity—Nancy's extension does not have to be an aural one), and the shadow (the flattening of the body and the reduction of the self). As she moves away from the mask, she turns her face toward the camera, but another shadow emerges to her left, as the body continues to come apart. While she continues to complain in voice-over about her situation, Diouana walks off screen. For a moment, all that is left in the shot are the mask and her lingering shadow. The body literally disappears, which matches her lack of agency in real life, as she must obey Madame's demands, but the voice remains unaffected by this material change, and goes on uninhibited and still aurally full. The control that Diouana exerts over her own voice becomes then a tool of resistance and a means to offset, at least partially, the loss of the physical body. This is one of those cases in which I believe that the acousmatic voice might work in an unorthodox way: instead of hovering free initially and then trying to return to the body, it does the opposite. Why can this voice, suddenly without a body, not attain the qualities invoked by Chion?

The next shot pans left inside the living room and shows the rest of the wall, which is empty. There is no clear point of view, but an argument could be made that the shot follows Diouana's eyes. However, given the lack of match-continuity, this basically amounts to a neutral point of view, with absolutely no physical body in the shot. Yet her voice fills the space with an aural body, and the room fills up, as it were, thanks to the words uttered by Diouana. The voice-over asks a rhetorical question that supports the emptiness of the shot: "Where are the people who live in this country?" In fact, the very act of asking these questions without answers suggests a material, aural trail. In other words, the question hangs in the air, just as it does in the consciousness of the spectators (who may even answer it in their own minds). The next shot takes the suggestion of emptiness to an extreme, because it reveals a window overlooking the south of France, through which one can only see the blackness of the night. The camera still pans left, as if trying to find proof of life in this darkness, or as if trying to catch up with the visual body it has just lost, while Diouana—still "invisible"—asks herself another question without answer, "Is this France?" To summarize, Diouana's body disappears, and even when it re-emerges in a later scene, it is a fragmented body, cinematically speaking. The voice-over, though, remains steady and unified in this scene; following Dolar's view of voice as an aural excrescence that goes beyond the visual body, Diouana's voice "leaves a trace" throughout the living room, projects itself into the darkness of the southern night, and ultimately punctures and punctuates the very fabric of the film.

Moreover, the acousmatic quality of this aural body recaptures Chion's mysterious powers, because, after all, isn't it magical to hear Diouana's voice without her lips moving?[12] In the end, it would seem that the visual body is abandoned (albeit not by choice), and a fuller, aural body takes shape. The latter allows Diouana to retain some level of control over her own subjectivity, but she still succumbs to the unfair and dehumanizing pressures of neocolonialism. To put this differently, Diouana fully *lives* through her voice, but does so only in response to the pressures exercised on her visual body by the neocolonial apparatus. Ultimately, her aural body does not garner enough power to overcome the visual limits imposed on her (emptied) body.

Touki Bouki

Mambety's hallucinatory *Touki Bouki* does not have a traditional voice-over, nor do any of the characters speak directly to the audience. The plot of the film is very simple: two young lovers, Anta and Mory, want to leave Senegal and go to France. Throughout the film, they search for ways to make this happen, but in the denouement only Anta embarks on a ship destined for Marseille, while Mory stays behind. Even though the audience does not have direct access to the characters' inner thoughts, there is one aural element that comes close to creating a similar effect: Josephine Baker's song, *Paris, Paris* (1949). The first time we hear this song on the soundtrack, the characters are well outside of Dakar, which makes the song a perfect example of contrapuntal music, opposing the visual shot of the surrounding nature, "against the wide expanse of Sahelian earth" (Adesokan 2011: 60). The result is a subversion of the idyllic scenery of Senegal, as Josephine Baker makes the claim that Paris "is paradise on earth." Michel Chion has described the film song in general as taking "the role of a pivot or turntable, a point of contact. The song opens a horizon, a perspective, an escape route for characters mired in their individual story" (2009: 428). In this description, Chion suggests that songs may carry a physical attribute—they make contact. In this particular case, the song makes contact not only with the audience (the song never descends from the nondiegetic level), but with the two diegetic characters. Indeed it is the song that drives their actions, which renders it quasi-diegetic. In other words, Stilwell's "fantastical gap" may emerge here without the usual play between the diegetic and the nondiegetic. This may be possible

---

[12] Chion's famous claim that cinema was never silent, but rather deaf, hinges on the movement of lips, too: seeing the actors' mouths move in silent cinema brings forth a kind of dream in which the audience understands ("hears") what it is being said (1999: 7–9).

because the voice of Josephine Baker turns corporeal as it transcends all boundaries and becomes a material event in the way meant by Altman. Mory and Anta appear to be listening to the instructions in the lyrics to Baker's song, even though the two entities—couple and song—should technically live on separate narrative planes. In other words, the singer's voice becomes an *acousmêtre* that offers literal guidance to the characters. Yet the song is also very clearly separate from the rest of the film, creating a sharp contrast both with the visual cues and with the overall mood. Consequently, a quid pro quo of sorts emerges with the diegetic characters supplying a physical foundation for the unseen body of Baker's voice, while Baker's song and voice aurally complete the meaning and purpose of Mory and Anta. Taken separately, neither side could reach full subjectivity; when put together, though, a hint of hope for the future of the African subject (almost completely lacking in Sembène's Diouana) begins to form.

Baker was born in 1906 in the United States, and she became a cultural icon in France in the 1920s. She is a severely stereotyped icon—images of her wearing bananas around the waist come to mind—but also a tremendous source of inspiration to artists of color, especially women, such as Beyoncé, who speak reverently of her. In the ethnographic study, *The Third Eye: Race, Cinema, and Ethnographic Spectacle* (1996), Fatimah Tobing Rony discusses Baker as a prime example of someone who could not quite assume a subject position because of one of the enduring stereotypes of indigenous people: "When Baker debuted in Paris, she was portrayed as monstrous" (1996: 199). Anne Anlin Cheng's excellent book *Second Skin* (2011) takes Josephine Baker's "monstrous" body and reframes modernism through its relationship with skin and surface. According to Cheng, Baker wears "her nakedness like a sheath" (2011: 1), by which she means that Baker's body is imbued with so much meaning, "over-exposed and over-determined [...] a layered construct" (7), that her nakedness actually disappears (58). Cheng essentially (and brilliantly) claims that Baker's nakedness in *Princess Tam Tam* (1935) reveals "*another* dress [...] Thus, in lieu of skin, we get cloth. In other words, the deflecting 'shine' of the fetish has been removed only to reveal not only the ghastly gap of castration but the smoothness of yet another seamless surface" (63). Cheng concludes that the second surface— the naked skin—confuses the colonial gaze, which is then forced to find an equivalence between "blackness" and the glittery outfits worn prior to being naked. So, in spite of the initial stereotype of a monster or the famous images of Baker inside a gilded cage (a singing bird in captivity, as it were), her body and nakedness transcend racist boundaries. Her voice, too, as an extension (*à la* Nancy and Dolar) of this always-meaningful body, may transcend boundaries.

As already suggested, Mambety carefully orchestrates the four interrupting moments when Baker's voice features in the film (each time with the same song). Amy Herzog calls this type of interruption a "musical moment," which "occurs when music, typically a popular song, inverts the image-sound hierarchy to occupy a dominant position in a filmic work" (2010: 7).[13] The dominance of the song is underlined by repetition, a refrain of sorts and remnant of oral traditions, that ends up controlling the narrative and perhaps even the actions of the characters. The first instance marks a crucial moment in the plot, because the song follows the characters' confusing lovemaking scene and essentially jumpstarts their adventure—this is the moment when they decide to leave Senegal. As the song takes over the soundtrack, the camera frames Mory and Anta in a medium shot, which limits our view of the visual surroundings, and thus forces us to consider the lyrics of the song more carefully. As the visual space shrinks, the aural space expands and, thanks to the "musical moment," takes over the narrative.

The song emerges a second time in another key moment, just as Mory leaves the stadium with a chest strapped on his bike. The couple had decided to steal the earnings from a wrestling event, and they hope the money is inside this chest. Narratively, this is significant because it marks the proverbial point of no return—from this moment on, Anta and Mory are criminals and they must flee the country. The soundtrack switches back and forth between Baker's song and Mory's voice-over as it mentions Paris and touristic destinations such as the Eiffel Tower or the Arc de Triomphe. As Mory's voice quiets down, the song swells up on the soundtrack, and they continue to alternate two more times, but the song never fades out completely. It just cedes aural primacy and remains beneath Mory's voice, giving support to his thoughts, while his thoughts on Paris justify the reappearance of the song in turn. This back and forth creates what I call a sonic rack focus effect.[14] Moreover, just as regular bodies may extend and make contact at their limits, as Nancy instructs us, the aural bodies of these two voices connect at their limits. What I want to underline here is that the two voices (sounds) do not work toward rendering the image full; instead, following an almost lyrical rhyming pattern (that is, three by three) they work together to complete each other's meanings and render the visual less consequential.

The third occasion on which Baker controls the soundtrack follows a quick visit to the travel agency where the characters get tickets for the *Ancerville*, a boat headed to Marseille. In this situation, too, the song comes back three

---

[13] Herzog's work is mostly confined to the musical genre, but it can be extrapolated here.

[14] For more see, Dima 2012.

separate times within the same episode, which extends to the two characters entering the harbor. This is another important moment, because Anta and Mory are finally making actual progress toward leaving. Yet the repetition of the song also makes it seem as if they are stuck, like a broken record, as it were. In retrospect, the incessant repetition of the lyric, "Paris, Paris, Paris," itself a repetition, perhaps turns ominous. Finally, the song's last occurrence comes after Mory makes the unexpected decision to stay. As the visual narrative focuses on the boat, Anta appears alone on the upper deck. The pairing of the song with a solitary Anta completes the quartet of musical interruptions in yet another tight, stanza-like structure: together, Mory, together, Anta. The meaning of "Paris, Paris, Paris" changes in each instance, and the meaning of the images on which it is superimposed also changes. The four musical moments also offer a downward trajectory: from hopeful to a very low note, because Anta could be seen as sad and distraught by Mory's change of heart. If initially the music could be considered to be empathetic (that is, in tune with the overall mood projected by the visual), by the time we get to the image of a lonely Anta, the song turns unempathetic and even ironic. In sum, Baker's "Paris, Paris, Paris" punctuates four crucial moments in the plot of the film—the beginning, the theft from the stadium, buying boat tickets then entering the harbor, and the ending—but its purpose is far more nuanced and complicated. Not only do the song and the voice support the visual narrative in the traditional sense (that is, they complete the meaning of the image, or they go into the same atmospheric direction), but they also spur on the visual action and seem to speak directly to the two main characters. In short, the voice and song meaningfully instruct, and therefore affect, the characters. In some ways, the song turns into an anthem for the couple and Baker's voice becomes a guiding *acousmêtre* that has a corporeal presence in spite of the fact that Baker is never visualized.

The unique case of Anta, Mory, and Baker begs a return to the question of diegetic and nondiegetic boundaries. Theorist Jeff Smith makes a radical contribution to the complex conversation about distinctions between the diegetic and the nondiegetic (music/sound) by focusing on the relation between diegetic music and narrative space, especially "aural fidelity" (sound's faithfulness to the source) and the "film's communicativeness" (2009: 2). According to Smith, discrepancies between levels of aural fidelity (that is, when the distance from the source of the audio increases without a marked change in the level of audio volume) do not necessarily mean a shift from diegetic to nondiegetic (13); indeed, sound always remains diegetic because the apparent transformation (what was previously thought to shift between states) is actually "produced as an effect of the film narration's communicativeness" (22). In such cases, music always remains within the confines of the diegesis. While this does not fully apply to *Touki Bouki*, the idea is intriguing because it offers further support to the hypothesis that the nondiegetic Baker may be on the same narrative level as the two diegetic characters. More importantly, Smith brings up Claudia Gorbman's term "metadiegetic music," which, he explains, is the type of music that "more consistently straddles the boundary between diegetic and nondiegetic because *imagined music*, unlike source music, does not require a physical source to produce it as concrete, materialized sound" (22; my emphasis). This is an intriguing possibility when taking into consideration the close relationship between the two characters and Baker's voice and song. In fact, the song only seems to emerge when the two characters are in the frame, and it does not overlap with other characters. Because Anta and Mory also seem to be guided by the song's call for Paris, it could very well be that the song is an example of metadiegetic, imagined music. Regardless, the three entities, Anta, Mory, and Baker, coexist on one continuous narrative plane, which yields a version of the African subject that, at least when compared to Diouana's case, appears to be more autonomous and in more control of the surrounding (aural) space.

The President

Jean-Pierre Bekolo's eclectic and idiosyncratic filmmaking style has made him one of the most important African directorial voices of this century. A director for whom "cinema is expression rather than education" (Murphy and Williams 2007: 197), Bekolo constantly pushes the boundaries of representation both visually and aurally. Of course, Bekolo definitely first stretches the possibilities of storytelling visually: the penchant for rapid-editing (that is, 1990s Spike Lee music video style) in *Quartier Mozart* (1992), the blue and reddish filters alongside the overall dark color scheme in *Les Saignantes* (2005), the obsession with extended superimpositions in *Naked Reality* (2017), or the emphasis on bright color schemes and slow-motion shots in *Miraculous Weapons* (2019). However, he also successfully experiments with the plasticity of sound and with its source, most clearly in *The President* (2013).

This film, a borderline mockumentary, given its interviews and general awareness of the camera, was banned in Cameroon because it overtly criticizes African dictators (Paul Biya specifically, yet without naming him directly). So, the plot envisions the disappearance of the president of Cameroon from the public eye, but falls short of following any classic narrative trajectory. The camera does follow a fictional version of the president who anonymously moves about the city of Yaoundé and its surrounding suburbs as he tries to connect with various people in order to see who might be worthy of succeeding him. This is how the audience meets another central character, a Cameroonian rapper, played by the very real activist and prolific singer, Valsero, nicknamed the General.

During his walks and introspective moments, the "fake" president had actually been listening to rap music, which leads to the first confusion: the song is played on the soundtrack, in the nondiegetic, but it could also very well be "imagined" by the president—a metadiegetic occurrence. Moreover, given that the president meets Valsero in the following scene, the spectators may attribute this first song to Valsero himself. Yet the music the president "hears" is by a different rapper, Smarty. The latter's hit "Chapeau du chef" [The Boss's Hat], in which he announces that the "roi va mourir" [king will die], plays almost entirely on the soundtrack (or in the president's mind). Moreover, an extradiegetic dialogue begins to take shape, because the president reacts to a real song, and ends up meeting another real rapper, Valsero, whom he essentially interviews as a potential replacement.

Valsero appears in the film initially dressed in the national soccer team's yellow jersey, but later he wears a T-shirt featuring Tupac Shakur (aka 2Pac, or Makaveli), as he addresses the audience directly. A direct connection to Tupac can now be made: the song on the soundtrack that follows the meeting with the president is Valsero's "Letter to the President" (2008), inspired by a homonymous Tupac song that came out in 1999.[15] Valsero sings his hit song in its entirety, but the aural intervention feels anachronistic, because he had already met the president. "Letter to the President" rolls on the soundtrack, while the camera follows a young man, headphones in his ears, riding a motorcycle through the Yaoundé traffic. In this case, too, there is plenty of confusion and overlap between narrative levels: the music is heard by this random character within the diegesis, so it is diegetic; it also flirts with the nondiegetic, thanks to the increased volume, although if one follows Smith's argument from above, aural fidelity maintains a song or sound inside the diegetic; finally, it most certainly brings forth the extradiegetic, the real world, through the physical presence of Valsero.

Following all these intricate aural links, Bekolo places Valsero in the middle of a busy neighborhood and has him deliver a rendition of another song, "I Am Young and Strong" (2010), performed a cappella, almost in its entirety. Such a long break in the narrative is certainly unorthodox. What happens then is that the song takes over the narrative almost entirely, especially because the visual "beneath" the songs tends to be largely static— Valsero barely moves. Shot in one take and framed in a medium close-up,

---

15 From 2Pac's third posthumous album, *Still I Rise* (1999).

Valsero's performance is both intimate (because of the tight framing)[16] and public (he is outdoors). People peek over Valsero's shoulder and into the camera, and they are the ones in focus as opposed to the singer. The rapper fades visually, which means that the narrative weight of his voice becomes foregrounded and thus elevated. Bekolo also adds a reverb effect to it, a lingering multi-point echo. A reverb occurs when sound moves around and its waves reflect off walls and other indoor surfaces, before reaching the listener with a slight delay. The reverb happens to be both a hyperbolized manifestation of Kay and Noudelmann's "echoing blow" from above and a materialization of Lyotard's and Altman's observations about sound as "matter." Naturally, Valsero being outside, there should be no reverb, so adding the effect takes the song from the street and into a studio; essentially, Bekolo puts the song into the nondiegetic while maintaining the visual body of the singer in the diegetic, and at the same time we remain aware that this is indeed Valsero, a real person. To return to one of the main points, the voice splits off from the body, even though the source of the sound is quite clear, forms its own aural body, and potentially even another magical *acousmêtre*.

With this intense scene, Bekolo finds a way to collapse the gap separating the diegetic from the nondiegetic. Indeed, with this performance, Valsero travels through all possible narrative levels. To recapitulate: he is diegetic when he talks to the president, but also extradiegetic because he plays himself; then, while in the diegesis he breaks the fourth wall by talking to the audience directly, so he enters a place of in-betweenness and ambiguity (again split between the diegetic and extradiegetic); later he fully moves to the nondiegetic through the song "Letter"; and finally, he reappears in the diegetic to rap to the camera, but the episode reads like a coda and an efficient way to combine all possible versions of the character. Valsero finds himself not quite on the inside, not quite on the outside, a simultaneously de-acousmatized and re-acousmatized *acousmêtre* that retains all of its powers, no matter the direction in which it moves. In fact, it is this type of directionless control over one's voice that bestows Valsero with immense power—his voice is never *lost*. Moreover, Valsero does not require the contribution of others in order to garner full agency, as was the case of Anta, Mory, and Baker; nor does his body belong to another, as with Diouana. Instead, he relies on multiple versions of *himself*, all of which communicate with one

---

16   The framing gets increasingly tighter at the end of the song, with the camera moving in more and more, and then tilting up to follow Valsero's finger pointing at the sky in a gesture reminiscent of the raised black fist of solidarity—an increasingly meaningful and needed signifier as of summer 2020.

another. In short, through Valsero's music and voice, Bekolo might give us one of the fullest and most self-affirming versions of the African subject yet.

Conclusion

Generally speaking, the body of the neocolonial subject suffers tremendous ordeals throughout the corpus of francophone African cinema. There are physical limitations and challenges; punishments imposed by colonial regimes; punishments self-imposed by a tormented psyche; traumas that haunt the individual body, as well as the national body; multidirectional acts of violence. In this vitriolic context, the body is often visually reduced to a shadow, like the one projected by Diouana in the empty French living room. The neocolonial subjects may suffer aurally, too (Diouana again, but also the wagoner from *Borom Sarret*, Mory's voice-over, or Sissako's voice-over in *Life on Earth*). The disembodied voices of these characters escape their bodies and, in the cases when the two entities (aural body and visual body) cannot be stitched back up together, the voices might act as a hollowing tool rather than one of self-affirmation. If we take Diouana's diegetic case and Josephine Baker's extradiegetic case, the bodies of these women might be hollowed out on purpose by their own voices, which fight off the symptoms of colonial and neocolonial injustices operated on those physical bodies. To put this differently, the battle over the physical body was already lost, so voices offer a more palatable alternative—a chance at aural "fullness." It turns out that the power of the voice, whether attached to a body or not, may also be liberating and can counteract the neocolonial effect of emptiness. The aural bodies that extend out of the (broken-down) visual bodies could give a sense of fullness to the African subject, making her or him whole *elsewhere*, in a space where the diegetic, the nondiegetic, and the extradiegetic collide and overlap. The process of rebuilding the African (neocolonial) body begins well outside of itself, with the aural body, and the hope is that one can move backward and smooth out the old (colonial) wounds and fragmentation of the physical, visual body. It is the skin of those aural bodies that turns out to be the protective veil required to navigate safely through the still dangerous neocolonial times. It is this skin that might establish the new limits of a *post*-neocolonial subjectivity.

Works Cited

Adesokan, Akin. *Postcolonial Artists and Global Aesthetics*. Indiana University Press, 2011.

Altman, Rick. "The Material Heterogeneity of Recorded Sound." *Sound Theory. Sound Practice*, edited by Rick Altman, Routledge, 1992, pp. 15–34.

———. *Silent Film Sound*. Columbia University Press, 2004.

Barker, Jennifer. *The Tactile Eye: Touch and the Cinematic Experience*. University of California Press, 2009.

Barlet. Olivier. *African Cinemas: Decolonizing the Gaze*. Zed Books, 1996.

Cheng, Anne Anlin. *Second Skin: Josephine Baker & The Modern Surface*. Oxford University Press, 2011.

Chion, Michel. *Audio-Vision: Sound on Screen*. Translated by Claudia Gorbman, Columbia University Press, 1994.

———. *The Voice in Cinema*. Translated by Claudia Gorbman, Columbia University Press, 1999.

———. *Film, A Sound Art*. Translated by Claudia Gorbman, Columbia University Press, 2009.

Deger, Jennifer. *Shimmering Screens: Making Media in an Aboriginal Community*. University of Minnesota Press, 2006.

Derrida, Jacques. *On Touching—Jean-Luc Nancy*. Translated by Christine Irizarry, Stanford University Press, 2005.

Diawara, Manthia. *African Cinema: Politics and Culture*. Indiana University Press, 1992.

———. "Popular Culture and Oral Traditions in African Film." *African Experiences of Cinema*, edited by Imruh Bakary and Mbye Cham, British Film Institute, 1996, pp. 209–219.

Dima, Vlad. "Aural Narrative Planes in Djibril Diop Mambety's Films." *Journal for Film and Video*, vol. 64, no. 3, 2012, pp. 38–52.

———. *Sonic Space in Djibril Diop Mambety's Films*. Indiana University Press, 2017.

———. *The Beautiful Skin: Football, Fantasy, and Cinematic Bodies in Africa*. Michigan State University Press, 2020.

Dolar, Mladen. *A Voice and Nothing More*. MIT Press, 2006.

Fanon, Franz. *Black Skin, White Masks*. Translated by Richard Philcox, Grove Press, 2008.

Gabriel, Teshome. "Towards a Critical Theory of Third World Films." *Questions of Third Cinema*, edited by Jim Pines and Paul Willemen, British Film Institute, 1989, pp. 30–52.

Harrow, Kenneth. *Postcolonial African Cinema: From Political Engagement to Postmodernism*. Indiana University Press, 2007.

Herzog, Amy. *Dreams of Difference, Songs of the Same: The Musical Moment in Film*. University of Minnesota Press, 2010.

Kay, Sarah, and François Noudelmann. "Introduction: Soundings and Soundscapes." *Soundings and Soundscapes*, edited by Sarah Kay and François Noudelmann, special issue of *Paragraph*, vol. 41, no. 1, 2018, pp. 1–9.

Lyotard, Jean-François. *The Inhuman: Reflections on Time*. Translated by Geoffrey Bennington and Rachel Bowlby, Stanford University Press, 1988.

Mbembe, Achille. *Critique of Black Reason*. Translated by Laurent Dubois, Duke University Press, 2017.

Murphy, David and Patrick Williams. *Postcolonial African Cinema: Ten Directors.* Manchester University Press, 2007.

Nancy, Jean-Luc. *Corpus*. Translated by Richard A. Rand, Fordham University Press, 2008.

Rony, Fatimah Tobing. *The Third Eye: Race, Cinema, and Ethnographic Cinema.* Duke University Press, 1996.

Shohat, Ella. *Taboo Memories, Diasporic Voices*. Duke University Press, 2006.

Smith, Jeff. "Bridging the Gap: Reconsidering the Border between Diegetic and Nondiegetic Music." *Music and the Moving Image*, vol. 2, no. 1, 2009, pp. 1–25.

Stilwell, J. Robynn. "The Fantastical Gap between Diegetic and Nondiegetic." *Beyond the Soundtrack*, edited by Daniel Goldmark, Lawrence Kramer, and Richard Leppert, University of California Press, 2007, pp. 184–202.

Ukadike, Frank. *Black African Cinema*. University of California Press, 1994.

Žižek, Slavoj. *"I Hear You with My Eyes*: or, The Invincible Master." *Gaze and Voice as Love Objects*, edited by Renata Salecl and Slavoj Žižek, Duke University Press, 1996, pp. 90–127.

CHAPTER FIVE

Timbuktu, Sonic Map of Desert Futures

Jill Jarvis

Timbuktu makes tangible the ways life is lived in the wake and under the pressure of violent change [...] There is a young woman who has been caught and found guilty of the crime of making music together in a room with three friends, another woman and two men. She is sentenced to forty lashes. In the midst of the vicious public beating her weeping breaks into song. (From *Zong* [which again means "song"] to Philip's *Zong!) This is, again, the time of the oral ruttier, and those songs help us find our way; they are our internalized maps in the long time of our displacement.* (Sharpe 2016: 127)

Tuning in to *Timbuktu*

Abderrahmane Sissako's film *Timbuktu* (2014) opens with an almost-silent tracking shot of a dorcas gazelle bounding swiftly across an ocher desertscape.

I would not have come to hear what I do in this film without shared listening and conversation with students, colleagues, and friends. I am especially grateful to Shanna-Dolores Jean-Baptiste, Marie Constance Hountondji, Cajetan Iheka, Sophia Nahli Allison, Marlika Marceau, and Marina Miller. I am also grateful to Abderrahmane Sissako, whom I accompanied as French-English interpreter during his visit to Princeton, New Jersey in April 2015, and from whom I learned a great deal in a short time about attentive listening.

The image lasts a few mesmerizing seconds before the faint rhythm of the gazelle's hoofsteps on sandy earth is shattered by the sharp report of AK-47 fire, a sound so abrupt that it triggers an acoustic startle reflex. Although I have watched the film a dozen times, I catch my breath; my body inadvertently flinches, heartbeat quickens; even my dog starts and whines. The frame cuts to a shot of a black flag with white Arabic text whipping from the roof of a speeding Toyota pickup filled with shouting men who are hunting the gazelle for sport. Their arrival on screen is an acoustic violation, a disturbing sonic invasion—the grind of a truck motor, the men's raucous voices, those relentless gunshots. The screen fades to black and the toponym TIMBUKTU appears in all-caps, white letters spare as picked bone. This stark image is accompanied by the needling staccato of machine guns. When the title shot fades, we see a row of carved wooden masks and sculptures being pelted by gunfire, wince at the sound of splintering wood. This opening sequence is alarming to watch, but it is physically painful to *hear*.

Originally titled *Timbuktu, le chagrin des oiseaux* [Timbuktu, the Sorrow of the Birds], Sissako's film is set in that legendary desert city at the southern shore ("sahel" in Arabic) of the Sahara in northern Mali at the moment that Timbuktu had been taken over by the militant Islamist group Ansar ad-Din in early 2012.[1] Although Sissako has described his film as a cinematic portrait of "an occupation from the inside," *Timbuktu* is structured as a dramatic tragedy that has only tangentially to do with Islamists.[2] The most resonant audiovisual sequences of *Timbuktu* marginalize the jihadis in ways that subtly dislodge reductive but enduring narrative frameworks for depicting violence and suffering in the African Sahara and Sahel.

---

[1] Ansar Dine (Ansar ad-Din) is a militant islamist group that was headed by a leader of the Tuareg separatist movement named Iyad Ah Ghaly; its members were from Mali, Algeria, and Nigeria. In March 2012, ten days after a coup d'état overthrew Malian president Amadou Toumani Touré, Ansar Dine and the National Movement for the Liberation of Azawad (MNLA) took over the northern cities of Kidal, Gao, and Timbuktu. In May 2012, Ansar Dine and the MNLA made a pact to form the Islamic Republic of Azawad. In 2013, the US Department of State designated Ansar Dine a Foreign Terrorist Organization, and in 2017 the group merged with Al-Qaeda in the Islamic Maghreb (AQMI). For a detailed overview of the 2012–2013 crisis in Mali, see Thurston and Lebovich 2013.

[2] Sissako has described the process of creating the film in multiple interviews, and uses this phrase in the following NPR interview: npr.org/sections/goats andsoda/2015/02/22/387554468/director-of-oscar-nommed-timbuktu-found-a-star-in-a-refugee-camp. See also rfi.fr/fr/culture/20140516-abderrahmane-sissako-timbuktu-revolte-entretien.

Sissako's cinematic style is so visually arresting that a spectator may not at first notice the film's acoustical complexity, yet sound is integral to my analysis of this film. I am undertaking here an experiment in close listening to cinema, an artform that is still approached in ontologically visual terms; as Michel Chion points out, we "see" and "watch" films rather than hear them.[3] Tuning in closely to the subtle soundings of *Timbuktu* compels us to interpret the film differently, and to understand Timbuktu's place in the world in ways that inherited political cartographies and disciplinary geographies obscure.

Film critics and scholars have marveled at the visual virtuosity of *Timbuktu*—its carefully framed, deep-focus long shots and stunning montages—and they have overlooked the significant ways that this film's sonic qualities interact with and qualitatively transform its images.[4] In a review entitled "Frames of Resistance," Manthia Diawara defends *Timbuktu* as a work of "visual poetry" whose "unabashedly 'imperfect' images we take with us and keep reworking in our mind, like poems" (2015: 6). He argues that Sissako's visual framing puts pressure on reductive tropes and silently enlists viewers as allies with the residents of Timbuktu: "Sissako's cinema binds us to them in an unspoken language," writes Diawara. "As we tremble with the images, faces, and landscapes of Timbuktu, we enter a new imaginary; we begin to understand these Malians' predicament under the jihadists' regime of senseless violence, and we are reborn as new spectators" (6).

---

[3] These points are from Michel Chion's *Audio-Vision: Sound on Screen*: "Cinema is routinely approached as a visual art; we typically say we 'watch' or 'see' a movie or series or TV program, ignoring the modification introduced by synchronized sound" (1994: xxi). And further: "Ontologically speaking, and historically too, film sound is considered as a 'plus' or add-on. The thinking goes like this: the cinema was endowed with synchronous sound after thirty years of getting along perfectly well without it, and with a soundtrack that has become even richer in recent years, crackling and pulsating—yet even now the cinema has kept its ontologically *visual* definition intact" (138).

[4] Soon after its release in 2014, *Timbuktu* became the most-viewed African film in cinematic history. US critics were nearly unanimous in their focus on the film's visuals: "But the glory of *Timbuktu* lies in its devotion to local knowledge, in the way it allows its gaze to wander away from violence toward images of beauty and grace" (A. O. Scott, *New York Times*); "visually dazzling and morally devastating" (Chris Nashawaty, *Entertainment Weekly*); "a transcendent political poem as intellectually rigorous as it is beautiful" (Tirdad Derakhshani, in *The Philadelphia Inquirer*); "heartbreaking, visually spectacular" (Andrew O'Hehir, *Salon*); "a work of almost breathtaking visual beauty, but it manages to ravish the heart while dazzling the eye simultaneously" (Glenn Kenny, RogerEbert.com); "abounds in extraordinary images" (Joe Morgenstern, *The Wall Street Journal*).

Yet this film's sonic qualities much more literally cause spectators to tremble. As Tina Campt points out in *Listening to Images*, sound is a "profoundly haptic form of sensory contact" (2017: 6), an "inherently embodied modality constituted by vibration and contact" (7). She tells us that sound "can be listened to, and, in equally powerful ways [...] can be felt; it both touches and moves people" (6). Indeed, the invasive ruckus with which *Timbuktu* opens produces an acoustic experience of threat that—by triggering a startle response, quickening the pulse—connects the listener to the hunted gazelle darting across the screen in an inadvertent, haptic way. These sounds literally touch and move us, eliciting a response more involved and immediate than spectating: "Listening requires an attunement to sonic frequencies of affect and impact," writes Campt. "It is an ensemble of seeing, feeling, being affected, contacted, and moved beyond the distance of sight and observer" (41–42).

Campt also recalls the scientific definition of acoustics and sonic perception as frequency, pointing out that *most* periodic frequencies are imperceptible to the average human ear, so that all sound "consists of more than what we hear" (7). Chion points out that aural perception operates more swiftly than does sight. *Timbuktu*, haunted by a lost subtitle that has not followed the feature film into its wide transnational circulation (The Sorrow of the Birds), attunes us to lower-frequency soundings that strike our senses almost without our knowing, literally before we register what we are seeing. *Timbuktu* is a kind of sonic relief map of layered frequencies that exert surreptitious power to touch, move, and reorient our senses. If anything, the jihadis' ruckus is something to tune out, not pay attention to, in the slow process of picking up on sounds that may be less perceptible, but not less affecting.

Visually, this film is almost too clear. Its relatively straightforward plot contrasts with the diffuse narrative style of Sissako's previous films *Bamako* (2006) and *Heremakono* (2003). In *Timbuktu*, a Tuareg family lives alone and tends their herd of eight cows in an encampment on the outskirts of town at a time when most other Tuareg have left. Meanwhile, a band of men from Algeria, Libya, Nigeria, and Mali have invaded with a take on Islamic law that they are trying to force on everyone in Timbuktu. Their bombastic voices amplified by megaphones drone new rules in French, Bambara, and Songhay through the town's red-dusted streets; their thumping boots and irreverent speech profane the sanctity of the Djinguereber Mosque. Much of the film is composed of montages featuring the women, men, and children of Timbuktu as they ignore, elude, and argue with the strangers who have laid siege to their city.

Tragedy unfolds when a fisherman named Amadou (played by Omar Haidara) spears and kills a cow named GPS who belongs to Kidane (Ibrahim Ahmed, also known as Pino), the guitar-playing Tuareg protagonist, after

GPS wanders out of young shepherd Issan's care and into Amadou's fishing nets in the Niger river. Kidane shoots Amadou when he confronts him about killing GPS. In keeping with the jihadi leader's ruling, Kidane is imprisoned, tried, and sentenced to death for murdering Amadou. Satima—Kidane's wife, played by Toulou Kiki—is shot and killed along with Kidane when she runs to embrace him at the moment just before his public execution near the prison. The film ends with shots of their orphaned child Toya (Layla Walet Mohamed) and her friend, the young shepherd Issan (Mehdi Ag Mohamed), as they run through the desert, hunted—visually tracked like the gazelle in the opening scene—by the jihadis with their guns.

To focus on visual composition makes it difficult to see beyond this bleak horizon. Most commentators stake positions in debates abouts the merits and shortcomings of Sissako's depiction of terrorists.[5] He has been both celebrated and excoriated, not least for reinforcing rather than challenging the preconceptions of predominantly European and American audiences eager to see "real" Muslim Africans defending civilization against Islamist invaders.[6] Images of intransigent Malians standing up to cruel if hapless jihadis resonated for spectators in the global north at a time in which the Sahara-Sahel had been "threat-mapped" as the most dangerous region in the world and the second front of a US-led "global war on terror."[7] Between December 2012 and July 2014—when filming was underway, mostly in Mauritania because Timbuktu was unsafe for Sissako's crew—the French military was engaged in "Operation Serval" to oust Islamist militants from northern Mali. Screened in the immediate aftermath of the January 2015 attacks on the Charlie Hebdo offices in Paris, *Timbuktu* ignited controversy and protests in France, Niger, and Mauritania. Diawara's and Sharpe's sensitive readings of the film defend its æsthetic subversions against antagonistic readings, yet they do not challenge a wider frame that renders the Sahara-Sahel above all a bleak and silent backdrop for violence, death, and tragedy.

---

[5] See, for a list of these, the works cited by Pasley 2016, and the round-table discussion among Adile Cazenave, Phyllis Taoua, Alioune Sow, and Kenneth Harrow. For a summary of the debate, see newyorker.com/culture/cultural-comment/a-movie-that-dares-to-humanize-jihadists-timbuktu.

[6] On this, see "*Timbuktu*—the Controversy. A Conversation among Adile Cazenave, Phyllis Taoua, Alioune Sow, and Kenneth Harrow" (2016) and Taoua 2015. Nicolas Beau attacked the film and accused Sissako of complicity with the Mauritanian political regime in "Abderrahmane Sissako, une imposture mauritanienne" (2015).

[7] On the long history of "threat-mapping" the Sahara-Sahel, see especially Andersson 2019 and MacDougall 2007.

By calling the film a "sonic map" I bring to the fore not visual representation but audio-visual performance and perception. Listening to the intricate soundings of this film attunes the ear in ways that transform sight; letting sound guide perception entails becoming aware of how else this film makes contact, touches, and moves. *Timbuktu's* sonic mapping is an alternative form of place-making that surfaces recessed networks of interdependency and relation.

Research on cinematic audiovisuality is a theoretically sophisticated field that has not reckoned with postcolonial and decolonial approaches.[8] In African film studies, æsthetic concerns have often been subordinated to political and pedagogical imperatives.[9] Listening closely to *Timbuktu* is a way to investigate the decolonial potential of sound studies. Here, I draw inspiration from Ian Baucom, who points out—in an essay called "Frantz Fanon's Radio: Solidarity, Diaspora, and the Tactics of Listening"—that because white supremacy and imperialism have worked by "policing, regulating, and interpreting the visible," we stand to learn much from what Fanon has to teach about the audible (2001: 16). The same may be said of Sissako. In the next section, I outline an interpretive practice of cinematic listening that culls insight from Campt, Sharpe, Baucom ("tactical listening"), Michel Chion ("transsensory perception"), and Stephen Feld ("acoustemology"). This guides me to parallel "close listenings" that amplify ecological and diasporic frequencies moving largely beneath the critical radar in responses to *Timbuktu*, and that point toward the infinitely *"more"* that eludes perception altogether.

Low-Frequency Listening Tactics

Close listening to *Timbuktu* yields some insights rather swiftly. At first, the place sounds like an empty desert disturbed by Ansar ad-Din's deranged, hyperactive noise, but upon listening with any attention we hear that the jihadis infringe on an extremely abundant acoustical environment. In fact, the only instance of actual silence in *Timbuktu* arrives at its end, a contrast that makes a listener keenly aware of how replete the entire soundtrack had been until this point.

---

[8] For an overview, see Richardson and Gorbman 2013. They cite in particular Claudia Gorbman's *Unheard Melodies* (1987), Michel Chion's *Audio-Vision* (1990), Caryl Flinn's *Strains of Utopia* (1992), and Anahid Kassabian's *Hearing Film* (2001).

[9] This is Kenneth Harrow's opening point in *Trash: African Cinema from Below* (2013: ix). Akin Adesokan makes a related point in the preface to *Postcolonial Artists and Global Aesthetics* (2011: xii).

In the final minute, the town water carrier who had brought Satima to Kidane on his motorcycle flees the execution site chased by that Toyota filled with yelling jihadis. Camels scream; birds shriek and scatter across the screen. Again, we see a tracking shot of the dorcas gazelle, dashing like a spirit across the sand, and hear Toya's ragged breathing. Then we see Toya stumbling alone across a spare landscape and Issan running in another direction. The water carrier disappears behind a dune trailed by a swarm of jihadis. The film's closing frame is a close-up of Toya's face as she runs pursued by the AK-47-toting hunters who have just murdered her mother, father, and the water carrier. We hear her footsteps, desperate breath, and fading voice as she sings to herself. The screen goes black.

No final gunshots ring out, only three full beats of dead silence, like a glimpse of the future from Toya's point of view. The impact is gutting. This sense of suspension is the product of contrast with what preceded (footsteps, heartbeat, breath, Toya singing) and what follows.[10] Dead silence gives way to the resonant thrum of a kora, a stringed lute made from a large gourd stretched with goatskin. This is an instrumental reprise of "Tombouctou fasso," the song performed earlier in the film by Fatoumata Diawara, a singer-songwriter who composed these Bambara lyrics and sings them in the role described by Sharpe that I have cited as epigraph. As credits roll across black screen, we listen to a bansuri flute echo of the song that got Diawara's character whipped. What many listeners will not know, but might feel, is that the lyrics of "Tombouctou fasso" paint a vision of a future Timbuktu, flourishing.

This echo is an entreaty to listen. Sissako's previous film, *Bamako*, ends with a formally similar sequence. That closing shot—it follows a suicide—combines radio silence and a black screen before credits and music roll, except that here a line from Aimé Césaire's "Les pur-sang" is typed out in white text: "L'oreille collée au sol, j'entendis passer demain" [Ear pressed to the earth, I heard tomorrow pass]. Much like what Ian Baucom detects in Frantz Fanon's "radiophonic" essay "La voix de l'Algérie," I take this fleeting citation of Césaire to signal the "compositional importance of the acoustic" across Sissako's works, and to orient our own ears to the future (Baucom 2001: 16). What Baucom writes of Fanon can be reprised here of Sissako: "It is as if he is not offering us a text but a radio receiver, as if he is not writing but scanning the bands of an empire's broadcast stations, gathering

---

[10] Chion elaborates: "The impression of silence in a film scene does not simply arise from an absence of noise. It results from a whole context, and from preparation—the simplest of which involves preceding it with a noise-filled sequence. In other words, silence is never a neutral void: it is the negative of sound we've heard beforehand or imagined, the product of a contrast" (1994: 56).

these scattered voices for our belated acts of listening, tuning our ears to the pandemonium of the incommensurate, the aural meeting places of the diaspora" (17). As Baucom notes, Fanon remixes Césaire as an act of both tactical listening and entreaty: "'And now how my voice vibrates,' Fanon remarks as he utters some lines from Césaire's *Cahier*. 'At my ear there is a song,' he subsequently informs us as his way of introducing his rendering of a lyric (126). 'Listen,' he reiterates (127). 'Listen' (130). 'Listen' (135)" (17).[11]

Tactically, it helps to get closer to the ground—so to speak—if we ignore *Timbuktu*'s visuals and even close our eyes to listen, listen, listen. Experienced acoustically, the film is a "relief map" of languages,[12] music, and other soundings in which myriad itineraries coalesce and converge. *Timbuktu* does not just plug in Dolby multitrack sound to accent and accompany its images, but operates as a kind of audiovisual sensorium that Michel Chion calls "transsensory"—that is, it "generates rhythmic, dynamic, temporal, tactile, and kinetic sensations that make use of auditory *and* visual channels" (1994: 145).

Without the visual control of subtitles, for instance, we detect a heteroglot range of different languages, accents, and registers spoken by characters—a rhythmic, dynamic, kinetic experience, even if we cannot decode linguistic sense. To a trained ear, these variations also create spatial awareness, almost like sonar echolocation. That is, the itineraries, histories, social positions, educations, and emotions of speakers can be picked up acoustically. The soundtrack is an aural cartography composed of Tamasheq, Songhay, Bambara, Maghrebi Arabic (Algerian, Tunisian, Libyan inflections), refined Classical Arabic, French (in Malian, Algerian, Tunisian, Haïtian variations), English (Nigerian), and Haitian Kreyol. Like most characters in the film and most audiences watching it, Sissako himself does not speak all of these languages, nor did he compose the film's dialogue himself; he and co-writer Kessen Tall collaborated with the performers so that they could generate

---

[11] Baucom's description of "tactical listening": "To listen thus is, then, not to commit to worshipfulness or passivity but to listen actively, critically, tactically—to filter the heart through the complex system of relays that wire the hearer's particularity, and then, like Fanon's listeners, to transmit what's been heard, to scatter the sounds that have gathered a community of listeners in anticipation of a subsequent moment of gathering" (2001: 37).

[12] This phrase is from Gayatri Spivak's description of Sissako's film *Bamako*, in "Rethinking Comparativism." She writes: "The new comparativism can read this film as a filmic discourse on epistemic discontinuity in the welding of place. We notice how much of the staging is in terms of a relief map of languages, colonial and local" (2009: 618).

their own interactions.[13] Kidane recognizes an Arabic-Tamasheq translator in the prison whose face is covered and says he is from Libya; why are you with these men, Kidane asks him in Tamasheq; he suspects the man to be from Léré, near Timbuktu. A gentle imam speaks in exquisitely refined Arabic, belying his own deep erudition and Timbuktu's long history as cultural beacon and textual archive.[14]

Linguistic multiphony in the film coexists with a score designed by the Tunisian composer Amine Bouhafa to bring together different musical histories, instrumental voices, timbres, and tones.[15] This sound mixing has the effect of rendering the human voice one of many instruments, and of heightening listener sensitivity to the distinctive voices of musical instruments that share a sonic plane with speech. Recorded in Tunisia, Turkey, France, and Hungary, the score features traditional West African instruments such as the kora and n'goni, as well as the duduk (a reeded woodwind instrument from the Caucasus), guitar, flute bansuri (a bamboo flute from the Indian subcontinent), piano, clarinet, and oud, along with the wind, string, brass, and percussion instruments of the Prague Philharmonic Orchestra.

---

[13] Sissako describes this process in published interviews, emphasizing the role of silence and what is left unspoken in dialogue: "Il ne faut pas tout montrer. Le silence, aussi, est important. Et « ne pas dire » est aussi un récit. Pour celui qui écoute, ou pour celui qui regarde" [You shouldn't show everything. Silence, too, is important. And "to not say" is also to narrate. For the listener, or the viewer] (avantscenecinema.com/entretien-abderrahmane-sissako-timbuktu).

[14] The status of Timbuktu as vast manuscript archive is a silent presence in the film. The manuscripts themselves, hundreds of thousands of them dating back to about the thirteenth century, filled interior spaces throughout the city, kept by families for generations; these manuscripts were being smuggled out of Timbuktu to Bamako by an organization called SAVAMA at the same time that Sissako was filming in Oualata, for related reasons. On the significance of the manuscripts, see the chapter "Timbuktu Studies" in *Beyond Timbuktu* (2016), by Ousmane Oumar Kane; see also the collection edited by Shamil Jeppie and Souleymane Bachir Diagne, *The Meanings of Timbuktu* (2008), in particular their opening chapters to the volume. On SAVAMA's ongoing preservation work in Bamako safe houses, see savamadci.net.

[15] Amine Bouhafa describes the composition process in a filmed interview with Benoit Basirico at Cannes in May 2014 (youtube.com/watch?v=-onhTj1_5co&feature=youtu.be). Bouhafa's work with Sissako was done in this spirit: "L'emploi de la musique doit être avec une certaine distance par rapport aux images ... on n'est pas dans une musique qui va accompagner l'action" [The use of music must be at a remove from the images ... we're not dealing with a music that accompanies the action].

Several of *Timbuktu*'s actors are practicing musicians, which makes the film itself a space of collaborative sounding and listening. Tuareg guitarist Ibrahim Ahmed (Pino), in the leading role of Kidane, sings and plays in secret with his family. *Timbuktu* also showcases performances by the Niger-born Tuareg musician Toulou Kiki, in the role of Satima, married to Kidane, whose original composition "Tiyota" is part of the score; by the Haitian choreographer Kettly Noël, whose performance as Zabou I discuss in the final section of this essay; and Fatoumata Diawara, whose "Tombouctou fasso" and sung lamentation are keynotes of the film's pathos.

Finally, a close listener will become aware that this heterogeneous soundtrack is often devoid of either music or speaking, but never silent. Even the quietest scenes and moments teem with lower-frequency sounds. Most of these sounds are nonhuman, marking out what Chion calls the "superfield," a sonic space created by ambient rumblings and rustlings that surround a film's visual field. The different spaces of Timbuktu are replete with diegetic sounds neither linguistic nor musical that produce highly specific senses of place. Different social spaces and relations register sonically: the Tuareg tent whistles with desert wind; the clink of Satima's bracelets, the sounds of tea-making and carefully collected water; the strum and pluck of Kidane's guitar and vocal harmonies within the family; the lowing of eight cows. Within Timbuktu resound calls to prayer from the mosques, crackling motorbikes, clucking chickens, crowing roosters, cooing doves, bleating goats, crying human babies—and an ever-present sonic substratum of hummings, chirpings, and tweetings of birds and insects. Only in the prison do these vivid sounds go silent, replaced by footsteps on cement and iron doors closing.

Timbuktu's relief map gradually refines our attunement to this sonic substratum composed of faint rustlings not obviously significant or even audible to untrained human ears. Like the film's linguistic and musical registers, its nonhuman sounds are variegated and distinctive; to appreciate this, simply consider that there are more than three hundred avian species found in Timbuktu. To any ear capable of distinguishing grebes, herons, egrets, bitterns, ibises, storks, avocets, cranes, doves, nightjars, spoonbills, plovers, and swifts from roosters and doves, this substratum of sound might be a qualitatively different kind of map.[16]

During decades spent recording birdsongs composed by the Bosavi people in the rainforests of Papua New Guinea, the musicologist Stephen Feld observed that it was "only a matter of seconds before a Bosavi kid [could]

---

[16] For an updated list of all 375 bird species found in Timbuktu, see avibase. bsc-eoc.org/checklist.jsp?region=MLtb&list=howardmoore.

identify a bird by sound, describe its location in the forest density, and tell a good bit more about the location of its food, nest, and partners. How does such knowledge happen?" (2015: 18). Such knowledge, Feld learned, was cultivated over generations through a shared repertoire of songs that were "vocalized mappings" of the forest told from a bird perspective, containing thousands of Bosavi lexical descriptions, toponyms, proper names of flora, fauna, topography, and evocations of light, wind, motion, and sound. These "poetic cartographies" reflected long histories of listening to birds as co-inhabitants of a shared space, and understanding birds as beings whose lives and afterlives intertwine with those of human beings (18–19).[17]

"Acoustemology," the word coined by Feld to help him think more precisely about this quality of knowledge, fuses "acoustics" with "epistemology" to ask "what is knowable, and how it becomes known, through sounding and listening" (2016: 93).[18] Listening acoustemologically to *Timbuktu*'s low-frequency sounds compels us to consider "what's to be learned from taking seriously the sonic relationality of human voices to the sounding otherness of presences and subjectivities like water, birds, and insects" in this way (Feld 2015: 19). Confronted by the film's title screen (TIMBUKTU) and the rat-a-tat of AK-47 fire, a twenty-first-century spectator in Europe or the US will not truly be surprised or moved, because this is what we implicitly expect. Whether or not we are aware of Timbuktu's symbolic and strategic positioning in the history of Africa's colonization, we come to the film with our senses trained by a perceptual dynamic centuries in the making that has rendered Timbuktu an ambivalent symbol of alluring emptiness, existential

---

[17] Feld explains his desire to "decolonize" the disciplinary paradigms of ethnomusicology by thinking in acoustemological terms in "Acoustemology." The songs he spent decades listening to in Papua New Guinea, he writes, "constitute a poetic cartography of the forest, mapping the layered biographies of social relationships within and across communities. The chronotopic historicity of sounding these songs is thus inseparable from the environmental consciousness they have produced. This is why, as knowledge productions—as listening to histories of listening—Bosavi songs are an archive of ecological and æsthetic co-evolution" (2015: 93).

[18] In a later essay, Feld undertakes a collaborative experiment in playback listening/recording with Ghanaian musician Nii Otoo Annan, moving this acoustemological experience much further, to think through how Annan's musical improvisations respond to the soundings of toads and crickets. "Take a moment," writes Feld, "to fantasize what the *Goldberg Variations* might sound like had Bach been born in Ghana, gone to sleep each night listening to *Bufo* toads, and devoted himself to the mastery of polyrhythms with the same dedication he showed to harmony" (2016: 98).

danger, and environmental desolation.[19] On its lower frequencies, *Timbuktu* activates a sonic subversion of this framework, attuning us to the sounding presence of intricate, interspecies ecosystems and diasporic networks that are fully vivid even though they move beyond the domain of sight.

The Quiet Sorrow of Birds

It might seem strange that a film about jihadi occupation so lingers over the death of a cow. Issan, the orphaned child who looks after the eight cows belonging to Kidane, guides them by vocal clicking and shushing as they descend to the Niger's bank to drink. Amadou, tending his fishing nets on the other side of the river, shouts to keep the cows away from his nets, his voice sharp over the sound of rushing water. Percussive music—a timpani, then a swelling orchestra—begins to pulse in time with Issan's escalating alarm as he cries out the errant cow's name (GPS! GPS!) as she wades into the nets. Amadou watches intently; picks up a spear. A woman working beside him screams his name—Amadou!—too late to stop his hurling the weapon. Issan wails; we hear but do not see the visceral cut of the spear perforate the body of GPS.

GPS moans, and the music stops abruptly so that the only sounds are hers, the splash of water as she falls, and the faint whisper of birds. GPS drops to her knees and then lies out on the riverbank, her body half-submerged. The mournful sound of a reed wind instrument plays quietly, a duet with the sound of GPS's own labored breath and the soft whirring of insects. Her death agony lasts nearly a full minute, opening a break in the film's temporal pace. We see a bright trickle of blood from her nostril, hear the insects and birds, watch a long-lashed eye close. The hum of insects and birds sonically enfolds the last soft exhalation of GPS.

This meditative slowing compels a spectator to acknowledge animal agony and singularity with attention usually reserved for human death. The scene's sonic staging also folds the higher-frequency jihadi narrative into a subdued and subtle field of relations that involve much more than only human lives.

After the last audible breath of GPS, the scene cuts. Steady rush of river water gives way to wind skimming over sand, and the faint voice of Issan who sobs as he runs toward the tent where Toya can hear his approach before she sees him. She awakens Kidane; Issan falls to his knees; Kidane listens to Issan's story. Kidane stands up, returns to the tent; Satima opens her eyes to

---

[19] Over centuries, the Sahara/Sahel in general and Timbuktu in particular have been mapped as spaces of existential threat to Western imperialist civilization in order to legitimize and facilitate colonial expansion and intervention. See Blais 2014; MacDougall 2007; Andersson 2019.

watch him unwrap a pistol. They speak for the last time; both of them will die as a result of the actions now in motion. Satima tells Kidane to go unarmed; they have a child. Kidane wraps the gun, stows it in his clothing. Satima watches him walk away toward the river, already obscured by the fabric of the tent as he disappears from her sight.

Later, Kidane wades across the Niger to confront Amadou. The only sound is the gurgle and rush of water and their quarreling voices. This confrontation is framed from a distance, the bodies of the two men silhouettes against evening sunlight and gleaming water. They grunt, struggle, and splash, bodies entangled. There is a visual glitch caused by a missing frame—the only instance of this in the film—directly before the sound of a single, sudden gunshot. Both bodies lie still in the water as a cacophony of startled birds trill and thrum. At a lower pitch, we hear a soft, steady whirring of insects and the liquid rush of the river. Kidane stands abruptly, stumbling away from Amadou's body.

The scene opens wide to an extraordinary long shot framed like a landscape painting. Kidane's silhouette is tiny against the broad span of the river, the trees on its banks, the glowing dusk. This shot lasts a full minute and a half as Kidane wades slowly across the river away from Amadou, who struggles to rise, falls, and is still. No music plays at first, yet the visual field pulsates with an aviary and insect superfield—crickets, frogs, myriad birds, the sound of water. Amadou's death is thus acoustically linked to that of GPS, like two spirits enfolded into a shared sonic hive. The equivalence does not reduce the value of Amadou's life to "mere" animal but connects human with nonhuman lives in a relational acoustic field.

An invisible network of ecological interdependencies reverberates in this sequence, undoing any mistaken sense of Timbuktu as intrinsically empty, disconnected, or desolate. Kidane and Satima have eight cows, a diminished herd on which they depend; Issan, an orphan, relies on their care. We hear his distress and grief when the cow named by and beloved to his friend Toya wanders out of his protection and into Amadou's fishing nets. Amadou's swift defense conveys alarm and precarity, as does Kidane's unwavering and reckless desire for confrontation. The stakes are high: the cherished cow of a Tuareg family needs water to drink yet threatens the nets on which Amadou's family relies for sustenance, and at the conclusion of this disturbance, GPS, Amadou, Kidane, Satima, and likely Issan and Toya will die. As with Amadou and GPS, there is a direct audiovisual thread connecting *Timbuktu*'s first scene—the gazelle—and its last, as the two children run hunted in the desert. Each one of these deaths is tragic, but not one of them senseless. We can clearly hear that they take place not in a desolate void but rather within an inhabited, vital, and delicate ecosystem to which Timbuktu's occupiers also belong.

Unidentified Flying Objects

The desert cities of Timbuktu and Gao are known by many Malians to be haunted with spirits that afflict women especially ("la folle de Gao" is a wry aphorism), so the character Zabou is not exactly an aberration, nor is she Sissako's creation. Zabou features in a series of scenes spliced into the sequence that connects the deaths of GPS and Amadou. She appears at once out of place and completely at ease, otherworldly yet assured; her hair stands untamed, she wears a long blue rag cape that trails several feet behind her like fantastical plumage and carries a rooster in the crook of her arm. Her voice is strong and strange.

Performed by the itinerant Haitian choreographer and dancer Kettly Noël—who lives in Bamako, where she runs the Donko Senko dance studio—this character is inspired by a real person, Zeynaba Arounhenna Maïga, a woman from a small town in northern Mali who worked as a burlesque dancer (stage name "Miss Zabou") at Le Crazy Horse cabaret in Paris in the 1970s and then returned to live in Gao.[20] Listening closely to Noël's performance as Zabou surfaces considerably more than meets the eye. It generates an acoustical and kinetic experience in which multiple itineraries can be felt to collide and commingle, like a "gathering of scattered voices for our belated acts of listening" that attunes our senses "to the incommensurate," to the "aural meeting places" of diasporic revenants (Baucom 2001: 17). When asked about her Haitian inflection of Zabou's character in *Timbuktu*, Kettly Noël says: "Nous avons de nombreux points communs. Zabou est un ovni, un brin mythomane, et on me considère parfois comme ça" [We have a lot in common. Zabou is a UFO, a bit of a mythomaniac, and people sometimes see me that way too].[21]

After GPS's death, before Amadou and Kidane confront each other, the scene shifts to town, where a man on a loudspeaker yells inane prohibitions in French. We cut to Zabou at her mirror in an open-air dwelling on a red

---

[20] The life of Zeynaba Arounhenna Maïga was the subject of a 2003 documentary film by Abdoulaye Ascofare entitled *Zabou, mannequin des sables*. The film poster includes a photograph of the real "Zabou," an older woman swathed in red cloth and many beaded necklaces, a large nostril ring, smiling broadly, with a white chicken perched on her shoulder (mubi.com/films/zabou-mannequin-des-sables). The stage name "Miss Zabou" can be found in the list of past performers on the Le Crazy Horse website, and a photograph of "Miss Zabou" taken by Giancarlo Botti in Paris in 1970 seems to be circulating online.

[21] See lemonde.fr/international/article/2018/04/05/d-haiti-au-mali-la-danse-transgressive-de-kettly-noel_5281233_3210.html.

banco rooftop. She sings and hums vodou songs to herself in Haitian Kréyol, arranging objects on what looks to be an altar. Doves coo, their shadows flitting across an earthen wall; chickens cluck; her rooster crows; the jihadi voice on the loudspeaker disappears into these sounds. Zabou bends to the rooster's cage, speaking lovingly to him ("doudou," "mon bébé") and calling him by name, Gonaïves. This name does not make it into the subtitles. It is a toponym, the place in Haiti's central district where in 1804 Dessalines declared independence from France after the long revolution waged by former slaves.

As Zabou carries on her singsong interaction with Gonaïves, a slow, percussive beat begins to play elsewhere—it might be a drum, or a pestle—an unplaceable sound, easily missed. We cut back to the street, where two donkeys carrying immense loads navigate narrow alleyways to the sound of that irritating voice on the loudspeaker proclaiming that adultery during Ramadan will bear the harshest penalty, death by stoning. The unidentifiable beat continues, a quiet but steady harbinger.

Several scenes later, after Amadou's death, we cut back to Zabou's rooftop. Her laughter rings out like a cackle as Gonaïves crows along. Three jihadis stand around her space—an assembly of old refrigerator, bare bedsprings, broken fan, glinting mirror shards, old playbills and news clippings. The jihadis seem at ease, quietly listening to Zabou who speaks French in an incantatory tone, her Haitian accent strong: It was a January 12, 2010, she says, at exactly 4.53 pm in Port-au-Prince. Zabou says that she appeared in Timbuktu from Port-au-Prince at the instant the earth cracked that day: "Le tremblement de terre, c'est mon corps, les fissures, c'est moi. C'est quoi le temps? Je suis fissurée" [The earthquake is my body; I am those fissures. What is time? I am cracked]. She addresses the rooster, opening his cage: "Gonaïves on est pareil. On est fissuré tous les deux. Fissuré partout" [We are the same. We are both cracked. Cracked everywhere].

One of the men, Abdelkrim (played by Tunisian-born French actor Abel Jafri), reasons with Zabou. You were here long before 2010, he says gently. Zabou tosses a piece of cloth at him—for luck, she says. He ties the cloth around his finger and Gonaïves crows again. Zabou's voice intensifies, her Haitian accent ebbing like a wave to sound Parisian, like Abdelkrim's: "fissurée de partout de la tête au pied des pieds à la tête des bras du dos du visage. C'est quoi, le temps, je suis fissurée" [cracked from head to toe from feet to head to arms to back and face. What is time, I am cracked].

This exchange is interrupted by a scene elsewhere: a close shot frames the exposed heads of a man and a woman buried up to their necks in sand. A circle of men stands around them, holding machine guns. The men step away, forming a wider circle. They kneel to pick up stones from the arid earth, then the shot moves back to the two heads in the sand. When it comes, the sound is acutely painful. It is heavy stone striking cranium, one rhythmic crack of tissue and bone, then another. This lapidation is the penalty for adultery announced by loudspeaker and portended by that unidentifiable drumbeat. The sound of cracking skull makes this the film's most excruciating moment to endure; here, I turn off the sound. This is also Sissako's most self-consciously realist depiction of an historical event; he had initially set out to make a documentary after reading a news article about a couple stoned to death in Aguelhok, Mali in July 2012.[22]

When the shot cuts back to Zabou's rooftop, it feels like a reprieve. The crack of stone on skull is supplanted by percussive beat of drum or pestle. The scene of lapidation is visually blocked, yet its treacherous rhythm continues in a way that haptically recalls the violence underway outside the frame. In this splicing, *Timbuktu*'s most mundane and surreal elements intertwine. Abdelkrim is on his knees in the sand on Zabou's floor; she lies on her bedsprings, watching him with a knowing smile, as if she foresaw this or made it happen. Abdelkrim's bare feet thump and scratch at the earth in time with the pulse, which now has the feel of a heartbeat or a ceremony. Abdelkrim becomes, for a moment, an exquisite dancing bird. His arms outstretch as if they are wings; he gathers sand to raise and let sift between feather-fingers as the music ends. The shot cuts back to the desert. Dozens of stones lie in the sand around the bleeding heads of the man and woman who have been killed. The pulse has gone quiet; the scene is still; all we hear now is wind.

These awful deaths are reframed by the acoustical and kinetic superfield that interrupts and fissures their unfolding. When Zabou speaks and Abdelkrim hunches his shoulders to dance to the haunting beat, we hear and feel Haiti. When Zabou speaks of the catastrophic 2010 earthquake—called by Haitians "gudugudu," the onomato-poetic term that imitates the sound of rock and buildings cracking—a multitude of crisscrossing itineraries surface. Her description implicitly invokes a vodou vision of death as a return to "Guinée" (Africa), yet that afterlife voyage is meant to take a year, a slow trek across the crypt of the Atlantic seafloor. Zabou's return was instantaneous, like the migration of a magical bird. Her flight path calls to mind a recessed archive of stories "existing on the edge of dream and memory, about enslaved Africans who could lift up and fly home," stories told over generations of

---

[22] After sending an interviewer to Timbuktu with whom the Ansar ad-Din leaders agreed to speak, Sissako watched the interview tapes and decided instead to make a cinematic fiction to have greater narrative and æsthetic control. See theguardian. com/film/2015/may/28/timbuktu-movie-jihadist-fighters-abderrahmane-sissako. The original news story is here: nytimes.com/2012/07/31/world/africa/couple-stoned-to-death-by-islamists-in-mali.html.

displaced and diasporic Africans, and subject of a future film presently being created by the experimental documentary filmmaker Sophia Nahli Allison.[23] Sissako's film's bleakest frames are sonically perforated in this way, cracking open unexpected portals (Port-au-Prince/Timbuktu; human/avian) and attuning our senses to recessed itineraries and articulations that lead somewhere other than death and despair.

Timbuktu's panoply of sound also blows open the inherited disciplinary limits of *francophonie*. Long mapped as a barrier that divides or a bridge that connects the continent, the African Sahara-Sahel is a consequential blind spot in scholarly disciplines and institutions still oriented by European colonial cartographies. The region's absent force as symbolic organizing barrier remains especially strong in francophone studies, which tacitly replicates a colonialist enterprise through spatial and racial distinctions that distinguish "Maghreb" from "sub-Sahara" and "Arab" from "Africa" in ways that render Saharan spaces—and vivid cultural nodes like Timbuktu— remote, empty, disconnected, and silent. The "Maghreb" tends to be cast as a primarily Mediterranean and ambivalently African space, defined in relation to imperial networks that connect it linguistically and culturally to Europe (and to France in particular) or to the Arabic-speaking Mashreq, whereas "sub-Saharan" tends to be positioned as the "real" Africa while the Sahara itself poses as geographical, conceptual, and disciplinary blank zone between these. The Maghreb-Subsahara-Antilles division that broadly organizes francophone postcolonial studies around this desert void also follows the old routes of French empire; it is often taken for granted that authoritative critical reflection on these spaces and their æsthetic production must circulate through the institutions and publication hubs of the former metropole rather than across and within networks of the global South. Finally, scholarship has charted the Africa-Antilles relation in a predomi- nantly one-way diasporic direction—picture Edouard Glissant's image of the fibril on the first page of *Poétique de la relation*, that thread of trans-Saharan tributaries flowing off the West African coast to funnel across the Atlantic Middle Passage and disperse across the Caribbean archipelago.

If we take mythomaniacal Zabou at her word—why not?—then at the very least her return flight undoes the entire historical trajectory of the French Atlantic slave trade in the blink of an eye. If we tune in to listen acoustemo- logically to *Timbuktu*—as the film's sonic substratum surreptitiously enlists

---

[23] On this aural archive of collective myth-memory, see the short film *Dreaming Gave Us Wings*, by Sophia Nahli Allison, included as a link in her essay "Revisiting the Legend of Flying Africans" (7 March 2019) here: newyorker.com/culture/ culture-desk/revisiting-the-legend-of-flying-africans.

us to do—then we will recognize that we must abandon or radically reorient the critical paradigms I have sketched above. We learn very quickly, if we did not already know it, that the Sahara and Sahel are replete with interconnected lives and entangled histories, and that Timbuktu *is* a center, not a periphery. Listening closely, we become aware that there are intrinsically meaningful itineraries and exchanges across and within the Sahara and between the continent and its diasporas that do not lead to or concern the global North at all. Sissako's film also trains our ears to recognize French sounds and syllables as part of an intricate acoustical ecology composed of languages, voicings, timbres, tones, and silences that include but in no way privilege the human.

In other words, *Timbuktu* resounds with irrepressible, inexhaustible sonic excess that might guide us to those fissures that open unexpected flight lines to other, better futures. Christina Sharpe notes this at the conclusion of *In the Wake*, where she sounds out what connects *Timbuktu* to *Zong!* and echoes a term from the poet Dionne Brand: "this is, again, the time of the *oral ruttier*," writes Sharpe, "and those songs help us find our way; they are our internalized maps in the long time of our displacement" (2016: 127; my emphasis).[24] A ruttier—from the French *routier*—is a long poem learned by sailors to navigate the sea by reciting the winds and tides, the locations of stars, flavors of saltwater, textures of seabed, species of birds, patterns of their migrations, sounds of their songs. *Timbuktu*, as aural ruttier, as navigational sonic map, points the way to a sure sense that human lives depend entirely on nonhuman lives, afterlives, and agencies for survival—on water, desert winds, cows, fish, roosters, insects, wild birds. In the absence of this knowledge, any possible future will indeed be very dark and very silent.

Works Cited

Adesokan, Akin. *Postcolonial Artists and Global Aesthetics*. Indiana University Press, 2011.

Andersson, Ruben. "The Timbuktu Syndrome." *Social Anthropology/Anthropologie Sociale*, vol. 27, no. 2, 2019, pp. 304–319.

Baucom, Ian. "Frantz Fanon's Radio: Solidarity, Diaspora, and the Tactics of Listening." *Contemporary Literature*, vol. 42, no. 1, 2001, pp. 15–49.

Beau, Nicolas. "Abderrahmane Sissako, une imposture mauritanienne." *Pambazuka News*, March 11, 2015, pambazuka.org/fr/governance/abderrahmane-sissako-une-imposture-mauritanienne.

Blais, Hélène. *Mirages de la carte: l'invention de l'Algérie coloniale*. Fayard, 2014.

Brand, Dionne. *A Map to the Door of No Return*. Vintage Canada, 2002.

---

[24] See Brand 2002: 213–218.

Campt, Tina. *Listening to Images*. Duke University Press, 2017.

Chion, Michel. *Audio-Vision: Sound on Screen*. 1990. Columbia University Press, 1994.

Diawara, Manthia. "Frames of Resistance: Manthia Diawara on the Films of Abderrahmane Sissako." *Artforum International*, vol. 53, no. 5, 2015, pp. 75–77.

Feld, Stephen. "Acoustemology." *Keywords in Sound*, edited by David Novak and Matt Sakakeeny, Duke University Press, 2015, pp. 12–21.

——. "Listening to Histories of Listening: Collaborative Experiments in Acoustemology with Nii Otoo Annan." *Musical Listening in the Age of Technological Reproduction*, edited by Gianmario Borio, Routledge, 2016, pp. 91–103.

Glissant, Edouard. *Poétique de la Relation*. Gallimard, 1990.

Harrow, Kenneth. *Trash: African Cinema from Below*. Indiana University Press, 2013.

Jeppie, Shamil, and Souleymane Bachir Diagne, eds. *The Meanings of Timbuktu*. South African Human Sciences Research Council Press, 2008.

Kane, Ousmane Oumar. *Beyond Timbuktu: An Intellectual History of Muslim West Africa*. Harvard University Press, 2016.

MacDougall, E. Ann. "Constructing Emptiness: Islam, Violence, and Terror in the Historical Making of the Sahara." *Journal of Contemporary African Studies*, vol. 25, no. 1, 2007, pp. 17–30.

Pasley, Victoria. "Beyond Violence in Abderrahmane Sissako's *Timbuktu*." *African Studies Review*, no. 92, 2016, pp. 294–301.

Richardson, John, and Claudia Gorbman, eds. *The Oxford Handbook of New Visual Aesthetics*. Oxford University Press, 2013.

Sharpe, Christina. *In the Wake: On Blackness and Being*. Duke University, 2016.

Sissako, Abderrahmane, dir. *Heremakono/Waiting For Happiness*. New Yorker Films, 2003.

——. *Bamako*. New Yorker Films, 2006.

——. *Timbuktu*. Cohen Media Group, 2014.

Spivak, Gayatri. "Beyond Comparison." *New Literary History*, vol. 40, no. 3, 2009, pp. 609–626.

Taoua, Phyllis. "Abderrahmane Sissako's *Timbuktu* and Its Controversial Reception." *African Studies Review*, vo. 58, no. 2, 2015, pp. 270–278.

Thurston, Alexander, and Andrew Lebovich. *A Handbook on Mali's 2012–2013 Crisis*. Institute for the Study of Islamic Thought in Africa (ISITA) Working Paper Series, Working Paper No. 13–0001, September 2, 2013, arch.library. northwestern.edu/concern/generic_works/6108vb43j?locale=en.

"*Timbuktu*—the Controversy. A Conversation among Adile Cazenave, Phyllis Taoua, Alioune Sow, and Kenneth Harrow." *African Studies Review*, vol. 59, no. 3, 2016, pp. 267–293.

CHAPTER SIX

Listening Back to the Sounds of Algiers in *Pépé le Moko* (1937), *Omar Gatlato* (1976), and *Viva Laldjérie* (2003)

Maya Boutaghou

The theoretical approach known as the "audio-vision" method is opening up new critical dimensions in the field of film studies by moving its main focus of analysis to filmic sounds (Chion 2019). This chapter seeks to interpret the soundscape of Algiers and its narrative of captivity in three films produced between 1937 and 2003. This approach is inspired by Liz Constable's seminal work on acoustic architecture (2009).[1] *Pépé le Moko* (1937) by Julien Duvivier, *Omar Gatlato* (1976) by Merzak Allouache, and, more recently, *Viva Laldjérie* (2003) by Nadir Moknèche, portray common themes in their sounds about the narrative of the city of Algiers. They offer a realistic approach to urban sonic life through the recording and reconstitution of its sounds. In listening back to the sounds of Algiers, an essential aspect of the city emerges.

This work will analyze sounds as forms that shape the imaginary of a place. A city on film is a reconstitution that can be realistic or unrealistic, magnified

---

I would like to thank Matthew Gonzalez (Columbia University) for his insights and thoughtful edits. This text found its full expression thanks to his rigorous *listening*.

[1] "To the ongoing task of defining the characteristics of 'new Algerian cinema,' a critical project in its early stages that leaves many definitional questions unanswered, I propose adding the growing significance of cinematic soundscapes as primary mediators of contemporary Algerian urban cultures" (Constable 2009: 180).

or not. By focusing now on the city's filmic sounds, a new way of revisiting past representations of a place is proposed to cultural critics. Throughout its cultural history, the collective imaginary of Algiers displays a certain narrative of violence and has been perceived as a city to escape from. In this chapter, I will concentrate on comparing sounds in films, while still using images to bolster my interpretation and to orient my analysis.

From 1937 to 2003, Algiers seems to symbolize a place of captivity. The sounds of the city also inform this narrative. In *Pépé le Moko*, the Casbah is the center of the diegesis. The film portrays an obvious opposition between the Casbah, as a place of captivity, and the European city, as a space of free circulation. In *Omar Gatlato*, that same feeling of captivity and oppression comes from the social condition of post-independence Algeria. Finally, in *Viva Laldjérie*, the aftermath of the civil war that occurred between 1991 and the early 2000s haunts the city. There have been a few studies about *Viva Laldjérie* (Crowley 2007; Durmelat 2007; Abderrezak 2007; Constable 2009; Boutaghou 2010; Jones 2012; Bentahar 2019) and *Omar Gatlato* (Shafik 2007). With the exception of the innovative critique of Liz Constable (2009), most critics do not address the centrality of sound in these films, or if they do, it is only to analyze the Algerian linguistic situation. Around *Pépé le Moko*, more critical work has been produced (Morgan 1994; Jordi 1998; Stepovich 2003; Ousselin 2004), but without really analyzing sound as a major part of the interpretation.

A close listening to the sounds of Algiers from a transhistorical perspective addresses two major pitfalls in many previous studies of Algerian cultural representations: the absence of both a translinguistic perspective inclusive of French and Arabic and a transhistorical perspective inclusive of colonial and post-independence periods. For the sake of the continuity of cultural History, and instead of contributing to its repetition of disruption and fragmentation, it is important now to address filmic representations beyond linguistic or disciplinary divides. Using the term "francophone" in this context should be understood as being inclusive of other languages and not a monolingual perspective on a historically multilingual city such as Algiers.

The present chapter highlights a comprehensive understanding of cinema in Algeria from 1937 to 2003. It challenges certain perceptions of what should be included in the postcolonial cultural study of Algeria. I maintain that a postcolonial approach is inclusive of the colonial period. My reading and analysis of *Pépé le Moko* is intended to subvert an Orientalist reading and to decolonize its approach. *Omar Gatlato* is considered to be an important movie in treatments of post-independence Algeria. It is rarely discussed alongside other movies, particularly because it challenges, once again, our understanding of a monolingual perception of cultural history. In a way, bringing together comparatively *Pépé le Moko, Omar Gatlato*, and *Viva Laldjérie* sets the stage for a clearer understanding of the plurilingual reality of Algeria as non-fragmentary and inclusive. These films together help us conceive of the francophone in its relational and inherently multilingual dimension, and they stand as an excellent example of a post-francophone perspective on filmic production (elhariry 2017). *Omar Gatlato* is almost exclusively in Arabic, with only a few words in French, making a strong observation about French being the language of the elite. On the other hand, *Viva Laldjérie* depicts working-class Algeria in French, which is not realistic. As we are paying attention to the sounds of the city, this critical linguistic dimension cannot be ignored, but neither is it the center of our analysis.

Sounds impart an intimate perception of the city. And like any major capital, Algiers exists through its sounds as well. Indeed, like images, sounds make a place emotionally accessible. The experience of sounds renders to the viewer/listener an important part of a place's existence, its implicit or explicit violence, but also its forms of resilience. Analyzing soundscapes using a semiotic approach allows us to identify underlying narratives about Algiers that were kept silenced, so to say, in previous studies.

Following Jennifer Solheim's "call to listen as a cultural phenomenon" (2017: 1), this study seeks to listen back to the sounds that represent Algiers. More precisely, it asks: How do such sounds translate the form of imprisonment and the need to escape that this city radiates? How do these sounds translate the distance between people? Inspired by Michel Chion, I will focus on three sources of sounds: *noise, music,* and *speech* (Chion 2019: 29). In each film, the evolving nature of captivity stems from cultural, social, and religious causes. Pépé, Omar, and Goucem, the main characters of the three films, are also each captive to the voice and the *speech* of the figure they love. The voice of this figure offers them illusions of escape from their social class and condition in the city of Algiers. For Pépé, it is the Casbah, or even a full escape out of the country; for Omar, it is the project known as "Climat de France"; and for Goucem, in the Art Deco district of Algiers, marriage is her escape. In the following pages, after I introduce these three films and my arguments about them more precisely, I will explore the idea of how the viewer/listener's "performance of listening" (Solheim 2017) to a film's ambient sounds is an integral part of diegesis.

Algiers, a Prison to Escape

Algiers bears captivity in its mythology, particularly in its early modern history and literature, with Miguel de Cervantes (from 1577 to 1580) as a major example of one of its captives. In the aforementioned films, Algiers can be perceived as a place of captivity through the "performance of listening." While my purpose is not to describe at length the history and political implications of captivity in the Barbary state, it is important to keep this past in mind as the return of an old and repressed representation of the city, revisited in films and never explicitly worded. I will therefore try to listen back to the sounds representing Algiers, to understand how the sounds narrate the story of Algiers as a place of captivity. Three sources of sounds are notable: *noise, music,* and *speech.* Depending on the circumstances and the level of the sounds, *music* and *speech* that are not intradiegetic can also be considered *noise.* Some sounds that I identify as *noise* add to the interpretation but without being central to the diegesis. The difference is how neat and understandable the sound is and how it collaborates with the diegesis. Being nondiegetic or offscreen does not mean a sound does not influence the meaning and perception of the audio-vision experience (Chion 2019: 73–74). In all three films, ambient *noise* is what amplifies the feeling of oppression, and certain *speeches* amplify the experience of captivity, echoing the overwhelming atmosphere of the place, sometimes explicitly expressing it. My reading deciphers the story of Algiers that its sounds tell us. In the three movies, Algiers exists as a character that can be heard.

In *Pépé le Moko*, the sounds of the city emanate from two sources: the Casbah, as the indigenous part of Algiers, and the European districts. The film belongs to the genre of poetic realism that Julien Duvivier and Marcel Carné developed in the 1930s. The main character, Pépé, is under investigation by the French police. When the film starts, he has been hiding in the Casbah for two years after escaping from the police in France. The first scene in the police department is a discussion about the unique nature of the Casbah as a territory within Algiers with its own rules and boundaries. Inès, Pépé's gypsy mistress, repeats several times that he is safe as long as he is in the Casbah. If he leaves the Casbah, he will be captured by the police. His paradoxical freedom is limited to the populous and multiracial native fortress. Except for the fictional street names, it is important to add that the reconstitution of the Casbah in the studio is very accurate, contrary to what some critics have stated (Morgan 1994: 637). After randomly meeting Gaby, a French tourist, Pépé is nostalgically reminded of Paris. Gaby becomes the impetus for him to leave the Casbah and risk his life in the European district where her hotel is. They both grew up in the Parisian neighborhood of les Gobelins. They share the same Parisian accent and the same marginal life. Pépé's nostalgic feelings reinforce the sounds of the Casbah as an oppressive weight. The film represents the Casbah and the European neighborhood as being antithetical to each other. The difference in how *music* and *noise* are perceived in the Casbah emphasizes several binary oppositions, such as those between the disorder of the Oriental native space and the order of the European colonial space, as well as the chaos of a lawless multiracial space and the colonial order of an exclusively white space.

Omar Gatlato is the story of a young man who lives in a project on the edge of what was once the European neighborhood of Algiers. This well-known project is called "Climat de France," built by the famous architect, Fernand Pouillon (1954–1957). Omar is in his early thirties and lives in a one-bedroom apartment with eight other family members. He shares the only bedroom with his divorced sister and her children while his parents and his younger sister sleep in the living room. After a long day of work in a crowded office, his only way to enjoy some freedom and privacy is to listen to *music* in his bed before going to sleep. The viewer is given a glimpse into the social reality of a new independent Algeria and everyday life in its capital. Contrary to *Pépé le Moko*, the divide is no longer between the European and the native but between the privileged of a socialist regime and the general population that experiences economic inequalities due to a massive exodus from rural areas to urban centers after Independence in 1962. One day, Omar listens to a feminine voice on a recording left on his new tape player. The woman who unknowingly left the recording, Selma, used it to record her impressions of the day, like a voice-memo journal. The film revolves around Omar's quest to find the origins of the feminine *voice* that he found in his tape player. He then wants to meet with Selma. This meeting is never realized.

Viva Laldjérie is the story of a family, a mother and her daughter, who escape Islamic terrorism in the suburbs of Algiers and find refuge in a hotel for single women in the center of the city (Boutaghou 2010). The three main characters are Fifi, a prostitute who is later murdered, Papicha, a former cabaret dancer, and Goucem, her daughter. The *noise* of Algiers is everywhere. The camera takes the viewer through the different neighborhoods of the Casbah and Art Deco Algiers. We follow the peregrinations of Fifi, Papicha, and Goucem in the city: from rue Didouche, to the "Stade du 5 Juillet," to the cemetery, "El Alia," to the former "Bibliothèque nationale."

The "performance of listening" guides our interpretation of Algiers as a place of captivity. Throughout the three movies, there exists an overlap and confusion between each of the three sources of sounds. *Speech* and *music* blend together to become one *noise*, losing meaning and augmenting another dimension of the films: their underlying symbolic narrative about Algiers, the city to escape from.

In *Pépé le Moko*, the opening credits of the film start with a call to prayer and is followed by a bolero, probably composed by Vincent Scotto. The first sequence is a conversation about the social identity of the Casbah, taking place in an otherwise silent office in the Police Department building in Algiers. This talking is a *noise* described by Chion as textual *speech* (2019: 219). The Casbah is defined by the officers as a fortress and a labyrinth. The mention of the Casbah is accompanied by what could be described as Oriental *music*. Mysteries and crimes are part of the identity of the Casbah as a lawless place. The Orientalist and racist clichés play into a definition of the Casbah as a prison, with its chaotic hybridity and its melting-pot essence, its secretive terraces, like puzzle pieces leading to the sea. The boundaries and divides between the two universes are accentuated by the choice of different genres of *music* to illustrate each world. Confirming the comments by the chief of the police: sounds reproduce the social divide between the world of the Casbah and the European city. The sounds of the Casbah are chaotic, loud, confusing, and finally, oppressive, reflective of the mental prison that the place represents for Pépé. Three moments of the movie are interesting in analyzing the meaning of sounds in this captivity: the introduction, the death of Pierrot, and the death of Pépé at the end of the film. The opening scene takes the viewer from the police office, a clean and quiet space, to the Casbah. Once the camera moves to the Casbah, in a following sequence, we hear Algerian *shaʿabī* (which means "the music of the people" in Arabic) music of the 1930s covering the chattering of prostitutes. The mingling between voices shouting, *music*, and the *noise* of the crowd characterizes the Casbah. In the following sequence, the music inspired by Rimsky-Korsakov's *Sheherazade* (1888) sounds "Oriental." It accompanies gunshots exchanged between Pépé's gang and the police. The *music* signals a mysterious space where sounds are the expression of a dormant violence. The European space is where the sounds are discernible and ordered: *speech* is isolated from *music* and *noise*. In the Casbah, all three sources of sounds are mixed and superimposed (Chion 2019: 45). This is the first thing that strikes the tourist or visitor to Algiers: the cacophony in the streets. After the first episode during nighttime in the Casbah, the viewer can hear, in the morning, the crowd walking in the narrow streets, the traditional music with drums, flutes, and a male singer whose words resonate with the beat, all of which are difficult to understand. Pépé walks in the company of the native detective, Slimane, whose mission is to capture him only outside of the Casbah. Within this lawless land, Slimane, who knows the Casbah, is "toléré" [tolerated] in the middle of the thieves. Drums in the background are first perceived as noise. If one pays attention, it is possible to hear the music and the singer's voice, like in a litany. The background sounds of the Casbah are very lively and loud: cries, *music*, and voices singing at the level of the dialogue between Slimane and Pépé, which creates a sense of confusion, of an absence of privacy that reflects biases about the Oriental space as crowded and noisy, confusing and dirty (Linderman

1996). The sounds seem to be natural, as if recorded in the streets, when in fact they were all reproduced on the soundstage. In this first part of the film there are a few characters who insist on the condition of Pépé as a prisoner of the Casbah: Slimane and Inès repeat the leitmotiv, "you cannot leave the Casbah, if you leave the Casbah, they will arrest you":

> Pépé: Quand donc je quitterai ce bled! [...].
> Inès: Encore?
> Pépé: Mais oui encore! Je suis comme l'Angleterre, mon avenir est sur mer.
> Inès: Tu t'ennuies avec moi?
> Pépé: Mais non Inès, je m'ennuie avec Alger.
> Inès: Si tu pars, je partirai avec toi!
> Pépé: Ah non alors! Ça non! Pas possible. J'en ai marre de la Casbah, si tu venais avec moi tu serais une espèce de Casbah portative [...].
> Inès: [...] tu sais bien que tu ne pourras jamais t'évader de la Casbah! Ils veulent t'arrêter. Ils ne se rendent pas compte que c'est déjà fait [...] Un pas dehors, y a plus de Pépé, descendu le Pépé [...].
> Pépé: Tu vas te taire, oui?
> Inès: Pour toi Paris c'est rayé, y a plus de Paris, y a plus de Marseille, y a plus rien, rien rien que la Casbah, plus rien plus rien.
> Pépé: Je ne veux plus t'entendre [...].
> Inès: Non! Je t'aime, t'entends, j't'aime, j't'aime.
>
> (*Pépé le Moko*, 23:46ff; my translation)

> Pépé: When am I to leave this *bled*? [...].
> Inès: Again?
> Pépé: Of course, again! I am like England, my future is at sea.
> Inès: Are you bored with me?
> Pépé: Of course not, Inès. I am bored with Algiers.
> Inès: If you leave, I will leave with you!
> Pépé: Oh no! Certainly not! It's not possible. I am fed up with the Casbah! If you come with me it's like having a portable Casbah [...].
> Inès: [...] you know well you cannot escape the Casbah! They want to arrest you. They don't know it's already done [...] One step outside, and gone the Pépé, shot dead the Pépé [...].
> Pépé: Can you stop talking?
> Inès: For you Paris is erased, there is no more Paris, no more Marseille, there is nothing, nothing but the Casbah, nothing nothing.
> Pépé: I do not want to listen to you anymore [...].
> Inès: No! I love you, do you hear me, I love you, I love you.

Pépé winds up in prison everywhere: in the Casbah, in a sociocultural prison, and outside of the Casbah, the police will capture him. As Pépé mentions, Inès is also an incarnation of the Casbah. She combines the passion and jealousy of the gypsy lover.

The death of both Pierrot and Régis is the other meaningful sequence. During this scene, the music is loud to the point of chaos. While the group of thieves is torturing Régis before he dies, the pianola plays loudly and covers the voices and the gun shots (Chion 2019: 6). This diversion between the images and the *music* is described as "anempathetic effect" (8). The day after the death of his friend Pierrot, Pépé, betrayed by Régis, gets drunk in the usual bar, Chez Chani [Chani's], where the gang used to meet. The sounds of the Casbah become more consuming. This sequence symbolizes the hubris of Pépé and his strong feeling of captivity. The viewer can hear in crescendo the drums playing on the streets when a beggar enters the café and asks for money. The beggar is blind, which accentuates an acoustic perception of the scene. It's a moment where Pépé feels he is losing his mind. His imprisonment in the Casbah without a chance of escape is heightened by the sounds of the environment. His claustrophobic life in the Casbah is communicated by the sounds that alienate the character more than the dirt or the people. Moreover, the sounds are more threatening during the colonial experience: they are the expression of languages that Europeans don't speak, or music they don't relate to, sounding at once unfamiliar, strange, and primitive. Sounds communicate their absolute cultural difference and fear. In the bar, the beggar starts asking for money in a nagging voice, his voice becoming unbearable to Pépé, who then throws a glass at him. This ultimate violence and immorality in a Muslim country indicates the mental breakdown Pépé is going through. The fact that the beggar is blind makes him even more vulnerable and in need of protection. For our purposes, the beggar's blindness amplifies sound as the only door to a perception of this world. The blind beggar loses his sense of direction, of course, relying only on sounds to walk in the streets. He doesn't understand that his voice drives others crazy. The voice of the beggar is accompanied by drums outside of the bar, the same drums we heard when Pépé walked with Slimane around the Casbah, now a little louder and more persistent. The last sequence in *Pépé le Moko* that expresses this sense of captivity in the soundscape is at the end of the film, when Pépé is at the harbor waiting for the boat, *Ville d'Oran*, to leave for France. At this moment, he is under arrest after being betrayed by Inès and captured by Slimane. While he asks for a few more minutes just to watch the departure of the boat with Gaby aboard, he sees her walking on the deck. The moment he shouts Gaby's name, the blaring foghorn drowns his voice out. His final plea doesn't reach her, and, at this moment, Pépé decides to commit suicide. In this sequence, the *noise* of the boat obscures the meaning of Pépé's final act before his death. This scream embodies his alienation.

In *Omar Gatlato*, Algiers is also depicted as an inescapable social prison, from which a mysterious *loving voice* and the *music* of the environment offer mental escape. Omar's attempts to flee his social condition become impossible. As in *Pépé le Moko*, the soundscape in *Omar Gatlato* is overwhelming. Omar does not want to leave Algiers, where he has no independence, and yet, throughout the movie, he perpetuates an illusion of a modern, urban life that he has no means to actually achieve. Algiers becomes a place of captivity that represses all of his dreams of modernity and adulthood. Omar is condemned to stay an eternal bachelor. If the Casbah is Pépé's prison, Omar's is the entire city of Algiers. Both the modern and the ancient parts of the city form one world: the capital of the newly independent Algeria. As mentioned earlier, Algiers, the capital of the new nation, had to adapt to a sudden influx of the population moving from rural areas to urban centers for economic reasons. In his one-bedroom apartment, Omar has no privacy, as he states (to the camera) in the opening sequence of the film. Already, at the beginning of the film, the listener/viewer hears in the background kids playing in the streets. In the apartment, the children's chattering, the radio playing *shaʿabī*, and, in the evening, the sounds of the TV constantly drown out Omar's *speech*. The only time he can have some privacy is when he goes to sleep in the room he shares with his nephews and his sister. The film, like *Pépé*, starts with an introduction to the neighborhood, the same textual speech sequence as in *Pépé le Moko*, a reminder that the "cité" he lives in was on the border between the European district and the Muslim district "Climat de France," in the heights of Bab el Oued, another very populous neighborhood. Omar describes the time before independence. He shares his memories of the sounds of gunshots during the anticolonial war. In the 1970s, the impossibility of escaping the crowd and the collective condition of Algiers is also visible in the city's public transport, where the European measure of personal space is not respected. Omar takes the bus every morning to go to the office he shares with three other employees. We can hear people talking all the time. The same feeling of invasiveness exists in the office where everyone listens to every conversation. After work, the viewer follows Omar to the movie theater, his only place of leisure. During this *mise en abîme*, we can hear the character in the Hindi film speak in French and sing in Hindi. The audience is exclusively masculine, revealing the gendered nature of space in Algeria in the 1970s.

An excess of voices and words is a prison that surrounds Omar: voices of people who are in his world, in the apartment, in the office, on the bus, in the theaters, and even on the streets when he walks to the bus station and has to chat with his neighbors. The collective prevents any form of individual space, private communication, and silence, which is where personal perceptions can grow. Omar is never alone. He is always with a group. The only physical space of freedom and leisure he is afforded is when he listens to his recordings of Hindi or *sha'abī* music in his bed when all the others are asleep. Later, the mysterious voice telling her story on an audiotape replaces the *music* and introduces some silence to his world.

In *Viva Laldjérie*, the viewer recognizes facts of post-independence Algiers. The traffic, a permanent touch of the cityscape, informs the sounds in the opening sequence of the movie. The viewer sees a crowd of Algerians walking. In the first sequence, where Moknèche takes a long and uninterrupted shot of the crowd in the center of Algiers, we can hear the natural sound of the streets in the background. After this first shot, the film starts with Goucem finishing her work week as a receptionist in a photography store. We meet her in the comfortable silence of the shop, isolated from the bustle of the street. Once on the street again, the *noisy* traffic and the recurrent sounds of ambulances in the city strikes the listener/viewer. Indeed, throughout the film, the *noise* of traffic, police and ambulance sirens signals the distinctive sounds of Algiers during the terrorist era. Algiers was particularly touched by the terrorist war and in this regard, it is reminiscent of sequences of *The Battle of Algiers*, with the series of urban terrorist attacks and the recurring sounds of ambulances. As in *Pépé le Moko*, the call for prayer orchestrates the time of day. The distinctive sounds of ambulances form the soundscape of Algiers during the 1990s. These sounds are present everywhere and at any time of day or night. When, for example, Papicha is in the cemetery, we hear the traffic in the background. When Fifi, the prostitute, escapes entering the car of an unknown driver in the middle of a wedding procession, the *music* and the car horns are mixed with voices shouting meaningless words.

Viva Laldjérie also conveys the sensation of narrow spaces being invaded by sounds. Goucem and Papicha live in a small hotel room, and the sounds of the TV and the children playing in the hallway are always in the background. From the door of her room, Goucem can hear Fifi laughing with her clients. The Art Deco clock produces its own sound in the hallway, reminding us of the life they live in common. At the same time, the listener/viewer perceives all the sounds that are a part of this changing reality. In *Omar Gatlato*, we can also hear TV series in French, displaying another way of life as an impossible dream for many Algerians. In *Viva Laldjérie*, sounds and images from Europe and the US are a part of this world, alluring and unattainable signs of comfort and freedom, magnified by their *sonic* aspect.

In the three films, *music* is played both as a part of the diegesis and nondiegetically. It belongs to the life of the characters, as artists, as dreamers trying to escape their reality. Musical sounds open up the possibility of escape. Music becomes a space of healing. It is also part of their interactions with the rest of the world. Below, I will analyze how *music* appears to be the way to escape the ever-present feelings of oppression and alienation that the invasive space of the Algerian city generates in these films.

Music as an Escape

In *Pépé*, the listener is exposed to different sources of *music*: *music* that is nondiegetic and *music* that is intradiegetic. From the start, two musical traditions alternate, European, mainly Spanish, and Maghrebi. Part of the nondiegetic *music* in this film was composed by Vincent Scotto and Mohamed Yguerbouchen. We can hear three genres of music in the film. There is the European music that sounds like a remake of Ravel's *Bolero*, and the traditional popular Algerian music, the *sha'abī* and street music, mainly drums. There are also several occurrences of characters playing *music* to mentally travel and escape the Casbah. For example, Maghrebi music is played in the Cabaret where Pépé and Gaby meet for the first time. This *music* reflects the multicultural mix, welcoming all traditions and all people. On the other hand, the European part of the city displays a sense of European and colonial uniformity, also reflected in its sounds.

Intradiegetic *music* is played purposefully by the protagonists. It occurs, for example, during the second encounter between Gaby and Pépé. While visiting the Casbah, Gaby's friends are at Chani's, using the phonograph to play music. The first disc they put on is labeled "native," "de la musique indigène," and the other is a more European dancing music, defined as "marrante," or "funny," by the protagonists. This is the moment where Gaby and Pépé dance together for the first time and they learn that they share a passion for Paris. Another occurrence of intradiegetic *music* is when Tania (the real singer, Fréhel, who plays the role of a former cabaret singer), listens to her own recording (Chion 2019: 220). By listening nostalgically to her singing voice, she travels back in her mind to France. The following day, when Pépé, already in love with Gaby, starts singing, the people on the street are stirred, they gather around, and begin to dance to his song in a bolero rhythm. This *music*, as often in films, informs the viewer about Pépé's inner feelings for Gaby, indeed, "sound interprets the meaning of the image and makes us see in the image what we would not otherwise see or would see differently" (Chion 2019: 34).

In *Omar Gatlato*, the only way to escape the difficult social and economic reality of post-independence Algeria is through *music*, and, at the end of the film, Omar has fallen in love with the voice of an anonymous woman (Chion 2019: 235). Omar listens to the music he records at live performances and film screenings. He explains in the opening scenes how listening to music is his way of letting go: "it touches him deeply," he says about himself in colloquial Arabic. Omar records any event he attends with music: Hindi music from Indian movies are part of his collection as well as Algerian popular music, *sha'abī*. *Omar Gatlato* is a hymn to popular culture in colloquial Arabic that was undervalued during the '70s and '80s, when the authoritarian Algerian regime imposed Classical Arabic on a nation whose primary language was *derija*, or colloquial Arabic. Merzak Allouache celebrates the beauty of popular culture in *derija*, as the language of the people, as opposed to the language of the political power in place. The film shows this opposition in a scene in a theater, during a performance that is rejected by an audience waiting to hear popular Algerian traditional music instead of a performance in Classical Arabic. This episode illustrates how the regime tried to impose a superficial culture on its people to reinforce an Arab nationalist narrative, particularly present in the region. Another interesting moment in the film is when, at the end of the workday, a group of young friends gather by night outside of their building, playing music on a guitar, listening to each other's silence and meditation. As in any Mediterranean city during the summer, the crowded streets are finally quiet. It is a good time to listen to music and dream. Finally, Omar's love for music is summarized in the film by the little box above his bed where he hides all his recordings. Before the dramatic ending, the discovery of a mysterious feminine voice will overtake Omar's love of music and become the center of his musing and attention for weeks.

In *Viva Laldjérie*, *music* played and listened to is also an escape from the violence and alienation of the city. Intradiegetic *music* is Algerian, traditional and non-traditional. The characters dance and sing, *music* always invites a performance involving the body. The nondiegetic *music*, with the piano as the main instrument, accompanies the characters in their circulation of the city by car or bike. Cheba Djanet's songs, as an iconic figure of *raï* nightclub music of the '90s, recur several times in the film (Bentahar 2019: 78); the lyrics openly express the desire of a woman for a man, her jealousy and desire to keep her lover. Intradiegetic *music* expresses untold stories, untold feelings and fears. The characters listen to music identified as typically Algerian, *sha'abī* and *raï*. *Music* as songs is again a way to escape the oppression experienced by Algerian citizens during the civil war and the fundamentalist terror. The relation to *music* is represented in two ways: as performance, to heal, and as distraction, to dream. Papicha, the main character in *Viva Laldjérie*, who is a singer and dancer, openly expresses the need for the arts to emotionally survive the horrors of the war. Goucem consumes *music* as a product to distract herself from her precarious current situation as a single woman in a repressed city. *Music* is inherently associated with dance. Nightclub *music* is also a mix of Western and Oriental consonance. It is loud and hectic. It translates the need to escape the difficult social reality that surrounds the desperate young Algerian generation in the late 1990s. In despair, Papicha's performance of singing, dancing, and listening to *music* is part of a healing process. It opens up doors to new interpretations. For Goucem, *music* is always loud, dancing is a relief available only when she goes to the one open club in Algiers. To her, *music* expresses a feeling of religious and social oppression. It's hectic and hysterical, sexually transgressive and provocative, "a little bit too much," according to her mother, whose definition of dancing and singing is a celebration of beauty and pleasure. At the end of the film, both Goucem and Papicha find their way to a kind of balance. Goucem will ultimately embrace her reality without trying to escape it. The artist, Papicha, will sing at the opening show of the Copacabana cabaret at the end of the film.

Finally, the last part of this chapter is concerned with the sound of the *loving voice*. The voice in this particular context is always associated with *speech*. In the three films, once again, the *loving voice* is the promise of an escape from Algiers as a place of oppression, a state of captivity. The *loving voice* produces ambiguous *signs*, wonders that are taken for reality by the characters who fall for them. For Pépé, Omar, and Goucem, listening to the voice of the lover complexifies the nature of *sonic signs*. It reveals their double semiotic nature as simultaneously *signifier* and *signified*. Indeed, how does the *voice* morph from a melody (sensual sonic experience) into *signs* that prompt each character towards action?

The Lure of the Loving Voice

Voices are another source of sound. Of course, generally speaking, voices articulate *speech* that the viewer/listener implicitly understands to contribute to a film's diegesis. However, in these three films, we limit our analysis to the *voice of the lover*. One can think of the Mediterranean trope of Odysseus, lured in by the singing voices of the Sirens. Indeed, Algiers is part of this mythology, too: the enchantment of Odysseus by the beguiling voices of the Sirens was not far from the coast of Algiers. The characters, Pépé, Omar, and Goucem, are trapped in an illusion constructed by voices that captivate their senses. In *Pépé*, voices reveal geographies of accents that were particularly relevant in Algiers during colonialism, when people were socially mixed, and their social origins erased. For example, Pépé and Gaby share a common origin revealed through the melody of their voice, their accent from les Gobelins. Soon the voice of Gaby becomes the sweet voice of the place he misses, Paris. The other *loving voice* in *Pépé* is Inès, the gypsy woman who embodies the Casbah and its alienation, as Pépé says: "une espèce de Casbah portative" [a kind of portable Casbah]. When Pépé and Gaby meet for the second and last time in the Casbah, he tells her that with her he cannot help but think of the sound of the "Parisian *métro*," or subway. This awkward comment connects Algiers to Paris in a binary construction: Algiers, the place to escape, Paris the desired place of freedom, represented by Gaby's alluring voice. The *loving voice* transports him from the *hic et nunc* to another dimension of time and space. Despite her jewelry, Gaby's accent is working-class, probably specific to les Gobelins, like in Algiers, where accents are related to space and are important to hear in order to interpret spatial relations properly. Gaby and Pépé deepen their bond when they name places they have both experienced in Paris. They are also both prisoners of their desire to be in a different social position. Gaby is captive to her greed for money and possession. When Pépé asks the famous question: "What did you do before the jewels?" and she answers: "I desired them," the viewer can hear the transfer of their common desire for the illusion of wealth.

Like a captive, Omar has no intimate space. *Omar Gatlato* starts with a sequence where we see him seated on his bed describing how, as the head of his household, he has no proper space for himself. He can only isolate himself from the reality of the small apartment when he listens to *music* and to the mysterious woman's voice. There are many voices around Omar. Several times, we see him calling from his office desk to speak to his best friend, attempting to find a shred of privacy. When he is home, his family talks and the TV is on, but there is no real conversation. The family is also a part of the collective *noise* of the city. When he stumbles upon the voice recording of a mysterious young woman, it soon becomes his way to escape his discontented reality. He will eventually try to contact her and find out more about her by calling his best friend. This call happens in the middle of the office with his colleagues listening in on his conversation. A few days later, he calls Selma from a public pay phone and promises to meet her for lunch the following day. The encounter will never happen. Omar cannot imagine himself with Selma in the one-bedroom apartment crowded with his family. In a kind of nightmare scene, the viewer sees the faces of all his friends laughing at him and saying that he cannot become the adult he wants to be with Selma. He will never meet Selma. His only real-life interaction with her is the one time they speak over a pay phone. Omar is unable to escape the social reality he is embedded in. The misery of his family life and his group of friends does not allow him to become an adult or try to have a family of his own. He knows that there is no escape from this social condition and renounces the idea of meeting Selma. Her voice remains the unfulfilled promise of a better life in a present with no exit. It represents an intimate space he could have shared, the allure of a better life. Omar will never escape Algiers and its social challenges.

In *Viva Laldjérie*, voices are very often heard over the phone. As in *Omar Gatlato*, the voices of lovers are always mediated by a phone line, a sign of social alienation and distance imposed by the current situation of restricted freedoms in Algeria. Since loving freely is not permitted, marriage is the only possible avenue for love. The viewer should note the way female characters hide their appearance but cannot hide their voices. When they are outside, they veil in a fake *hijab* but their *speech* is direct and expresses all their frustrations. Fifi, Anis, and Goucem are connected to the world by phone because of the illegitimate and marginal position they hold in society. The voice of Papicha is praised: "you have a beautiful voice," says one of her former admirers. The laughing voice of Fifi, recorded as a voicemail that we hear many times, is the only sign of life after she dies. The changing nature of the voice from seductive to harsh, from sweet and loving to mad and angry, is also worth noting in the film. *Viva Laldjérie* plays with the sound of each voice to a greater extent than the other two films, reminding us that in a Muslim country, love can be sparked just by hearing a voice. Particularly in North African cultures, feminine voices are the expression of an old gendered wisdom and internal vernacular among women. But Fifi, Goucem, and Papicha are displaced and grieving their situation of loss, where they have to reinvent a new wisdom in their lives without men. Their voices express the truth they are pushed to hide. The nuance and emotion in their voices express their experiences and their dreams. Their voices are traces connecting them to their past. This is expressed in the iconic scene where Papicha drunkenly sings with Cheba Djanet in a bar full of men. She is publicly mourning her husband, who was murdered by a terrorist. The Islamist period in Algeria prohibited women from singing, dancing, and laughing in public. Onstage, in front of a crowd of conservative men, these three women perform the rebellious act of revealing the essential nature of the feminine voice in Algiers through their urbanity and freedom.

As songs often do, the *loving voice* populates their world with unfulfilled dreams. When Goucem tries to meet with her lover, Anis, and cannot reach him by phone, the unfulfilled promise of the *loving voice* is finally revealed in *Viva Laldjérie.* She will leave him endless voicemails that he will ultimately answer with a letter confessing he intends to remarry and will keep her as his mistress. Anis writes a letter as a way to keep at a distance the emotions that the voice cannot easily hide. He can finally speak the truth. An subsequent sequence presents Goucem reading, accompanied by the sound of Anis's voice in her head.

In each of these three films, the *loving voice* as an acoustic *signifier* enchants, distorts any tentative perception of the world. Words are reduced to their melody, to the enchantment of their sound, their sonic *signifier*. These three characters are blind to the signs of their failure; they resist the truth, mesmerized by the melody of the *loving voice*. The viewer/listener sees them progressively becoming trapped by their senses. Pépé and Omar will not survive the *alluring voice*. Their false interpretation of it in a sense exemplifies the attention they give (and that we as viewers/listeners give) to the *signifier* instead of the more complex perception of all the *signs*. It will lead to Pépé's death and Omar's disenchantment. Goucem is the only one who will recover, by facing her reality and accepting her life in Algiers. After the traumatic death of her friend, Fifi, she comes to terms with the harsh reality of her social condition in Algiers and, freed from the illusion of Anis's *loving voice*, she can move on knowing that she will never marry him. These three characters exemplify in different ways the overt attention often paid to one aspect or another of the *sign*. They lose the ability to perceive the *real*. Indeed, the materiality of sounds should not impair one's sensitivity to *signs*. This sonic materiality offers subtlety to the fine balance between the constellations of *signs* and the *real*, opening up new interpretations. Mesmerized by the sonic image of words pronounced by the *loving voice*, Pépé, Omar, and Goucem are prevented from listening and interpreting other *signs*. Their deep emotional connection to the *sonic signifier* (as in the case of Pépé and Gaby, who speak with the same accent about the same places), precludes their perception of the *real* and leaves them unable to interpret it properly. This disillusion, like a form of death, internal or external, is the result of the discrepancy between their interpretation of the *signs* and the *real*.

Listening back to the sounds of Algiers to more profoundly understand the filmic representation of the city throughout its colonial and post-independence history adds another theoretical dimension to the audiovisual experience beyond the linear perception of the image. Sounds lend a depth and complexity that enriches the flatness of the image and the inevitable risk of a simplistic interpretation. The filmic sound emphasizes the memory of the place. Listening to the soundscape of Algiers reveals aspects of these three films that we can miss if we do not upend the hierarchy between image and sound. The "performance of listening" is a new way of experiencing a film. It creates space for new interpretation. It reminds the viewer that he or she is also a listener who (re)constructs a memory of the city defined as much by its soundscape as by its visual representations. We hear Algiers as we hear Cairo, Paris, or New York City, and by hearing them we can visualize them.

To listen closely is to get closer to what filmmakers perceive of a city at a given time. It is the combination of image and sound that marks our experience and construction of a place's meaning. By isolating one or the other, we are not doing justice to the entire æsthetic experience. Applying the "performance of listening" to these three francophone films reveals forgotten traces of urban experiences. The interpretation of soundscapes adds to the meaning of the city as it indexes distinctive sounds that are part of a traceable narrative about the materiality of Algiers as a changing urban space.

The continuity I have suggested in the choice of these three films reconciles perceptions of the place through its sonic representations. Listening to the city through filmic representations is paying closer attention to the *signifier*. Through sounds, the *signifier* is again at the center of interpretation. Last but not least, film studies in the Maghreb often focus on linguistic representations; paradoxically, language has never been studied as sound sensations. In this chapter, focus has been given to sounds at large. This broader perspective opens up the *signifier* to interpretation, instead of the conventional focus on the *signified*. It forces us to listen back to the materiality of sounds and how they also form images. The three movies discussed here are part of a continuous mythology about Algiers, the city of the captive, the city of piracy. The main characters of these movies, Pépé, Omar, and Goucem, as captives to their sonic illusions, invite the listener/viewer to *perform listening to sounds* as *signs* beyond the allure of the Sirens.

Works Cited

Abderrezak, Hakim. "The Modern Harem in Moknèche's *Le Harem de Mme Osmane* and *Viva Laldjérie*." *Journal of North African Studies*, vol. 12, no. 3, 2007, pp. 347–368.

Bentahar, Ziad. "The Deceptive Absence of Arabic in Nadir Moknèche *Viva Laldjérie*." *Francopsphères*, vol. 8, no. 1, 2019, pp. 73–83.

Boutaghou, Maya. "Alger montre ses marges: la mère, la fille et la prostituée dans *Viva Laldjérie* de Nadir Moknèche." *Femmes marginalisées et insertion sociale*, edited by Fatima Sadiqi, Imprimerie Imagerie Pub Néon, 2010, pp. 33–46.

Chion, Michel. *Audio-Vision: Sound on Screen*. Translated by Claudia Gorbman, Columbia University Press, 2019.

Constable, Liz. "Hearing Cultures: Acoustic Architecture and Cinematic Soundscapes of Algiers in Merzak Allouache and Nadir Moknèche." *Contemporary French Civilization*, vol. 33, no. 1, 2009, pp. 179–208.

Crowley, Patrick. "Images of Algeria: Turning and Turning in the Widening Gyre." *Images, Imagination: Algérie*, edited by Mireille Rosello, special issue of *Expressions maghrébines*, vol. 6, no. 1, 2007, pp. 79–92.

Durmelat, Sylvie. "L'Algérie est à réinventer ou femmes d'Alger hors de leur appartement dans *Viva Laldjérie* de Nadir Moknèche." *Expressions maghrébines*, vol. 6, no. 1, 2007, pp. 93–112.

elhariry, yasser. *Pacific Invasions: Arabic, Translation, and the Postfrancophone Lyric.* Liverpool University Press, 2017.

Jones, Christa. "Daring to Love: Nadir Moknèche's *Viva Laldjérie* and Laïla Marrakchi's *Marock.*" *The French Review*, vol. 86, no. 1, 2012, pp. 80–91.

Jordi, Jean-Jacques. "Alger 1830-1930 ou une certaine idée de la construction de la France." *Méditerranée*, vol. 89, nos. 2–3, 1998, pp. 29–34.

Linderman, Deborah. "*Pépé le Moko* and the Discourse of Orientalism." *Literature and Psychology*, vol. 32, no. 1, 1996, pp. 1–17.

Morgan, Janice. "In the Labyrinth: Masculine Subjectivity, Expatriation, and Colonialism in *Pépé le Moko.*" *The French Review*, vol. 67, no. 4, 1994, pp. 637–647.

Ousselin, Edward. "From le Moko to le Pew: Pépé's Transmogrifications." *The French Review*, vol. 77, no. 5, 2004, pp. 902–911.

Shafik, Viola. *Arab Cinema, History and Cultural Identity.* American University in Cairo Press, 2007.

Solheim, Jennifer. *The Performance of Listening in Postcolonial Francophone Culture.* Liverpool University Press, 2017.

Stepovich, Romi. "*Pépé le Moko.*" *The Moving Image*, vol. 3, no. 1, 2003, pp. 171–173.

Voices

CHAPTER SEVEN

Sounds of Palestine

Olivia C. Harrison

Representation in Sound

In the final minutes of *Waltz with Bashir,* Ari Folman's animated documentary about a former Israeli Defense Force (IDF) soldier's quest to remember what role, if any, he played in the 1982 massacres of Sabra and Shatila, the viewer finally sees, and hears, the Palestinians.[1] In a jarring, transmedial use of the point-of-view shot, the flinching gaze of the film's protagonist, a stylishly sketched, nineteen-year-old soldier, suddenly gives way to archival film footage of Shatila in the hours after the massacre. Moments before the cut from animation to archival film footage, we hear a single voice emerge from the indistinct wailing of the women advancing toward the protagonist. The sound of her voice carries into the archival film footage and seems to match up with that of a grieving woman who addresses the camera directly, her Arabic left untranslated in the film. But just as suddenly as the cut from animation to documentary, the Palestinian woman's voice is muted as the camera pans to film the silent bodies of the slain. Representation in sound

---

[1] On September 16–18, 1982, shortly after the Israeli siege of Beirut in summer 1982, several thousand Palestinian men, women, and children were tortured and killed by Christian militias (Katā'ib) in the refugee camps of Sabra and Shatila in Beirut, with the logistical support and tacit approval of the IDF, which was stationed outside the camps. Shatila has become a metonym for the massacres.

falters before the image of death. Or does it? Closer attention to the use of sound in *Waltz with Bashir* complicates the question of if, and how, one might represent Palestine in sound.

A critically acclaimed Israeli, French, and German co-production, *Waltz with Bashir* is perhaps the best-known representation of Shatila in France, even though the film centers around the impossibility of representing Palestinian death.[2] The irony of an Israeli film mediating Palestine for a French audience cannot be lost on pro-Palestinian activists who for decades have sought to make the Palestinian question *audible* in France. From 1968 to the present day, street protests, slogans, non-theatrical film screenings, and experiments in popular theater have formed the soundtrack of solidarity with Palestine in France.[3] And yet these vocal forms of solidarity with Palestine have barely registered in public discourse. Untranslated in *Waltz with Bashir*, the Palestinian woman voiced in animation and then recorded *viva voce* might, then, be read as an allegory for the inability to decipher the sounds of Palestine in France. At the same time, *Waltz with Bashir* is symptomatic of both the ethical paralysis that is emblematic of the age of trauma, and the tendency that Gayatri Spivak long ago diagnosed of First World intellectuals (here, filmmakers) to speak for the subaltern.[4] Writing about a woman whose political decision to commit suicide was misunderstood as an act of shame, Spivak famously wrote: "She 'spoke,' but women did not, do not, 'hear' her" (2010a: 22).[5] What would it mean to hear the subaltern? To what extent, and

---

[2] *Waltz with Bashir* sold nearly half a million tickets during its theatrical release in France in summer 2008, and garnered superlative reviews on the crowd-sourced site AlloCiné.

[3] On pro-Palestinian activism in postcolonial France, from migrant workers and theater troupes in the early 1970s (les comités Palestine, l'Action Culturelle des Travailleurs) to contemporary antiracist militants (les Indigènes de la République) and performance artists (Mohamed Rouabhi), see Harrison 2014.

[4] In David Lloyd's analysis, Spivak's seminal essay "Can the Subaltern Speak?" continues to provoke both "ethical consternation" and "dismayed paralysis" in the reader: "It is as if the question 'what is to be done' [in relation to the subaltern] here transforms into the assertion 'There is nothing I can do.'" For Lloyd, the real question posed by the essay is "Can the intellectual represent the subaltern?" (2019: 96–97).

[5] I am quoting Spivak's revised version of "Can the Subaltern Speak?" In the first version of the essay, Spivak warns us against the metaphor of listening, which implies that there is a lost subject—a voice—that can be retrieved. "In seeking to learn to speak to (rather than listen to or speak for) the historically muted subject of the subaltern woman, the postcolonial intellectual systematically 'unlearns' female privilege. This systematic unlearning involves learning to

how, can sound enable a critique of the politics of representation? These questions are all the more pressing, I want to suggest, in dealing with the representation of Palestinians, colonial subjects still, some seven decades after the foundation of the state of Israel on the ruins of historic Palestine. How might one hear the sounds of Palestine that have been muted, drowned out, or replaced by the very voices that claim to represent them?

Sound, of course, is a sense of perception. It is also a medium of representation. In order to fully grasp the politics of sonic representation in *Waltz with Bashir*, we need to take seriously the conditions through which hearing can take place. What would it mean to hear (*entendre*), in the dual sense of perceiving and understanding, the voice of the Palestinian woman in the film footage? How can we restore the sound that has been muted in the closing shots? How might we imagine audiovisual representation of the subaltern otherwise?

In what follows I explore what I am calling *the sounds of Palestine* in three sets of texts that address the question of representation in sound: *Waltz with Bashir*; Jean-Luc Godard and Anne-Marie Miéville's 1976 film *Ici et ailleurs* [Here and Elsewhere]; and Jean Genet's Palestinian writings. In different ways and to different effects, these texts are centered around the impossibility of representing the dead—not one's own dead, it should be noted, but the dead other, whether friend (*Ici et ailleurs*, *Un captif amoureux*) or enemy (*Waltz with Bashir*). The different subject positions of the authors of these texts— critical allies of Palestine in the first two cases, historical opponents in the last—partly explains the different approaches they take with regard to the representation of the colonized other. As an Israeli veteran, Ari Folman is directly implicated in the death he represents in animation, and remediates in film. Godard, Miéville, and Genet, on the other hand, citizens or residents of a country that played a direct role in the colonization of Palestine, disidentify with France, and Europe more broadly, but they cannot identify with the Palestinians.[6] At the heart of the crisis of representation staged in these texts, then, is the fraught history that has produced—and continues to

---

critique postcolonial discourse with the best tools it can provide and not simply substituting the lost figure of the colonized" (Spivak 2010b: 267). In other words, to listen is not necessarily to hear.

6 A Swiss national, Miéville was running the Librairie Palestine in Paris when she met Godard, just back from the Palestinians camps and bases in Jordan, Lebanon, and Syria, where he, Jean-Pierre Gorin, and Armand Marco filmed the footage that would be edited to make *Ici et ailleurs*—a film about the impossibility of filming the Palestinian revolution from France. Miéville's voice, as we will see, is instrumental in formulating a critique of representation in sound.

produce—what Edward Said has called "the question of Palestine," perhaps the most visible and enduring reminder, and remainder, of the colonial question in the twenty-first century. Analyzing the sounds of Palestine in these texts is not, I want to suggest, a matter of recuperating the authentic voice of Palestinians. What I aim to do instead is analyze the politics of representation in sound, in order to identify the conditions that would make it possible to hear (*entendre*) the Palestinians.

We are by now familiar with the pitfalls of representing the colonized other, thanks to Said, Spivak, and other pioneers of postcolonial studies. With few exceptions, however, postcolonial critiques of representation have gravitated around textual, and more recently, visual representation. How do the terms of critique shift when we tackle the question of representation in sound? What, in turn, does the shift to sound as medium enable us to understand differently about the politics of representing the colonized? Sound, I will argue, is what marks the failure of representation in the texts I analyze below. But the ways in which this impossibility is staged vary drastically, with important political and æsthetic effects. I focus in my readings on three distinct acoustic forms: voice in *Waltz with Bashir*; volume in *Ici et ailleurs*; and silence in Genet's "Quatre heures à Shatila" [Four Hours in Shatila] and *Un captif amoureux* [Prisoner of Love]. Against the naturalization of the human voice as an unmediated form of representation, I explore the use of volume and silence as media that stage a critique of representation in sound. Careful attention to the use of sound in these texts, I argue, enables a critique of the twin pitfalls of representation in sound I identified above: ethical paralysis and representation as substitution (speaking for).

Voice

Waltz with Bashir falls prey to these twin pitfalls, despite its bona fide attempt to give voice to the Palestinians. This is largely because the film naturalizes sonic representation, even as it sketches a stark demarcation between animated sound and documentary sound, the sound of life and the sound of death. Propelled by the filmmaker's quest to recover his memories of the war, the animated film comes to an abrupt stop, we are made to understand, when his long-repressed memories of the destroyed camp return, filling the hand-drawn soldier's squinting eyes with audiovisual footage of the ruins of Shatila, and then, in another abrupt cut, muted images of the bodies of the slain, piled atop one another, poking out from the debris, slumped on the floor in improbable positions. Because his friend has already suggested that the Palestinian camps represent "the other camps" for the filmmaker—"Auschwitz," he confirms—the conclusion to be drawn from the ending of the film is clear: there can be no animation after Shatila.[7]

It is true that there are three frames depicting the dead in the final sequence of the animated film: the face of a little girl ensconced in rubble; a room strewn with the bodies of a slain family; the bodies of young men piled up chest-high. But the slow, mournful stringed instruments that accompany the resurgence of memory in the film mark these images as the memory of one of the film's secondary characters, not the film's autobiographical protagonist. Memory, for the filmmaker, is characterized by the absence of music, by untranslatability, by silence. He cannot draw his own victims, he cannot speak for the Palestinians. The archival film footage of mourning and dead Palestinians marks the impossibility of animation in the face of Palestinian death.

The visual cut from animation to archival film footage in *Waltz with Bashir* is profoundly disturbing. It is also marked at the level of the soundtrack. Throughout the animated scenes, the main characters of the film—most of them former IDF soldiers, friends of the filmmaker who help him piece together his missing memory—narrate their experiences of the 1982 Lebanon war in colloquial Hebrew, to the sound of machine guns, rocket-propelled grenades, car-crushing tanks, contemporary pop songs, and the film's original musical score. Sound in the animated film is both indexical (the flies buzzing around the eyes of a slaughtered horse, which catapult an IDF soldier into the full realization that he is at war; the "hissing" of rocket-propelled grenades which, according to the war correspondent Ron Ben-Yishai, sound like "a Native American arrow-shooting range"; the sound of a knife being sharpened before the massacre) and "empathetic" (the swelling violins that accompany the surge of memory) (Chion 1985: 123). Sound is in large measure what animates the film, reconstituting the protagonist's past one painful memory at a time. Until he is confronted with what he has been looking for all along, that is: the memory of Shatila, which propels the animated film into documentary, and sound into untranslatability and silence. Voice, as we will see, is the sound that bridges animation and documentary, even as it marks the impossibility of animation after Shatila.

Visually speaking, the representation of the Palestinians on screen is what opens the floodgates of memory. If the film's characters speak of Palestinian

---

[7] To riff on "no poetry after Auschwitz," the oft-quoted aphorism attributed to Theodor Adorno ("to write poetry after Auschwitz is barbaric," in the original formulation [1981: 34]). I cite the English closed captions when quoting from *Waltz with Bashir*. Translations of other sources are mine unless otherwise noted.

Figure 7.1. Wailing women in Shatila. Screenshot of *Waltz with Bashir*.

Figure 7.2. Shot: the gaze of the IDF soldier. Screenshot of *Waltz with Bashir*.

"terrorists" and civilians at several points, it is only in the final sequence that the Palestinians are visible, first as animated characters, then as survivors caught on film. But what happens to sound in the cut from animation (shot) to documentary (reverse shot)? The final animated image of the Palestinians is a forward dolly zoom of a throng of women marching toward the protagonist, barely visible in the distance (Fig. 7.1). We hear them wailing, but their voices are indistinct. The camera cuts through the crowd and accelerates toward the

Figure 7.3. Reverse shot: "Where are the Arabs?" Screenshot of *Waltz with Bashir.*

protagonist, who is gripping his gun, chest heaving in fear and trepidation as he guards the barricaded exit of the camp (Fig. 7.2). Without warning or transition, this final animated frame is replaced by raw footage of Palestinian women perambulating among the wreckage. In the montage of the film, this is the point-of-view shot that shows us what the protagonist sees. In an imperfect sound bridge, the indistinct wailing of the animated soundtrack is replaced by the voices of Palestinian women recorded in real time as they take stock of the destruction of the camp.

The soundtrack is clearly meant to tie the film footage and animated sequence together. Seconds before the cut, an indistinct voice emerges from the throng of women pushing forward, saying barely audible words that seem to match up with one of the voices of the Palestinian women we see next in the archival footage. Caught on camera by one of the few reporters on the ground, the grieving woman's muttering becomes increasingly distinct, until she turns to face the camera and shouts to those who are watching: "wayn al-ʿarab, wayn al-ʿarab? wayn al-ʿarab, wayn? sawwaru, sawwaru, sawwaru, waddu [...] sawwaru, waddu ʿala bilad al-ajanib!" [Where are the Arabs, where are the Arabs? Where are the Arabs, where? Film, film, film, send it (...) film, send it to the foreign countries!] (Fig. 7.3).[8] But the montage of archival footage in the animated film drastically reframes her address: no longer an

8 I am grateful to Mahmoud Hosny for helping me decipher the woman's Palestinian Arabic in this scene.

injunction to the foreign reporter who is broadcasting the footage of Shatila to an international audience, her words are now addressed to the IDF soldier turned filmmaker, who cannot remember what he must have seen and heard as he lit the flares that allowed the massacre to take place.

For the first time in the film, a Palestinian's voice is heard, an Arabic voice is recorded. And yet the film dispenses with closed captions or Hebrew voice-over, as if what she was saying did not need to be translated. The Palestinian has the last word, but the images speak for themselves. In visual terms, what she is saying is framed as a response to what we see next, the grainy super-8 shots that replace the first archival film: the bodies of slain Palestinian men, women, and children, motionless and wrapped in a shroud of silence, save a pulsating rhythm that marks the beat of what sounds like a human breath. The original soundtrack has clearly been muted, so this "sound-over" does not mark the presence of the cameraperson.[9] If we follow the logic of the point-of-view shot, it can only be the breathing of the animated film's protagonist, or of the filmmaker himself, dumbstruck by the images he can finally remember. The cut to documentary is thus accompanied by both recorded sound—Palestinian voices, in distinct but untranslated Arabic—and an artificial silence punctuated by introspective sound, meant to mark the filmmaker's refusal to speak for the Palestinians, even as he finally witnesses their death. Palestinians need not be represented, they can represent themselves, *Waltz with Bashir* seems to be suggesting. And yet what they are saying is not understood (*entendu*).[10]

---

[9] Michel Chion distinguishes "son off" [sound-over] from "son hors-champ" [off-screen sound] in terms of diegetic space: "nous choisirons pour notre part d'appeler: *son hors-champ*, seulement celui *dont la cause n'est pas visible simultanément* dans l'image, *mais qui reste pour nous situé* imaginairement *dans le même temps que l'action montrée, et dans un espace contigu* à celui que montre le champ de l'image [... et] *son off*, seulement celui qui *émane d'une source invisible située dans un autre temps et/ou un autre lieu* que l'action montrée dans l'image" [we chose to call *off-frame sound* only the sound *whose cause is not simultaneously visible* in the image, *but that remains* in our imagination *situated in the same time as the action depicted, and in a space that is contiguous* to that shown in the frame of the image (... and) *sound-over* only that which *emanates from an invisible source situated in another time and/or space* than the one depicted in the image] (1985: 32). If the sound that animates the muted images of dead Palestinians in this final sequence pertains to what Mladen Dolar calls the "non-voice" (2006: 23), it nevertheless signifies in the place of the Palestinians.

[10] My reading of this sequence hews closely to Kamran Rastegar's analysis of *Waltz with Bashir* as a "perpetrator-trauma" film that flirts with moral equivalency between victim and perpetrator. "The Palestinian victims, largely

Notwithstanding the film's self-effacement in the closing sequence, it should be clear that Palestine is multiply mediated in *Waltz with Bashir*: in the two reels of archival film footage, of course (the film credits the British film archives ITN and BBC worldwide), but also in the montage of animated images and archival footage, and in the film's treatment of the sounds of Palestine. Why translate the voice of a Palestinian woman if her wailing already signifies her grief, triggering the protagonist's memory and bringing the quest with which the film began to a close? Why keep the original soundtrack of the images of the dead—which might have included footsteps in the rubble, the buzzing of flies, even the grainy quality of the absence of sound that we call silence—when it is the filmmaker's shock that this scene seeks to register? The object of the film is Israeli trauma, not Palestinian suffering.

I do not mean by this to cast doubt on the important role the film has played in Israel. *Waltz with Bashir* is one of the few films to tackle the important topic of Israeli complicity in the massacres. Nor does it shy away from comparing the Warsaw ghetto and Shatila, the Jewish genocide and the ethnic cleansing of Palestinians, breaching what the Moroccan writer Edmond El Maleh (1982) called *l'interdit* (the unsayable) in the wake of Shatila: the interdiction imposed upon Jews who invoke the memory of the Holocaust to condemn Israeli state violence. The very decision to include archival footage of the camp after the massacre is a bold one, given the moratorium on Palestinian suffering in Israel. And the filmmaker's refusal to speak for the Palestinians can be read as a political gesture in itself, an acknowledgment of complicity in the violence that is recorded in the archival footage included at the end of the film.[11]

---

unidentifiable, finally speak at the end of the film, but it is not clear if they are heard or comprehended" (2013: 75). Richard Dindo's film *Genet à Chatila* (1999) uses the same footage of the woman shouting, "wayn al-ʿarab," but to vastly different effects. A young Franco-Algerian woman travels to Shatila looking for Palestinian refugees and former *fedayeen* (guerrilla fighters) who might have met Genet. She is invited to watch footage taken by reporters after the massacre, and sits with her hosts, silently weeping before a small television monitor set up in one of the narrow alleys of the camp. Here, too, the footage is left untranslated, but the Palestinian survivors and Franco-Algerian witness who are watching it understand both what is said and the context of its utterance.

[11] In her reading of *Waltz with Bashir* as a film about forgetting, not memory, Gil Hochberg argues that the archival footage at the close of the film provokes the viewer to ask, "Do *we* (finally) see?" (2015: 149). Compelling as her reading is, Hochberg's "we" remains aligned with the protagonist's subject position, not that of the victims who remain unheard (unstranslated, silent) in the final sequence of the film.

Without downplaying the importance of the film's subversive politics for an Israeli and international public, however, I want to interrogate the crisis of representation staged, through sound, in the film's final sequence. What does it mean that the viewer can hear but not understand the Palestinian survivor? That we can see but not hear the dead bodies she mourns? The buzzing of flies hovering around the agonizing horse's eyes in the animated film finds no equivalent in the archival footage. The dead are forever silent—doubly so because the film does not explain their presence to begin with. The massacre was carried out by the Phalangists to avenge their assassinated leader, Bashir Gemayel, one of the characters explains, and they were able to do so thanks to Israeli flares. But why are the Palestinians in Lebanon? The only clue we have about the reasons for their presence is the Palestinian woman's untranslated interjection: "where are the Arabs?" Heard in an Israeli context, these words echo uncannily with Israeli state discourse, which refuses to take responsibility for the Palestinians who fled their homes in the wake of the violent establishment of the state of Israel in 1948. Is the Palestinian woman suggesting that the Arabs should have helped the Palestinians? That the Arabs are responsible for them? The last words of the film, pronounced by a person whose authenticity cannot be called into question—she is a survivor of the massacre—seem to implicate the Arabs, not the Israelis. Remarkably, there is no mention in the film of *al-nakba*, the catastrophe that uprooted three quarters of a million Palestinians from their lands and flung them into refugee camps across the Arab world, only to be joined by later waves of refugees following each new Israeli war. The Palestinian woman speaks, but her story is silenced. Her presence in an Israeli film is thus doubly ironic: she is visible, and audible, in a film produced and released in what used to be her homeland, where her words are either incomprehensible or decontextualized. Israel and Palestine belong to different regimes of representation, giving new audiovisual relevance to Jean-Luc Godard's pithy formulation in his 2004 film *Notre musique* [Our Music]: "le peuple juif rejoint la fiction, le peuple palestinien, le documentaire" [the Jewish people pertains to fiction, the Palestinian people to documentary].[12]

---

[12] In a masterclass in post-war Sarajevo, Godard illustrates the cinematic technique of shot/reverse shot through two formally similar, but in his telling narratively opposed, photographs of migrants knee-deep in the sea: the color photograph of Jews disembarking in 1948 represents "fiction" (the myth of the nascent nation-state); the black-and-white photograph of Palestinians carrying their possessions in shallow waters represents "documentary" (witnessing in the era of human rights). Although it is consonant with his longstanding critique of the Israeli state, Godard's provocation is, I would argue, intended here as

Against the intended ethics of the film's transmedial conclusion—its refusal to speak for the Palestinians—I propose another interpretation of the use of voice in *Waltz with Bashir*. For the film's message is based precisely on the decision not to translate or contextualize the words of the grieving Palestinian woman. The inclusion of archival footage of the camps is what lends the film "an aura of narrative specificity," to cite Spivak's critique of the instrumentalization of subaltern voices (2010a: 23). The voice of the Palestinian woman and the silence of the bodies she mourns do not speak for themselves. They serve, rather, as audiovisual confirmation of the protagonist's memory, which is itself a screen memory for "the other camps." In this story, the Palestinians have a voice, but they do not have "permission to narrate" (Said 2000: 243). Naturalized in this way, voice becomes an alibi for the traumatized filmmaker unable to understand the survivor of a massacre he helped engineer.

Volume

As I suggested above, the critical success of *Waltz with Bashir*, a few short years after the outbreak of the second Intifada, risks displacing a rich history of engagement with the Palestinian question in postcolonial France, where the thorny question of how to represent Palestine dates back at least to the late 1960s and the period following the 1967 Arab-Israeli war and May '68. The remainder of this chapter is devoted to two of the main figures who have placed the Palestinian question at the heart of contemporary French culture and politics: the iconoclastic filmmaker Jean-Luc Godard, and Jean Genet, *enfant terrible* of French literature. Sound, I will argue, is central to the critique of representation they deploy in their Palestinian texts.

In November 1969, Jean-Luc Godard and his collaborators in the Dziga Vertov film collective were commissioned by the fledgling Palestinian national liberation movement Fatah to make a film about the Palestinian revolution, titled *Jusqu'à la victoire* [Until Victory]. Shortly after the film crew's return to Paris, the events known as Black September—the massacre, by Jordanian troops, of several thousand Palestinian *fedayeen* and civilians in September 1970—put an end to the project as it had initially been conceived. After the Dziga Vertov group disbanded, Jean-Luc Godard and Anne-Marie Miéville

---

a critique of the mode of representation naturalized in the shot/reverse shot technique, and thus also a critique of the naturalized Jew/Arab dichotomy. This dichotomy is further unraveled in the same scene when Godard shows two images of Jewish concentration camp detainees, one a "Jew" and the other a "Muslim"—as detainees on the cusp of death were called—an onomastic coincidence first noted in voice-over in *Ici et ailleurs*, the film I turn to next.

began working on an experimental film, *Ici et ailleurs*, structured, like *Waltz with Bashir*, around the impossibility of representing the dead. But the object of the filmmakers' quest is not to retrieve the memory of a massacre. Rather, the impossibility of representing the dead is itself the object of the film. Sound, and in particular the acoustic gradations of volume, becomes the medium for a complex engagement with the politics of representation.

A montage of shots filmed by Godard, Jean-Pierre Gorin, and Armand Marco in the Palestinian military bases in Jordan, Lebanon, and Syria from February to July 1970, and fictional scenes shot by Godard and Miéville in Grenoble in 1974, *Ici et ailleurs* makes use of direct sound (the Palestinians), voice-over translation (Miéville), voice-over commentary (Godard and Miéville), and silence to deconstruct representation in sound. Elsewhere I have written about the film's elaborately staged critique of the making of an agit-prop film, focusing on the deconstruction of the visual medium of film itself: the illusion of movement and life produced by the montage of still images (Harrison 2018). Here I focus on the use of sound as a critique of audiovisual representation. Film does not capture the real. It does not even produce it. It displaces it, by literally reducing the volume of Palestine and substituting it with other sounds. "Le son est trop fort et couvre la réalité" [the sound is too loud and covers reality], as the voice-over puts it in the film's final seconds. Volume, here, is a metaphor for representation as substitution in the film: speaking over, not for, as, or to, the subaltern. But it is also the very medium that allows for the deconstruction of sound as representation. For it is the voice-over commentary of Godard and Miéville, alternately translating, layering over, or drowning out the sounds of Palestine, that delivers this critique. The play and modulation of volume in the film, from silence to silencing with many gradations in between, allows us to hear sonic representation as substitution.

Ici et ailleurs begins by marking the distance between 1970, when the images of Palestinian *fedayeen* were shot, and 1974, when they were edited by Godard and Miéville. The first frame is composed of pixelated block letters flickering against a solid black background—"mon / ton / son image" [my / your / his or her (sound) image][13]—as the voice-over of Godard intones: "En 1970 ce film s'appelait *Victoire*. En 1974 ce film s'appelle *Ici et ailleurs*" [In 1970 this film was titled *Victory*. In 1974 this film is titled *Here and Elsewhere*]. The sounds and images that follow—women and men training with automatic weapons, a semi-literate woman haltingly reading a Fatah pamphlet, children marching

---

[13] This is an untranslatable wordplay on *son*, sound, a homonym of *son*, his or her. The sounds and images taken by the filmmakers are, in fact, theirs, even though they are presented as the sounds and images of Palestine.

in military formation to the Palestinian national anthem—are sequenced according to the prerogatives of the Palestinian revolution, dubbed by Miéville, and commented by Godard. "On avait organisé tout ça comme ça," explains the filmmaker. "Tous les sons et toutes les images, dans cet ordre-là" [This is how we organized everything. All the sounds and all the images, in that order]. But the representational premise of Miéville's voice-over translation— already denaturalized in her prosodic imitation of the semi-literate woman's halting Arabic—breaks down when the same rush footage plays again, but muted. Instead of the soundtrack of *Jusqu'à la victoire*, we hear Godard's voice compute the Fatah slogans that were to structure the film, in a monotone voice sharply at odds with the lyricism of the Palestinian resistance:

> la volonté du peuple, plus, plus la lutte armée égale la guerre du peuple, plus, plus le travail politique égale l'éducation du peuple, plus, plus la logique du peuple égale la guerre populaire prolooongée, prolooongée [*sic*], prolongée jusqu'à la victoire du peuple palestinien.

> the will of the people, plus, plus the armed struggle equals the war of the people, plus, plus the political work equals the education of the people, plus, plus the logic of the people equals the popular war prolooonged, prolooonged, prolonged until the victory of the Palestinian people.[14]

Godard's voice-over makes audible the silencing of Palestinians in a film that purports to make them speak. The Palestinians cannot speak for themselves, they must be represented.

If voice-over marks one end of the spectrum of volume, silence marks the other. Eight minutes into the film, silence interrupts the soundtrack of the Palestinian revolution when color images and direct sounds of Palestinian men, women, and children singing, ploughing the land, typing up tracts, training for combat, and learning to read are abruptly replaced by silent blue-tinged close-ups of the faces of dead *fedayeen*. The only transition between the moving and still images are block letters flickering on what looks like an analog screen, computing the passage from life to death: "ceci est devenu cela" [this became that]. Pixelated words superimposed on the still images of the dead, followed by a series of muted title cards, elucidate the

---

[14] In his memoir *Le Bien des absents*, the Palestinian historian and writer tasked with serving as guide and interpreter for the Dziga Vertov group, Elias Sanbar, recounts a scene in which an Egyptian doctor-turned-*fedayee*, Mahjoub, explains that it is important to stretch out the vowel of the word *prolongée* in order to "hear" its velocity (2001: 46). The uncredited translation of Mahjoub's elongated vowels in the voice-over is one of the first moments in the film to draw attention to the (re)mediation of Palestinian voices.

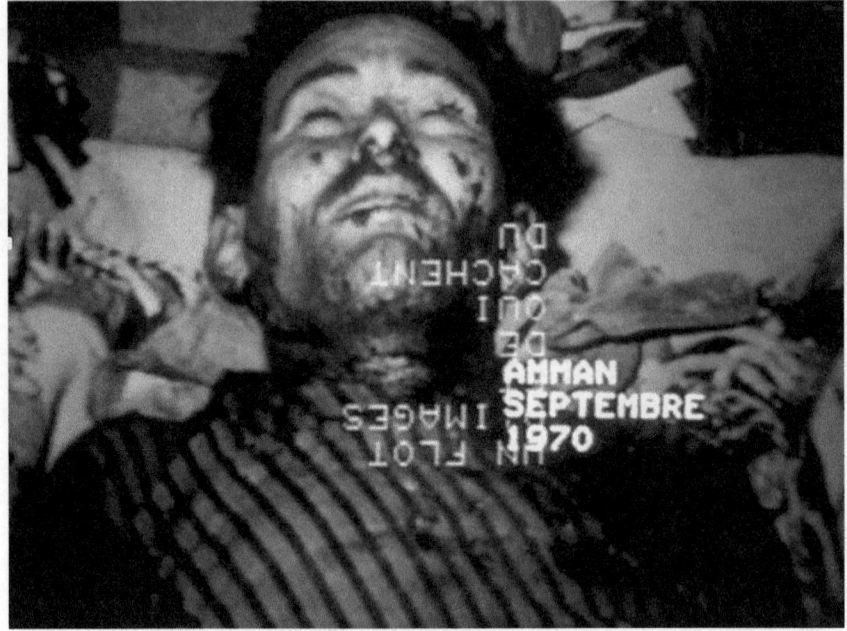

Figure 7.4. "A stream of images and sounds that hide silence."
Screenshot of *Ici et ailleurs*.

contrast between sound and silence: "La mort est représentée dans le film par un flot d'images / un flot d'images et de sons qui cachent du silence" [death is represented in the film by a stream of images / a stream of images and sounds that hide silence] (Fig. 7.4).

Intradiegetically, the editing suggests that the massacres of Black September put into crisis the project of filming the Palestinian revolution: how can French filmmakers "here" purport to celebrate victory in the face of annihilation "elsewhere"? As if to drive the point home, the sound gradually fades out during a shot of a Fatah leader speaking with a microphone, as the camera tracks left to film the Palestinian men and boys he is addressing. "Le film a filmé des acteurs en danger de mort" [the film filmed actors at risk of death], explains one of the title cards. The moving image gives way to the still image, direct sound to silence. But the suspension of sound also makes audible the medium of representation itself. As the camera lingers on the motionless faces and bodies of the slain—doubly motionless because the camera is recording still images—we hear the unmistakable staticky sound of the film reel turning. "Silence, on tourne," as the French idiom has it. If the stream of images and sound that compose the rush footage of *Jusqu'à la victoire* "hides silence," it is also because the audiovisual medium of film

Figure 7.5. "Turning up the volume."
Screenshot of *Ici et ailleurs*.

replaces the sounds of Palestine. The rest of the film proceeds to stage the silencing of Palestine through the manipulation of volume.

I focus on a sequence that begins with a question posed by Godard: "mettre le son plus fort, en réalité, comment ça se passe?" [turning up the volume, how does it work in reality?]. A little girl turns up the volume of the television set "pour effacer [...] le bruit de la famille, et celui de l'école" [to erase (...) the noise of the family, and that of school]; a factory worker hunches over the din of a pinball machine; a taxi driver turns up the volume of his car radio to find out if he has won the lottery; as if to cue us in to the importance of sound, a domestic worker increases the volume of her portable radio so that she can hear an advertisement for a sound system that captures "les modulations de fréquence [...] restitue intégralement et dans toute leur pureté les graves et les aiguës" [the modulations in frequency [...] restores entirely and in all their purity the bass and treble]. In the shot that follows, the voice-over "décompose un de ces movements" [decomposes one of these movements]—the girl reaching for the volume knob on the television set—into not one but two movements, illustrated by a close-up shot of the treble and bass frequency indicators on an analog stereo system (Fig. 7.5). The volume of the parents' argument is on one indicator, the volume of the television program—a Hollywood film dubbed into French—on the other. The camera cuts to an even closer shot of one of the frequency indicators as the sound of the dubbed film is replaced by Adolf Hitler's gravelly, booming voice. Volume is linked to fascism, as the voice-over explains: "Toujours un moment ou un point dans le temps où un son prend le pouvoir sur les autres [...] Il a pris le pouvoir parce qu'à un moment donné, il s'est fait représenter par une image" [Always a moment or a point in time when a sound seizes power from the others (...) It seized power because at a given moment, it was represented by an image].

Volume is fascistic. And yet the filmmakers are not off the hook. The shots that follow offer an audiovisual montage of sound and image, producing "une chaîne ininterrompue d'images, esclaves les unes des autres" [an uninterrupted chain of images, each enslaved to the other] accompanied by two or three distinct soundtracks at varying levels of sound: a wall of television monitors projects still and moving images of Richard Nixon, Moshe Dayan, Henry Kissinger, television news anchors, soccer matches, May '68 protestors, and the mutilated bodies of Palestinians. What does it mean for sound to be represented by an image? "Prendre le pouvoir est possible quand [...] l'image à son tour se fait représenter par un autre son, comme un ouvrier se fait représenter par son syndicat" [Seizing power is possible when (...) the image in turn is represented by another sound, in the way a worker is represented by his or her union]. But the image that Godard is commenting on in this voice-over is not the image of a worker or a union. It is a shot of a Fatah commander declaiming a speech about the revolution, in untranslated Arabic, filmed by the Dziga Vertov collective. The title card that follows— "ici (image) / ailleurs (son)" [here (image) / elsewhere (sound)]—ironically exposes the attempt to naturalize sound as the authentic emanation of the filmed subject. Sound does not represent the other. It drowns the other out. Godard's monotone continues: "On a fait comme pas mal de gens, on a pris des images, et on a mis le son trop fort" [We did what a lot of people do, we took images, and we turned the volume up too high].

The following shot directly implicates the filmmakers in the manipulation of volume. An extreme close-up shows the hand of a man, and then the hand of a woman—Godard's and Miéville's?—slowly raising the volume knob of a Sony sound system as we hear the chorus of "l'Internationale" resound: "c'est la lutte finale" [this is the final struggle] (Fig. 7.6). Punctuated by the communist anthem, which booms out each time the volume is raised, the voice-over continues:

> avec n'importe quelle image: Vietnam, toujours le même son, toujours trop fort, Prague, Montévidéo, mai '68 France, Italie, révolution culturelle chinoise, grèves en Pologne, torture en Espagne, Irlande, Portugal, Chili,

Figure 7.6. "Always the same sound, always too loud."
Screenshot of *Ici et ailleurs*.

Palestine, le son tellement fort qu'il a fini par noyer la voix qu'il voulait faire sortir de l'image.

with just about any image: Vietnam, always the same sound, always too loud, Montevideo, May '68 France, Italy, Chinese cultural revolution, strikes in Poland, torture in Spain, Ireland, Portugal, Chile, Palestine, the sound so loud that it ended up drowning out the voice it wanted to extract from the image.

The final fifteen minutes of the film offer an explicit critique of the Dziga Vertov group's attempt to represent Palestine in sound and image. Miéville, who was not part of the collective's expedition, offers her voice-over commentary on a series of shots from the rush footage, only one of which has been shown before (the muted Fatah leader speaking to the people over a microphone). In one scene, a little girl recites a poem by Mahmoud Darwish in the ruins of Karameh, the site of an iconic Palestinian battle against the IDF.[15] In another, an illiterate woman repeats a Fatah text that is being

---

[15] According to Rebecca Dyer and François Mulot, the Darwish poem recited in the ruins of Karameh is "Azhaar al-damm" ("Roses of Blood"), not "I will resist," as the voice-over claims in this scene (2014: 76).

read to her. The last presents a pregnant woman in Beirut saying that she will devote her son's life to the revolution. Miéville is critical of what she calls "political theater" in all these scenes: the little girl is "innocent," her performance less so; the illiterate woman is bored and wants to get back to work; the Fatah leader is far from the people he is supposed to represent. But the main object of her critique is Godard. The screen goes black and we hear Godard's voice—now in direct sound—asking the mother-to-be to repeat her text, sit straighter, adjust her veil. We see a second take, and then a third, but now the sound is muted. Miéville's voice-over explains that this woman was not, in fact, pregnant. She was a Lebanese student who accepted to play the role Godard gave her out of solidarity with the Palestinian cause. "Les textes parlent, parlent, mais ne parlent jamais du silence" [The texts speak, speak, but they never speak of silence]. In literal terms, silence here is the off-screen sound that was to be edited out of the film. But it is also tantamount to silencing: it is the substitution of one sound for another.

We return one last time to the close-up shot of two hands raising the volume on a sound system, immediately before the longest continuous shot in the film: a long take of a troupe of *fedayeen* discussing tactics as they rest in a banana grove near the Jordan River after an unsuccessful nighttime operation. We hear their muted voices, birds chirping, the wind rustling the leaves. Godard's voice layers over the soundtrack to ask Miéville what they are saying, and she resumes the role of interpreter she had at the start of the film. But now we know her translation is not unmediated. Her voice has lost the transparency it had when we first heard it. The *fedayeen*, she explains, "are critiquing the way they crossed the river under the fire of Israeli machine guns." What is tragic is that they are talking about their own imminent death, Godard remarks. What is tragic, Miéville retorts, is that you didn't say anything about it. The camera continues to film after the *fedayeen* stop speaking. Godard comments: "c'est vrai que même du silence, on ne l'a jamais écouté en silence. On a tout de suite voulu crier victoire, et en plus, à leur place" [it's true that even silence, we never listened to it in silence. We wanted to cry out victory right away, and what's more, in their stead].

In a moving text written two decades after the filming of *Jusqu'à la victoire*, the Dziga Vertov group's Franco-Palestinian interpreter, Elias Sanbar, describes the making of this scene. Looking at the rush footage brought back from the Middle East, Godard had the "intuition" to lower the volume of the voice addressing the camera in the foreground—the filmmakers had asked one of the *fedayeen* to deliver an "autocritique" for the camera—and asked Sanbar to translate the *fedayeen*'s now audible conversation in the background (Sanbar 2001: 49). In lieu of autocritique, what they discovered was a heated confrontation with the leader who had sent them out to battle unprepared, resulting in the deaths of several of their fellow combatants. "Nous étions abasourdis," writes Sanbar:

> lui parce qu'il ne m'avait pas alors demandé de traduire ce que disaient ces hommes, et moi, moi dont c'était la langue maternelle, profondément culpabilisé de n'avoir alors strictement rien entendu, tant les théories et les convictions inébranlables m'avaient frappé de surdité. (1991: 116)

> We were in shock, he [Godard] because he had not asked me to translate what these men were saying at the time, and me, whose mother tongue it was, racked with guilt that I had heard absolutely nothing, so completely had these unshakable theories and convictions deafened me.

According to Godard's biographer, Antoine de Baecque, this belated attempt to decipher, and translate, the sounds of Palestine would be the springboard for the film *Ici et ailleurs* (2010: 527).

The soundtrack of the film that wasn't made would have silenced the *fedayeen*. Instead, Godard and Miéville decompose the movements of sound, the ways in which the volume of one sound increases to cover the others. Miéville asks:

> D'où vient-il que nous avons été incapable d'écouter et de voir ces images toutes simples, et que nous avons, comme tout le monde, dit autre chose à propos d'elles, autre chose que ce qu'elles disaient, pourtant? Sans doute est-ce que nous ne savons ni voir, ni entendre, ou alors, que le son est trop fort, et couvre la réalité.

> Why is it that we were incapable of listening to and seeing these simple images, and that like everyone else we said other things about them, other things than what they nevertheless said? It's probably because we do not know how to see or hear, or because the sound is too loud, and covers reality.

Unable to reconstitute the sounds of Palestine, *Ici et ailleurs* makes us hear the silence in the soundtrack of *Jusqu'à la victoire*.

Silence

Sound is a medium of representation. But can it be represented? I turn in this section to a silent medium, the written text, that represents all the gradations of sound, including silence.[16] Like *Waltz with Bashir* and *Ici et ailleurs*, Jean

---

[16] For a discussion of sound in silent media, see David Toop: "I hope to show that sound—and by sound I mean the entire continuum of the audible and inaudible

Genet's Palestinian writings begin with the impossibility of representing the dead. But the dead do not remain silent in Genet's prose. Beneath the silence of the corpses of Shatila, Genet hears the sounds of the *fedayeen* he lived with, and loved, in the early 1970s. Writing is what makes possible the translation from silence to sound, and from hearing to understanding. And yet the very medium Genet uses makes it impossible to take for granted representation in sound.

In his witness account of the Sabra and Shatila massacres, Genet ponders the impossibility of representing the dead, not because of an ethical or political impasse—after his first visit to the Palestinian *fedayeen* camps in the fall of 1970, Genet would write of nothing else—but because of the limits of intermedial representation:

> Une photographie a deux dimensions, l'écran du téléviseur aussi, ni l'un ni l'autre ne peuvent être parcourus [...] La photographie ne saisit pas les mouches ni l'odeur blanche et épaisse de la mort. Elle ne dit pas non plus les sauts qu'il faut faire quand on va d'un cadavre à l'autre. (1983a: 4–5)

> A photograph has two dimensions, so does a television screen; neither can be walked through [...] A photograph doesn't capture the flies nor the thick white smell of death. Neither does it say the leaps you must make to get from one corpse to another. (1983b: 4–5; translation modified)

In an impossible attempt to reproduce the author's sensorial perceptions as he picks his way through the cadavers—kinesthesia, smell, touch, sound—"Four Hours in Shatila" registers the haunting silence of death, described not as the absence of sound, but as the visceral evidence of a transitive *silencing*. Silence is perpetrated in the act of violence itself, but it is also the product of an active failure to hear violence. Silence screams in Genet's prose:

> Le visage noir et gonflé, tourné vers le ciel, montrait une bouche ouverte, noire de mouches, avec des dents qui me semblèrent très blanches, visage qui paraissait, sans qu'un muscle ne bougeât, soit grimacer, soit sourire ou hurler d'un hurlement silencieux et ininterrompu [...] Ce qui manquait en ce lieu, je m'en rendis compte, c'était la scansion des prières. (1983a: 7–8)

> Her black and swollen face, turned toward the sky, revealed an open mouth, black with flies, and teeth that seemed very white to me, a face that appeared, without moving a muscle, either to grin or smile or else to cry

---

spectrum, including silence, noise, quiet, implicit and imagined sound—can be identified as a sub-text, a hidden if uncertain history within otherwise silent media" (2010: xiii).

out in a silent and unbroken scream [...] What was missing in this place, I realized, was the rhythm of prayer. (1983b: 8–9; translation modified)

Genet makes us see the cadaver in agonizing detail. But he also enables us to imagine the sonic dimensions of death. The writer listens for the sounds of violence—blows, gunshots, screams, wails, death rattles—silently registered in the bodies he witnesses. For the killing cannot have been silent. The silence of death—unrecorded by the cameras of photojournalists—becomes a metaphor for Israeli complicity: "Les massacres n'eurent pas lieu en silence et dans l'obscurité. Éclairées par les fusées lumineuses israéliennes, les oreilles israéliennes étaient, dès le jeudi soir, à l'écoute de Chatila" [The massacres did not take place in silence and darkness. Lit by Israeli flares, Israeli ears were listening to Shatila as early as Thursday evening] (1983a: 11; 1983b: 15; translation modified). Trapped in the silent reverberations of the din of massacre, Genet becomes Palestinian. "Depuis que les routes étaient coupées, le téléphone silencieux, privé de communication avec le reste du monde, pour la première fois de ma vie je me sentis devenir palestinien et haïr Israël" ["Since the roads had been cut off and the telephone was silent, deprived of contact with the rest of the world, for the first time in my life, I felt myself become Palestinian and hate Israel"] (1983a: 9; 1983b: 10). The silencing of the Palestinians, and the metaphoric silence (in reality, the refusal to hear) of the accomplices and witnesses of the killings, are what prompt him to speak for, and as, a Palestinian. In lieu of ethical paralysis—I cannot speak for the Palestinians—Genet chooses identification: I will speak as a Palestinian.

Silence as a transitive verb is the pretext for everything Genet will write about Palestine, from his first stays in the military bases in Jordan to his visit to the camps of Sabra and Shatila in the days following the massacres, and his own death, four years later. His writings about Palestine, from "Les Palestiniens" to "Quatre heures à Chatila" and *Un captif amoureux*, are an attempt to animate Palestine, translating all the registers of the human sensorium—sound, sight, smell, touch, texture—through writing, and this despite the impossibility of the task. "Même avant d'y arriver, je savais que ma présence au bord du Jourdain, sur les bases palestiniennes, ne serait jamais clairement dite: j'avais accueilli cette révolte de la même façon qu'une oreille musicienne reconnaît la note juste" ["Even before I got there I knew that my visit to the banks of the Jordan, to the Palestinian bases, could never be clearly expressed. I had greeted the revolt as a musical ear recognizes a right note"] (1986: 17; 2003: 9). How can this acoustic recognition be rendered into language? And how can the living pretend to speak for the dead? Genet stages the aporia of representation through the allegorical image of a puppeteer attempting to ventriloquize the dead from beyond the grave:

> Guidées par des ficelles ou agitées par les doigts du montreur sous des costumes de soie, les marionnettes sont seules probablement à réussir un spectacle véritablement crépusculaire, funèbre, finalement macabre. Le titre de ce spectacle est un avertissement: Théâtre d'ombres. C'est par des personnages en carton, en bois, par de muettes poupées d'étoffe [...] que la mort fut évoquée, la mort mais surtout les morts eux-mêmes, tout l'empire des morts, cela sera presque naturel, le mutisme résistant à tout, c'est en quoi chaque mort dès qu'on l'évoque en le nommant se transforme. Et ces personnages de carton ou de doigts habillés [...] sont à des distances certainement infranchissables de cette voix qui raconte une histoire ou croit leur prêter une voix en prétendant que voix et histoire sont celles des poupées [...] Ces personnes que je crois faire vivre ou revivre en tendant l'oreille pour entendre ce qu'elles me disent, restent mortes. L'illusion littéraire n'est pas vaine [...] un livre a aussi pour ambition de laisser voir [...] le squelette et la poudre de squelette qui se prépare. L'auteur aussi, comme ceux dont il parle, est mort. (1986: 499–502)

> It's probably only with puppets, worked by strings or the fingers of the puppeteer beneath their silken costumes, that you can produce a really ghostly and funereal, a truly macabre show. The very name—shadow show—warns you what to expect. Death was conjured up by characters made out of cardboard or wood, by mute fabric dolls [...] and not merely death, but the dead themselves, the whole empire of the dead. It's natural, really: muteness survives everything. It's what every dead person turns into as soon as you mention their name. And these characters made of cardboard or dressed-up fingers [...] are an unbridgeable distance away from the voice telling their story, or trying to give them a voice, pretending story and voice are those of the dolls [...] They remain dead, the people I try to resuscitate by straining to hear what they say. The literary illusion is not pointless [...] One thing a book tries to do is show [...] the skeleton and the skeleton dust to come. The author too, like those he speaks of, is dead. (2003: 351–353; translation modified)

The meaning of this last sentence is not merely autobiographical (Genet knew he was terminally ill when he was writing *Prisoner of Love*, and died in the midst of proofing the manuscript). It also confirms what Genet discovered in Shatila: to hear the silence of Palestinian death is to become Palestinian. In this allegory of writing as puppetry, dying as a Palestinian becomes the condition for narrating Palestinian life.

What are we to make of this impossible identification in death? And of the paradox of Genet's persistence in restoring the sounds of Palestine from beyond the grave? Without resolving these questions, the text dwells in the paradox of infrasonic representation. One of the most moving passages in *Prisoner of Love* describes Genet listening to the improvised songs of the *fedayeen*, some of them as young as fourteen:

> Choisies et improvisées par l'enfant—comme le reste du chant était improvisé—les vocalises sans consonnes étant généralement très aiguës, il me semblait que trois Reines de la Nuit à moustache légère, en tenue léopard, chacune éloignée et perdue, se retrouvaient dans le matin et dans le vibrato, et cela avec l'assurance, l'imprudence, l'indifférence des reines d'opéra, oublieuses de leurs armes, de leurs vêtements, de leur statut de soldats alors qu'une rafale de Jordanie pouvaient les rendre muettes pour toujours par un tir plus précis et autant harmonieux que leur chant. Peut-être croyaient-elles, ces Reines, que la tenue léopard les faisait chanter en silence, ou dans une langue et une musique émettant des infrasons? (1986: 67)

> Chosen and improvised by the children—just as the rest of the singing was improvised—the trills were devoid of consonants and mostly very high pitched. It was as if three lost Queens of the Night, wearing faint moustaches and battle dress, came together in the morning and in the vibrato with the confidence, recklessness and detachment of prima donnas, oblivious of their weapons, their clothes, and their status as soldiers, who at any moment might be rendered forever mute by a hail of bullets from Jordan more accurate and just as melodious as their own singing. Perhaps the Queens believed their camouflage uniform made them sing in silence, or in a language and music that emitted infrasound? (2003: 45; translation modified)

At the antipodes of what, in his first text about the Palestinians, Genet called "les marches militaires composées pour les armées colonialistes" [military marches composed for colonialist armies]—the pompous military music played on "clandestine radios" to parrot the sounds of European armies—improvised Palestinian songs are the stuff of "cultural revolution" (1991: 94; 2004: 75–76; translation modified). Though they cannot be heard—their songs are "infrasonic"—synesthesia allows the listener to touch and smell the voice of the Palestinians:

> Les voix, ce matin au moins, étaient aussi sûres que les sons du hautbois, de la flûte, du flageolet, des sons si vrais qu'ils permettaient de sentir avec le nez l'odeur du bois dont sont faits les instruments, d'y reconnaître le sens de la fibre de ce bois [...] Pour la première fois de ma vie, un chant

arabe en liberté sortait de bouches, de poitrines, il était porté sur un souffle vivant que les machines—disques, cassettes, radios—tuaient à la première note. (1986: 68–69)

The voices, that morning at least, were as sure as the sound of oboes, flutes and flageolets—sounds so true you could smell the wood the instrument was made of, feel its grain [...] For the first time in my life, Arabic singing came freely out of people's mouths and chests, borne on a living breath that machines—discs, cassettes, radios—killed at the very first note. (2003: 45–46; translation modified)

As he smells and touches the voice of the *fedayeen*, Genet begins to identify with the Palestinians: "for the first time in my life, Arabic singing came freely out of people's mouths."[17] It is through this grammatical slippage in referentiality (Genet's life, Arabic voices) that we can understand Genet's becoming Palestinian. Against the representational claims of mechanical reproduction, Genet attempts to ventriloquize the sounds of Palestine through writing.

This is not to say that Genet was not acutely aware of the aporia of representation. Writing, like the recording devices he mentions, marks the absence of the very object it seeks to represent, even as it produces a distortion akin to the static of a transistor radio:

Et ce livre que j'écris, remontée dans mes souvenirs d'instants délicieux est, mais le dirais-je? l'accumulation de ces instants afin de dissimuler ce grand prodige: « *il n'y avait rien à voir ou à entendre* ». Est-il alors une sorte de barricade dressée afin de cacher ce vide, accumulation de quelques détails vrais qui par contagion donnent vraisemblance aux autres? (1986: 124–125)

And this book I'm writing, an upsurge in my memory of delightful moments, is—but can I say it?—an accumulation of such moments designed to conceal this revelation: *"there was nothing to see and hear."* Is this book a kind of barricade to hide the void, an accumulation of a handful of accurate details to lend plausibility by suggestion to the rest? (2003: 86–87; translation modified)

In the absence of the voice itself—his Palestinians are long dead—Genet writes as a Palestinian, restoring the grain of the voice and the sound of silence in the imperfect medium of writing.

---

[17] Barbara Bray's idiomatic translation disambiguates Genet's contracted prose by inserting a distinction between subject and object not found in the French: "for the first time in my life, *I heard* Arabic singing" (my emphasis).

And yet, unlike the Palestinians in *Waltz with Bashir* and *Ici et ailleurs*, the silent victims have a narrative in Genet's texts. "Four Hours in Shatila" begins not with the massacre, but with a lyrical evocation of the time Genet spent among the then living *fedayeen* in the early 1970s—the same *fedayeen* who "chantaient en se répondant de colline en colline" [were singing to each other from hilltop to hilltop] (1986: 65; 2003: 44; translation modified). In an obvious way, the simultaneously mirthful and melancholy images of the living that frame "Four Hours in Shatila" provide a dramatic contrast with the dead. But they also reanimate the prostrate bodies and turn them into objects of love. This is how Genet qualifies his feelings for the dead as he leaps over their bodies: "mon amitié, mon affection pour leurs cadavres pourrissants était grande aussi parce que je les avait connus. Noircis, gonflés, pourris par le soleil et la mort, ils restaient des feddayin" ["my friendship, my affection for their rotting corpses was also immense because I had known them. Blackened, swollen, decayed by the sun and by death, they were still *fedayeen*"] (1983a: 16; 1983b: 21). Hijacking the reportage and witnessing genres that he nevertheless deploys for his own purposes, Genet reads political survival into biological death: the silent corpses resist by virtue of being there. In a catachrestic rearticulation of the Palestinian idea of *sumud* [steadfastness], resistance is enacted not through arms, but through mere existence. And in their silence, Genet hears sound. The songs of the *fedayeen* that Genet evokes in *Prisoner of Love* provide a revolutionary soundtrack for the silenced Palestinians, turning the dead into the living and, surreptitiously, victims into resistance fighters. Ten years after he first "touched" the voice of the *fedayeen*, Genet hears the transitive silence of the victims of Shatila.

Sounding the Future

As a medium of representation, sound fails in the films and texts I have discussed above. In *Waltz with Bashir*, the voice of a Palestinian woman triggers the return of the repressed, but for the perpetrator-cum-bystander whose inability to hear, the sounds of killing turns her untranslated injunction to bear witness into a silent reproach. Sound in *Ici et ailleurs* is exposed as the medium that enables the Western filmmaker to speak not for, but over the Palestinians. Only in Genet's Palestinian writings do we glimpse a positive, if paradoxical, articulation of sound as representation. For it is the impossibility of representing the sounds of Palestinian life—the improvised songs of the *fedayeen*—that animates the silence of the dead.

So, can the Palestinians be heard? This, I hope to have shown, is less a question of the adequacy or inadequacy of sound to the task of representation. It is precisely because sound cannot claim to transparently represent its purported source that we must work to analyze representation in sound as carefully as artists, scholars, and activists have analyzed textual and visual representation, until recently the twin foci of postcolonial and critical race scholarship and decolonial and antiracist activism. Nor is this only a question about representing the other. Sound, as a medium that both implies and departs from its source, puts pressure on the naturalized link between self and representation. If the texts I have discussed mark the failure of sonic representations of Palestine by non-Palestinians—indeed, in the case of *Waltz with Bashir*, by someone whose very identity is articulated against the possibility of Palestinianness—this is not to say that sonic self-representation is transparent, unmediated, or unproblematic. The films of Palestinian directors Elia Suleiman and Kamal Aljafari, for example, problematize unmediated representations of sound, underscoring the pitfalls of sonic self-representation in a context where self—Palestinianness—remains more contested than ever.

I'd like to suggest in closing that from a Palestinian perspective, the silver lining of sound's failure to represent is the very plasticity of sound as an object. Metaphorically and acousmatically speaking, the sounds of Palestine are ubiquitous. To focus on French and francophone cultural production alone, the sounds of Palestine echo across the decades with the sounds of migration, indigeneity, and antiracist struggle in France: a Moroccan migrant reads a newspaper article in halting Arabic in Moumen Smihi's short film, *Si Moh, pas de chance*; in Godard's *Notre musique*, we hear Native Americans recite the poetry of Mahmoud Darwish in the ruined library of Sarajevo; a French-Algerian actor performs Darwish in Mohamed Rouabhi's play, *Darwish, deux textes*; a Palestinian from the West Bank compares his lot to that of a Tunisian *harrag* in Maki Berkache and Nathalie Nambot's documentary, *Brûle la mer*.[18] As we know, the Palestinian question is a planetary one. Like the plastic qualities of sound, it exceeds the map of Palestine and the coordinates of its diaspora. Sound, in this sense, might also offer an unexpected metaphor for Palestine, in the sense Edward Said gives the name in *The Question of Palestine*: Palestine as utopia, literally a non-place, that allows the sounding of "a novel future" (1979: 125). But this should not lead to any facile conclusion about the metaphoric promises of sound as an immanent and unmediated medium of representation. On the contrary, against the naturalization of sound as an index of authenticity, I have argued that we need to analyze and critique representation in sound before we can begin to understand what it would mean to hear (*entendre*) the sounds of Palestine. Beneath the soundtrack of the revolution, against

---

[18] I am grateful to Peter Limnick for introducing me to the films of Moumen Smihi. On "Smihi's soundscapes," see Limnick 2020: 73–106.

the grain of an artificial silence, echo the sounds of Palestine. A vast sonic *médiatèque* is waiting to be analyzed by those ready to hear them.

Works Cited

Adorno, Theodor. *Prisms.* Translated by Samuel Weber and Shierry Weber Nicholsen, MIT Press, 1981.

Chion, Michel. *Le Son au cinéma.* L'Étoile, 1985.

De Baecque, Antoine. *Godard: biographie.* Grasset, 2010.

Dindo, Richard, dir. *Genet à Chatila.* Les Films du Paradoxe, 1999.

Dolar, Mladen. *A Voice and Nothing More.* MIT Press, 2006.

Dyer, Rebecca, and François Mulot. "Mahmoud Darwish in Film: Politics, Representation, and Translation in Jean-Luc Godard's *Ici et ailleurs* and *Notre musique.*" *Cultural Politics*, vol. 10, no. 1, 2014, pp. 70–91.

El Maleh, Edmond Amran. "Au seuil de l'interdit: interrogations." *Revue d'études palestiniennes*, 1982, pp. 18–34.

Folman, Ari, dir. *Waltz with Bashir.* Sony Pictures Classics, 2008.

Genet, Jean. "Quatre heures à Chatila." *Revue d'études palestiniennes*, no. 6, 1983a, pp. 3–19.

——. "Four Hours in Shatila." *Journal of Palestine Studies*, vol. 12, no. 3, 1983b, pp. 3–22.

——. *Un captif amoureux.* Gallimard, 1986.

——. "Les Palestiniens." *L'Ennemi déclaré: textes et entretiens*, edited by Albert Dichy. Gallimard, 1991, pp. 89–99.

——. *Prisoner of Love.* Translated by Barbara Bray, New York Review of Books, 2003.

——. "The Palestinians." *The Declared Enemy: Texts and Interviews*, edited by Albert Dichy, translated by Jeff Fort, Stanford University Press, 2004, pp. 71–80.

Godard, Jean-Luc, dir. *Notre musique.* Les Films du Losange, 2004.

Godard, Jean-Luc, and Anne-Marie Miéville, dirs. *Ici et ailleurs.* Sonimage, 1976.

Harrison, Olivia C. "Performing Palestine in Contemporary France: Mohamed Rouabhi's Transcolonial *Banlieue.*" *Modern and Contemporary France*, vol. 22, no. 1, 2014, pp. 43–57.

——. "Consuming Palestine: Anticapitalism and Anticolonialism in Jean-Luc Godard's *Ici et ailleurs.*" *Studies in French Cinema*, vol. 18, no. 3, 2018, pp. 178–191.

Hochberg, Gil Z. *Visual Occupations: Violence and Visibility in a Conflict Zone.* Duke University Press, 2015.

Limnick, Peter. *Arab Modernism as World Cinema: The Films of Moumen Smihi.* University of California Press, 2020.

Lloyd, David. *Under Representation: The Racial Regime of Aesthetics*. Fordham University Press, 2019.

Rastegar, Kamran. "'Sawwaru Waynkum?' Human Rights and Social Trauma in *Waltz with Bashir.*" *College Literature*, vol. 40, no. 3, 2013, pp. 60–80.

Said, Edward. *The Question of Palestine*. Vintage Books, 1979.

——. "Permission to Narrate." *The Edward Said Reader*, edited by Moustafa Bayoumi and Andrew Rubin, Vintage Books, 2000, pp. 243–266.

Sanbar, Elias. "Vingt-et-un ans après." *Trafic*, vol. 1, no. 1, pp. 109–119.

——. *Le Bien des absents*. Actes Sud, 2001.

Spivak, Gayatri. "Can the Subaltern Speak?" *Can the Subaltern Speak: Reflections on the History of an Idea*, edited by Rosalind Morris, Columbia University Press, 2010a, pp. 21–78.

——. "Appendix: Can the Subaltern Speak?" *Can the Subaltern Speak: Reflections on the History of an Idea*, edited by Rosalind Morris, Columbia University Press, 2010b, pp. 237–291.

Toop, David. *Sinister Resonance: The Mediumship of the Listener*. Continuum, 2010.

CHAPTER EIGHT

Transcending Exoticism? Sound and Voice in Dai Sijie and François Cheng

Shuangyi Li

Francophone Chinese writers such as François Cheng (b. 1929), Gao Xingjian (b. 1940), Dai Sijie (b. 1954), and Shan Sa (b. 1972)—all of whom are first-generation migrants in France—have enjoyed the highest French and Western institutional recognitions, from the Prix Femina and the Grand Prix de la Francophonie to the Nobel Prize for Literature. The seminal *Dictionnaire des écrivains migrants de langue française (1981–2011)* places a special emphasis on francophone Chinese writers' surprisingly prolific contribution to contemporary French literature (Mathis-Moser and Mertz-Baumgartner 2012: 43–45). The eminent scholar Karen L. Thornber considers such "literature by writers from countries not part of France's former colonial empire" to be "one of the most promising new areas of Francophone studies" (2009: 223). Indeed, there have even been attempts to see francophone Chinese literature as an "emerging genre," with shared thematic and stylistic preoccupations and recurrent translingual features (Bisinger 2016; Détrie 2004).

As I have argued elsewhere, it may be more productive to conceptualize this literature as *exophone* writing (Li 2019: 360). Not only does the notion of exophony highlight these writers' non-nativeness to French—their dominant language of literary creation (except for Gao)—which therefore makes their writing's status "outside" ("exo-") their native tongue; as a literary and cultural phenomenon, exophony may also be associated with *exoticism*, which is both a theme that they actively explore in their works and a linguistic and literary æsthetic that characterizes their writings. As Mathis-Moser and Mertz-Baumgartner quite rightly point out,

> les auteurs exophones ont un rapport plus décomplexé à la France et au français [...] ils sont des passeurs entre l'Orient et l'Occident—rôle dont témoignent leurs activités comme traducteurs d'œuvres littéraires. (2012: 43)

> exophone writers [for example, Cheng, Gao, and Shan] have less of a complex in relation to France and French [...] they are ferrymen between the East and the West, a role that is affirmed through their activities as translators of literary works.[1]

This observation suggests that exophone writing may sit somewhat at odds with a more restricted understanding of francophone postcoloniality. One is indeed tempted to make a certain distinction between postcolonial and exophone writings: if the former, with its antagonistic and subversive nature, is generally perceived to undergo a process of "writing back" to the imperial center, the latter may be seen as affirmatively "writing in" from *outside* the empire, pledging a kind of intertextual allegiance whilst embodying a sense of alterity.[2] Exophone writing emphasizes the articulation of a cosmopolitanism in a globalized world and, to borrow Mads Rosendahl Thomsen's characterization of migrant literature, "brings a certain strangeness to something familiar" (2008: 99). There is a strong sense of *rapprochement* between a familiarizing French other and a distancing Chinese origin and self.

Yet, such a distinction is far from watertight, especially if we think of "the postcolonial," following Stuart Hall, "at the limit." For, the "post" may signify not only "after" but also "going beyond" the colonial, the latter implication of which resonates in fact with the idea of "going outside." Franco-Chinese exophone writings may not be direct products of Western colonization of China in politico-economic or spatial terms, but they do relate to postcolonial writings as "'emergent' new configurations of power-knowledge relations" that "are beginning to exert their distinctive and specific effects" (Hall 1996: 254). They both reread their historical relations with the West as "part of an essentially transnational and transcultural 'global' process," advocating a "decentred, diasporic or 'global' rewriting of earlier, nation-centred imperial grand narratives." Postcolonial and exophone writings, whether "back" or "in," refuse the "'here' and 'there,' 'then' and 'now,' 'home'

---

[1] Unattributed translations are mine.

[2] The identification of migrant and exophone writing as "writing in" is adapted from Porra 2007: 24.

and 'abroad' perspective" (247), despite the writers' divergent attitudes (for example, subversion vs. respect) to such a "colonial" or "adopted" language as French.

Exoticism, seemingly non-colonial, is an unignorable quality conducive to the commercial success and rapid institutional integration of Franco-Chinese writers' works in France and beyond. However, critics (including myself) have previously approached the issue of exoticism in Franco-Chinese literature from an overwhelmingly *visual* perspective. This is first conveniently encouraged by these writiers' artistic vocation and profession in visual arts: Chinese calligraphy (Cheng), ink wash paintings (Gao and Shan), and cinematography (Gao and Dai). The visual traits of the Chinese writing and literary poetics, in addition, prove to be an inexhaustible source of inspiration and creativity for these writers' French-language texts. The visuality of the sinograph, rich in symbols and metaphors, has an immediate impact on the poetic and æsthetic dimension of Franco-Chinese literary and artistic productions, further enhancing the inextricable relation between text and image.[3]

But can Franco-Chinese literature also "speak"? Or is there such a thing as a Franco-Chinese "voice"? Does the kind of creative exoticism embedded in Franco-Chinese literature also have a special auditory æsthetic that we should be attuned to? After all, etymologically, the suffix of "exophone" denotes the "sound" rather than the "image" of a language. A deeper cause of our current *oculocentric* approach to Franco-Chinese literature lies in the long-held, quasi-Orientalist view and misconception of the Chinese language, which routinely downplays or suppresses the voicing of sinographs. Such a cross-cultural linguistic myth or fantasy—predominantly Western but also widely circulated in Asia—expresses what Andrea Bachner dubs "muteness envy," which fixes the attention to the exotic image of the language. Indeed, from G. W. F. Hegel's alphabetic chauvinism to Jacques Derrida's antiphonocentric celebration (as argued in *De la grammatologie*), much of Western philosophy and theory signals a general "muting of the sinograph" and "an erasure of its connection to speech." As Bachner continues, "both for detractors and for supporters of the sinograph, Chinese frequently signifies as the prime example of pure writing, whereas its pronunciation does not interest, or is framed as an inferior, mutable add-on" (2014: 94–95).

In comparison, with access to both the sound and the image of Chinese *and* French, Franco-Chinese writers are seen not only to play with Western fantasy, but also to rework and reconfigure, cross-culturally, the dynamic relationship between *phone* and *graph* in their literary works, especially in

---

[3] For a brief explanation of this point, see Croiset 2009: para. 22.

relation to exoticism. Indeed, their biculturality often enables them to think beyond such binary tensions and reflect more synthetically on the universal human experience of language. This chapter aims to enrich our current sensory approaches to Franco-Chinese literature by paying more attention to its auditory æsthetic. I will demonstrate how these writers' translingual elaboration of auditory details further accentuates the performative but also, to some extent, metaphorical nature of their fictional utterances and language. My examples are primarily drawn from Dai's and Cheng's works, as these two authors demonstrate a more sustained interest in incorporating issues of sound and voice in their translingual storytelling and transcultural intellectual reflections, albeit in very different ways. My analysis will move from Dai's sensitivity to exotic linguistic sounds and accents to Cheng's novelistic and philosophical elaboration on musical, mystical sounds and poetic voices, such as his Daoist-informed French formulation of *la voix-voie* [the voice/way].

Performing Exotic Sounds and Accents

Dai's debut French-language novel *Balzac et la Petite Tailleuse chinoise* (2000) tells the story of two "rusticated youths"—Luo and Ma—sent down from the provincial capital of Chengdu to a remote mountain village for "re-education" during the Cultural Revolution, where they meet the Little Seamstress and secretly read forbidden books from the West in Chinese translation. Dai later adapted the novel for the screen in 2003. His literary exoticization begins with his deliberate juxtaposition of two culturally divergent proper names in the title. While "la Petite Tailleuse chinoise" may be seen as a facile appellation that evokes the Orientalist image of a petite, docile Chinese woman among Western readers (Zhang 2016: 97), Dai's exoticization of "Balzac" is first and foremost enacted through its unusual pronunciation by the Chinese protagonists. He actively works on what Roland Barthes formulates as "symbolic phonetics" behind a writer's (in Barthes's case, Proust's) exploration and making of proper names as onomastic signs, particularly in the sense that the exotic sound (or the *exo-phone*) of "Balzac" in Chinese is attached to quasi-mythical associations and metaphors and implies transgressions (Barthes 2009: 64–65), with special meanings imputed to the sign through the vehicle of sound. This is how the protagonist describes his first encounter with the name before he even reads Balzac's novel:

« Ba-er-za-ke ». Traduit en chinois, le nom de l'auteur français formait un mot de quatre idéogrammes. Quelle magie que la traduction! Soudain, la lourdeur des deux premières syllabes, la résonance guerrière et agressive dotée de ringardise de ce nom disparaissaient. Ces quatre caractères, très élégants, dont chacun se composait de peu de traits, s'assemblaient pour former une beauté inhabituelle, de laquelle émanait une saveur exotique, sensuelle, généreuse comme le parfum envoûtant d'un alcool conservé depuis des siècles dans une cave. (Dai 2000: 71)

"Ba-er-zar-ke." Translated into Chinese, the name of the French author comprised four ideograms. The magic of translation! The ponderousness of the [first] two syllables as well as the belligerent, somewhat old-fashioned ring of the name were quite gone, now that the four characters—very elegant, each composed of just a few strokes—banded together to create an unusual beauty, redolent with an exotic fragrance as sensual as the perfume wreathing a wine stored for centuries in a cellar. (Dai 2002: 52)

Dai deliberately defamiliarizes the sound of "Balzac" for his francophone and Western readership by putting forward its phonetic transliteration in Chinese. As a sign, the name "Ba-er-za-ke" carries no pre-established or conventional meaning either for the Chinese protagonist—due to his "ignorance totale de ce pays nommé la France" ["complete ignorance of that distant land called France"] (2000: 72; 2003: 53)—or for Dai's Western readership precisely because of such a phonetic defamiliarization. Dai avails himself of the translingual context of storytelling to æstheticize the sound in a way that works towards a creative form of exoticism. The protagonist invests—almost by instinct—a highly subjective and personal meaning in this unusual quadrasyllabic name,[4] based on the heavy, explosive sound that he associates with belligerence and aggression. Francophone readers with no knowledge of Chinese are then invited to imaginatively appreciate the protagonist's further semantic elaborations on "ba-er-za-ke" through other senses by contrast, analogy, and association. Thus, the auditory "ponderousness" is said to be visually translated into simple written Chinese that reflects elegance; and the contrastive synergy between the auditory and the visual are then transformed into a metaphor for "exotic" and "sensual" fragrance and flavour, therefore transgressing into the olfactory and gustative realms of experience. Such a signifying process goes infinitely beyond denotation. In other words, through its sound and the ensuing sensory transgressions—Barthes's symbolic phonetics—"ba-er-za-ke" is made to feel exotic to the Chinese protagonist as much as to Dai's francophone readership.

In fact, the protagonist's unique auditory experience in fiction is shared by certain critics of the novel, who largely ascribe its international success

---

4   Most Han Chinese personal names consist of two or three syllables/characters.

to the special sonority of "Balzac" in the title for non-francophone speakers, as the Japanese scholar Susumu Niijima observes:

> Ce nom bizarre de Balzac qui claque sec à l'oreille [...] Si le livre avait été intitulé *Romain Rolland et la Petite Tailleuse chinoise*, aurait-il eu le même succès? Évidemment non. Pas au Japon, en tout cas. Le mot Balzac, sa sonorité étrange, semble fonctionner comme un mot magique ouvrant sur de nouveaux espaces, excitant l'imaginaire, comme les noms de Mishima ou de Tanizaki, pour les lecteurs occidentaux, connotent probablement le Japon et les prolongent d'un coup au cœur de sa culture et de son univers. (2017: 197)

> The strange name of Balzac which sounds inscrutable to the ear [...] If the book had been called *Romain Rolland and the Little Chinese Seamstress*, would it have had the same success? Obviously not. Not in Japan anyway. The word Balzac, its strange sonority, seems to function as a magical word opening to new spaces, stimulating imaginations, like a Mishima or a Tanizaki for Western readers, which would probably connote Japan and plunge them suddenly into the heart of its culture and its universe.

Yet, interestingly, the name of Balzac in the title was only added during the French editorial process, and was primarily intended by the publisher to appeal to the readership in France by evoking a familiar canonical author while tantalizing them with a Chinese character in an utterly unfamiliar cultural setting (Xavier 2016: 88, 117).

In this debut novel, Dai seems keen to play with the linguistic myth that associates European alphabetical scripts with sounds and accents and the Chinese script only with images. For example, the three Balzacian novels the narrator secretly offers to his male companion are *Le Père Goriot*, *Eugénie Grandet*, and *Ursule Mirouët*—three almost quintessential French proper names (each with a typical French accent [*è, é, ë*]) which produce exotic sounds to the protagonists' ears through the phenomenon of symbolic phonetics. By contrast, for his signature beneath the dedication, the narrator simply "dessin[a] trois objets" ["drew three figures"] that semantically correspond to the three characters of his Chinese name (Dai 2000: 137–138; 2002: 103): 马 (*ma* for "horse"), 剑 (*jian* for "sword"), 铃 (*ling* for "bell"). However, only the first character can be said to have a decidedly pictographic origin. In reality, what Dai creates in the French text is merely an ordinary rebus employing pictures to depict words, but it is evidently used in this context to flirt with the idea of a certain exotic pictographic feature popularly believed to charac- terize Chinese writing. Furthermore, exoticized as a Chinese "pictographic" riddle, the narrator's name effectively becomes "unpronounceable" and consequently "invisible" for Western readers (as the pinyin spelling *ma* is never used in the text). This has led a couple of critics in their otherwise excellent scholarship to claim that "we never find out in the novel" the name of the narrator, "who is called Ma in the film" (Chevaillier 2011: 61), or that "il s'agit de la voix d'un personnage dont on ne connaîtra jamais le prénom" [it has to do with the voice of a character whose name we will never know] (Cañas 2011: 194). Of course, for someone who knows even just a little Chinese, the narrator's Chinese name is both visually concrete and aurally present in the French text.[5] As we will see, this blatant and misleading form of linguistic exoticization evolves in Dai's subsequent French novels.

The pivotal activity of storytelling in *Balzac* is primarily carried out as *vocal* performances, which are freely adapted, yet modally distinctive, from the forbidden literature the protagonists secretly *read* and the films they are officially sent to *see*. In fact, the novel displays some distinctive qualities of a *Künstlerroman* as the protagonist-narrator progressively learns to be an accomplished storytelling artist. He initially contrasts his terrible stage fright ("trac") with the storytelling genius of his male companion Luo, who is able to deftly adjust his tone of voice and gestures to different characters, asking the listeners questions, making them respond and correcting their answers (Dai 2000: 31; 2002: 19). Disappointed by his own performance, the narrator is later sensitized to the power of a storyteller's voice to move the listener "majestueusement" ["majestically"] to tears, as he observes how Luo intones a proverb and "pouvait manipuler le public en changeant simplement la place d'une voix off" ["was able to electrify an audience by means of a perfectly timed voice-over"] (2000: 55–56; 2002: 37). As the narrator becomes a fully independent storyteller (from Luo), he picks a French novel of his own liking and is keen to exercise his newly acquired vocal skills: "Je me redressai, m'assis au bout du lit, et me préparai à prononcer la première phrase, la plus difficile, la plus delicate; je voulais quelque chose de sobre" ["I slid out from under the covers and sat at the foot of the bed, pondering the most difficult, delicate task: how to phrase my opening line. I wanted to set the tone with something straight-forward and arresting"] (2000: 154; 2002: 144). As his voice "résonn[e] dans l'obscurité d'encre de la pièce" ["rings out in the inky blackness of the room"], the narrator does not hesitate to accentuate foreign-sounding names as an oral storytelling strategy to arouse the old tailor's interest in the exotic, "tous ces nom français, ces lieux lointains" ["all the foreign (French) names and faraway places"] (2000: 155; 2002: 115–116). Names such as Marseille, Edmond Dantès, Monte-Cristo, and even Jésus,

---

5 The famous tonal instruction on "mā, má, mǎ, mà" quite literally features in the first lessons of all beginners' courses of Chinese.

spark the old tailor's imagination to such an extent that this listener later ends up creating his own version of Mediterranean fashion in the clothes he makes for the mountain villagers (2000: 158; 2002: 117). In this last example, exoticism is first conveyed almost exclusively through sounds and voices as the storyteller and the listener do not see each other in the darkness of the room at night, and it exerts a cross-modal impact on the mountain villagers' everyday life.

In many ways, Dai's narrative, as well as his storytellers', is not so much concerned with the exact contents of individual novels and stories, but rather with how their stories come to mean at all to the audience through their speech acts in a given situation. To appropriate Barbara Johnson's formulation of "performative utterance" in Stéphane Mallarmé's "La déclaration foraine," one could perhaps argue for a "performative storytelling": to tell the story is visibly to perform the action of telling a story which, "unorthodox as it may be, is uncontestably made to fit into its side show circumstances" (Johnson 1980: 55).

Dai's seemingly dichotomic engagement with exoticism through languages significantly evolves in his subsequent novels. In *Par une nuit où la nuit ne s'est pas levée* (2007a) [*Once on a Moonless Night*, 2009], he takes a more comprehensive approach to language, elaborating notably on issues of sound and mediality, in addition to visual concerns.[6] Dai himself describes *Par une nuit* as "avant tout un roman sur la langue" [first and foremost a novel about language] (2007b), about human languages in general. Dai invents a lost and mysterious language called Tumchooq (meaning "bird's beak") and the narrative revolves around the tortuous uncovering and deciphering of an ancient Buddhist manuscript written in this language, which has been torn into two parts. The title of the novel is taken from the incipit of the manuscript. The female French protagonist-narrator successively learns English, Mandarin, Tibetan, Bambara, and Hebrew, in Europe, Asia, and Africa. The family history of her mixed-race Chinese lover, whose name is also Tumchooq (due to his French sinologist father's obsession with this language), is intertwined with the twentieth-century trajectory of this manuscript. His pursuit of the manuscript brings him into contact with Tibetan, Sanskrit, and Burmese.

Rather than dwelling exclusively on image-informed cross-cultural semantics, exoticism in this novel is conveyed as multi-sensory and quasi-phenomenological experiences of languages and learning languages, in which

---

[6] The visual qualities of sinographs are explored through Freudian and Lacanian psychoanalysis in his second novel, *Le Complexe de Di* (punning on *le complexe d'Œdipe*) (Prix Femina 2003).

the auditory, such as sound, accent, and voice, takes precedence. This is how Tumchooq first introduces his Chinese mother's name to the French narrator:

Le prénom de ma mère, comme elle se plaît elle-même à le dire, se compose d'une seule syllabe à la fière insolence, une unique voyelle qui refuse toute alliance avec ses pairs du système vocalique, encore moins avec une consonne, et sonne à l'oreille comme une pure revendication: E. Peu de mots, dans notre langue, ont la même prononciation. Le E de ma mère signifie « bombyx du mûrier », et se compose de deux idéogrammes, celui de droite signifiant « ver », celui de gauche « moi ».[7] (2007a: 122)

My mother's first name, as she herself delights in saying, is made up of just one proud, insolent syllable, a single vowel which refuses alliance with any of its vocalized peers and certainly not with a consonant, giving it a strong ring of protest: E. There are few words in our language with the same pronunciation. My mother's E means "Mulberry Bombyx," the silkworm moth, and is made up of two ideograms, the one on the right meaning "worm," the one on the left meaning "me." (2009: 85)

The protagonist's description of his mother's single-character Chinese name initially through a phonetic system (for example, syllable, vowel, consonant), and with a quasi-instinctive *phonetic* meaning attached to it (for example, "a strong ring of protest"), largely goes against our usual (Western?) image-focused expectation of a Chinese character and indeed of Chinese in general, Tumchooq's "mother tongue." The actual sino*graphic* form and meaning of the mother's name come only afterwards. Clearly, the *phone* and the *graph* do not *mean* the same.

While the meaning of the written language form is standardized, it is the sound and accent that highly particularize the individual's relation to language and, by extension, other human beings. The narrator describes his Chinese lover's "terriblement efficace" ["terribly effective"] teaching of the street [*hutong*][8] names of an area in Beijing as follows:

Tûmchouq me les faisait *lire* avec lui *à voix haute*, rue par rue, quartier par quartier. Certains noms, par la composition de leurs idéogrammes, brillaient d'une élégance aux nuances exquises, d'autres *m'envoûtaient* par

---

[7] A quick note to clarify that Dai actually got this character wrong, the character 蛾 is written in the reverse order, that is, "ver/worm" on the left, and "moi/I" on the right.

[8] *Hutong* is a kind of traditional alley in Beijing and has a long and rich cultural history. It is often considered a quintessential element of the city, and therefore an obvious object of geographical and architectural exoticism.

leur sonorité subtile, sensuelle, parfois exubérante, *surtout quand c'était lui qui les prononçait, mon Tûmchouq au joli accent pékinois*. (2007a: 348; my emphasis)

Tumchooq made me *read them out loud* with him, road by road, quarter by quarter. Some of the names, the way their ideograms were combined, sparkled with exquisitely nuanced elegance, others *captivated me* with the sound they made: subtle, sensual, occasionally exuberant, *particularly when he said them, my Tumchooq with his attractive Peking accent*. (2009: 256)

Although this passage seems to present the visual and the auditory as concurrent sensory experiences of the Chinese language, when the narrator returns to the site years later noticing the disappearance of those streets, it is the local pronunciation—not the written characters—of the street names that she recalls and misses:

Dans ce quartier de l'ère nouvelle, je me demandai si quelqu'un avait noté combien de hutong avaient disparu. Mille? Deux mille? quel regret! Ne serait-ce que pour leurs noms, si riches en consonnes rétroflexes, que seuls les natifs de Pékin pouvaient prononcer, si riches en diphtongues et autres sonorités exquises. (2007a: 350)

I wondered whether anyone had made a note of how many *hutong* had disappeared in this neighborhood, which now belonged to a new era. A thousand? Two thousand? What a shame! Even if only for their names with their wealth of retroflex consonants, which only natives of Peking could pronounce, their diphthongs and other exquisite sounds. (2009: 258)

In fact, the French narrator's recollection of this once-familiar site and its everyday activities is essentially configured according to human voices and through Tûmchouq:

Plus je marchais, plus j'étais frappée par l'absence des petits vendeurs ambulants qui, jadis, se succédaient du matin au soir [...] Tûmchouq savait imiter à merveille les cris des vendeurs de patates douces grillées [...] ou ceux des vendeurs d'abricots aigres et sucrés, qui faisaient saliver en été, ou ceux de galettes frites dans l'huile [...] ou encore ceux des vendeurs de plantes aphrodisiaques réputées vous faire pisser plus haut qu'un poteau électrique. (2007a: 348)

The further I walked, the more struck I was by the complete absence of simple street pedlars when there used to be an endless stream of them from morning till night [...] Tumchooq could do a brilliant impression of the ones who sold grilled sweet potatoes [...] or those selling sweet and sour apricots, which made you drool in summer; or hot, crispy, deep-fried cakes [...] or even those selling aphrodisiac plants reputed to make a man pee higher than an electricity pylon. (2009: 256)

Such a sensory phenomenon is formulated elsewhere by the narrator as "une réminiscence sonore" ["an auditory memory"] (2007a: 367; 2009: 270). In stark contrast, she now only hears "le bruit des bulldozers résonnant comme le tonnerre dans l'air étouffant de la nuit, et des coups de klaxon, longs, nerveux, agressifs" ["the rumble of bulldozers reverberating like thunder in the stifling night air and the long, irritable, aggressive toot of car horns"] (2007a: 349; 2009: 256). Dai's fictional configuration of the French narrator's auditory experience subtly reworks the conventional Western oculocentric approach to Chinese language and cultural signs and sites.

Yet the pivotal language of the novel is not Chinese but the mystical Tumchooq, a language that is described as "mi-musique d'anges, mi-chant de sirens" ["half angel music, half siren song"]. The protagonist Tumchooq learns this language by repeating after his French father, "mais sans en comprendre le sens exact ni la logique" ["although (he) didn't understand its exact meaning or logic"], and he reports that it is through the "pronunciation" and the "sonority" that his father is able to link the Tumchooq language to Prakrit, Pali, Persian, and Parthian (2007a: 180–181; 2009: 128–129). Correspondingly, the narrator's initial encounter with this language (through the character Tumchooq) is marked by a distinctive sense of aural enchantment that ultimately leads to a synesthetic experience described through metaphors:

Quand il eut fini sa dédicace en tûmchouq, il la lut plusieurs fois, syllabe par syllabe; sa voix résonnait dans la boutique de légumes, et sa sonorité raviva en moi le sentiment que j'avais éprouvé le soir où, pour la première fois, j'avais entendu son nom, sous un voile de pluie fine, confinée en brume. Les mots par lui murmurés sonnaient comme une formule secrète au son inconnu, qui suscitait en moi un léger vertige, une douce ivresse, comme des grains de sable flottant où baignaient tous mes sens. (2007a: 151)

When he had finished his dedication in Tumchooq, he read it out several times, syllable by syllable; his voice reverberated around the greengrocer's shop and the sound of it reawakened the feeling I had the evening I first heard his name, beneath a veil of fine rain, bordering on mist. The words he murmured sounded like a secret formula full of unfamiliar sounds, producing a vertiginous dizziness in me, a sweet intoxication, like drifting grains of sand bathing all my senses. (2009: 107)

As Barthes explains, such a "phonetic motivation requires an interior naming: the language surreptitiously returns to a relation that was— mythically—postulated as being immediate" (2009: 63). From then on, the narrator's fascination with the person becomes inseparable from the language he embodies. In fact, the narrator eventually identifies with the character Tumchooq so strongly that she declares to herself in a highly allegorical remark: "C'est moi, Tûmchouq" ["I am Tumchooq"] (Dai 2007a: 243; 2009: 177). The enchanting sound of Tumchooq also seems to possess the power to connect to a couple of other languages she acquires. Thus, the Hebrew words "dont on ne note que les consonnes, les voyelles restant enfouies dans la tête du lecteur comme un secret de famille" evoke "inévitablement le manuscrit du sûtra en tûmchooq" ["written only in consonants, the vowels staying buried inside the reader's head like a family secret inevitably (reminded her) of the manuscript on the Tumchooq sutra"] (2007a: 286; 2009: 209); the sonority of certain Tibetan phrases "à la beauté imprévisible [...] évoque un peu celle de la langue tûmchouq" ["with unexpectedly beautiful sentences (...) which reminds me of the Tumchooq language"] (2007a: 252; 2009: 184). Both Tibetan and Hebrew, despite their apparent differences from alphabet to writing order, are traditionally thought to carry special religious and spiritual significance: while the former is "imprégnée de Bouddhisme" ["imbued with Buddhism"] (2007a: 250; 2009: 182), to acquire the latter is "à franchir le seuil sacré du temple, à entamer un nouveau parcours vers une destination inconnue" ["to step over the sacred threshold into the temple, to embark on a new journey of indeterminate length to an unknown destination"] (2007a: 285–286; 2009: 210). Yet it is through sound, or the sound of Tumchooq, that their supposedly divergent spiritual qualities converge in the protagonist.

There is a sustained exoticization of languages throughout the narrative of *Par une nuit*. Whereas the visual manifestation of languages is presented as given, predetermined, and prescriptive, the aural experience of languages is portrayed as highly individual, intuitive, and imbued with spiritual significance, waiving any attempt at rationalization. The fictional, mystical language of Tumchooq, in which the Buddhist manuscript is written, occupies a kind of empty medial position that connects languages around the globe primarily through sound. Such a sonic configuration of linguistic exoticism highlights both the linguistic and cultural specificity and the universal human experience of language. Transcendence in Dai can therefore be quite concretely understood as a progressive problematization and complication of "here" and "beyond" in our perception of linguistic and cultural differences through sound, while (re)inscribing in them a sense of mysticism and spirituality.

The actual content of the manuscript, a Buddhist parable, the second half of which is deciphered by the narrator in the end, does not bear any apparent semantic relation to the main story. Yet, crucially, it ends with "une voix" ["a voice"] that tells a falling traveler to let go of his hands; the traveler takes a leap of faith and follows, and he subsequently realizes that the ground is just thirty centimeters beneath his feet. To faithfully follow this *voix* may also mean to follow a whole new *voie* [way]—from its physical to ontological sense—and this is how François Cheng engages with sound and voice in his French exophone writings.

The *Voix-Voie* of Exoticism

Rather than elaborating on any specific physical sound of French or Chinese, Cheng leans towards a thematic approach to sound and voice in his fictional and theoretical writings. Sound and voice are sometimes seen as synonymous to human language in its broadest sense, yet at other times conceptualized as a fundamental form of our spiritual being in, and soulful engagement with, the world through poetry and music. Quite different from Dai's novelistic examples of performative utterance or storytelling that illustrate how sounds and voices come to *mean*, Cheng metaphorically and philosophically prioritizes the invisible, immaterial, and spiritual qualities of sound and voice. No longer does the creative tension arise from the dynamic between *phone* and *graph* in contrastive languages. As we will see, it is the translingual creative reconfiguration of the notion of sound and voice that allows Cheng to understand and conceptualize the fundamental experience of human life as a soul's journey through poetry and music cross-culturally.

Cheng's French homophonic formulation of *voix-voie* is directly informed by the meaning of *dao* 道 in Daoism (as well as in Confucianism), which, in Chinese, means both "to say" and "the way."[9] Daoism is often translated as "la Voie" in French. Such a translingual linkage between the voice and the way plays an active role in his novelistic character's philosophical reflections, as the protagonist Dao-sheng in *L'Éternité n'est pas de trop* [*Green Mountain, White Cloud*] remarks: "Toutes ces voix convergent pour former une immense Voie. Oui, la Voie, le Tao. Et justement, j'y pense, le Tao en chinois n'a-t-il pas un double sens: chemin et parole, marcher et dire?" ["And all these voices join to form one enormous path. Yes, *the* Way—the Tao. I believe it no coincidence that in Chinese *Tao* has a double meaning: both 'way' and 'word,' both 'walking' and 'speaking'"] (Cheng 2002: 139;

---

[9] The association originally comes from Jacques Lacan, with whom Cheng worked intensively from 1969 to 1973 (Bertaud 2011: 57).

2004: 120). Don Ihde observes in *Listening and Voice: Phenomenologies of Sound* that "in the beginning was voice and the voice was speech and speech was Language" (2007: 185). Cheng also believes that man is fundamentally "être de langage" ["a being of language"], and the notion of *voix-voie* allows Cheng to understand and formulate his different way of life and existence through his acquired French language, "des murmures maternels des mots secrets mus par une autre sonorité. J'étais, pour tout dire, devenu quelqu'un d'autre, indéfinissable peut-être, mais autre" [some maternal whispers of secret words moved by another tone. I had, on the whole, become someone else, perhaps indefinable, but other] (Cheng 2010: n. pag.). Here, it is evident that for Cheng, the self-othering and transformative power of language lies essentially in its sound and tone. Between the "murmures maternels" and the "autre sonorité," there is a spiritual resonance and communion, which may lead to a certain transcendence. Indeed, Cheng's notion of *voix-voie* is infused with a mysticism of language:

> Je parlais du mystère du langage humain; je suis prêt à affirmer à présent que c'est dans le langage, toujours au sens large, que réside notre mystère. C'est bien au moyen de notre langue, à travers notre langue, que nous nous découvrons, que nous nous révélons, que nous parvenons à nous relier aux autres, à l'univers des vivants, à quelque transcendance en laquelle certains d'entre nous croient. (2010: n. pag.)

> I was talking about the mystery of human language; I am ready to affirm now that it is in language, always in the broad sense, that our mystery resides. It is by means of our language, through our language, that we discover ourselves, that we reveal ourselves, that we manage to relate to others, to the universe of the living, to a certain transcendence in which some of us believe.

Poetry, then, epitomizes the highest form of expression of such a linguistic mysticism; it is "l'art du langage même" [the art of language itself] (n. pag.). Cheng's *voix-voie* applies specifically to his vocation as a poet who seeks a common ground or, better still, a communion, between his two cultural heritages. On the one hand, he follows the æsthetic of Classical Chinese poetry inhabited by the spirit of *chan* (better known as Zen in the West)—the fruitful marriage between Indian Buddhism and Chinese Daoism—which "cherche à *laisser parler* le paysage et les choses, à laisser transparaître entre les signes un état de communion où *l'invisible* a sa part" [tries to *let the landscape and things speak*, to reveal between the signs a state of communion where *the invisible* has its share] (n. pag.; my emphasis). On the other hand, he is thoroughly informed by the Western "Orphic Way" of poetry, "Orphée, le poète à la lyre, ordonne par son incantation le mouvement des rochers, des arbres et des animaux et, par là même, insère le destin de l'homme dans l'ordre de la Création" [Orpheus, the poet with a lyre, through his incantation orders the movement of rocks, trees, and animals and thereby inserts the destiny of man in the order of Creation] (n. pag.). Cheng's own account of both Chinese and Western poetic traditions emphasizes the vital yet invisible role of sound and voice that gives life to things, and which connects our being to the world.

The latter Orphic Way is most notably championed by Mallarmé's "explication orphique de la terre" [Orphic explication of the Earth] (qtd. in Cheng 2010: n. pa.) as the poet's only duty. For Mallarmé, "la Poésie est l'expression, par le langage humain ramené à son rythme essentiel, du *sens mystérieux* des aspects de l'existence" [Poetry is the expression, in human language restored to its essential rhythm, of the *mysterious* meaning of the aspects of existence] (qtd. in Bertaud 2011: 237; my emphasis). While Mallarmé's "explication orphique" appears to concern itself primarily with meaning, Cheng's specifically aural reconfiguration of the Orphic *voix-voie* has another important source, Victor Segalen, to whom Cheng devotes several essays collected in a volume entitled *L'Un vers l'autre* (2008). Segalen approaches the myth of Orpheus explicitly from the perspective of sound, voice, and music, as exemplified in the novella *Dans un monde sonore* and the play *Orphée-roi*. To cite a revealing remark from the foreword of the latter play, "Orphée ne fut pas un homme, ni un être vivant ou mort. Orphée: le désir d'entendre et d'être entendu. Le pouvoir dans un monde sonore" [Orpheus was not a man, nor any human being, living or dead. Orpheus is the Desire to hear and to be heard, the Power in a world of sound] (Segalen 1995: 668). The dramatic text of *Orphée-roi* was supposed to be realized in musical form through Segalen's close collaboration with Claude Debussy.[10]

Although Segalen's sustained interest in non-Western music is also well-documented, as exemplified in his essay "Voix mortes: musiques maori" (1907), the poet's "China"—its music, language, and landscape—is extraordinarily silent.[11] As Philip Weller comments, "Segalen regarded the profound silence of China as something nearly absolute: unremitting, unsettling, at times even disturbing" (2000: 123). Segalen's most explicit poetic engagement with the Chinese language is seen in *Stèles* (1912), a collection of sixty-four bilingual poems, each consisting of a preceding Chinese epigraph and poetic

---

[10] Debussy had to abandon the idea of composing the music, and the text was finally published in 1921, about two years after Segalen's death.

[11] Charles Forsdick considers this contrast to be a "stylized" progression from orality to literacy as Segalen's journal moves from Polynesia to China (2000: 145).

lines in French. The (Classical) Chinese characters æsthetically laid out on these pages are devoid of any sonic sensibility, as Segalen is searching for a purely Chinese "form" in his poetic conception. Each poem is supposed to formally resemble the text from a Chinese tomb stone slab, which Christian Doumet characterizes as "une parole pétrifiée" [a petrified speech] (informed by Jacques Rancière's formulation of "la parole muette" [the mute speech]) (Doumet 2000: 40–41). As Christopher Bush rightly points out, Segalen "explicitly sets out to use China as a set of dehistoricized formal possibilities, deploying elements of traditional Chinese culture as 'forms' with which to compose his own poetic language" (2010: 74).

Segalen's approach to China, Chinese, and Chineseness is an excellent example that exposes his paradoxical conception of exoticism, famously formulated as the æsthetics of Diversity (*une esthétique du Divers*). On the one hand, the utter dearth of "Chinese sound" represented "precisely this radical, impermeable 'otherness' that he had come to China to seek out" (Weller 2000: 125), as it corresponds to "la perception aiguë et immédiate d'une incompréhensibilité éternelle" [the acute and immediate perception of an eternal impenetrability] (Segalen 1995: 751). The mysterious, the mystical, the superhuman, the divine, and so on can thus be maintained through such an exoticism. Segalenian exoticism advocates an "antiglobalization æsthetic that would preserve the alterity of the Other," opposing "the logics of assimilation and appropriation" (Bush 2010: 75), because, as Charles Forsdick decisively states, "at the root of Segalen's exoticism [...] is a universal aversion to Western intervention" (2000: 145). On the other hand, it also runs the risk of perpetuating many of the Western Orientalist constructions and misconceptions of the Other—in this case, the deliberate muting of the sinograph.

This, however, is not Cheng's reading of Segalen. In *L'Un vers l'autre*, Cheng is determined to construct a relational understanding of Segalenian poetics beyond mere "Chinese forms," as he sees in Segalen "un effort non moins intense d'ouverture, de bouleversement, d'assimilation et de transformation" [no less intense an effort at opening up, dramatic change, assimilation, and transformation], and he describes the "charme étranger" [strange charm] of the Segalenian style as coming from "cet espacement de soi au travers de l'autre" [this distancing from self through the other] (Cheng 2019: 65). Notions such as "dialogue" and "communion" permeate Cheng's voicing on Segalen. One can argue that Cheng makes use of Segalen's extensive cross-cultural experience and intellectual thinking to articulate his own cultural enterprise more generally. In many ways, he sees it his duty and vocation to make those muted Chinese voices heard in his French writings. Ultimately, as we will see, the invisibility and immateriality of sound and voice enable

Cheng to not only open up a transcultural intellectual dialogue but also experience a *spiritual* communion, through poetry and music, from the *voix* to the *voie*, expressing a palpable desire for a planetarian transcendence. As he reflects on Segalen in the following:

> Assurément, la Terre est le lieu de notre destin [...] En son sein, devenus des êtres de langage, nous avons entrepris un dialogue de fond avec nos semblables, avec l'univers des vivants et, comme irrésistiblement, avec une forme de transcendance. (Cheng 2019: 104)

> Most certainly, the earth is the place of our destiny [...] In her womb, we've become beings of language, we have engaged in a profound dialogue with our fellow beings, with the universe of the living and, quite irresistibly, with a form of transcendence.

In view of such remarkable intellectual influence from Cheng's double cultural heritage, I would now like to turn to the theme of *voix-voie* in Cheng's novel *Le Dit de Tianyi* (1998) [*The River Below*, 2000]. The issue of sound and voice, through the acts of ritualistic calling, asking, answering, as well as poetic singing and musical listening, becomes key to the understanding of the protagonist's spiritual and soulful journey between China and Europe, during which both a Segalenian and an un-Segalenian sense of exoticism pervade.

The French title already reflects such a notion, as the "dit" [saying] of Tianyi can also be understood as his Daoist "way." The novel starts with a voice: "Au commencement il y eut ce cri dans la nuit" ["In the beginning there was the cry in the night"] (Cheng 1998: 15; 2000: 3). At a first glance, it seems that Cheng deliberately turns the biblical "void" and "darkness" on earth into an atheistic cry in the night. It is a pre-semantic word consisting of only breath and sound, which is captured in an act of listening and described only in auditory terms, "un long cri se fit entendre. D'abord plaintif, lointain, puis de plus en plus proche et strident, il finit par se muer en une sorte de mélopée à mots répétés, monotone, lancinante mais infiniment berçante" ["we heard a long cry. Plaintive at first, distant, then closer and closer; strident, soon it had turned into a kind of repetitive chant, an insistent monotone, but infinitely soothing"]. The identification of this auditory source is also depicted in the language of the creation myth: "C'était une voix de femme, jaillie aurait-on dit de ses entrailles, ou de celles de la terre, tant elle résonnait d'échos immémoriaux" ["The voice was woman's, so resonant with immemorial echoes that it seemed to spring from her entrails or from the bowels of the earth"]. The feminine voice (*voix*) is thus ontologically associated with the Way (*voie*) of Mother Earth. Subsequently, "âme" ["soul"] turns out to be the first semantically intelligible word that the protagonist Tianyi hears—"Âme errante, où es-tu, où est-tu? [...] Âme errante, viens ici, viens ici" ["Wandering soul, where are you, where are you? (...) Wandering soul, come here, come here"] (1998: 15; 2000: 3).

What is at stake in this opening passage is Cheng's translingual reconfiguration—through *voix-voie*—of a Daoist ontology and sensibility that are founded on the idea of the *Souffle* ("breath," "air," or *qi* 气 in Chinese), which, in Cheng's words, "ont avancé une conception unitaire et organiciste de l'univers créé, où tout se relie et se tient, le Souffle étant l'unité de base qui anime et relie entre elles toutes les entités vivantes" [have advanced a unitary and organicist conception of the universe created, where everything is connected and held together, the Breath being the basic unit which animates and links together all living entities] (2010: n. pag.). The initial characterization of this female voice sprung from the womb of Mother Earth is in fact a direct reference to the "Mysterious Female" or the "Esoteric Feminine" in Chapter 6 of *Laozi*, a founding text of Daoism.[12]

However, what is concretely taking place in this scene is a Daoist and folk ritual of soul-summoning: a widow is making an effort to call back the soul of her recently deceased husband so that the soul, separated from the body at the moment of death, may stop wandering, come back, and rest in peace. But if a living being verbally answers such a call, he or she "perd son corps dans lequel s'introduit l'âme errante du mort, lequel, du coup, réintègre le monde vivant" ["loses his body, which is quickly entered by the dead man's wandering soul that then returns to the world of the living"]. The child protagonist naïvely answers the summoning voice, "oui, je viens; oui, je viens" ["yes, I'm coming; yes, I'm coming"], and then, in a moment of hallucination as it were, "sees" himself leaving the body, "déjà mort" ["already dead"]. From then on, the protagonist is convinced that a wandering soul has attached itself to him and feels "étranger" ["a stranger"] to himself: "j'avais conscience que mon corps antérieur avait été pris par quelqu'un, et ce corps étendu là [...] était celui d'un autre, auquel mon âme s'était, coûte que coûte, accrochée" ["I was aware that my previous body had been taken by someone; what lay on the bed (...) was another person's body, to which my soul had attached itself, come what may"] (Cheng 1998: 16–17; 2000: 3–4). Thus, this misunderstood verbal call and answer, a seemingly accidental vocal performance of language, results in an ontological transformation between life and death, between self and other. This scene serves as both an allegory and a metaphor of our fundamental relation to the world through sound and voice. Phenomenologically, from the repeated "viens

---

12 For a helpful overview of this theme, see Chen 1974.

ici" to the repeated "oui, je viens," the voice of the World finds response, an "echo," in the subject's own voice that takes up the language of the World through "a primary listening." As Don Ihde continues, the self is "a correlate of the World, and its way of *being-in* that World is a way filled with voice and language" (2007: 116–117).

In many ways, the opening scene represents a novelistic initiation of an important thesis that Cheng advances throughout his writings, as he, for instance, remarks in *Le Dialogue*: "le propos de la vie n'est pas la domination mais la communion [...] il faut connaître une sorte d'effacement originel avant d'accéder à l'être, au voir, au pouvoir de chanter" [life's intention is not domination but communion (...) one must know a kind of erasure of origin before reaching out to one's being, seeing, the power to sing]. In this context, Cheng is explicitly comparing the Chan Buddhist poetics with the Orphic Way. He subsequently cites Rainer Maria Rilke's *Sonnets to Orpheus* and explains how Rilke

affirme la primauté du Souffle, par lequel Apollon, ou l'Ange, ou le Poète célébrant relie le double royaume de la vie et de la mort [...] pour nous initier à la Voie qui mène du fini vers l'infini, du visible vers l'invisible [...] le Poète [...] invite chacun de nous à entrer dans le courant de la Transformation. (2010: n. pag.)

affirms the primacy of the Breath, by which Apollo, or the Angel, or the celebrating Poet connects the coupled kingdom of life and death [...] to initiate us into the Way that leads from the finite to the infinite, from the visible to the invisible [...] the Poet [...] invites each of us to enter the current of Transformation.

Written words may be seen as fixed and finite, so it is through invisible sound and the act of singing or chanting that the Poet breathes infinite life into them, which, in turn, transforms our sense of being. Like Tianyi's "wandering soul," Orpheus's journey, as André Velter writes in the preface to Cheng's *À l'orient de tout* (2005), is "une expérience de la dépossession, de l'abandon, de la perte de soi" [an experience of dispossession, abandonment, loss of self], and it "décide de l'existence tout entière comme elle décide du surgissement de la parole poétique et de sa légitimité" [decides the whole existence as it decides the outburst of poetic speech and their legitimacy] (2005: 12). In other words, Tianyi, Orpheus, and Rilke all breathe, utter, and call out poetically to recuperate, to become, and to be.

It must be pointed out that Cheng's novelistic elaboration on the soul-summoning alludes to one of the earliest anthologies of Classical Chinese poetry, *Chu Ci* [*The Songs of the South*] (3rd century BCE), which

Cheng often mentions in his other writings.[13] *Chu Ci* is particularly known for its shamanistic and supernatural ideas and characteristically features the presence of the mysterious and the exotic. Many of the verses, such as "Yuan you" 远游 [Far-off Journey], "Zhao hun" 招魂 [Summons of the Soul], and "Da zhao" 大招 [The Great Summons], deal explicitly with Daoist esoteric, out-of-body, spiritual traveling experiences, including flights to various places on earth and in heaven. Read in this light, Tianyi's tortuous cross-cultural journey between and within China and Europe, and to a large extent that of Cheng himself, seems to incarnate such mystical experiences which are at the same time exotic and self-othering. Indeed, in the additional preface Cheng wrote in Chinese for the Chinese translation of *Le Dit, Tianyi yan*, he describes retrospectively the process of this particular literary creation as a "spiritual journey" 心路历程, referring explicitly to *Chu Ci* (2009a: 2).[14]

Orpheus is a legendary musician, and this important detail decidedly *in-spires* ("to take in spirit") Cheng to develop a specifically musical notion of the soul in his configuration of the *voix-voie orphique*, especially when, on numerous occasions, he cites Rilke's famous line from *Sonnets to Orpheus*, "Chanter, c'est être" [To sing is to be]. In effect, music broadens the "linguistic" language-as-word, and a musical characterization of the soul is inclined towards a certain universality of human experience, which further enriches the transcultural dynamics in Cheng's works: "Languages bind together and separate humankind. Otherness and strangeness is dramatic in the difference of tongues, but there is also the human ability to learn to 'sing' in any language" (Ihde 2007: 118). Cheng also draws on the musical definition of the soul proposed by his predecessor Jacques de Bourbon Busset at the Académie française:[15]

> Usant d'une image musicale, il dit que l'âme est la « basse continue » de chaque être, cette musique rythmique, presque à l'unisson du battement de cœur, et que chacun porte en soi depuis sa naissance. Elle se situe à un

---

[13] For a quick overview of how this ritual is described in *Chu Ci*, see Wang 2011: 41–44.

[14] Quite curiously, Cheng's conception of literature here seems to bear an affinity with Hélène Cixous's "cri de la literature" in *Ayaï*: the soul is transmitted from poet to poet, "aux commencements des commencements, il y aura eu la première note de notre douleur [...] *AYAÏ!* Le mot universel, l'Appel [...] Et aussitôt vient la Réponse [...] La mort attaque" [In the beginnings of beginnings, there would have been the first note of our suffering (...) *AYAÏ!* The universal word, the Call (...) And just as soon comes the Response (...) Death attacks] (2013: 23–24).

[15] Jacques de Bourbon Busset is the deceased French Academician whose seat was filled by Cheng.

niveau plus intime, plus profond que la conscience. Parfois en sourdine, parfois étouffée, jamais interrompue cependant, et à certains moments d'émotion, ou d'éveil, elle se fait entendre. Se faire entendre et résonner, c'est sa manière d'*être*. Résonner, voilà le mot juste. Résonner en soi, résonner à la « basse continue » d'un autre, résonner à la « basse continue » de l'univers vivant, c'est sa chance d'être immortelle. (Cheng 2008: 56)

Using a musical image, he says that the soul is the "continuo" of each being, the rhythmic music, almost in unison with the heartbeat, that each of us carries within from the time of our birth. It is located on a deeper, more intimate level than consciousness. Sometimes muted, sometimes hushed, it is never interrupted, and at certain moments of strong emotion or awakening, it makes itself heard. To make itself heard, to resonate, is its manner of *being*. To resonate, yes, that is the right word. To resonate within, to resonate with the "continuo" of another, to resonate with the "continuo" of the living universe, that is its chance to be immortal. (2009b: 49–50)

Soul as a musical being, soul as resonance, soul as a fundamental way of experiencing the world by answering and reacting to its "call," which results in the soul's own transformation, ceaseless, yet elusive and unpredictable: Cheng's elegant formulation of the soul in relation to sound, voice, and music prefigures some of the major contemporary theoretical works on world relation, such as Hartmut Rosa's *Resonance* (2019).[16] Such a formulation not only adds another layer of understanding to the "wandering soul" in the opening passage of *Le Dit*, it also encourages us to pay special attention to the Orphic protagonist's experience of music during his "spiritual" journey.

Tianyi and his male companion's first encounter with Western orchestral music during the Sino-Japanese War is marked by an exotic appeal of the unknown and an uncanny sense of wonder. The cello is described as an "être si mystérieux [...] aussi attirant qu'impénétrable" [mysterious creation (...) as appealing as it is impenetrable].[17] Words like "fasciné" ["fascinated"],

---

[16] In brief, Rosa employs "resonance" to conceptualize our way of *encountering* the world, a mutually transformative relationship between the subject (already in the world) and the world which is, in turn, "conceived as *everything that is encountered* (or *that can be encountered*)" (2019: 34).

[17] The exoticism of Western musical instruments also features in Dai's *Balzac*: "[le chef] fit courir ses doigts calleux sur une corde, puis une autre [du violon ...] La résonance d'un son inconnu pétrifia aussitôt la foule, comme si ce son forçait chacun à un semi-respect" ["(the headman) ran his calloused fingertips over one string, then another (of the violin ...) The strange resonance froze the crowd, as if the sound had won some sort of respect"] (Dai 2000: 10; 2002: 5).

"halluciné" ["carried away"], and "la folle illusion" ["deluded by the mad hope"] (Cheng 1998: 92–93; 2000: 60–61) are repeatedly employed to describe the protagonists' experience of the performance. Tianyi remarks: "Si la littérature et la peinture nous étaient plus ou moins accessibles par la traduction et la reproduction, la musique nous demeurait quasiment inconnue" ["although literature and painting were accessible to us through translation and reproductions, music remained virtually unknown"] (1998: 90; 2000: 58). Yet, as a transcultural experience, music "needs no translation or explanation whatsoever for being 'understood' by everybody" (Pothast 2008: 64). The immediacy of music, Beethoven's *Pastoral Symphony*, is felt as "l'intrusion inopinée—ou miraculeusement opportune—du Dehors" ["the unexpected—or miraculously opportune—intrusion of the Outside"] (Cheng 1998: 90; 2000: 58). "To listen is to be dramatically engaged in a bodily listening that 'participates' in the movement of the music," and there is a "*loss of distance* which occurs in dramatically sounded musical presence" (Ihde 2007: 155–156). While Beethoven's symphony is described as "ce chant aux accents si souverains, si conquérants [...] était proche cependant du battement de cœur de ces deux marcheurs perdus dans la nuit de Chine" ["a song with tones so sovereign, so conquering (...) Yet how akin it was to the heartbeat of two walkers lost in the Chinese night"], those of Dvorak get through to the "plus intime, '[le] creux des entrailles'" ["the most intimate and the innermost of the heart"] (Cheng 1998: 91; 2000: 59). At the same time, Beethoven's music *transposes* the protagonists to "les champs de blé et les pâturages de la lointaine Europe" ["the wheat fields and pastures of far-off Europe"] (1998: 93; 2000: 59); and Dvorak's music, "originaire d'Europe centrale" ["native of central Europe"] (1998: 95; 2000: 62), "si lointaine, si 'étrangère'" ["from afar, so foreign"], is "d'emblée proche, aussi proche que certains morceaux chinois anciens [...] Tant que durait la mélodie, le pays natal semblait être à portée" ["immediately close, as close as some ancient Chinese pieces (...) As long as the melody lasted, my native region seemed within reach"] (1998: 92; 2000: 59–60). Indeed, just like the "aventure de l'âme singulière et à l'errance" ["restlessness of spirit and the peculiar adventure of each (wandering) soul"] (1998: 96; 2000: 62) that Tianyi has always believed in, music empowers the subject to travel in time and space. In a highly Orphic moment, the protagonist states: "L'écoutant, je me laissais porter par la vague émotion, celle qui me faisait sentir que d'un instant à l'autre j'allais retrouver les êtres chers qui m'attendaient: ma mère, ma sœur, l'Amante" ["Listening, I was carried on the music's wave of emotion, which made me feel that at any moment I would be reunited with the loved ones who waited: my mother, my sister, the Lover"] (1998: 92; 2000: 60). While Tianyi's sister is lost forever, his mother and Lover will later wait to be retrieved from the Underworld:

his journey to Tchoungking to rejoin his dying mother is described as "une longue descente aux enfers" ["a long descent into the underworld"] (1998: 182; 2000: 123), and his return to China to find the Lover "une véritable descente aux enfers" ["a veritable descent into hell"], explicitly compared to the myth of Orpheus (1998: 275; 2000: 191). In fact, lacking a legitimate *voice* because of his foreignness to the language and customs, even Tianyi's arrival in Paris is described as another journey to hell (1998: 196–197; 2000: 136). However, it is thanks to the Dvorak concerto that he makes the romantic acquaintance of the clarinetist Véronique, "un être qui sache [lui] sourire" ["a woman who smiles (at him)"] in "cet enfer parisien" ["the Parisian hell"] (1998: 256; 2000: 178). And it is thanks to the company and encouragement of this musician-lover that he begins to "entendre [sa] voix, à trouver sa voie" ["hear (his) voice, to find (his) way"] (1998: 262; 2000: 181), as a painter. Such diegetic details are not only configured according to the Orphic "pattern," they also allude to the "Esoteric Feminine" of Daoism (*la Voie*), as Tianyi recalls his poet-companion's remark: "C'est peut-être juste ce que pensait un Dante, ou un Goethe: nous serons sauvés par la Femme" ["This may be just what a Dante or a Goethe was thinking: we shall be saved by Woman"] (1998: 94; 2000: 61). In fact, Cheng continues to explore this theme in his more recent work, *De l'âme: sept lettres à une amie* (2016), in which he positions the soul, essentially feminine, sonic, and musical, in a ternary system of thought that overcomes the body-mind binary:

> Tout se calme. Je suis là seul, mais je suis de ce côté de la vie [...] Une musique douce se fait entendre. Puis une chanson nostalgique, entendue jadis, chantée par une voix de femme [...] Là, elle me poigne corps et âme [...] de la planète Terre [...] foncièrement maternelle et maternante [...] monte un chant qui rappelle que chaque âme qui l'habite porte en elle une berceuse depuis sa naissance. Cette berceuse, qui résonne avec le chant originel, ne cesse de chanter en elle [...] (2016: n. pag.)

> Everything is calm. I'm here alone, living on this side of life [...] Mellow music is heard. Then a nostalgic song, heard long ago, sung in a woman's voice [...] There, she captures my body and soul [...] from the planet Earth [...] profoundly maternal and motherly [...] rises a song which reminds us that each soul which inhabits it carries within it a lullaby since birth. This lullaby, which resonates with the original song, never ceases to sing with her.

From the Chinese polysemic *dao* to the French homophonic *voix-voie*, this translingual incident allows Cheng, in both his creative writings and reflective essays, to conceptually expand the notion of sound and voice far beyond their physical properties. Unlike Dai's creative approach to contrastive linguistic sounds in the author's ultimate "homage to language" (*langue*) (2007b), the cross-cultural theory on sound and voice proposed by Cheng seeks to understand and explicate our fundamental sense of being in the world *through* human language (*langage*), particularly in the forms of poetry and music, which, in turn, come to define our soul and communicate our spiritual experiences of the world.

I started this chapter by conceptually qualifying Franco-Chinese literature as exo*phone* writing, which aims to accentuate its auditory æsthetic that has often been "muted" in traditional oculocentric approaches to such literature. Whereas previous debates on exoticism in Franco-Chinese literature often centered around problems of visual stigmatization and clichéd cross-cultural representation (Deppman 2010: 125–126), the exoticism conveyed through sound and voice examined in this chapter largely hinges on individual and personal associations, experiences, and observations, from Barthesian symbolic phonetics to cross-cultural poetic and musical being as soul. While visual exoticism may be easily accused of reducing the complexity of cross-cultural realities, the aural exoticism in my analysis is not only seen to significantly enrich our perspectives on the visible and the finite with tangible meanings, but also enables us to investigate the performativity of utterance (in Dai) and to reconnect our being to, or to resonate with, the world through the invisible, the immaterial, and the spiritual (in Cheng). Whether in Dai's novelistic evolution or Cheng's spiritual journey across cultures, the issue of sound and voice allows Franco-Chinese writers to consciously and creatively readjust their individual æsthetic distance between self and other in their literary works. They attempt to assimilate their exotic objects in meaningful and lateral ways while re-enchanting them with, and reinscribing them in, a new kind of mystique and mysticism (for example, the mystical language of Tumchooq and the wandering soul through the *voix-voie*) that is palpably oriented towards a dialogue, a communion, and a transcendence to come.

Works Cited

Bachner, Andrea. *Beyond Sinology: Chinese Writing and the Scripts of Culture.* Columbia University Press, 2014.

Barthes, Roland. *New Critical Essays.* Translated by Richard Howard, Northwestern University Press, 2009.

Bertaud, Madeleine. *François Cheng: un cheminement vers la vie ouverte.* 2009. Hermann, 2011.

Bisinger, Lena. *Rencontre interculturelle dans le roman franco-chinois: invitation au voyage d'un genre émergent.* Logos Verlag, 2016.

Bush, Christopher. *Ideographic Modernism: China, Writing, Media.* Oxford University Press, 2010.

Cañas, Beatriz Mangada. "Dai Sijie: écrire en français pour évoquer dans la distance le pays quitté." *Çédille: revista de estudios franceses,* no. 7, 2011, pp. 190–203.

Chen, Ellen Marie. "Tao as the Great Mother and the Influence of Motherly Love in the Shaping of Chinese Philosophy." *History of Religions,* vol. 14, no. 1, 1974, pp. 51–64.

Cheng, François. *Le Dit de Tianyi.* Albin Michel, 1998.

——. *The River Below.* Translated by Julia Shirek Smith, Welcome Rain, 2000.

——. *L'Éternité n'est pas de trop.* Albin Michel, 2002.

——. *Green Mountain, White Cloud: A Novel of Love in the Ming Dynasty.* Translated by Timothy Bent, St. Martin's Press, 2004.

——. *Cinq méditations sur la beauté.* 2006. Albin Michel, 2008.

——. *Tianyi yan* 天一言. Translated by Nianxi Yang, People's Literature Publishing House, 2009a.

——. *The Way of Beauty: Five Meditations for Spiritual Transformation.* Translated by Jody Gladding, Inner Traditions, 2009b.

——. *Le Dialogue: une passion pour la langue française.* 2002. Desclée de Brouwer, 2010. [Kindle, n. pag.]

——. *De l'âme: sept lettres à une amie.* Albin Michel, 2016. [Kindle, n. pag.]

——. *L'Un vers l'autre.* 2008. Albin Michel, 2019.

Chevaillier, Flore. "Commercialization and Cultural Misreading in Dai Sijie's *Balzac et la Petite Tailleuse chinoise.*" *Forum for Modern Language Studies,* vol. 47, no. 1, 2011, pp. 60–74.

Cixous, Hélène. *Ayaï! Le cri de la littérature.* Galilée, 2013.

Croiset, Sophie. "Passeurs de langues, de cultures et de frontières: la transidentité de Dai Sijie et Shan Sa, auteurs chinois d'expression française." *Trans-,* July 8, 2009, trans.revues.org/336.

Dai, Sijie. *Balzac et la Petite Tailleuse chinoise.* Gallimard, 2000.

——. *Balzac and the Little Chinese Seamstress.* Translated by Ina Rilke, Vintage, 2002.

——. *Par une nuit où la lune ne s'est pas levée.* Gallimard, 2007a.

——. *Rencontre avec Dai Sijie.* Gallimard, 2007b, gallimard.fr/catalog/entretiens/01058735.HTM.

——. *Once on a Moonless Night.* Translated by Adriana Hunter, Vintage, 2009.

Deppman, Hsiu-Chuang. *Adapted for the Screen: The Cultural Politics of Modern Chinese Fiction and Film.* University of Hawai'i Press, 2010.

Détrie, Muriel. "Existe-t-il un roman chinois francophone?" *Magazine littéraire*, March 2004, pp. 65–66.

Doumet, Christian. "Corps-signe." *Reading Diversity/Lectures du Divers*, edited by Charles Forsdick and Susan Marson, University of Glasgow French and German Publications, 2000, pp. 39–49.

Forsdick, Charles. *Victor Segalen and the Aesthetics of Diversity*. Oxford University Press, 2000.

Hall, Stuart. "When Was 'The Post-Colonial'? Thinking at the Limit." *The Post-Colonial Question: Common Skies, Divided Horizons*, edited by Iain Chambers and Lidia Curti, Routledge, 1996, pp. 242–260.

Ihde, Don. *Listening and Voice: Phenomenologies of Sound*. SUNY Press, 2007.

Johnson, Barbara. *The Critical Difference: Essays in the Contemporary Rhetoric of Reading*. Johns Hopkins University Press, 1980.

Li, Shuangyi. "Novel, Film and the Art of Translational Storytelling: Dai Sijie's *Balzac et la Petite Tailleuse chinoise*." *Forum for Modern Language Studies*, vol. 55, no. 4, 2019, pp. 359–379.

Mathis-Moser, Ursula, and Birgit Mertz-Baumgartner, eds. *Passages et ancrages en France: dictionnaire des écrivains migrants de langue française (1981–2011)*. Honoré Champion, 2012.

Niijima, Susumu. "La traduction japonaise et *Balzac et la Petite Tailleuse chinoise* et son retentissement au Japon." *Balzac et la Chine, la Chine et Balzac*, edited by Véronique Bui and Roland Le Huenen, Presses universitaires de Rouen et du Havre, 2017, pp. 193–197.

Porra, Véronique. "De l'hybridité à la conformité, de la transgression à l'intégration: sur quelques ambiguïtés de la représentation identitaire dans les littératures de la migration en France à la fin du XXe siècle." *La Littérature 'française' contemporaine: contact de cultures et créativité*, edited by Ursula Mathis-Moser and Birgit Mertz-Baumgartner, Gunter Narr Verlag, 2007, pp. 21–36.

Pothast, Ulrich. *The Metaphysical Vision: Arthur Schopenhauer's Philosophy of Art and Life and Samuel Beckett's Own Way to Make Use of It*. Peter Lang, 2008.

Rosa, Hartmut. *Resonance: A Sociology of Our Relationship to the World*. Translated by James C. Wagner, Polity Press, 2019.

Segalen, Victor. *Œuvres complètes I*. Robert Laffont, 1995.

Thomsen, Mads Rosendahl. *Mapping World Literature: International Canonization and Transnational Literatures*. Continuum, 2008.

Thornber, Karen L. "French Discourse in Chinese, in Chinese Discourse in French: Paradoxes of Chinese Francophone Émigré Writing." *Contemporary French and Francophone Studies*, vol. 13, no. 2, 2009, pp. 223–232.

Velter, André. "Le troisième souffle." *À l'orient de tout*, by François Cheng. Gallimard, 2005, pp. 7–14.

Wang, Eugene Y. "Ascend to Heaven or Stay in the Tomb: Paintings in Mawangdui Tomb 1 and the Virtual Ritual of Rivival in Second-Century BCE China." *Mortality in Traditional Chinese Thought*, edited by Amy Olberding and Philip J. Ivanhoe, SUNY Press, 2011, pp. 37–84.

Weller, Philip. "'Sound—Silence—Space': Between Segalen and Debussy." *Reading Diversity/Lectures du Divers*, edited by Charles Forsdick and Susan Marson, University of Glasgow French and German Publications, 2000, pp. 115–142.

Xavier, Subha. *The Migrant Text: Making and Marketing a Global French Literature*. McGill-Queen's University Press, 2016.

Zhang, Hua. "Writing across Languages and Reading across Culture: Is There a Recipe for the Sino-French Novel?" *China from Where We Stand: Readings in Comparative Sinology*, edited by Kate Rose, Cambridge Scholars Publishing, 2016, pp. 91–100.

CHAPTER NINE

A Walk on the Wilde Side: Rock Music and Listening as Narrative Strategy in Marjane Satrapi's *Persepolis*

Jennifer Solheim

As an emerging discipline in the 1980s and '90s, francophone studies was productive in highlighting vital cultural work previously unrecognized in scholarship, which often framed such works as a dubious legacy of France as a colonizing force and its civilizing mission. Yet, in setting francophone cultural works apart from the rest of French literature and culture through geopolitics, *francophonie* remains the one area of French studies not organized temporally. This holds true in the categorization of literature in French bookstores, podcasts, and other literary endeavors as well. While works from mainland France by writers of French origin are categorized and considered by historical era or century, with emerging literary voices in French from the colonial world, the organization becomes spatial, regional, and geopolitical.

Removing francophone literature and culture from the temporal setting that governs the rest of French literary and cultural history serves a systemic political purpose. The rhetoric of right-wing politicians like Marine Le Pen and culture war critics such as Eric Zemmour (who, as the son of Algerian Jews, complicates received notions of French vs. Francophone) cudgel the idea of a white, Christian France as "us" and immigrants and the broader French-speaking world as "them," stereotyping the latter category as non-Christian religious extremists and denying the legacy of colonialism, thus revising or ignoring the intimate ties that France imposed and imposes through coloni-zation and globalization (Wampole 2020: 11, 14–15). So if francophone works are seen likewise as apart, separate, or distinct from French works in time, then there are fewer opportunities for readers to draw social connections that might offer productive critiques of implicit bias and French privilege as part of an ongoing institutional legacy of colonization.

To establish francophone studies as distinct from French historical time disrupts the chronological narrative established when following historical eras: there is a *suite de logique* to French studies that abruptly ends when we shift to the francophone context that is, nonetheless, rooted in French history as well. "Postcolonial" might seem to situate modern works historically, yet it also has a flattening effect, and maintains francophone cultures as distinct from the broader French historical context.[1] Why shouldn't *all* works written in French after 1962 be considered postcolonial? This blind spot speaks to the privilege of continuing on, social and culturally, in a more or less uninterrupted way, while former colonies in the wake of liberation were left struggling to define and structure statehood, selfhood, and social identity. As an organizing principal for French literature, historical time sets a tempo with which francophone works are always already out of step—and thus, organizationally speaking, incongruous.

As narratives that must establish a historical context, then, many francophone works employ global hits contemporaneous to the story, putting a narrative strategy of listening to work for the audience. By weaving music into cultural narratives—whether literary, theatrical, cinematic, or graphic— authors, filmmakers, and playwrights establish a temporal cadence through listening, both as performed within the work, and by the audience. For example, "Passe-moi la flûte," the Lebanese anthem made famous by Fairuz, runs through the narrative of Yasmina Khadra's novel *Les Sirènes de Bagdad* (2006), which is set in Iraq. The song catches the narrator's attention as his musician cousin responds to the violence of the second American invasion of Iraq with music; hearing Fairuz again in the airport thwarts the narrator in his plot to carry a lethal virus with which he has been injected to London. In the 2019 Mati Diop film *Atlantique*, the supernatural refugee story is framed by scenes in a dance club that's either lively with music and dancers, or silent by day—but in each scene, the club is the place where crucial information is revealed to the protagonist about her lover lost at sea. As a third example, in both the stage productions and film adaptation of Wadji Mouawad's *Incendies* (2003 and 2010), music situates the audience temporally in a story that moves between an unnamed country much like Lebanon in the midst of its civil war of 1975–1990, with The Police and Supertramp, and Québec in the early aughts, with PJ Harvey and Radiohead.

---

[1] For more on this distinction in postcolonial studies, and the rhetorical distancing of the hyphen in "post-colonialism," see Mishra and Hodge 1991 and 2005.

These works do not seek a place within the French historical canon; rather, they establish their own narrative tempo. Similar to the melding of North African and Euro-American musical structures, instruments, and languages to create the genre of Beur music, these cultural narratives graft Euro-American musics onto geopolitical settings. For the audience, then, the characters in these works embody a kind of universalism—both politically and narratively—with specific music, set in their particular place and time. Music in these works is diegetic—part of the narrative, heard by the characters— and listening to the music establishes and punctuates narrative time, which sets a beat alongside the historical organization of French literature. The music draws the audience into the story and character concerns, unmarking these works as globally distinct. As Oliver Sacks describes in *Musicophilia*, "listening to music is not just auditory and emotional, it is motoric as well [...] we keep time to music, involuntarily, even if we are not consciously attending to it" (2007: ix, xi). The representation of not only the music but listening to it offers a shared human experience between characters and audience in the feel of musical time, the movement in rhythmic time that is ingrained in our psyches and physiologies.

Accordingly, my analysis offers not a study of sound but a study of listening as a narrative strategy in Marjane Satrapi's *Persepolis* (originally published in four volumes, 2000–2003). In this autobiographical graphic narrative set during the Islamic Revolution in Iran, music plays a vital role for the central character, Marjane, as coping mechanism and means of understanding and being in the world. In this essay, I analyze the Kim Wilde chapter in *Persepolis* Volume 2, to take up the role of listening to music in the narrativization of character development. A representation of listening and reacting to music offers the *performance of listening*, which "establishes the *narrative as listener*," where "the narrative of the work itself [...] intercepts sounds and silences" (Solheim 2017: 10). To illustrate the narrative performance of listening in *Persepolis*, I work throughout with film sound theorist Michel Chion's concept of synchresis, "the forging of an immediate and necessary relationship between something one sees and something one hears at the same time" (2019: 224). Synchresis arises in these panels and pages through characters listening and reacting to what they hear—both music and speech—upon alternately sparse and culturally evocative settings.[2] Marjane and the other characters don't simply refer to bands and performers, nor is music just part of the background noise and cultural context. Rather, the characters react to the music—and what it represents. Marjane sings along,

---

[2] For an explanation of how the performance of listening requires setting, sound source, and listener in cultural works, see Solheim 2017: 10–17.

dances to it, turns it off, turns it down, turns it up. Her parents, the dealers on the black market, and the guardians of the Revolution who appear near the end of the chapter react to it morally and ethically as well, questioning or advocating the music's value, selling or buying it on the black market, confiscating and threatening arrest over possession of it. These reactions are part of the synchresis between sound, setting, dialogue, and action. Characters' reactions often occur in the same panels where the music plays, lending a kinetic quality to the performance of listening in *Persepolis*. The synchresis of music and character reaction and action establishes narrative time and tempo, too. Musical, graphic, and linguistic synchresis is central to the analysis of Persepolis that unfolds in the coming pages.

Music is part of the social ecosystem in *Persepolis*, akin to what Michael Allan notes of Frantz Fanon's "Ici La Voix de l'Algérie," which "brings to light the importance of a robust media ecology informed by attention to transformations in sense perception" (2019: 192). Fanon describes the reactions of Algerians listening to Classical Arabic on the radio, a language they "do not fully understand," as the voice "recalls the nature of revolution" (192). To listen to "the voice of Algeria" on the radio transforms Algerian listeners through broadcast reception, transforming the radio from "mouthpiece of the French occupation to voice of the Algerian resistance" (188). As a psychologist, Fanon's relation of the gathering of a group around a radio and the individual bodily reactions of the listeners as a transformation offers a kind of psychological synchresis—the necessary relationship between what is seen and what is heard by the psychologist. We can read *Persepolis* in a similar way: as part of a coming-of-age story, the narrative portrays Marjane transformed through the performance of listening. In representing her actions and reactions to music on the page, both in graphics and language, we see a young woman negotiate worlds with which she is perpetually—at times, dangerously and tragically—out of step. Music gives structure to narrative time in the work, and she takes solace in tempo(ral) and lyrical sense within an increasingly disorienting world.

Notably, however, while Marjane is informed neither morally nor æsthetically by music, her drive toward consuming music culture is commercial. The "sonorous stereotype" (Szendy 2012: 28) of Kim Wilde's "Kids in America" refrain, repeated in key panels in the *Persepolis* chapter named for the British pop star, becomes unique to the character Marjane: she takes solace in the phantasmagoric "we" of the song's refrain, yet she never finds community within the increasingly oppressive and dangerous public world of Tehran and insular life at a private French school, and is ultimately exiled from her family.

Satrapi presents us with a teenage narcissism in the narrative perspective that focuses not on the cultural possibilities in Iran, but on the censorship of

American and European culture in Iran. For the adolescent protagonist, Kim Wilde's "Kids in America" becomes a "'Marseillaise' of the psyche" (Szendy 2012: 62). But the phantasmagoria that arises from anglophone rock is not limited to the music. It extends to products: posters, a jeans jacket, Nikes, and band buttons. As Szendy points out, "the censorship of music in general, under the Taliban regime in Afghanistan, for example, seems to have as its object *what music represents* other than itself, that is to say, what it refers to: as if, in this particular case, it transmitted a general text, the 'libretto' of Western capitalist culture" (59). As the Kim Wilde chapter unfolds, Marjane assumes English-language rock music as an object of resistance, and by extension the fashion and cultural objects associated with the music.

Listening and reacting to music informs Marjane's character and how she develops, which I theorize as sonic and psychological synchresis, character embodiment of phantasmagoria and emergent cultural practice, an Althusserian interpellation, and finally, a Szendian inthymnacy. These processes narrate the development of Marjane's character through the Kim Wilde chapter, which sets the stakes for the narrative arc of the graphic novel: a privileged adolescent girl from a bourgeois yet politically progressive family, her generational path is set on a different course in her reactions to the censorship of music by a governmental regime and the phantasmagoria that the censored hit songs conjure. The debates about music and taste influence Marjane to take up the emergent cultural practice of the black market, which results in a confrontation with the guardians of the Revolution. This scene leads to the chapter's concluding performance of listening, in which Satrapi foreshadows her national and cultural exile. Inthymnacy arises in the final panel through a narrative accretion of different performances of listening: the psychological synchreses portrayed in several early scenes in this chapter gives way to a phantasmagoria, which in turn leads Marjane into an emergent cultural practice in the black market and subsequent embodiment of what censored music represents. In other words, we see the beginning of Marjane's exile in the Kim Wilde chapter, when her very body becomes contraband. Ultimately, it is this exile that leads to the inthymnacy of the Kim Wilde song "Kids in America."[3]

---

[3] One might argue that the character Marjane was always already in exile in cultural revolutionary Iran, a country that was never a French colony. Satrapi attended the Lycée Français in Teheran before her parents decided to send her to Vienna for the outspoken teenager's safety. As Simidchieva 2017 has argued that *Persepolis* could and should be considered a Persianate work, so, too, might we extend the term francophone to *Persepolis*, particularly given the disorientation of the francophone field from the historical organization of French studies.

Phantasmagoria and Family Complicity

The Kim Wilde chapter is set in Tehran in 1983, after the borders of Iran have opened to travel in spite of the ongoing Iran-Iraq War, and continuation of a fundamentalist cultural and governmental regime that forbids cultural imports from much of the outside world, but in particular the US and Europe. Adolescent Marjane, from whose perspective the story is related, doesn't give her audience an insight into Persian cultures; her attention to what is forbidden bears a teenage narcissism. This attention also speaks to Szendy's notion of the phantasmagoria that arises when hit songs are censored. It's not simply from the censorship of music that a phantasmagoria arises, but more particularly the censorship of what the music represents: a "psyche within the market" (Szendy 2012: 57). In the opening scenes of the Kim Wilde chapter, a phantasmagoria of family complicity against the fundamentalist regime plays out through the conspicuous consumption of censored music and cultural objects. The following discussion brings Marjane into complicity with her parents through a conversation about the merits of the musical contraband, in multiple senses of the term: the music and related fashion and cultural objects forbidden by the regime are smuggled into Iran. But beyond this, in listening to rock music and consuming the trappings of the culture, Marjane embodies the idea of contraband as well: through her comportment and style of dress, her very body becomes not only subversive, but also illegal and detainable. Her embodiment of contraband—in other words, her embodiment of music, and of what the music represents—shows her development as a social and political being out of sync with the world around her, and thus both isolated and endangered. It is a return to the music that helps Marjane reorient herself—which reinforces further a phantasmagoria of belonging through Kim Wilde's "Kids in America" at the end of the chapter.[4]

When the family discusses Taji and Ébi's upcoming weekend in Turkey, the panels are devoid of background: we only see parents in conversation with daughter Marjane, whose head and shoulders in the foreground are twice as large as her parents. As we see the daughter react to the news that she's being left with her grandmother, the parents are featured head to ankle

---

[4] In fact, I would argue that the asynchronous narrativization of character is part of what makes *Persepolis* such a commercially successful work in France and globally: beyond the linguistic affiliation, this asynchronous narrative, categorized geopolitically rather than temporally, is recognizable within francophone culture, and further as a coming-of-age narrative of teenage alienation. These aspects make *Persepolis* a universal story on its own terms, within its own specificity.

in the background. She deflects her disappointment: "Pff ... c'est trop nul la Turquie! Y a que des ringards qui y vont. Tant qu'à voyager, allez un peu plus loin, en Europe ou aux États-Unis par exemple!" ["Turkey's for the birds. Only uncool people go to Turkey. If you're taking a trip, why not go to Europe or the United States?"] (2007: n. pag.; 2004: 126).[5] Marjane only knows Europe and America through the filter of culture smuggled from Turkey. Her parents demonstrate understanding of Marjane's identification with censored music and culture; Taji defends their choice: all "tout ce que tu trouves de chic ici" ["all the hip stuff you like"] comes from Turkey, since, the exposition details, imports from the West were halted in Iran.

The next panel shows Marjane excitedly making a list, counting on her fingers while Ébi takes notes: "Une veste en jean, du chocolat, un poster, non deux, un de Kim Wilde et un de Iron Maiden" ["A denim jacket, chocolate, a poster, no, two posters, one of Kim Wilde and one of Iron Maiden"] (2007: n. pag.; 2004: 126). This is the first evocation of music in the chapter, and while neither the characters nor readers hear music, it's clear that Marjane's parents are listening. Taji stands centered in the background, saying, "Iron Maiden? Les quatre brutes là?" ["Iron Maiden? Those four brutes?"]. Ébi responds, "Ce n'est pas des brutes. J'aime beaucoup ce qu'ils font" ["They're not brutes. I really like what they do"]. Taji responds, "Tu aimes ça?" to which he replies "J'adore!" and Marjane, situated in the right corner of the panel, looks up at her mother with a wide-eyed I-told-you-so look and says, "Tu as vu?" ["You like that?" "I love it!" "See, mom?"] (2007: n. pag.; 2004: 126). The debate here is about the moral and æsthetic qualities of Iron Maiden, not about whether or not it's acceptable to smuggle contraband into the country. That they will do so is a forgone conclusion, and Marjane's phantasmagoria of complicity and belonging starts to take shape around the idea of music through the debate about taste.

The next panel portrays Taji and Ébi in a record store plastered with posters, including AC/DC, the Rolling Stones, and Iron Maiden. This detailed panel contrasts with the family discussion about Turkey and Iron Maiden, featuring objects from music cultures that Marjane covets. The posters, racks of records, stickers plastering the checkout desk are synchretic reminders of the connection between what this music represents—a willful teenage resistance, rebellion, and freedom—and social and political oppression, represented by their cultural absence.

Thus there is no need for exposition in the next panel: as Marjane's parents walk from the store with posters rolled under the arms, Ébi says,

---

[5] The 2007 French edition published by L'Association, which compiles the four volumes of *Persepolis* into one volume, is unpaginated.

"C'est tellement dur pour les enfants en Iran! Les pauvres petits!" ["It's so hard for the kids in Iran. The poor things"]. "Dis, tu aimes vraiment Iron Maiden?" Taji asks. "Tout à fait!" he replies. "Quel hypocrite!" she says ["Do you really like Iron Maiden?" "Absolutely." "You hypocrite!"] (2007: n. pag.; 2004: 127). This discussion offers a sonorous stereotype in Taji's dismissal of Iron Maiden: both parents have enough understanding to either laud or dismiss heavy metal as an antagonistic cultural force, pushing back against its censorship, the muting force of the cultural revolution.

In the subsequent two-page, multi-paneled scene, the parents conspire to sew the posters into the lining of Ébi's coat to get them through customs, which makes the shoulders of the coat stick out at comically suspicious right angles. This image offers another kind of synchresis: how censorship mutes both culture and sense. Taji insists that they look like shoulder pads—"Tu es à la mode" ["It's stylish"] (2007: n. pag.; 2004: 128)—and they go through customs to have their luggage searched and to be threatened by the officer. Wearing her mandatory headscarf, Taji asks the officer, "Mais enfin monsieur, on a l'air de contrebandiers ou quoi?" ["Sir, do we really look like smugglers?"] (2007: n. pag.; 2004: 129). A long pause indicated by a series of ellipses in a dialogue bubble offers synchresis of graphic silence and suspended action that rachets up the tension, an embodiment of the cultural oppression and menace that silences those subject to it. Finally, the officer lets the parents through.

Listening arises in these panels through the band name Iron Maiden, the poster, and, as we will see shortly, music itself. This listening—in other words, this cultural engagement—functions within the storytelling convention of "show, don't tell"—yet in the representation of music as the fodder of resistance that draws the family into complicity with one another, the music also speaks as a narrative strategy. In seeing her parents' active resistance to cultural oppression by smuggling music and cultural objects, Marjane is further cultivated and emboldened as a cultural consumer and politically outspoken adolescent girl.

In the opening panel of the next scene—the first to portray Marjane listening to music—she plays air guitar with a tennis racket. Her new posters are taped to the wall, and she first imitates the defiant stance of Iron Maiden, body square, arms across her chest. In the next panel, she imitates Kim Wilde's seductive pose, with her hands on her hips, turned in a three-quarter posture. These poses offer further insight into Marjane's phantasmagoria of music and music culture: she can strike the pose, but she needs to acquire more music and merch. Kim Wilde might not yet have been discussed or heard, but the repetition of her name alongside Iron Maiden's represents an earworm in this chapter: it's clear now that for Marjane, music and music culture are intimate forces, familial, political, and mercantile.

Emergent Culture and The Black Market

The consumption of decadent Western rock and consumer products like merchandise defies the regime of censorship. In other words, the censored music represents Western capitalist culture and mercantile practices (Szendy 2012: 59), offering Marjane a scenario in which she feels empowered through contraband. With the sense of empowerment, the phantasmagoria of censored music has arisen. In the next scene, Marjane actively seeks out music for herself, resulting in an emergent cultural practice. Raymond Williams explains in *Marxism and Literature*: "By 'emergent' I mean, first, that new meanings and values, new practices, new relationships and kind of relationship[s] are continually being created," but "since we are always considering relationships within a cultural process, definitions of the emergent, as in the residual, can be made only in relation to a full sense of the dominant" (1977: 123). Together with social and political changes in Iran, and Marjane's parents' morals and choices for themselves and their daughter, the phantasmagoria of music as resistance amounts to emergent cultural practices of consumption.

To go to the black market, Marjane dresses in her new Nikes and denim jacket, pins her Michael Jacket button to the lapel, "et bien sûr mon foulard pour sortir" ["and, of course, my headscarf (to go out)"] (2007: n. pag.; 2004: 130). Taji sits in the living room reading, and Marjane asks, "Alors, tu me trouves comment?" "Belle, très mignonne!" Taji replies ["So what do you think?" "Nice! Very cute!"]. Marjane tells her she's going out to buy tapes, and Taji tells her to be back within an hour. "Je serai là dans deux heures" ["I'll be back in two hours"], Marji says, and then narrates, "Pour une mère iranniene, ma mère était très permissive. À part moi, je ne connaissais que deux ou trois autres filles qui avaient le droit de sortir seules à treize ans" ["For an Iranian mother, my mom was very permissive. I only knew two or three other girls who could go out alone at thirteen"] (2007: n. pag.; 2004: 131). There is foreshadowing in this exposition: they have not yet fully reckoned with the potential dangers an outspoken adolescent girl alone in public might face under the new regime.

In the next panel, Marjane walks past a gauntlet of black-market vendors, with the expositional comment that

> Le problème de la nourriture était déjà résolu depuis un an par la croissance du marché noir. Par contre pour trouver des cassettes, c'était un peu plus compliqué. Sur l'Avenue Gandhi, on arrivait à s'en procurer. (2007: n. pag.)

Food shortages had been resolved by the growth of the black market. However, finding tapes was a little more complicated. On Gandhi Avenue you could find them sometimes. (2004: 132)

This exposition tacitly acknowledges Marjane's privilege; she is never concerned about having enough to eat. Her hunger is for culture, to consume contraband. Her hunger is embodied in this panel scene through the synchresis of the vendors' hisses and whispers, alongside their mustaches— none have beards, signifying opposition to the regime—and further visual details. The first vendor, a dwarfish man with slanted eyebrows, offers "Estevie Vonder." Second comes a tall, skinny, frowning vendor, also with a mustache, who offers "Abba, Bee Gees." Marjane's walk is suspended between this second vendor and a third, who offers "Yazoo." The fourth vendor says "Julio Iglesias," pointing to his jacket, while the fifth cups his hand beside his mouth to whisper "Pink Floyd." Another vendor pops out from behind him, saying, "Jikael Mackson." A final vendor holds open his coat to reveal pockets stuffed with wares: "videos, music, cards, lipstick, nail polish, chess set, pantyhose, chocolate ..., ..." (2007: n. pag.; 2004: 132). The array of early '80s popular music references is further contextualized by games, diversions, and beauty products, the latter of which is depicted in later scenes of *Persepolis* as another means of political opposition in everyday life for privileged Iranian girls and women such as Marjane, who straddle Iranian and other cultures through the educational and cultural opportunities afforded them, hidden beneath their mandatory *chador*s. The panel in the black market shows the full arc of Marjane's hit song phantasmagoria and foreshadows her coming of age: from her rebellion through popular music as a preteen to embracing feminizing beauty standards when she returns to Iran from Vienna, this black-market scene imbues both music and beauty care products with political potency. As a narrative performance of listening, music and related cultural consumption reinforces and helps Marjane embody her political awareness and outspokenness.

The next two panels are suffused with a black background as Marjane buys Kim Wilde and Camel tapes from yet another mustache-wearing vendor, who gives a quick glance left and right before he pulls them from his jacket. Marjane imitates his glances as she slides the tapes into her denim jacket. There is a comic intensity to the looks on Marjane's and the vendor's faces in these two panels which suggests that, from our protagonist's perspective, the black market is more of an adventure than a risk. Yet, in contrast with the white-background panels where the Satrapi family debate the cultural value of Iron Maiden, here the black background offers another kind of synchresis between the shadows and silence, represented by the lack of dialogue and the furtive glances. This synchresis is comedic, spoofing expressionist films that Satrapi claims as an influence. It also foreshadows the disorientation to come.

Interpellation and Disorientation

It's worth pausing to consider the synchresis of silence and imagery that arises from the panel as Marjane leaves the black market for home. Aside from the panels featuring her parents in the record store in Turkey, and then emerging from customs to see Marjane and her grandmother on the other side of the glass, the panel in which Marjane has just left the black market is the only one that features a detailed background. City buildings are rendered in black-and-white squares, and the street is rendered in black. Marjane is in the fore of the panel; she is smiling, mouth closed, and a dialogue bubble indicates that the earworm refrain of "Kids in America" is running through her head, "We're the kids in America whoa ..." (2007: n. pag.; 2004: 132). On the street, behind her back, there is a car with three frowning women in *chadors*, one of them pointing at Marjane. The synchresis between the city setting and the Kim Wilde earworm offers both character development and a tonal shift: Marjane believes she's safe and sound, that the risk—and the adventure of emergent cultural practice—is over. She is situated here as her parents were in the record store, in the phantasmagoria of Kim Wilde, and she's feeling the "we" in the refrain. She knows where she is and where she is going. Everything makes sense.

The next panel offers a jarring synchresis between the finger pointed at Marjane and the command of the *chador*-clad women, who now stand on the street: "Arrête-toi" ["You! Stop!"]. The female guardians of the Revolution, Marjane explains in exposition, is a new branch that "se joignit aux hommes pour arrêter les femmes qui n'étaient pas correctement voilées (comme moi par exemple)" ["had been added in 1982 to arrest women who were improperly veiled. (Like me, for example.)"] (2007: n. pag.; 2004: 132). These two panels suggest syncretic disorientation: the guardians look like the indoctrinating schoolteachers to whom Marjane and her friends have been giving trouble for years. Yet in this context, the women in *chadors* become a part of the police force that has been threatening and murdering Satrapi family and friends. The synchresis of the pointed finger and the imperative "arrête-toi" is an Althusserian interpellation: Marjane is literally stopped in her tracks by the words, which both represent and embody the broader social structures and strictures at work within the cultural revolution in Iran. She is obliged to stand and listen.

The narrative action and dialogue in the next panels offer further syncretic disorientation of character and place. The looming guardians question Marjane's dress and appearance. One panel features a high-top sneaker and that pointing finger of the guardian again, who calls them "chaussures de punk" ["'punk' shoes"] (2007: n. pag.; 2004: 133). Marjane defends herself against the accusation that her shoes are punk with a quivering lip and the claim that they are basketball shoes and she's on the school team. "Il fallait mentir! Il n'y avait pas d'autre alternative" ["There was no alternative. I had to lie"] (2007: n. pag.; 2004: 134). Until this point, rebelling against the regime through music and fashion had been a hobby of sorts. At school, she was scolded; at home, cultivated, corrected, yet also lauded. Here, outside the black market, the phantasmagoria that has produced an emergent cultural practice—and Marjane's embodiment of contraband, or the capitalist culture the music represents— has led to judgment and sentence. The guardians see through her right away. The second retorts, "Ah oui ... ça se voit à ta taille!" ["Oh sure, I can tell by your height!"] (2007: n. pag.; 2004: 134). There is a sinister note to this judgment of Marjane's physical size: she's being judged for her female body (rendered smaller than the guardians) and the way she presents it to the world as an embodiment of rebellion through rock (or, as Marjane would say, "punk") culture.

The interpellation continues, and Marjane continues to fabricate excuses. In the next panel, the third guardian shakes Marjane by the lapels of her denim jacket, saying, "Et avec cette veste, tu fais du basket aussi??" ["And you wear this to play basketball as well?"]. Then she takes a closer look at Marjane's button. "Qu'est-ce que je vois? Michael Jackson? Ce symbole de la décadence?" ["What do I see here? Michael Jackson! That symbol of decadence?"] (2007: n. pag.; 2004: 133). Marjane claims the button features Malcolm X—even though the button reads "Michael Jackson"—and again, the guardians are having none of it.

Throughout these panels, synchresis forges disorientation between the music merchandise and fashion that Marjane wears and has strived to acquire as part of her emergent cultural practice, the dialogue, and the guardians' physical manhandling of Marjane. One of the guardians yanks Marjane's headscarf over her face, yelling, "Baisse ton fichu, petite pute!" ["Lower your scarf, you little whore!"]. In the next panel, she points at her legs and asks if Marjane isn't ashamed to wear "un jean moulant comme ça" ["tight jeans like these"]. The dialogue and actions might suggest an ocular focus, but remember that the music is censored for *what it represents*— the decadence of American and European cultures—and for Marjane, the clothes are as much a part of cultural expression as the music. Marjane is both physically and psychologically disorientated by the guardians' interpellation. Of her tight jeans, Marjane cries, "Il a rétréci!" ["They shrank!"] (2007: n. pag.; 2004: 133) as she struggles to pull the scarf back from her eyes and stands on one leg, wobbling, off-balance. The world around her has become unintelligible. The guardians' dialogue is confrontational, insulting, aggressive, and interpellates Marjane herself as contraband—she embodies what the music represents.

It becomes clear that from the moment she was first stopped by the guardians, she had already been sentenced, the confrontation a parody of a court trial, for in the next panel the guardians order Marjane into the car and say they are taking her to the "committee," which she explains in exposition is the headquarters of the guardians of the Revolution. Marjane's back is to the guardians, but the readers can see her eyes wide and her mouth quivering with fear. Here, as with the first panel in this scene when she's got the Kim Wilde refrain in her head, Marjane's back to the guardians hits a synchretic mute button: they won't listen to her explanations; they can't *hear* her, in any sense of the word. But the reader does. What the censored music represents has been transformed, both for Marjane and for the reader: it's no longer just cultural contraband that represents the decadent West. The music offers a stand-in for Marjane's emotions: contentment and a sense of place in the world has given way to mounting fear, disorientation, and bodily danger. As Marjane explains to the reader in the next panel:

> Au comité on pouvait ne pas prévenir mes parents, on pouvait me garder quelques heures ou quelques jours, on pouvait me fouetter, bref tout pouvait m'arriver. Il faut agir. (2007: n. pag.)

> At the committee, they didn't have to inform my parents. They could detain me for hours, or for days. I could be whipped. In short, anything could happen to me. It was time for action. (2004: 134)

Throughout the first volume of *Persepolis*, the young Marjane has heard stories from her parents, her grandmother, and her beloved Uncle Anoush (who was imprisoned and murdered by the current regime, with Marjane as his final visitor) about political imprisonment, torture, and execution. These stories take on mythical status in her life and indeed influence Marjane personally and politically. The connections in the narrative between these family stories and her desire to rebel are tightly bound. In this scene, what she has heard is now borne out through her own experience: after a childhood spent staging political rallies and demonstrations in the living room, and following her imitation of Kim Wilde's pose and the gesture of the black-market vendor, as well as her fashion choices, in the confrontation with the guardians of the Revolution, she experiences for the first time the threats to which she, as an individual, ostensibly sovereign being, is subject. This, too, is part of her process of exile: she has come to embody not only what the music represents, but also family tradition, which she knows through the stories she's been told over tea, or at bedtime, since she was a child. They are Marjane's birthright, and she embodies these myths through both sonorous stereotypes and emergent cultural practices. But her embodiment is not without cost. The guardians' arrest, judgment, and sentence set Marjane on an exilic path well before she leaves Iran.

Narrative Inthymnacy

The concluding panels of the Kim Wilde chapter are imbued with an implicit poignancy: Marjane returns home. Taji asks why she has been crying, but Marjane does not tell her. Instead, she retreats to her bedroom. The final panels of the chapter take on an *inthymnacy*, as Szendy defines it: "the becoming-hymn of hits is elaborated not only on national and international political stages but also on the stage of the individual psyche [...] musical obsessions that, in each one of us, play the role of an 'Internationale' of intimate collaborations" (2012: 64). The penultimate panel of the Kim Wilde chapter depicts Marjane's hand inserting a tape into a boom box. The exposition reads, "Je m'en suis quand même bien sortie. Les gardiennes de la Révolution n'ont pas trouvé mes cassettes" ["I got off pretty easy, considering. The guardians of the revolution didn't find my tapes"] (2007: n. pag.; 2004: 134). In the final panel, a dialogue bubble with jagged edges takes up the top quarter, and sharply angled points indicate that Kim Wilde's "Kids in America" is blasting from the boom box while Marjane sings along at the top of her lungs, swollen eyes screwed shut, hands balled into fists, and arms swinging as her open black mouth intones, "We are the kids of America whoao." Significantly, an eighth note symbol flanks the line rather than punctuation. Notably, within this experience of inthymnacy, the note symbols indicate rhythm—but not melody. The exposition at the bottom of the panel concludes the chapter: "On se calme comme on peut" ["To each his own way of calming down"] (2007: n. pag.; 2004: 134).

To calm herself, she turns to a pop hymn of youth rebellion that has moved beyond representing capitalist culture: this is the hymn of Marjane's coming-of-age, shaped through judgment and exile. Marjane's identification with the broad, encompassing refrain of "We are the kids in America whoao" becomes a subject position through which to navigate her disorienting experience with the guardians of the Revolution. As censored contraband, the lyric "we" in the song provides cover for Marjane. The "we" and "America" become generic: this could be any youthful "we," in any local struggle against oppression.

In *Persepolis*, rock music cultivates a phantasmagoria of the marketplace for Marjane: complicit with her politically outspoken parents, who are more than happy to procure censored music, merch, and fashion for their daughter,

Marjane wants more of all of it, and so she dresses to resist and heads to the black market. The consumption of music and complementary fashion results in a phantasmagoria that leads to crucial character development. In the final panel, where she sings and dances with fists clenched, mouth open, and eyes screwed shut to "Kids in America," we see an aspect of character realized much like in the panel after the black market, before the guardians confront her. In inthymnacy with Kim Wilde, the audience sees Marjane transformed by her experiences. And in this final panel, we see how the synchretic meaning of "Kids in America" is transformed as well, through Marjane singing along, restoring rhythm, cadence, and tempo—there is sense in sound, even if Marjane has realized that she is not necessarily safe and sound.

As if on a mixtape, music moves in this story between narrative and character, just as it does in real life. We can all identify with Marjane in that final panel of the Kim Wilde chapter, and the fact that the eighth notes suggest rhythm but not melody here offers a final close reading of the significance of inthymnacy in *Persepolis*: there is no melodic narrative in the confrontation with the guardians of the Revolution. The event took place in narrative time, but it also feels offkey, recalling the misfit of postcolonial works within dominant cultural traditions, even with their linguistic affiliation. Marjane can't make narrative sense of the actions of a dictatorial regime against the people, aside from resisting them. It's in the rhythm of music and the absence of melodic narrative that she finds a way to respond to the horrific unintelligibility of the world around her. This is the tradition of the performance of listening within francophone culture more broadly: a representation of listening that orients the narrative through musical and exilic, rather than historical, time.

Works Cited

Allan, Michael. "Old Media/New Futures: Revolutionary Reverberations of Fanon's Radio." *PMLA*, vol. 134, no. 1, 2019, pp. 188–193.

Chion, Michel. *Audio-Vision: Sound on Screen*. Translated by Claudia Gorbman, Columbia University Press, 2019.

Mishra, Vijay, and Bob Hodge. "What Is Post(-)colonialism?" *Textual Practice*, vol. 5, no. 12, 1991, pp. 399–414.

——. "What Was Postcolonialism?" *New Literary History*, vol. 36, no. 3, 2005, pp. 375–402.

Sacks, Oliver. *Musicophilia: Tales of Music and the Brain*. New Knopf, 2007.

Satrapi, Marjane. *The Complete Persepolis*. Translated by L'Association and Anjali Singh, Pantheon/Random House, 2004.

——. *Persepolis*. L'Association, 2007.

Simidchieva, Marta. "Marjane Satrapi's Persepolis through the Lens of Persian Historiography." *International Journal of Persian Literature*, vol. 2, no. 1, 2017, pp. 87–137.

Solheim, Jennifer. *The Performance of Listening in Postcolonial Francophone Culture*. Liverpool University Press, 2017.

Szendy, Peter. *Hits: Philosophy in the Jukebox*. Translated by Will Bishop, Fordham University Press, 2012.

Wampole, Christy. *Degenerative Realism: Novel and Nation in Twenty-First Century France*. Columbia University Press, 2020.

Williams, Raymond. *Marxism and Literature*. Oxford University Press, 1977.

Outro

The "Tchip" Heard 'Round the World

Edwin Hill

Sonic culture, thus situated, renders the urban audiosocial as a system of speeds and channels, dense pressure pockets, vortices of attraction, basins of acoustic immersion and abrasion, vibratory and turbulent: a whole cartography of sonic force. (Goodman 2010: 9)

Channel 1. Information Frequencies: "Halte au 'tchip' en classe!"

On June 2, 2015, a certain sound caught our collective ear, and bugged everyone out: the *tchip*. **"Halte au 'tchip' en classe!"** [Stop the "tchip" in the classroom!] headlined *Le Parisien*. "C'est un son de mépris d'origine africaine désormais largement utilisé par tous les ados, y compris à l'adresse des profs. A tel point que des lycées ou des collèges ont décidé de le bannir" [It's a sound of contempt from Africa now widely used by all teenagers, including when they address teachers, so much so that high schools and middle schools have decided to ban it].[1] *Presse Océan* called it **"La mode du 'tchip' en classe"** [The "tchip" in the classroom fad] (June 4, 2015). This "sound of contempt," spreading with the speed of the latest fashion, hit the news wires like it hit the

---

[1] All translations are my own.

nerves of French teachers: quickly and repeatedly. **"Le 'tchip': une pratique qui exaspère les professeurs"** [The "tchip": A habit that infuriates teachers] wrote *Le Figaro* (June 3, 2015). **"Le 'tchip' interdit dans certains collèges et lycées en France"** [The "tchip" banned in some middle schools and high schools in France] (France 24, June 3, 2015). And this "infuriating" sound, and the way it was being banned, became a noisy curiosity, its affective vibration crackling into and through news wires and digital media, buzzing its way across and beyond the boundaries of the French republic. Across Europe people queried, what is this sound coming from over there? Who and whose is it? How is it made and what could be its proper use? And why "tchip" with quotation marks? Why does the media seem to clip up the word like so much dirty laundry, or perhaps a Most Wanted poster? The whole hubbub sounds very French. (They're always making noise about something, right?) This "tchip" must not be *du français propre*, French clean and proper; seems it's been hung out to dry by all of the French teachers but still hasn't come back dirt-free! The international press often left the word without translation in the headlines. **"Francia: 'Tchip Tchip,' il verso africano che irrita i prof; Sculole bandiscono nuovo slang sprezzante degli alunni"** [France: "tchip tchip," the African sound irritating all the teachers; schools ban the students' new slang of contempt] (*ANSA Notiziario Generale in Italiano*, June 2, 2015). **"French schools ban 'teeth sucking'; Schools across France impose a ban on 'le tchip', French for teeth-sucking, a sound made by sucking in air through pursed lips common in African and Afro-Caribbean culture"** (*The Telegraph*, June 4, 2015). **"French schools ban African 'teeth-sucking'"** (*The Daily Telegraph*, June 5, 2015). **"Les codes pour bien tchiper"** [The codes for *tchip*ing right] (*L'Express*, June 4, 2015). **"Too much sauce on the tchips"** (*Sydney MX*, June 5, 2015). **"Mind your lip! French schools move to ban African pupils from cultural practice of 'teeth-sucking' saying it is vulgar and offensive"** (*Mail Online*, June 8, 2015). **"À Evry, l'interdiction du tchip au lycée divise"** [In Evry, the high school *tchip* ban is controversial] (*Le Monde*, June 11, 2015). **"Le 'tchip' et les ados: un bruit de bouche venu d'Afrique"** [The teen *tchip*: A mouth noise from Africa] (*La Croix*, September 23, 2015). The *tchip*, this "mouth noise from Africa," was heard round the world, triggering a cascade of emotions, from irritation and anger to love and laughter, with all sorts of funky feelings in between. In the meantime, a "sonic color line" (Stoever 2016) was drawn that "produces codes, and polices racial difference through the ear, enabling us to hear race as well as to see it" (10). But, this institutional line of separation is also a diasporic line of relation already networked through the Hexagon. *Tchippage* of all sorts already saturated the sonic channels of French popular culture and the cultural politics of emotion. In this chapter, we listen to a few of its frequencies.

Channel 2. Diasporic Frequencies: Le Tchip! Nous ne l'entendons pas tous de la même oreille!

Le tchip, simply put, "refers to the gesture of drawing air through the teeth and into the mouth to produce a loud sucking sound" (Rickford and Rickford 1976: 302). Named variously in vernacular culture as *suck-teeth*, *kiss-teeth*, *chups*, *steups*, *stchoops*, *tchwipe*, and *kuipe*, *tchip* practices are heard around the world because they extend across the African diaspora. Linguists are clear: the *tchip* has no linguistic function strictly speaking, and no predetermined or linguistically fixable semantic content. The rare dictionaries that attempt to account for it end up listing an open-ended set of scenarios rather than a precise set of semantic definitions. So, imagine: a teacher imposes an annoying task, a high school counselor tells you your bad attitude won't be acceptable for the workplace, a classmate tests your limits in front of friends, a pencil rolls off your desk and falls out of grasp—these unruly objects (teacher, counselor, classmate, pencil) expose themselves to a *tchip*, generally a sonic affective expression of skepticism, discontent, frustration, disdain, anger, and even rage in its most negative affective modes. Equipped with a sound-symbolic component (Figueroa and Patrick 2001) and a combination of facial expressions, eye and head movements, and bodily postures, the diasporic sonics of this affective gesture corroborate the notion that "emotions should not be regarded as psychological states, but as social and cultural practices" (Ahmed 2004: 9).

Where it gets sticky (as Ahmed might say) with the affective dynamics of the *tchip*, pointedly suggested in the news stories above, is in its *frequencies*, key for understanding how these suck-teeth practices express frustration but also frustrate others. *Tchippage* tends to *agacer* [annoy, irritate] its target with its high frequencies—by which I mean its high pitch but also its capacity to repeat itself and spread to others, inhabiting and taking over new hosts, sticking to them through dynamics of iterativity. The frequencies of *tchippage* overwhelm targets with so many "contrariétés, vexations, ennuis légers mais désagréables parce que répétés et continus" [contra-rieties, vexations, and annoyances that are slight but disagreeable due to their continuous repetition] ("Agacement" [Annoyance] *Trésor de la langue française informatisé* (*TLF*), becoming "un bruit qui nous affecte désagréa-blment, un bruit qui nous paraît inharmonieux" [a noise that affects us in a disagreeable way, a noise that seems unharmonious/rude] ("Agacer" [to irritate/annoy], *TLF*). The *Trésor de la langue française* dictionary explains that the verb *agacer* tends to take high-pitched noise, a repeated movement, or an acidic taste as its subject, and parts of the human body like the nerves or nervous system and sensory organs as its object. For example, "this repetitive, high-pitched noise is getting on people's nerves." The omnipresent *tchip* not only signals irritation, it transfers that irritation back at its willful objects in very specific ways. "Légère douleur irritante" [Slightly painful irritation] or, in psychological discourse, "Irritation à la fois nerveuse et morale" [An irritation of the nervous system and psyche] ("Agacement," *TLF*). Sianne Ngai's insights concerning relationships between psychological irritation and physical irritation prove useful here. The affective dynamics of *tchip*'s vibrational frequencies tend to "blur [the boundaries] between psychic and corporeal (or internal and external) experience" (Ngai 2004: 174–208). *Tchip* frequencies overwhelm the ear and take over the tongue, but they also get under the skin, scathing it, making it irritable in turn. Reinforcing the "sonic color line," the *tchip*'s affective push plugs into vibrational forces whose modes of feeling—*agacé, énervé*, irritated—turn up *sensitivity to skin*—especially skin's contact with other skins and other surfaces—and *sensitivity of the ear*—the slightest of sounds becomes amplified, the affective flows and economies of the other become unbearable noise. Touch the skin of a person who has just been burned by a *tchip* and you may trigger an explosive reaction. However, if this sonic force, at first glance—or rather first listening—seems "noticeably weaker than what Philip Fisher calls the 'vehement passions,'" in the way Sianne Ngai thinks of irritation, the *tchip*'s affective frequencies—its public performance of sonic dissent, its capacity to spread and repeat, its fricative combat with clean articulation, its disruption of official language and speech, its way of taking over *la langue*, its way of cutting through all the *b***s**** without making much of a sound ... I call it *black static*. It's the sound that's not supposed to be there, the sound that escapes containment, and even detection at times, but that most often makes a sonic show of itself to affectively disrupt the dominant message. *Tchip*'s affective forces correlate directly with the infinite ways in which people perform the sound. Variations in the length, pitch, and tone, as well as the bending of the pitch, its contextual timing, its affricative thickness, the bodily postures and facial expressions that accompany it, and so forth, all forcefully direct its affective power.

Sociolinguists often prefer to refer to the sound with the term "KST" for Kiss/Suck Teeth in brackets to emphasize that this sound is plurilingual and, in a sense, extra-linguistic. To write the word is to select a linguistic base, composed of letters and grammar, that belies the true status of this performative interjection. As sociolinguists Figueroa and Patrick note, the "sounds of (KST) do not lend themselves to literary description, and attempts are rarely committed to paper" (2001: 5), however there are relevant, if somewhat rare, examples. While these sociolinguists have focused on anglophone contexts, we find examples in francophone letters, especially in the French West Indies, as well. Martinican writer Raphaël Confiant approaches the sound as he imagines Paul Gauguin's time in Martinique, and specifically his encounters with Creole women, in the novel *Le Barbare enchanté* [The Enchanted Savage]. Confiant's Gauguin describes the *tchip* as a "claquement de langue que seules savent produire les négresses créoles" [a tongue clicking sound only the black Creole women can make] (2003: ch. 3). This is a sound that "n'a rien à voir avec le 'tsst!' de nos femmes d'Europe car il peut vous ébranler l'homme le plus aguerri. Soit il vous met en rage—les nègres cognent beaucoup leur compagnes—soit il vous contraint à battre en retraite, la bouche chargée d'injures rentrées" [has nothing to do with the "tsst!" of our European women. It can shake up even the toughest of men. Either it enrages you—the *nègres* often beat their women—or it forces you to back down and mutter your insults under your breath]. The *tchip* of Creole *négresses* produces an *ébranlement* [shaking], where *ébranler* [to shake] functions to "Imprimer un mouvement d'oscillation" [Imprint/ impress a movement of oscillation] and, in the process, "Rendre moins assuré, moins ferme" [Render less assured, less steady] ("ébranler," *TLF*). Confiant's analysis picks up on the ways in which *tchip* sonic practices *press* against the body, not to scratch it or break it, but to shake it to its core with a vibrational force capable of either pushing him over the edge, or of sending him packing and biting his tongue.[2]

The willful protagonist of Raphaël Confiant's novel *Eau de café* (1991) delivers her *tchip* in a different way: within the act of storytelling. It serves to mark her disdain for the stereotypically weak and passive postures of the Creole *doudou*, as well as to shake up any skeptical listeners. You think she won't seize the pen (or the microphone) and author her own life's story?

> C'est que vous me confondez avec ces petit capistrelles lotionnées qui espèrent un homme depuis que le sang s'est mis à leur fifiner entre les cuisses et qui rongent leur vie au rebord d'une fenêtre si les jours chassent les jours et que pas une ombre ne se dessine dans l'allée qui conduit à leur case. Moi-même, *tchip!*, je n'ai pas besoin de ces encombrantes cargaisons de rêve [...] Ce n'est pas Eau de Café qui marchera dans vos macaqueries, messieurs et dames! (Confiant 1991: ch. 9)

> You must be confusing me with these little lotioned-up teases who have been waiting for a man ever since blood first started dribbling between

---

[2] Patrick Chamoiseau recalls "in heart-wrenching detail how the young boys planned their verbal approaches in the tiniest detail, only to be delivered the Creole Tchip, which would instantly reduce them to a gibbering mess" (Thomas 2017: 96).

their thighs and who bite their nails by the windowsill if days pile up without the trace of a shadow coming their way down the alley. Please, *tchip!* I don't need these cumbersome fantasies [...] You won't find Eau de Café caught up in this foolishness ladies and gentlemen!

Set up by the Creole interjection *moi-même* (which I have translated simply as a sarcastic "please"), the *tchip* participates in the Creolization of French in the narrative. Intervening with its own exclamation point mid-phrase, it marks a pivot in the sentence, reorienting it towards the flesh-and-bones rhythm of the storyteller's flow, part of Confiant's transformation of written text into oral storytelling. This *tchip* rejects the "encombrantes cargaisons de rêve" [cumbersome fantasies] that animate dominant gender scripts, announcing, swearing even before all, that she's *not the one*. As is common praxis, this *tchip!* stages its dissonance and dissent spectacularly, in public ("messieurs et dames!"). Her *tchip* mocks and breaks up the stereotypical post/colonial stereotype that would imagine young black Creole women as simultaneously oversexed and passive, waiting endlessly by the window for their dreamy prince charming to sweep them off their feet. The conjured *capistrelles lotionnées* call attention to the class dynamics involved in her alternately embodied, performative posture of Creole womanhood. This protagonist isn't afraid of getting her hands dirty or her skin scathed. If kiss-teeth practices give breath to "characters, common in West Indian literature" who seem constituted as "bundles of negative emotions waiting for release" (Figueroa and Patrick 2001: 10), in the case of *Eau de café*, it signals a gendered and racialized "willfulness" (Ahmed 2014). Despite your skepticism, and despite even the conditions of her narrative authorship, this black female protagonist boldly steps forward and seizes the opportunity before her. We can hear the *tchip!*—especially associated with black women of working-class or rural background, as well as with the Creole language and now "black" and *banlieue* speech more generally—as a sonic gesture that pings at intersectional junctures in matrices of power.

While linguists and sociolinguists provide important insights into kiss-teeth practices, it's important to note, as Dominique Fattier writes in *Contribution à l'étude de la genèse d'un créole: l'Atlas Linguistique d'Haïti, cartes et commentaires*, "ce son n'a pas de fonction linguistique dans la langue" [this sound doesn't have a linguistic function in the language] (1998: 94). Unlike its anglophone diasporic counterparts, the (French) *word* for the *tchip* sound is marginalized and even stigmatized, even if saying the word still offends much less than actually making the sound. (A "Je vous tchipe, monsieur!" [I tchip at you, sir] will likely not fall foul of official *tchip* bans at schools). The lexeme, perhaps more Creole than French, carries the baggage of an illegitimate linguistic history and post/colonial trajectory. Indeed, the interesting thing about banning *le tchip* is that dominant white hexagonal French culture has never heard of it, much less heard and registered its meaning. Although often referred to as onomatopoeic, linguists tend to locate it as a (French) Creolization of the Portuguese or Spanish *chupar*. In any case, silencing the *tchip* resonates with the post/colonial French history of repressing Creole expression and standardizing white French speech in classrooms. At the same time, the way media outlets and other testimonies compared and associated *le tchip*'s with the expression *wesh wesh* [slang similar to "yo" or "'sup"] suggests that dominant discourse racializes and juvenilizes the word and its practice, relegating it to the urban peripheries of acceptable expression, while also dismissing it as "the latest thing" (not to do) that all the kids are doing. In short, as the ban, the scare quotes and italics, and dominant discursive listening networks make clear, the *tchip* has not been granted its full cultural citizenship papers in France.[3] Yet, rooted deeply and widely in the affective archives of the African diaspora, *tchip* practices are far more than the latest fad. While most commonly associated with adults reprimanding children, kiss-teeth practices often involve "scene[s] of class tension and conflict" (Patrick and Figueroa 2001: 5), and, as the examples above show, these practices often serve as a tool for resetting gendered (physical, emotional, and ideational) boundaries, or transgressing and rearranging them. The *tchip* signals and enacts a rebellion against bourgeois patriarchal order and social hierarchies. Long story short, it's not just an expression; it's out here doing things on the street.

---

[3] In explaining "Tuipe, kuipe (faire un bruit avec la bouche)" [*Tuipe, kuipe* (make a noise with the mouth], Dominique Fattier writes: "Concrètement, il s'agit d'émettre une sorte de clic, que les Haïtiens utilisent pour marquer leur désapprobation. Ce son n'a pas de fonction linguistique dans la langue. Le verb est probablement un néologisme construit à partir d'un radical onomato-péique" [Concretely, it has to do with a sort of click that Haitians use to mark their disapproval. This sound has no linguistic function in the language. The verb is most likely a neologism constructed based on an onomatopoeic stem] (1998: 94).

Channel 3. Fashion Frequencies: Noir et Fier

je tchipe
tu tchipes
il tchipe
elle tchipe
nous tchipons
vous tchipez
ils tchipent

I *tchip*
you *tchip*
he *tchips*
she *tchips*
we *tchip*
you *tchip*
they *tchip*

Hold up! [*Tchiiiiiip!*] I spotted it the summer of 2017 at the Paris AfroPunk festival. It hung among the various Afro-themed goods for sale by vendors near the entrance of the festival's main concert venue. Among the fabrics, jewelry, and posters, and the bass vibrations pulling me ultimately, inevitably, towards the speakers of the stage, it immediately grabbed my attention: a white t-shirt with, down the front in one vertical line, a conjugation of the (marginally) French "verb" "to tchip"! The subject pronouns and the verbs were in black, except for the conjugations which were in red. Reading from top to bottom, the message feels like a social declination as much as a grammatical one. It's as if *le tchip* has spread from me to you to her and her and so on. The t-shirt made me think of the ways in which this sound practice, largely characterized as an expression of negative affect, the pushing away—if not a stiff shove—of an encroaching other now seemed inviting, like a way to connect people, to bring them together. This t-shirt was a friendly, even flirtatious, thing, a *clin d'œil*, like: Do you see me? I see you, I hear you, you hear? It called out to me, stopped me in my tracks, and pulled me in. I bought (into) it. For me, these threads lay claim to *le tchip* as part of the urban fabric, inseparable from of the French (linguistic) facts of life. At the same time as it marks a Creolization, cannibalization even, of French speech—filling in but also pointing out gaps and holes in expression—it suggests a certain diasporic orientation to the city and to "the world." These facts of life point towards histories of dissent and descendancy that escape or otherwise run counter to the dominant record. It makes a claim on physical and linguistic space as well as style and knowledge right here in the middle, or rather on the peripheries, of Babylon.

Or course, what I had encountered was not the sound itself, it was the (French-Creolized) unofficial linguistic signifier for the sound. These letters, this woven word, and its message, literally shook to the sonic pulses hitting the vendors' stalls from the venue's open doors. These bundles of sentiment resonate naturally with the affective vibrations of the scene. Its sale and sentiment find themselves at home in the context of this festival, in relation to what Steve Goodman might call its "(sub)politics of frequency," the ways in which its "sonic processes seek to intensify low-frequency vibration as a technique of affective mobilization." Goodman explains:

> The production of vibrational environments that facilitate the transduction of the tensions of urban existence, transforming deeply engrained ambiences of fear or dread into other collective dispositions, serve as a model of collectivity that revolves around affective tonality, and precedes ideology. (2010: xx)

Perhaps this "model of collectivity that revolves around affective tonality" becomes especially important in the Paris editions of the AfroPunk festival, a (Brooklyn-based) event situated to cash in manifesting a hub of diverse transnational, plurilingual, and diasporic expression, "the other black experience." Sunday July 16, 2017, the day I attended, featured performances by artists ranging from Laura Mvula and Kiah Victoria to Yasiin Bey and Robert Glasper to DJ Anaïs B and Disiz La Peste. *Tchip* musical vibes were particularly resonant in this affective sound space. The people were *chic* and grunge, provocative and spiritual, open and beautiful in a thousand different ways. The *tchip*, and the *tchip* t-shirt, hung well here. The *tchip* tee found its place among a range of Afro-centric and diasporic themed t-shirts that each in its own way signaled an ongoing history of diasporic dissent and dissonance.

I also got another t-shirt that night, this one for free: all black with the phrase "AFRO PUNK IS NOFI" in white lettering. Like "Afro Punk" itself, it wasn't immediately clear exactly what the expression meant, but I liked the price (free) and the fit! The shirt fit my body, my type. It stuck to me (pulled bodies, clung to them), and moved (got sold, moved bodies, spread). It speaks to those who share a certain critical orientation towards the world. Many people asked me what "Nofi" meant before I was forced to look it up online. It turns out NOFI stands for "Noir et Fier" [Black and Proud] the name of a company that specializes in Afro-centric and African diasporic themed fashion, and that designed the *tchip* t-shirt. The company's marketing strategy, as the free give-away attests, makes it its business to assemble and tap into a range of diasporic affective push and pull forces, where against-ness frequencies or outsider-ness and towards-ness frequencies or inward-ness function simultaneously to create buzz and sales. Admittedly, the AfroPunk Festival has changed drastically since its first edition in 2005, now often appearing more like mainstream branding rather than grassroots community building. As Rachel Lifter writes in regard to the AfroPunk Fest look, while the festival promotes itself as a champion of alternative modes and expressions of blackness, its valorization of individual style and expression "is also a historically specific ideal through which young women—and, here, men, and non-binary people, as well—are interpellated into the contemporary fashion system" (2019: 112). *Le tchip* is a mode of self-fashioning whose entanglements with popular culture and style complicate conventional visual and sonic codes of blackness, but also the notion that the *tchip* embodies some pure force of anti-establishment resistance and positionality. Still, the t-shirt I fell for makes evident the ways in which *tchip* practices come in handy for the expression of "the creative agency of speakers and their abilities to disassemble and reassemble indexical 'bundles' or packages" (Goodwin and Alim 2010: 181). Similarly, the *tchip* among French youth serves to situate them with respect to codes of authenticity, coolness, and independence. Ultimately, in today's world, we might speak of *le tchip* as beyond self-fashioning and moving to self-branding. It coordinates and publicly expresses an attitude and more, a coherent and personal approach towards life, plugged into consumer and leisure culture as well as social media personality. Spreading, moving, and cutting through sound cultures is what *le tchip* can do.

Channel 4. Music Frequencies: Grooves and Gros Mots

While rooted deep in African diasporic experiences, this sound functions in a range of new ways as it navigates the urban topographies and soundscapes, the linguistic, cultural, and affective flows operative in contemporary France. Despite its seemingly (that is, heard as) foreign and even hostile relation to French culture and institutions, as well as "the French language," *le tchip* entered mainstream French culture long ago. Like the t-shirt above, the *tchip* seems to have retained its marginal bona fides even as it has been woven into French auditory culture. Television and movies have long since made it the privileged sound symbol stereotype for authentic (read: exotic) black women.[4]

---

[4] The French Netflix teen superhero series *Mortel* jumps to mind. The black teenager's mother, who is, of course, a vodou priestess, constantly *tchip*s as she looks askance at the world.

Still, more creative minds, like the French Martinican rap artist Greg Frite and the French Congolese comedian Christian Nsankete, have capitalized on the *tchip* in more interesting ways, amplifying its sound while often re/directing its affective force, not unlike like what AfroPunk Fest and NOFI have done with their t-shirts. Greg Frite, aka Black'Boule, is one-third of the golden age of French hip-hop group Triptik. Comprising MCs Dabaaz and Drixxxé, along with DJ Pone, the group's second album *Microphonorama* (2001), with tracks like "Panam," "Bouge tes cheveux," and "America," became something of a French hip-hop classic. Greg Frite's rhyme structures and wordplay, mid-tempo grooves and rhythmic flow, still resonate with that era. What he sacrifices in complexity he gains in clarity and *kickage*. Frite's flow is as straightforward and direct as his lyrical messages, which often offer his take on language, identity, and urban space, that is, when they're not just club bangers and feel-good booty shakers. His work taps into old school hip-hop's playful frequencies and upbeat vibes. While some tracks betray an anxiety of American and English linguistic influence ("Franglais," *Les Gros Mots*, 2014), lyrically and narratively Greg Frite pointedly grounds himself in Greater Paris, its neighborhoods and *banlieues*, ports of entry and metro stops, but also its sense of self, its public and private life (for example, "Panam" from the album *Microphonorama*). Through it all, Greg Frite's texts show a love of words and language, and his flow situates hip-hop—perhaps more specifically, the hip-hop cypher—as a crucial place where language and expression can be cared for and exchanged. On the album *Gros Mots* (2014, Quintessence Music/Believe Recordings), Greg Frite plugs *le tchip*—word, text, and sound (see music video)—into the (sub)frequencies of global linguistic hip-hop flow (Goodwin and Alim 2010). The *tchip* naturally finds itself at home in the affective expressions of the cypher (or the dirty dozens, for that matter), an æsthetic practice built on the desire to "totally destroy somebody else with words" (MC Kurupt, qtd. in Spady, Alim, and Meghelli 2006: 7).

Accordingly, while Greg Frite's musical *tchip* practices remain essentially playful, the lyrics make clear that *le tchip*'s power is no joke. But if you want to get down with it, that is, if you want to "disassemble and reassemble [your current] indexical 'bundles' or packages" (Goodwin and Alim 2010: 181)—before someone else does it for you—then you need to know how to appreciate it and do it right:

> Rien de tel qu'un bon [*tchiiip*]
> Pour marquer son agacement ou sa désapprobation
> Si quelqu'un fait le bouffon, t'entends [*tchiiip*]
> Devant un prix exorbitant, ou dans une queue, quand tu attends
> L'inverse de l'ovation, c'est le [*tchiiip*]

Pour mépriser les cancans ou maîtriser les enfants
Tellement prisé maintenant, tout le monde [*tchiiip*]
Plutôt simple et si plaisant, le tchip est omniprésent
[...]
Une onomatopée hier communautaire
C'est d'Afrique aux Caraïbes que la formule opère
[...]
Parmi les plus grandes montées en l'air qu'aient connus nos nerfs.

[Refrain]
Tu aimerais tant savoir faire le [*tchiiip*]
Colle ta langue derrière tes dents
Tes lèvres opèrent un pincement
Garde te salive pour le [*tchiiip*]
Ta mâchoire est verrouillée
L'ennemi prêt à dérouiller.

Nothing like a good (*tchiiip*)
To show your frustration or your irritation
If someone acts a fool, you hear (*tchiiip*)
Faced with a sky-high price, or with a wait in line
The opposite of applause is a (*tchiiip*)
To scoff at hype or put the kids back in line
It's so trendy now that everyone (*tchiiip*)
So simple and so fun, the *tchip* is omnipresent
[...]
An onomatopoeia that was yesterday a community's
From Africa to the Caribbean the expression gained its fluency
[...]
One ways our nerves blow up through the ceiling.

[Refrain]
Wouldn't you like to know how to [*tchiiip*]
Stick your tongue behind your teeth
Give lips your lips a good squeeze
Keep your spit to make one of these [*tchiiip*]
Keep your jaw sealed tight
Your enemy ready to take flight.

Greg Frite's "Tchip" taps and tunes in to the audio virology of suck-teeth practices, that is, their propensity to spread. *Tchip* practices catch hold like an earworm but also spread like a viral feeling or hit song. If you hear and see others doing it often enough, you will probably eventually find yourself doing it too. (This chapter itself may do the same: trigger its own *tchips* upon *tchips* from the reader and those that listen to her.) "A fundamental expression, it remains outside the grammar, unremarked yet indispensable— we cannot resist using it even among the uninitiated, while outsiders to Diaspora culture who learn it, find that it instantly fills an expressive gap" (Figueroa and Patrick 2001: 3). This sonic gesture hooks onto the body by locating gaps in a whole field of affective expression. Mess around with *le tchip*, you end up catching feelings, you know? [*tchip*]. Kiss-teeth gestures and practices have a tremendous capacity to "stick and move," to borrow phrasing from Sarah Ahmed, whose work deeply informs this chapter's readings. Greg Frite plays into that *catchiness* as the basis of this track, charging the way this sonic gesture "instantly fills an expressive gap" with desirability and sexual innuendo. *Le tchip* is the hook on this song in more ways than one. While the lyrics explain what the sound is, where it comes from, and what sets it in motion, they also sketch out a set of scenarios where you expect this sound, and what you might expect to happen next. In the meantime, the sound itself serves as a basic, recurring element of the rhythm track. More specifically, a juicy pitch-bending *tchip* fills the space and time of a rhythmic break on every other fourth beat of the song. It demands that Frite regularly smooth the sound into his lyrics in a meaningful way, but also sets up a recurring element inviting participation by listeners. On the dancefloor, I imagine this *tchip* beat triggering freezes and poses, slides and slow motion, drops and body waves, as well as rhythmic cut eyes, twisted up lips, and other bodily postures and facial expressions that commonly accompany this sonic gesture. Just as the track's *tchips* encourage listeners to participate lyrically, the *tchip* commandeers bodies, inspiring all manner of improvised and citational gesture and play. Greg Frite's "Tchip" fits snuggly alongside his multidimensional project "Les Gros Mots," which includes the album as well as a mini-series of rap and music videos aired in the *Le Before* program on Canal+ that explain expressions from popular culture and "street" slang. What we might call Frite's "black, blanc, beur" ethos leads him to take *le tchip* in a far less sonically and progressively black radical direction than we might encounter at the AfroPunk Fest. His project comes from the perspective that we need to share the same words in order to get along, and that we needn't have fear of these forms of expression, nor, by extension, must we fear the people who use them. Still, for this listener, his plays on and with popular speech at times borders on the kind of ridiculous humor that resonates too much with the mockery of imitation. His *tchip* is funky sometimes, but it has no bite.

Channel 5. Comedy Frequencies: Le Tchip est en danger! Rendez nous le tchip!

They say kiss-teeth is an art ... [*tchiiip*]; maybe a martial art. There might not be formal competitions, but impromptu matches pop off all the time. It happens whenever the other fails to respect "territories of the self" (Goffman 1971). The *tchip*'s sonic performance affectively gestures (you) towards a resetting of these self-territories. The *tchip* signals, allows for, and rather demands that we check the (affective and vibrational) flow of our (racialized and symbolic) social order. The comedian and YouTube sensation Christian Nsankete, aka Dycosh, excels at deploying *le tchip* to disrupt the post/colonial French ear, while poking fun at the tensions and contradictions in our everyday ways of reading people, in his video sketch "Rendez Nous le TCHIP," posted on YouTube on April 4, 2014.[5] The setup is a television news story that will cover the "controversy" of non-African diasporic people taking up *le tchip* practices. They go live to their reporter on the street who is getting the pulse of the street on this (farcical) hot issue. He stops to speak to two men hanging out in the neighborhood:

> Doudou Mwen Fâché (Infirmier - Hôpitaux de Paris): Rendez-nous le tchip! Je vais vous dire pourquoi. La dernière fois j'étais en soirée, en soirée tranquille. La Blanche vient me voir, elle me dit: « Est-ce que tu peux zouker avec moi? » J'ai dit « Oui. » J'ai dit « Oui, » *Nou ka zouké, nous ka zouké* ... A un moment je lui marche sur les pieds, mais sans faire exprès! Sans faire exprès! Je lui marche sur les pieds. La meuf me tchipe! Je lui ai dit: « Comment ça tu me tchipes!? Déjà, je t'*autorise*, je t'*autorise* à danser le zouk avec moi, mais en plus de ça tu me *tchipes*!? »

> Doudou Mwen Fâché (Nurse – Paris Hospital): Give us back the *tchip*! I'll tell you why. This one time I went out to a party, it was cool. This white lady comes up to me, and she says: "Will you dance a zouk with me?" So I said, "Yes." I said, "Yes." So, *we zookin', we zookin'...* And, at a certain point, I step on her foot, but not on purpose! Not on purpose! I step on her foot, and the chick sucks her teeth! I said, "What you sucking your teeth for? First off, I *gave you permission*, I *gave you permission* to dance a zouk with me, and then you suck your teeth at me!?"

I decline to attempt to reproduce it in the transcription above, but Dycosh performs his character Doudou Mwen Fâché ("I'm Angry Sweetie" in Creole)

---

5 Watch the sketch at youtube.com/watch?v=G0vLMSc7JlY. For the rest of Dycosh's videos, see his YouTube channel, youtube.com/user/dycoshtv/featured.

with an exaggerated Creole accent, with French *r*'s smoothed out to *w*'s, lively intonations, and amusing facial expressions. In his story, an invitation to dance is made and accepted; then, a foot is stepped on. *Tchip!* Here especially, Sara Ahmed's terms in *The Culture Politics of Emotion* provide insight:

> *We need to remember the "press" in an impression.* It allows us to associate the experience of having an emotion with the very affect of one surface upon another, an affect that leaves its mark or trace. So not only do I have an impression of others, but they leave me with an impression; they impress me, and impress upon me. I will use the idea of "impression" as it allows me to avoid making analytical distinctions between bodily sensation, emotion and thought as if they could be "experienced" as distinct realms of human "experience." (2004: 6)

It may have been an accident, but you have made a sore impression on me—specifically on my foot! And now you've made a bad impression of us on the dancefloor, in front of everyone. *Tchip!* she exclaims, not "aïe" [ouch]. This pain is physical and musical, psychological and social; many boundaries have been breached. The rules of the social game manifest in this chance choreographic encounter, like the racial fantasies that potentially undergird it, have been broken. The *tchip* gives shape to this experience by marking him as an unruly object, and an unworthy dance partner. Her *tchip* pings the party's affective atmospherics: this black man's body is unruly; it doesn't do what it's supposed to do. While for Dycosh's Antillean persona, "the white woman" should have considered herself lucky to dance a zouk with a black (Antillean) man in the first place, her *tchip!* has put him *in his place*, or rather, locates him as frustratingly *out of place* musically, physically, and perhaps even culturally. Potentially calling into question his cultural and racial authenticity, as well as his masculinity, in front of everyone at the party, her *tchip* leaves him irked and halfway speechless (rather like the description Confiant describes above), not to mention partnerless. Doudou means to hear her *tchip* as an example of the ways in which white people steal black culture, even using it to take advantage of black people, but even in his own story, her *tchip* rings true, clear through his storytelling. The mere fact that she has left Doudou Mwen Fâché with a bruised ego and a bad taste in his mouth proves the effectiveness of *la Blanche*'s sonic blow. We have already aligned ourselves with her sound judgment, despite his antics.

"Cawamel Désiré Ahmed (Chômeur Professionnel)" [Caramel Desired Ahmed (Professionally Unemployed)], performed by Maghrebi comedian Ahmed Sparrow, now tells his story … in a thick Creole accent, including exaggerated, stereotypical yet spot-on French West Indian intonations, speech patterns, gestures, and rhythms. It turns out that Cawamel is the

French zouk champion, and runner-up in the world championships. He tries to back up his buddy, but here he is, another non-black, non-Antillean who masters the zouk dance better than Doudou. Cawamel has been officially recognized and legitimated, his name Creolized, his speech vibes with the same affective postures and feedback tones as Doudou, who calls upon him, ironically, to co-sign his indignation at the white woman's nerve. Doudou remains unaware of the irony, but his supposed outrage at the white woman's insolent *tchip* is thus revealed to be even more pathetic than it first appeared. The men then hilariously debate the meaning of a "poke" on social media, specifically whether or not Cawamel has been *tchip-poke*'d. The sketch pokes fun at these two clueless men (of a certain age), their laughable attempts to "figure out women," their off-putting out-of-touchness, and their expectations for how people should move and sound. Dycosh's ability to cinch the clichéd, racialized gender script of the "white girl in black space" through reference of her *tchip* suggests how out of touch we are in our thinking about how peri/ urban spaces sound and who we think those sounds belong to.

The television news framing device allows for several sketches within the same video, each purporting to take live testimony on the street about the state of *tchippage*. By the end of the video, we've heard the *tchips* of Shakra Tandoori Zgari, working at the corner market, who interrupts the interview about the *tchip* with his own live *tchip* at a hooded youth sneaking some fruit from the bin: "Eh! Repose ça! Repose ça enfoiré! *Tchip!*" [Hey! Put that back! Put that back, asshole! *Tchip!*]. The clip's finale features Dycosh's most famous character, the Congolese sapologist (and sapeur pompier [fireman]), debonair dandy Eli Kitengué ("Equilibre!" [Balance!]). The interview turns nasty when Eli realizes the soundman has been subtitling him. "Arrête de me sous-titrer! Mais! *Tchip!* Arrête de me sous-titrer!" [Stop subtitling me! Hey! *Tchip!* Stop subtitling me!] he exclaims, rolling his *r*'s along the way before physically struggling with the film crew over the camera and microphone. This *tchip* motion sends the entire news report reeling as another example in a suite of sound failures and *ratés*. Ultimately, the *tchip* triggers this series of *décalages* between sounds and bodies (and machines). Rather than some intra-group code, Dycosh's sketches suggest the ways in which people from all walks of life and all backgrounds adopt *tchip* practices to navigate the frictions of everyday life in the multi-ethnic spaces of Greater Paris. Ultimately, as the reporter's outrageous exclamations make clear ("Rendez-nous le tchip!" [Hand over the *tchip!*]), while the adoption of *tchip* practices by non-diasporic groups feels like cultural reappropriation (because, well, it is), when we listen back, we can also hear it as sonically indexing zones of multi-ethnic encounter and exchange, friction and creolization. Dycosh's critique of the cascade of emotions socially, culturally, and institutionally triggered from *tchippage* served as a critical opening in his career, securing the success of his YouTube channel, which has over 27 million views. Like the AfroPunk Fest, the NOFI t-shirt design, and Greg Frite's musical projects, Christian Dycosh's humorous commentary leaps into the break, or a breaking down, of dominant discourse that the *tchip* produces—that "expressive gap" that can and must be "instantly filled"—to successfully navigate these zones of encounter. In the process of re/locating the sonic coordinates of black diasporic life, these artists tap into *le tchip*'s ability to reorient our bodies in and towards the world. Capitalizing on its audio virological tendencies and re/directing its affective forces, their *tchippage* grabs our attention and pulls us in, freezes us and makes us get down, then confuses us and makes us crack up at the sonic absurdity of it all. More than simply considering it theft or stereotype, these artists and others have taken the contemporary popularity, and popularization, of *le tchip* as an opening for creative expression and cultural commentary. Here, *le tchip* sounds the (potentially radical) blackening of the *métropole*, suggesting the ways in which African diasporic practices deeply inform French social and cultural life. On the next channel, we will hear how *le tchip* has been deployed to inform French political life too.

Channel 6. Political Frequencies: The Taubira Tchip

It might not (always) be black rage, but black static, this parasitic sound, can politically buzz and bite. Adopting ruses of Creole camouflage and the tactics of black fugitivity, it can go off the grid, fly under the radar to avoid enemy fire, but still deliver a stinging clap back.[6] Christiane Taubira, the French-Guyanese politician, former Minister of Justice, knows this well. The darling of the French left demonstrated her skills in a conference with students at the Université Paris Dauphine on March 17, 2015. The hosts of the Dauphine Discussion Débat Association, Loréna Lebœuf and Tom Michon, ask Taubira to give the first adjective that comes to mind for a series of words/names:

> Lebœuf: Marine Le Pen.
> Taubira: [*tchip!*]

She turns her head and looks away, while some in the audience laugh, then suddenly covers her mouth completely with her hand. Eyes wide, she looks back and forth between Michon and Lebœuf. Awkward silence filled by

---

6 In *Stolen Life*, Fred Moten describes black fugitivity as "a desire for and a spirit of escape and transgression of the proper and the proposed. It's a desire for the outside, for a playing or being outside, an outlaw edge proper to the now always already improper voice or instrument" (2018: 131).

nervous laughter ensues for a several seconds. Have the hosts, the audience, heard and understood? It's unclear. Finally, she removes her hand a bit but keeps pinching her nose. Is she holding back laughter? Is she holding her nose in disgust, turning it up in contempt? Will she add something to explain? (Is she really this surprised and shocked by the mention of this name?) Labœuf's co-host picks up the thread: "Non. Pas d'adjectif. Le silence ... Deuxième personne ..." [No. No adjective. Silence ... Second person ...]. Only those already fluent in this diasporic practice—which seems not to be the case for Michon, Labœuf, and much (but definitely not all!) of the live audience—will have heard and understood the stinging disregard with which Taubira had just handled her perennial opponent, leader of France's then National Front party, Marine Le Pen. The Taubira *tchip* has disrupted the discursive flow, breaking down the interview game, and it has delivered a blow, yet the transcription will record her response as silence.

However, Taubira's *tchip* seems less spontaneous when one considers that she had already explained this strategy in an interview on i-Télé weeks before (February 10, 2015). In the context of this interview, after playing a video montage of the violent anti-black racist discourse aimed at her during her time as Minister of Justice, journalist Laurence Haïm asks Taubira if these attacks hurt her, if they perhaps make her cry sometimes. (*Tchip*-worthy questions in their own right.)

> Taubira: Il y a quelque chose que l'on fait dans la société créole, dans *les* sociétés créoles, donc en Guyane mais ailleurs aussi. C'est un langage très féminin, et c'est ce que ça m'inspirerait: ça s'appelle un 'tchip' ...
> Haïm: Un 'tchip' ...?!
> Taubira: Un tchip. [*tchip!*]
> Haïm: [*tchip!*]
> Taubira: C'est un concentré de dédain.
> Haïm: C'est ce que vous inspire Marine Le Pen?
> Taubira: C'est qui ça?

> Taubira: There's something that we do in Creole society, Creole societies, so in French Guyana but elsewhere too. It's an expression used by women, and that's how I respond to all that. It's called a 'tchip' ...
> Haïm: A 'tchip' ...?
> Taubira: A tchip. [*tchip!*]
> Haïm: [*tchip!*]
> Taubira: It's a concentration of disdain.
> Haïm: That's how you respond to Marine Le Pen?
> Taubira: Who?

Taubira's definition of her *tchip* as a "concentré de dédain," highlights the dynamics of affective and sonic intensity involved in this sonic gesture. This "concentrated disdain" aims its disgust at a set of associations she finds repugnant, physically, intellectually, and emotionally, if the pinched nose from the original *tchip* tells us anything. Perhaps Taubira's statement that she *tchiped* "instinctively" is an explanation rather than an excuse, suggesting, as linguists have done, the (semi/sometime) involuntary nature of *tchip* practices (another demonstration of the *tchip*'s affective capacity to move people and spread to others). Once you pick them up, *tchip* practices become practically reflexive, jumping from your mouth when something sends your body to recoiling and riposting before you've had a chance to formulate your thoughts. The Taubira *tchip* recoils, but also parries the blow and allows for a pivot. Instead of discussing Marine Le Pen, or taking the time to dignify the antics of the far right with a full response, she *tchips*. Why? Because, as Greg Frite puts it, "When someone acts a fool you hear [*tchiiiiiip*]." She doesn't name-call, but *tchippage* in fact designates Le Pen as a buffoon, then feigns to not know who she is at all. By explaining *le tchip*, calmly, succinctly, and with a smile, Taubira essentially brushes her shoulder off, and turns a question about her (assumed) victimization by anti-black racism into a teaching moment. Before, her blow was delivered (un)silently, escaping commentary due to the fact that it was largely unheard and/or didn't register with the public. Here, the *tchip* not only pivots, it becomes the pivot with which she pushes the discussion towards. Opening up a discussion about cultural difference and critical dissent in the French republic, Taubira reframes the discussion in her own terms. Haïm seems charmed to learn the expression and practice doing it. (I can already see white French women with campaign election tees: *I tchipe with her!*) Positioning the *tchip* in relation to gender as well as the Creole diaspora, Taubira leads us to consider the misogynistic violence in the anti-black racist attacks she endures as a politician and public spokesperson.

Arguably the most prominent black politician in France, the French far right have made Taubira their obsession, frequently attempting to gin up outrage at instances of her supposed disrespect (read: disobedience) of the racialized performative demands of French citizenship. One such occasion was when the National Front demanded she resign as Minister of Justice for not singing the French national anthem during an official commemoration of the abolition of slavery on May 10, 2014. They managed to make enough of a fuss for it to end up on all the political debate panels and national television news shows. After Taubira replied via social media that she doesn't always feel like participating in a "karaoké d'estrade" [stadium karaoke], National Front VP Florian Philippot pounced, tweeting: "Derrière le terme karaoké d'estrade de Taubira pour évoquer le chant de la Marseillaise, il y a tout le mépris du peuple" [Taubira's use of the term "stadium karaoke" to describe the French national anthem shows a complete disdain for the people]. The French right Twitter-verse buzzed in agreement:

Laure Candlot: "Pitoyable ... Pauvre France" [Pathetic ... Poor France].

Florian Philippot: "Si Valls n'annonce pas ce soir le limogeage de Taubira, nous saurons que la haine de la France est au sommet de l'Etat #limogeage" [If Valls doesn't announce Taubira's dismissal tonight, we will know that hatred of France has risen to the highest ranks of government #dismissal].

La Droite au cœur: "Le mépris c'est maintenant: Pour #Taubira la Marseillaise est un 'karaoké d'estrade.' Cette femme est juste une honte." [The utter disdain: For #Taubira the national anthem is "stadium karaoke." This woman is simply shameful].

Marine Le Pen: "Ce dérapage inacceptable est en effet une preuve symbolique de premier ordre de son mépris pour la France" [This unacceptable blunder is in fact the indisputable symbolic proof of her contempt for France].

This outcry was not exclusive to the extreme right; the leader of the center-right UMP, Jean-François Copé, declared himself "among millions of French people [...] deeply shocked"[7] by Taubira's words and behavior, which for Le Pen are "symbolic proof" of the highest order. The tweets involve heavy projection, especially casting Taubira as part of an intellectual elite that holds "the people" in contempt [*mépris*] and (thus) hates the French nation. It suggests her attitude points towards the way the government has been taken over at the very highest levels by people who are out of line, and taking the country down the wrong path. France is to be pitied for the shameful treatment it receives from "this woman." Christiane Taubira, perhaps not unlike the black girls and teens at the vocational school in Evry, is accused of not *obeying* the rules of civic duty in the Latin sense of the word:

The verb "to obey" derives from the Latin word for hearing: to give ear. To obey is to give your ear to the law. A history of disobedience could be thought as a history of willful ears, or ears that block the message of the justice of the law, of ears that hear the right as wrong. To hear a wrong is to hear wrongly; it is to be willing to be heard as in the wrong. (Ahmed 2014: 137)

---

[7] "French Minister's National Anthem Snub Sparks Resignation Calls," May 12, 2014, modified May 13, 2015, france24.com/en/20140512-france-justice-minister-christiane-taubira-la-marseillaise.

Taubira's *tchip* takes up this struggle over the "lawful ear," constituting a refusal to hear and sound right, and a "willing[ness] to be heard as in the wrong." The right-wing French machine might be right to hear the Taubira *tchip* as coming from this "history of willful ears, or ears that block the message of the justice of the law," as Ahmed writes, even as Taubira held the highest justice department job in the French republic. Figueroa and Patrick's critique of KST soundings in courtroom settings follows for the institutional settings under consideration in this discussion of Taubira, even when she acts in her official function as the French Minister of Justice. When a juror repeatedly kisses her teeth during a trial in Trinidad, "she speaks out of turn, relies on hearers to co-construct meaning, and expresses her own personal stance" (Figueroa and Patrick 2001: 12). *Tchip* practices disrupt the conditions of possibility for a proper hearing, its static disturbs or "block[s] the message" of French nationalist ideologies. For the latter, Taubira, as the official ear of the law, can never offer a clean processing of *l'audience*, the hearing.

Taubira's appearance on the late-night French TV talk show *On n'est pas couché* (February 6, 2016) follows the pattern above. Goncourt-winning author and co-host Yann Moix takes Taubira to task on the difficulty and style of her prose in her work *Murmures à la jeunesse* [Murmurs to the Youth] (2016).

> Yann Moix [quoting from *Murmures*]: « Que sait-on de l'amour indomptable si l'on n'a entendu Nina Simone menacer de cette voix de madrépore [...] ».[8] Comme les madrépores ce sont des récifs de coraux, je ne comprends pas comment un corail peut chanter ... mais ... peut-être que ... [...]
>
> Laurent Ruquier: Là c'est vrai que je suis allé dans le dictionnaire pour vérifier qu'est-ce que c'était qu'une voix de madrépore. Alors, c'est quoi?
>
> Taubira: Vous n'avez jamais entendu le chant de l'eau sur les coraux? Bon, peu importe.
>
> Moix: Alors là, vous me bluffez [...] On peut chanter sous sa douche mais sous l'eau c'est plus difficile quand même ... Vous êtes d'accord ...?
>
> Taubira: Moi, je trouve qu'il y a un très grand mépris dans votre propos.

> Yann Moix [quoting from *Murmures*]: "What can one know about wildly passionate love if one has never heard Nina Simone threaten with

---

[8] Full quote: "Que sait-on de l'amour indomptable si l'on n'a entendu Nina Simone menacer de cette voix de madrépore *I put a spell on you*, ou, l'ayant entendue, si l'on n'a senti son cœur se dilacérer millimètre par millimètre" (Taubira 2016: n. pag.).

her madreporic voice [...]." Since madrepores are coral reefs, I
  don't understand how a coral reef can sing ... but ... maybe ... [...]
Laurent Ruquier: I have to admit I had to get out the dictionary to check
  that one, the voice of coral reefs. So, what is it?
Taubira: You have never heard the water sing on coral reefs? Really, oh
  well, never mind ...
Moix: Oh, very impressive! [...] One can sing in the shower but singing
  under water is a little bit tough, don't you think?
Taubira: What I think is that there's a lot of contempt in your words.

Taubira has decided to calmly cut to the quick, essentially calling out the
toxic white masculinity that animates Moix's critical reading. Several tense
exchanges ensue, with him constantly interrupting her throughout. Then
Moix returns to his objections over the title, finding it emblematic of the
lack of logic and coherence in imagery and, ultimately, ideological vision, that
undergird the entire work:

Moix: Mais pourquoi *murmures?* [...]
Taubira: [Parce que] Je crois que si je chuchotais vous écouteriez plus.

Moix: But why *murmurs?* [...]
Taubira: [Because] I think that maybe if I whisper you'll listen harder.

The Taubira *tchip* and *murmure* seem very proximate to her final quip to
Moix in the passage above. As Ruquier notes in the ensuing discussion,
whispering to make an audience listen more intently is a performance
method in theater. In evoking *tchips*, whispers, and *murmures*, Taubira,
known for her rhetorical and debate skills, foregrounds an "expression non
formulée (de sentiments, d'affects)" [inarticulate expression (of sentiments
and feelings)] ("Murmure," *TLF*). Rather than an angry, or racially injured,
black scream, Taubira encourages French youth to "baisser le ton" [turn
it down a notch] and to imagine the future as far from written. Taubira's
evocation of Nina Simone's menacing "madreporic voice," and later "the
song of water on the coral reefs," fittingly bother Moix. In a book dedicated
to French youth—and written in the aftermath of her resignation from
the Ministry of Justice over the proposed law to strip people convicted of
terrorism of their French citizenship—Taubira proposes a sonics whose
feeling for the world is deeply informed by histories of diaspora. Her pointed
sonic tactics evoke, and mean to situate her within, an ideological posture
built on the ethos of an entire generation, one profoundly shaped by a set
of ideas but also feelings. The latter are perhaps best represented in records,
literature, and philosophy as much as in politics, and its mapping of the
world is composed of transnational matrices, post/colonial trajectories, and,

ultimately, relentless optimism. Such optimism sustains a proclaimed belief in French republican ideals, its forms of democratic participation, and its modes of debate and exchange, despite attempts to negate blackness, which would amount to the negation of that optimism, by French institutions and their nationalist tendencies. Against a politics of exclusion based on fear, Taubira seems to call on French youth, especially black and brown French youth, to tap into a global corpus of works connected to the liberation movements and dreams of freedom of generations past and present, her generation's but also their own. Here, she seems to suggest, they'll find not only the inspiration to fight on, they'll find one another.

This *tchip* doesn't register with the familiarity of a *wesh wesh*. Instead, it offers a political performance whose engrained sense of things registers deeply with African diasporic and diasporic adjacent populations. Taubira's *tchip* practices subtly draw on what Sara Ahmed calls a "willfulness archive [...] full of acts of disobedience" (2014: 134). Perhaps some will hear this performance as street smarts, but others will feel it in its deep connections to African diasporic cultural values, norms, and æsthetics. Listening back, the Taubira *tchip* registers as a brilliant deployment of kiss-teeth practices. Performed, or perhaps we should say *improvised*, spontaneously live and demonstrated subsequently in an internationally broadcast TV interview from Washington, DC, explained and followed up on by a short pedagogical film, and situated within a transnational and diasporic cultural ethos, Taubira seems to have rolled out this diasporic tactic as part of a broader strategy for tapping into the political bandwidth of *tchippage*. Taubira herself explains her thoughts about the endless expressions of racial hatred she endures: "Whether they hurt me or not is beside the point. What counts is how much they hurt the little girls who [...] look like me. What counts is how much they hurt someone who has succeeded at school but gets no reply to job applications ..." (qtd. in Lichfield 2014).

Channel 7. Education Frequencies: Tchip and the Surveillance of Affective Tonality

Let's return to the "girls who look like" Taubira, and who sound like her too. Since the 2000s, black French girls and teens have been type cast as problem children in the Republic (Steil 2019). Films like *La Squale* (dir. Fabrice Genestal, 2000), *Bande de filles* (dir. Céline Sciamma, 2014), and *Divines* (dir. Uda Benyamina, 2016) depict black girls as agents of disruption in public, private, and professional settings and spaces. These girls are too loud! They've got too much attitude! Ultimately dominant French discourse un/genders black girls' and teens' bodies by flagging them as visually and audibly noisy, threateningly masculine, and excessively difficult. Never mind the vile anti-black and misogynistic violence coming from the white French patriarchy, the girls and teenagers of sub-Saharan African and West Indian descent are naturally capable of tearing into the most hard-boiled white flesh. These girls, unlike the cliché of studious Arab girlhood, usher in a new phase of the blackening of the Hexagon. The assimilation and integration of these black adolescent girls requires the repression of their (stereotypical) conflict talk. This attitude adjustment specifically targets girls and teens from working-class and low-income families; after all, do we see or hear the codes and expressions of disdain coming from bourgeois youth being singled out for proscription? French schools that prohibit suck-teeth practices—while ignoring French interjections of exasperation such as *pppffff* or *hhhhrrrr*—instantiate a sonic color line with intersectional specificity. This ban effectively singles out African diasporic cultures and practices, and especially the sounds and bodies of black girls and teenagers, specifically those from the working-class, and then reifies *tchip* practices as solely a sound of hostility. H. Samy Alim "locat[es] the school as a primary site of language ideological combat" (2007: 214), and suggests the ways "that educational institutions have been attempting to gentrify and remove BL [black language] from its speakers with similarly unfulfilled promises of economic mobility" (215). French schools have a deep colonial history of drawing sonic color lines, in fact. The *tchip* ban participates in this systemic and historic marginalization of students' local speech sounds and practices. Black and brown students in France continue to endure, as Alim explains, "teachers' attempts to eradicate their language and linguistic practices [...] in favor of the adoption of White cultural and linguistic norms" (215). Further, this sonic color line goes beyond the sole purview of linguistic performance, reinforcing "processes whereby 'being emotional' comes to be seen as a characteristic of some bodies and not others" (Ahmed 2004: 4).

The intersectional implications of *tchip* prohibitions mostly get lost in the media coverage and debate that ensued. The teacher who encouraged the ban at the Charles Baudelaire vocational school in the outskirts of Greater Paris estimated that the student population at this school was 80% black in certain tracks (*filières*), with black girls ("filles noires") accounting for 100% of the bac pro Accueil [professional hospitality] track. In other words, the banning of *le tchip* de facto targets poor and working-class black (and black-ish, that is, self-styled black) girls and teenagers. Taking this into account, one understands how this "sonic color line" would attempt to strip and stigmatize a tool that proves particularly handy for, and used by, working-class black female students. This intersectional insight points us towards critical connections with the other ways in which the bodies of black girls and teenagers get racialized, un/gendered, and policed in Europe and North America, from the characterization of their hairstyles as "too ethnic," "too masculine," unprofessional, or otherwise unacceptable by teachers and administrators in high schools in the United States, to laws banning the *hijab* in French schools, deeply affecting black girls and teenagers. The way these girls get tracked towards certain sectors of the French labor market, as indicated by the percentages of black girls in certain types of training at the Baudelaire high school, speaks to the colonial legacy of French education and migration policies, particularly demonstrable in the case of the organized migration and systematic training and employment of French West Indian women by the state from the 1960s to the 1980s. BUMIDOM, the Bureau pour le développement des migrations dans les départements d'outre mer [Bureau for the Development of Overseas Department Migration], tracked and trained Martinican and Guadeloupean women for domestic labor, *aide-soignant* positions, and, much more rarely, administrative positions. At the same time, undergirding its mission was the notion that this education extended beyond skills to include the moral and cultural values of mainland France. While anxiety over black female sexuality and fertility fueled BUMIDOM's agenda for French West Indian migration and work, today's representations betray the anxieties of security discourse and the "crisis" of incivility, negrophobia and negrophilia, class tension and the fragility of white masculinity.

Given that the kiss-teeth/*tchip* is hard to write down, describe, or inscribe in language, residing at, but encroaching upon, the limits of recognized (post/imperial) language, French educational institutions have made it their post/colonial mission to contain it. In their racial neoliberal logic, the question of the *tchip* ban has nothing to do with blackness, let alone gender; instead it's about being an *aimable* and *serviable* black worker, demonstrating not only the ability but the desire to follow white, French codes of professional conduct. There's no room for black female discontent, or black women's feelings at all for that matter, in the workspace. Here, civic duty and "employability" get bound up with a politics of emotion animated by the intersectional legacies of French post/colonial republican history. In conjunction with the almost-but-not-white dynamics of traditional assimilation models and practices, this assimilation-as/for-labor-integration requires that black girls find "their place" in white dominant society by performing certain racial scripts. Borrowing a famous formula, we might say, educational neoliberalization = emotional thingification. The prohibition of the *tchip* demonstrates how policing affective tonality operates at the core of post/colonial assimilation projects, and how the latter are coupled with the notion of integration as the willingness and ability to occupy the exact position in matrices of power designated for you by the state. The *ratées*, the ones with funky feelings and sounds, must adjust their attitudes for the republican machine to function properly.

In terms of the particular school singled out in media coverage for this story, it seems a teacher of African descent essentially outed the students at Charles Baudelaire vocational high school in Evry, letting white teachers know that the students (these black girls) were insulting them up and down all day in class. "J'ai expliqué ça à mes collègues" [I explained that to my colleagues], the teacher explains.[9] And, it's true that any *tchip* directed at a teacher coming from a student can be dripping with insolence and disobedience. Just as the information, music, and political channels above all felt the need to explain what a *tchip* is and how it works in the first place, this sound has now been heard and felt in institutional contexts of power, where, as witnessed in examples above, it can be "perceived as an act of insubordination: between servants and masters; civilians and police, military, or judges; workers and employers. A low-status person, kissing their teeth upon receiving an order from a high-status person, is understood to commit an act of defiance, disobedience or even revolt" (Figueroa and Patrick 2001: 12). At the same time, the *tchip* ban, as part of the raced and gendered stigmatization of post/colonial expression and cultural history, carries profound implications for subject formation, as Frantz Fanon has taught us. The "sonic color line" (Stoever 2016) doesn't just outlaw a sound, it circumscribes the expectations of the raced and gendered body, it suggests—anticipates, waits for, desires— that these bodies tend to step out of bounds, that they require extra scrutiny, extra codes of conduct, and amped up technologies of surveillance. The *tchip* ban adds to the pressures of white heteronormativity, deciding what a body can and should do, how it should look and sound, and perhaps especially, how it should feel about it all. Because as it racializes and genders these bodies, the *tchip* ban participates in the surveillance of affective tonality (Goodman 2010). Poor performance of the latter leads to a declining investment in the French republican dream, the social hierarchies it holds in place, and the place assigned to young black women within it all. If we can understand confidence as "the seemingly neutral 'tone' of capitalism itself," as Ngai

---

[9] I am intentionally leaving out the name of the teacher in my critique. First of all, the name is quoted/spelled differently in different reports, but most of all my argument has nothing to do with this particular person. Instead, it has to do with an institutional system of listening. This particular quote comes from France 24: "Le 'tchip' interdit dans certains collèges et lycées en France," June 3, 2015, france24.com/ fr/20150602-tchip-afrique-antilles-interdit-lycees-colleges-france-education.

suggests in *Ugly Feelings*, then we can hear the *tchip*'s off-putting againstness as pushback that directs its affective investments elsewhere. Perhaps the *tchip* we hear from black girls and teenagers in Parisian suburbs fundamentally resonates with the Taubira *tchip*. It's the sound of rebellion, discontent, and frustration, yes, but also a rallying cry, or rather a rallying whisper, full of self-knowledge and steadfast willfulness that will open up onto untold new horizons and modes of social relation in the future.

Works Cited

Ahmed, Sara. *The Cultural Politics of Emotion*. Routledge, 2004.

——. *Willful Subjects*. Duke University Press, 2014.

Alim, H. Samy. "Critical Hip-Hop Language Pedagogies: Combat, Consciousness, and the Cultural Politics of Communication." *Journal of Language, Identity & Education*, vol. 6, no. 2, 2007, pp. 161–176.

Confiant, Raphaël. *Eau de café*. Grasset, 1991. [Kindle, n. pag.]

——. *Le Barbare enchanté*. Écriture, 2003.

Fattier, Dominique. *Contribution à l'étude de la genèse d'un créole: l'Atlas Linguistique d'Haïti, cartes et commentaires*. Doctoral thesis, 1998, u-cergy. fr/fr/laboratoires/lt2d/publications/these-creole.html.

Figueroa, Esther, and Peter Patrick. "The Meaning of Kiss-Teeth." Unpublished working paper, 2001, repository.essex.ac.uk/167/1/KSTpapwww.pdf.

Goffman, Erving. *Relations in Public: Microstudies in the Public Order*. Basic Books, 1971.

Goodman, Steve. *Sonic Warfare: Sound, Affect, and the Ecology of Fear*. MIT Press, 2010.

Goodwin, Marjorie Harness, and H. Samy Alim. "'Whatever (Neck Roll, Eye Roll, Teeth Suck)': The Situated Coproduction of Social Categories and Identities through Stancetaking and Transmodal Stylization." *Journal of Linguistic Anthropology*, vol. 20, no. 1, 2010, pp. 179–194.

Lichfield, John. "Christiane Taubira on a French Identity Crisis: 'France Is in Distress. There Is a Kind of Rage Out There.'" *Independent*, February 16, 2014, independent.co.uk/news/world/europe/christiane-taubira-on-a-french-identity-crisis-france-is-in-distress-there-is-a-kind-of-rage-out-9132231.html.

Lifter, Rachel. *Fashioning Indie: Popular Fashion, Music and Gender*. Bloomsbury, 2019.

Moten, Fred. *Stolen Life*. Duke University Press, 2018.

Ngai, Sianne. *Ugly Feelings*. Harvard University Press, 2004.

Rickford, John R., and Angela E. Rickford. "Cut-Eye and Suck-Teeth: African Words and Gestures in New World Guise." *The Journal of American Folklore*, vol. 89, no. 353, 1976, pp. 294–309.

Spady, James G., H. Samy Alim, and Samir Meghelli. *The Global Cipha: Hip Hop Culture and Consciousness*. Black History Museum Press, 2006.

Steil, Laura. "*Boucan!* Loud Moves against Invisibility in Postcolonial France." *Critical African Studies*, vol. 11, no. 1, 2019, pp. 121–135.

Stoever, Jennifer Lynn. *The Sonic Color Line: Race and the Cultural Politics of Listening*. NYU Press, 2016.

Taubira, Christiane. *Murmures à la Jeunesse*. Philippe Rey, 2016. [Kindle, n. pag.]

Thomas, Bonnie. *Connecting Histories: Francophone Caribbean Writers Interrogating Their Past*. University Press of Mississippi, 2017.

Notes on Contributors

Maya Boutaghou is Associate Professor of French at University of Virginia, where she is also Andrew Mellon Faculty at the Institute of the Humanities and Global Cultures. She is the author of *Occidentalismes, romans historiques postcoloniaux et identités nationales au XIXe siècle* (Honoré Champion, 2016). Other publications include a work on the reception of Ernest Renan's *Qu'est-ce qu'une nation?* (Honoré Champion, 2020) and the edited volume *Représentations de la guerre d'indépendance algérienne* (Classiques Garnier, 2019). She has edited special issues of *L'Esprit Créateur* (*The Algerian War of Independence and Its Legacy in Algeria, France and Beyond*, 2014), *Cultural Dynamics* (*The Minor in Question*, 2020), and *Les Lettres Romanes* (*Littératures francophones et pouvoir herméneutique*, 2021), and coedited a special issue of *Contemporary French and Francophone Studies* (*Mapping Francophone Postcolonial Theories*, 2018). Her writing has been published in *Expressions Maghrébines*, *French Studies*, *International Journal of Francophone Studies*, and *Dalhousie French Studies*.

Thomas C. Connolly is Associate Professor of French at Yale University, where he specializes in nineteenth- and twentieth-century French and francophone poetry. He studied at Oxford University and the École normale supérieure (Ulm), before obtaining his PhD in Comparative Literature from Harvard University. He is the author of *Paul Celan's Unfinished Poetics: Readings in the Sous-Oeuvre* (Legenda, 2018), and the special editor of a double issue of *Yale French Studies* (137–138) entitled *North African Poetry in French* (2020).

Vlad Dima is Professor of African Cultural Studies at the University of Wisconsin, Madison. He has published numerous articles, mainly on French and francophone cinemas, but also on francophone literature, comics, American cinema, and television. He is the author of *Sonic Space in Djibril Diop Mambety's Films* (Indiana University Press, 2017) and *The Beautiful Skin: Football, Fantasy, and Cinematic Bodies in Africa* (Michigan State University Press, 2020). His next book, *Meaning-Less-Ness in Postcolonial Cinema*, will be published in 2022.

yasser elhariry, Associate Professor of French at Dartmouth College, is the author of *Pacifist Invasions: Arabic, Translation & the Postfrancophone Lyric* (Liverpool University Press, 2017), and the editor of *Cultures du mysticisme* (*Expressions maghrébines*, 2017), *Critically Mediterranean: Temporalities, Aesthetics & Deployments of a Sea in Crisis* (with Edwige Tamalet Talbayev, Palgrave, 2018), *The Postlingual Turn* (with Rebecca L. Walkowitz, *SubStance*, 2021), and *Khatibi Now!* (with Matt Reeck, *PMLA*, 2022). A recipient of the William Riley Parker Prize, his essays have appeared in *New Literary History*, *Yale French Studies*, *L'Esprit Créateur*, *Francosphères*, *Contemporary French and Francophone Studies*, *Contemporary French Civilization*, *Parade sauvage*, *French Forum*, *Hyperion*, *Jacket2*, and several edited volumes.

Olivia C. Harrison is Associate Professor of French and Comparative Literature at the University of Southern California. Her publications include *Transcolonial Maghreb: Imagining Palestine in the Era of Decolonization* (Stanford University Press, 2015), an anthology-in-translation of the Moroccan journal *Souffles-Anfas* (Stanford University Press, 2015), and essays on Maghrebi literature, Beur and *banlieue* cultural production, and postcolonial theory. She is currently completing a monograph about the intersection of antiracism and Palestine solidarity movements in France, and researching the recuperation of minority discourses by the French far- and alt-right for a book tentatively titled *The White Minority*.

Edwin Hill is Associate Professor at the University of Southern California with joint appointments in the Department of French and Italian and the Department of American Studies and Ethnicity. His research focuses on African diasporic musical and cultural histories, Black transnationalism, and the sonic entanglements of modernity and post/coloniality. He published his first book manuscript, *Black Soundscapes White Stages: The Meaning of Francophone Sound in the Black Atlantic*, with Johns Hopkins University Press in 2013.

Jill Jarvis is Assistant Professor in the Department of French at Yale University. Her first book, *Decolonizing Memory: Algeria and the Politics of Testimony* (Duke University Press, 2021), weaves together close readings of literary, juridical, theoretical, and activist texts to illuminate both the nature of state violence and the stakes of literary study in a time of unfinished decolonization. A co-convener of the Desert Futures research collective, she is also at work on *Signs in the Desert: An Aesthetic Cartography of the Sahara*, a book that challenges the longstanding disciplinary divide that partitions North from sub-Saharan Africa by building a case for how contemporary writers, filmmakers, and other multimedia artists are transforming the reductive ways in which the African Sahara has long been mapped.

Shuangyi Li is a Lecturer in Comparative Literatures and Cultures at the University of Bristol. He is the author of *Proust, China and Intertextual Engagement: Translation and Transcultural Dialogue* (Palgrave, 2017), which won the ICLA Anna Balakian Prize 2019 for the best first monograph in the field of Comparative Literature published in the last three years by a scholar under the age of forty. Shuangyi received his PhD at the University of Edinburgh, and had also studied at the École Normale Supérieure Paris and the Université Catholique de Louvain. He is currently completing his second monograph, *Travel, Translation and Transmedia Aesthetics: Franco-Chinese Literature and Visual Arts in a Global Age*, forthcoming with Palgrave in 2021.

Martin Munro is Winthrop-King Professor of French and Francophone Studies at Florida State University. He previously worked in Scotland, Ireland, and Trinidad. His publications include *Writing on the Fault Line: Haitian Literature and the Earthquake of 2010* (Liverpool University Press, 2014); *Tropical Apocalypse: Haiti and the Caribbean End Times* (University of Virginia Press, 2015), and an edited volume of Caribbean ghost stories. In 2019, he published a translation of Michaël Ferrier's *Mémoires d'outre mer*, and he is currently translating other novels by Ferrier. In 2020–2021 he was a Fellow at the National Humanities Center in North Carolina. He is Director of the Winthrop-King Institute for Contemporary French and Francophone Studies at Florida State.

Raphaël Sigal is Assistant Professor of French at Amherst College. He is the author of *Artaud, le sens de la lecture* (Éditions Hermann, 2018). His second book, *Shoalzheimer* (Quidam Éditeur) will come out in early 2023.

Jennifer Solheim is the author of the *The Performance of Listening in Postcolonial Francophone Culture* (Liverpool University Press, 2018), and her fiction and essays have been published in *Bellevue Literary Review*, *Confrontation*, the *Los Angeles Review of Books*, *The Pinch*, and *Poets & Writers*. She was also bassist, singer, and songwriter in several indie punk bands, including The Smoothies (Southern Records) and Minim (Dyslexic Records). She is the Associate Director of the BookEnds Program at Southampton Arts of Stony Brook University, and a Contributing Editor at *Fiction Writers Review*. Over the past decade, she has taught on a contingent basis at the University of Illinois–Chicago in both English and French and Francophone Studies, and she also serves as a UIC Honors College Faculty Fellow.

Edwige Tamalet Talbayev is Associate Professor of French and Director of Middle East and North African Studies at Tulane University. A scholar of Maghrebi literature and Mediterranean Studies, she is the author of *The Transcontinental Maghreb: Francophone Literature across the Mediterranean* (Fordham University Press, 2017) and the co-editor of *The Mediterranean Maghreb: Literature and Plurilingualism* (*Expressions maghrébines*, 2012) and *Critically Mediterranean: Temporalities, Aesthetics, and Deployments of a Sea in Crisis* (Palgrave, 2018). She is currently at work on several projects that examine borders and migration from the standpoint of water as an epistemological site. She is Editor of *Expressions maghrébines*, the peer-reviewed journal of the Coordination Internationale des Chercheurs sur les Littératures Maghrébines.

Index

Page numbers in **bold** refer to figures.